the romance of commerce and culture

U. S. supplies, packed in paper, speed the liberation of The Netherlands and colonies

CONTAINER CORPORATION OF AMERICA

Willem de Kooning, Container Corporation magazine advertisement, United Nations series, January 1945. Courtesy of CCA (Smithsonian American Art Museum).

the romance of commerce and culture

Capitalism,
Modernism,
and the
Chicago-Aspen Crusade
for Cultural Reform

Revised Edition

james sloan allen

University Press of Colorado

Published by the University Press of Colorado
5589 Arapahoe Avenue, Suite 206C
Boulder, Colorado 80303

Previously published by The University of Chicago Press, Chicago, Illinois, 1983

The University Press of Colorado is a cooperative publishing enterprise supported, in part, by Adams State College, Colorado State University, Fort Lewis College, Mesa State College, Metropolitan State College of Denver, University of Colorado, University of Northern Colorado, University of Southern Colorado, and Western State College of Colorado.

The paper used in this publication meets the minimum requirements of the American National Standard for Information Sciences—Permanence of Paper for Printed Library Materials. ANSI Z39.48-1992

Library of Congress Cataloging-in-Publication Data

Allen, James Sloan.
  The romance of commerce and culture : capitalism, modernism, and the Chicago-Aspen crusade for cultural reform / James Sloan Allen.— Rev. ed.
    p. cm.
Includes bibliographical references and index.
  ISBN 0-87081-654-3 (pbk. : alk. paper)
  1. Arts, American—20th century. 2. Arts and society—United States. 3. Technology and the arts—United States. 4. Arts—Marketing—United States. 5. Popular culture—Illinois—Chicago. 6. Popular culture—Colorado—Aspen. I. Title.
  NX504 .A53 2002
  700'.1'03097309041—dc21

                                                                                        2002003986

Design by Daniel Pratt
Typesetting by David Archer

Cover image: 1937 Container Corporation magazine advertisement by A. M. Cassandre, courtesy of CCA (Smithsonian American Art Museum).

11 10 09 08 07 06 05 04 03 02   10 9 8 7 6 5 4 3 2 1

To Elizabeth H. Paepcke in memorium,
To my wife,
And to Ortega's Elegance

contents

preface

to the second edition

When the first edition of *The Romance of Commerce and Culture: Capitalism, Modernism, and the Chicago-Aspen Crusade for Cultural Reform* appeared in the early 1980s, its title subjects were undergoing epochal changes. American capitalism was creating a consumer culture on a mass scale that within the next two decades would encircle the globe, thanks to the advent of information technologies like satellite television, the personal computer, and the Internet, as well as to the end of the Cold War and the collapse of communism in Eastern Europe and the Soviet Union. The earnest aesthetic and cultural aspirations of modernism were yielding to a postmodern spirit that inclined toward a blithe eclecticism in the arts—incorporating consumerism and popular culture—and social criticism that sanctioned cultural relativism on the one hand and assailed the power of consumer capitalism on the other. America was gaining an increasing dominance in world politics, economics, and culture that became unrivaled with the end of the Soviet Union in the early 1990s. And Aspen, Colorado, along with the Aspen Institute and most of the other institutions whose stories the book also tells, were being transformed as American culture moved toward the twenty-first century.

In this edition, I have brought these and other historical threads loosely up to date in a new epilogue. I have also made minor revisions throughout the book, but I have not attempted to rewrite it from the perspective of the twenty-first century and of the scholarship of the last twenty years. That has not been necessary. The history this book details remains what it was—that of an emblematic episode in the modern relations between commercialism and cultural life. And the widening interest in this topic among historians and social critics over the past two decades (to which I make occasional reference), including the fashionable "postmodern critique" of the culture of consumer capitalism, has put this episode in a rich historical context while also underscoring how the early- and mid-twentieth-century romance of commerce and culture recorded here foreshadowed what we now see all around us.

acknowledgments

The writing of this book would not have been possible without the cooperation of many people—many of whom have since passed away, but whom I acknowledge here as in the first edition. First among them is the late Elizabeth H. Paepcke, who opened the extensive archives of her late husband, Walter, granting me carte blanche to use them as well as her thoughtful recollections, and whose generosity, warmth, and rare elegance opened many other doors for me and made my work a pleasure and an education. I also owe a special debt to my former teacher and continuing mentor, Jacques Barzun, for introducing me to Elizabeth Paepcke, and for alerting me to the demands and rewards of writing cultural history and of writing well. Extraordinary kindnesses and cooperation were extended to me during my research by Mortimer J. Adler, Joella and Herbert Bayer, Henri Temianka, and Charles Saul, all of whom also graciously provided useful materials, as did Katharine Kuh, Herbert Pinzke, Eugene Lilly, Tom Sardy, Robert O. Anderson, and the now-extinct Container Corporation of America through the persons of Bill Bonnell, John Massey, and Lony F. Ruhmann. (The advertising art of the Container Corporation is now held by the Smithsonian American Art Museum.) I am grateful as well to Thomas G. Thompson for many insightful conversations, to Sidney Cheresh for some deft detective work, and to Mark and Phyllis Allen for valuable information and invaluable encouragement.

For the generous and amiable interviews they granted me, I thank Mortimer J. Adler, Robert O. Anderson, Jacques Barzun, Herbert Bayer, Joella Bayer, Mr. and Mrs. Fritz Benedict, Ferenc Berko, Bill Bonnell, Peggy Clifford, Charles T. Coiner, Norman Cousins, Norman DeHaan, Antonia P. Dubrul, Ralph Eckerstrom, Mrs. Laurence Elisha, Alvin Eurich, Gaylord Freeman, William Gomberg, William Gorman, Mr. and Mrs. Robert Gronner, Alice P. Guenzel, Sydney Harris, Mrs. John Herron, Robert L. Hoguet, James Hume, Mrs. Robert M. Hutchins, Elmer Johnson, Charles Jones, Katharine Kuh, Eugene Lilly, Jenny Lyngby, John Massey, Jane Mayer, Sterling M. McMurrin, Samuel Mitchell, Paul H. Nitze, Elizabeth H. Paepcke, Herbert Pinzke, Tom Sardy, Charles Saul, Arthur Siegel, Joseph E. Slater, Henry L. Stein, Henri Temianka, Friedel Ungeheuer, Vitya Vronsky, F. Champion Ward, Harry Weese, Robert Jay Wolff.

I am grateful to the following institutions for permission to quote from works published under their imprint: The MIT Press (Sibyl Moholy-Nagy, *Moholy-Nagy: Experiment in Totality*, 2d edition, © 1950 and 1969 by Sibyl Moholy-Nagy; and Hans M. Wingler, ed., *The Bauhaus: Weimar, Dessau, Berlin, Chicago*, English adaptation © 1969 by The Massachusetts Institute of Technology); The Aspen Institute for Humanistic Studies (letter from Ortega y Gasset to Walter P. Paepcke, 26 October 1949, in *1974: 25th Anniversary Year*); Macmillan Publishing Company and Weidenfeld & Nicolson (Mortimer J. Adler, *Philosopher at Large: An Intellectual Autobiography*, © 1977 by Mortimer J. Adler).

For permission to quote from unpublished documents, I gratefully acknowledge Ansel Adams, Mortimer J. Adler, Robert 0. Anderson, Vitya V. Babin, Jacques Barzun, Joella Bayer, Charles Benton, Norman Cousins, Elizabeth Reuther Dickmeyer, Clifton Fadiman, Gerald R. Ford, R. Buckminster Fuller, Andreas Giedion, William Gomberg, Ronald Goodman, Ise Gropius, Richard Hocking, Vesta Hutchins, Michael Imison (for the Noel Coward estate), Elmer Johnson, Philip Johnson, Mrs. George Fred Keck, Eugene Lilly, Myres S. McDougal (for the Harold Lasswell estate), Rhena Schweitzer Miller, Hattula Moholy-Nagy, Beaumont Newhall, Soledad Ortega, Elizabeth H. Paepcke, Patricia Ross, Amos Wilder, Helen Wolff, the University of Chicago Archives.

Finally, to my wife, Elizabeth Cheresh Allen, who read and judged my every word, I owe the lucidity of many passages, uncountable other critical contributions, and the romance and contentment of my life.

introduction

Ever since the tides of scientific rationality, political democracy, and industrial capitalism began sweeping across Western culture more than two hundred years ago, that culture has been divided against itself. Partisans of the new order have prized its openness to reason and to individual merit and its material productivity. But critics have decried it for bringing cultural disintegration and the hegemony of a social class—the bourgeoisie—awash in spiritless materialism, vulgar tastes, and dull uniformity.

The critics have been fewer in number but more conspicuous than their opponents, for the critics have included most of the gifted artists and intellectuals of the past two centuries. And never did their hostility erupt with greater passion than in the second half of the nineteenth century and the first half of the twentieth. During these years, artists and intellectuals of the political left as well as the right made antagonism to the bourgeois regime a prime inspiration of their work, and set the renovation or regeneration of culture as the ruling end of that work.

The story of modernism has often been told through the career of this "adversary" spirit in the late nineteenth and early twentieth centuries. Fed by contempt for conformity, modernist authors made a fetish of disturbing truths and innovative literary styles, while painters, architects, and composers spurned convention in their quest for elemental aesthetic forms, and intellectuals charted the seas of human irrationality and cosmic nihilism. Yet for all its intensity, that adversary spirit did not wholly characterize the modernists' disposition toward the world around them. Not only did these artists and thinkers rage against that world and often, in Dostoevsky's memorable words in *Notes from Underground,* exalt their own "lofty suffering" above the "cheap happiness" of the hated bourgeoisie, or middle class (to which most of them belonged); but they also knew their share of that world's advantages, and many tasted a portion of "cheap happiness" too. Thus the poet Charles Baudelaire cursed the prudish manners and pedestrian tastes of the bourgeoisie, but he also celebrated the "heroism of modern life" and hymned the pleasures of the *flâneur* strolling the streets of modern Paris. T. S. Eliot bemoaned modernity as a spiritual wasteland, but he also clung to the secure routine of modern work and to puritan middle-class morality. Hermann Hesse made his Steppenwolf despise the spiritless and tacky popular culture of the twenties, but he also had him learn to revel on the dance floor and accept with a smile the shallow and inescapable modern "radio music of life." Jean-Paul Sartre philosophized about the meaninglessness of existence and denounced the bourgeoisie as "skunks" and grew nauseated at their inanity, but he also admitted to laughing alongside them at the cinema and sharing their enjoyment of cafés and popular songs. Some painters (like Gauguin and Picasso) extolled the unadulterated aesthetics of primitive art, but others (like Édouard Manet, the Italian futurists, and the American pop artists) took their inspiration from the modern middle-class life itself—cafés, city streets, consumer products, etc.—and others still (like László Moholy-Nagy, Fernand Léger, Piet Mondrian, and Le Corbusier) identified their cherished aesthetics of abstraction with machines and the modern metropolis. Architects and designers, most notably those associated with the Bauhaus school of design, bewailed the fragmentation and vulgarity of modern culture, yet they proposed to restore unity and improve tastes by teaching good industrial design.

The artists and intellectuals of the modernist era therefore stood not in simple opposition to the world they inhabited but in uncomfortable ambivalence toward it. Like most people of their time, they hated modernity and they loved it. They hated its cultural disunity and spiritual aridity, yet they desired its material advantages and demanded its liberties for the individual. So rooted in the conditions of modernity is this ambivalence that attempts to resolve it have often sought to turn its causes into cures. Industrial production and consumer capitalism, detested dehumanizers of labor and destroyers of quality, could become for some the means of unifying mankind and elevating taste; mass advertising and public relations, begetters of foolish wants and stupefying conformity, could become agents of cultural reform; and the commercial middle class, historic enemy of art, mind, and spirit, could become the ally, friend, and benign master of artists and intellectuals.

The Romance of Commerce and Culture discloses some dynamics of this modern ambivalence by telling the story of a few ambitious endeavors to resolve it during roughly the first half of the twentieth century. The story plays across seemingly disparate fields of American cultural history—consumer capitalism; art and design; educational theory; cultural criticism; and the making of Aspen, Colorado, as a center of cultural reform and of fraternization for America's intellectual, managerial, and political elites. The seeming distance between these fields vanishes when the paths connecting them come to light. For these paths led through Chicago in its golden age and Aspen in its formative years, and, in part, through the lives of several men who, at one time or another and in one coalition or another, saw themselves joined in combat against cultural disintegration, dehumanization, and bad taste and who often found themselves deploying in battle the techniques of consumer commerce.

The first of these men, Walter Paul Paepcke, founded the Container Corporation of America and guided it to eminence in the culture of consumer capitalism—the first company to combine the aesthetics of modern art and the genius of mass advertising to fashion a corporate image. Chapter 1 traces these accomplishments within the consumer revolution that made them possible. The second man, László Moholy-Nagy, an influential teacher at the Bauhaus in Germany, brought the Bauhaus ideas of industrial and graphic design, art education, and cultural reform to Chicago and, backed by Walter Paepcke as friend and sponsor, made them live again in the New Bauhaus (later the Institute of Design). Chapter 2 charts the passage of the Bauhaus from Europe to America, illuminating the alliance of art and industry that the Bauhaus helped forge and the quest for cultural integration that gave the Bauhaus its singular character. Two other men, Robert M. Hutchins and Mortimer J. Adler, made the University of Chicago the preeminent institution in the reform of higher education for two decades, and then, armed with a vision of cultural unity and a knack for public relations, carried their ambitions beyond the university with the Great Books movement and the fifty-four-volume *Great Books of the Western World*. Chapter 3 records the history and intent of these ambitions.

The next four chapters follow these men as they joined others to impress their messages of cultural reformation on post–World War II America and in so doing strengthened the bond of cultural ends and commercial means in American society. Chapter 4 describes Paepcke's conversion of Aspen from a faded mining boom town into a nascent recreational and cultural center.

The next two chapters record the efforts of Paepcke, Hutchins, and others to heal the culturally disintegrated and recently war-torn world by holding an international festival of art and ideas in Aspen commemorating the two-hundredth anniversary of the birth of the cosmopolitan humanist Johann Wolfgang von Goethe. The first of these chapters follows the translation of the festival's high philosophic purposes into a unique and adroit mass publicity campaign; the second looks at the event itself and its relation to mid- twentieth-century American culture and against critical portraits of the leading participants—including Albert Schweitzer, Ortega y Gasset, Giuseppe Borgese, and Thornton Wilder. So successful was the festival in winning public notice and in edifying its many participants that several of them resolved to stage a sequel the following year and possibly to establish a permanent institution in Aspen dedicated to advancing their cultural ideals. This resolution fathered the Aspen Institute for Humanistic Studies, born the next year and molded into an influential organ of American cultural life by the labors and ideas of Paepcke, Ortega, Hutchins, Mortimer Adler, Henry Luce, and others. Chapter 7 traces the progress of the institute from its idealistic conception to its pragmatic program of seminars for America's corporate, political, and intellectual leaders.

The next two chapters look at the Aspen Institute as a mirror of several important elements of American culture in the 1950s. Chapter 8 examines the emergence in Aspen, and America, of a class of intellectuals and executives occupied with defining the character of American culture and with strengthening America's stature in the postwar world. These were the "leaders" who Paepcke and his colleagues hoped would carry the Aspen message into all parts of American life. Chapter 9 traces the intellectual history of the arts—particularly photography and design—in Aspen through the ideas of the prominent artists and critics who gathered there to probe the relation of art to commerce and to assess the accomplishments and failures of modernism. The new Epilogue then surveys developments from the 1960s to 2001 that complete the story—including the fate of the Container Corporation, the growth of the Aspen Institute for Humanistic Studies into an international forum for discussions of public policy, the emergence of Aspen as a capital of late-twentieth-century celebrity culture, and the passing of the generation and the character type prevalent in this book.

This history wears no ideological badge. But it lends itself to two distinctly different readings. One reading will find here the story of how capitalism and high culture ended their age-old antagonism in a pattern of alliances beneficial to both sides. These alliances enabled the artifacts and ideas of modernism and humanism to enter the mainstream of middle-class American life, thereby rendering culture more nearly whole and easing the ambivalence toward modernity of artists, intellectuals, and sensitive bourgeois alike. The other reading will find a record not of mutually beneficial alliances but of how capitalism gained hegemony over high culture by turning artists and intellectuals into its agents, thereby robbing them of their ability to criticize or pose alternatives to the kingdom of consumer commerce. Yet, different as these readings are, they complement rather than contradict each other. For together they reflect the ambiguous legacy in twenty-first-century America of the romance of commerce and culture.[1]

I

modernist
culture
and its critics in
chicago

I

modernist marketing:

the consumer revolution and the container corporation of america

Americans of the early twenty-first century live in a landscape of art. City parks and plazas sport massive abstract constructions—monuments, not to notable persons or events, like the sculptures of former days, but to *art*. Exterior walls glow with eye-catching murals, while boyish graffiti in images, names, and scribbles swarm across unguarded public edifices and vehicles, eliciting praise from popular critics for their spirited artistry. Elementary schools not only provide hours for art but give over their halls and windows to its display. Towns and villages sponsor annual art festivals, and urban museums swell with crowds hungry for glimpses of the latest blockbuster show, whether ancient Egyptian or Chinese treasures, illuminated medieval manuscripts, or postimpressionist still lifes. Corporations spend millions commissioning artists and collecting masterpieces, which they proudly exhibit in banks, lobbies, and offices, while middle-class homes boast reproductions of masters old and new chosen to fit the decor. Seldom does a day pass without our hearing or pronouncing the vogue phrases of the art culture: "creative person," "aesthetic appeal," "good design," and the like. Members of even the most practical professions find it appropriate to describe their work in art-related terms, like the dentist on New York's Seventh Avenue who advertises his services as "oral aesthetics."

Yet remarkable as this widening cult of art is, more remarkable is the dissemination of art throughout daily life by art's former enemy, commerce. No longer confined to the realms of aesthetics and edification, art has become a nutrient of the consumer economy fed to us by art's commercial offspring: product and graphic design, advertising art, architecture, and popular entertainment.

The adversarial relations that existed between high art and capitalism from the late eighteenth century are all but dead. Their death was foreshadowed long ago by exponents of arts and crafts, industrial arts, and most prominently by the Bauhaus, whose members showed "the way beyond 'art.'"[1] In the 1970s, the erstwhile doyen of New York's bohemian art world, Andy Warhol, could happily announce: "After I did the thing called 'art' . . . , I went into business art, . . . and I want to finish as a business artist," for "good business is the best art."[2]

Warhol's "business art" may signify the final passing of the venerable conflict between art and bourgeois commerce. But this passing does not signify the defeat of art, much less of modern art. On the contrary, it signals the assimilation of artistic modernism, with its abstract, experimental aesthetics and earnestly contemporary spirit (if not its metaphysical and moral vision), into the common tastes and temper of the culture at large. The modern alliance of art and commerce thus contains the story, in part, of how art gained its cultural ascendancy and how modernism and the consumer economy joined forces.

This story begins with the consumer revolution of the second half of the nineteenth century. It was then that the introduction of new products and new methods of marketing sparked the radical reorganization of the economy and the culture that continues today. And it was marketing rather than products that fueled the revolution. For a consumer economy thrives on desires, not needs, or, better, on desires that become needs when aroused by the twin engines of modern marketing: promotion and distribution. Once the railroad, the telegraph, and then the telephone provided the rapid transportation and communication systems necessary for mass promotion and distribution, the consumer revolution was on.

Department stores grew up almost overnight in every large city. Some, like R. H. Macy's, B. Altman's, and Bloomingdale's in New York (closely following and soon surpassing their Parisian counterparts, the *grands magasins de nouveautés*, led by the pioneering Bon Marché), expanded from single-line retail outlets during the 1860s and 1870s into full-scale department stores. Others, like Arnold Constable, Lord & Taylor, and Alexander Stewart of

New York, John Wanamaker's of Philadelphia, and Marshall Field and Carson Pirie Scott of Chicago, emerged during the same period from wholesale houses. Nearly all the major department stores in this country and elsewhere date from those vital decades near the end of the nineteenth century and the beginning of the twentieth. These stores, which offered relatively easy credit, "democratized luxury" (in the words of Emile Zola);[3] and in spirit as well as in the palatial edifices that housed them, they were truly temples of commerce.

Chain stores also sprouted to exploit new merchandising opportunities. The first of these stores, the Great Atlantic and Pacific Tea Co., had a hundred outlets just ten years after its founding in 1859; and a few decades later, having spanned the country and widened its range of products far beyond tea, it was well on its way to becoming the nationwide supermarket chain known as A&P. Other chains followed in the 1870s and 1880s, among them Woolworth's and Kress's, as well as the remarkable operation of Thomas Lipton in Britain, which eventually embraced production, transportation, and retail stores—and helped make tea and jam staples of the British diet.

Customers at a distance from urban department and chain stores had not long to wait for the mail order house to begin enticing them with capacious catalogues of inexpensive and varied articles and promises of sure and speedy delivery. These enticements, first issued in the 1870s from the offices of Montgomery Ward in Chicago, led to some of the greatest successes of modern marketing. In 1887, the Montgomery Ward catalogue listed over 24,000 items; and by 1900, mail order houses, concentrated in Chicago, had far surpassed the business of any department store. Ward's chief competitor, Sears, Roebuck and Company—then barely ten years old and already pulling ahead of Ward's in sales—had a sales volume of $40 million, more than a third higher than Marshall Field, and double that of Macy's.

The freshly formed powers of distribution were paying off. New merchandise (ready-made clothes, furniture, appliances, hygienic devices, prepared and packaged foods, and objects of diversion, like toys and cameras) was flowing; prices, thanks to mass production and marketing, were declining; and consumer desires were beginning their endless upward rise.[4]

But the improved distribution of goods still depended for success on awakened or heightened consumer desires. It is no wonder that retailers began seeking more effective means of promoting products, and that once the mechanics of distribution were in hand, advertising became the engine of marketing.

Recognizing the need for mass advertising, retailers early pressed for more space and graphic freedom in their newspaper copy. Hoping to skirt the Eastern newspapers' "agate rule," which restricted advertising print to tiny, agate-sized letters for the sake of the publisher's dignity, R. H. Macy, for example, left conspicuous blanks and clustered the letters to make bolder figures, notably the Macy star, in the store's advertising copy. As the agate rule yielded and illustrations slowly appeared, advertisements grew in size, number, and graphic variety. With the publication in 1879 of the first full-page advertisement (for John Wanamaker's New York store), the future interdependence of retailing, advertising, and the print media was assured; by 1900, as Daniel Boorstin has remarked, "the department store had become a mainstay of the big-city daily newspapers throughout the country."[5]

Meanwhile, the expanding requirements of promotion had called to life the modern advertising agency, led by N. W. Ayer & Son of Philadelphia, which, in 1875, created the "open contract," granting sole responsibility to the advertising agent for shaping and placing a company's advertising.[6] Many other aids to marketing materialized around the same time, including consumer trade magazines like *Dry Goods Reporter* (1871) and *Grocers' Criterion* (1873), the professional advertiser's journals *Printers' Ink* (1888) and *Advertising and Selling* (1894), and business societies like Chicago's Commercial Club (1871) and the Mercantile Club (1889). Soon after the turn of the century, the exigencies of promotion created still more professions dedicated to comprehending and winning consumers. "Public relations" (a term coined in 1908 by Theodore Newton Vail, president of American Telephone and Telegraph Company, and a profession first practiced in 1906 when the journalist Ivy L. Lee was hired to improve the public image of some unpopular coal mining interests) became a "science" under the hand of Sigmund Freud's nephew Edward Bernays, who insisted "there is no detail too trivial to influence the public in a favorable or unfavorable sense."[7] "Market research" had its birth as "commercial research" when Charles Coolidge Parlin traveled the country in 1911 for the publisher Cyrus H. K. Curtis in search of patterns in consumer markets, and then published his findings in the seminal books *Department Store Lines* (1912) and the five-volume *Automobiles* (1914). "Marketing" itself gained professional status through the many business schools founded near the turn of the century (including those at New York University, Dartmouth, and Harvard) and through the first national marketing association, created in 1915, and its professional journal, the *Journal of Marketing*. The rise of modern marketing also forced a shift in economic theory away from production to consumption—away, for instance, from the idea that the value of products resides in the costs of production and toward the idea, elaborated in the late nineteenth century as "marginal utility," that this value derives from subjective consumer demand or desire in relation to supply. And it prompted Thorstein Veblen to pen his diatribes against the eclipse of production by *business* and to form his angry theories of "conspicuous consumption," "pecuniary emulation," and "waste." It is no surprise that advertising expenditures jumped tenfold during the last three decades of the nineteenth century to reach $500 million. Ten years later those expenditures had more than doubled again; by 1950, they had surpassed $5 billion, and at the century's end, they were approaching $200 billion.[8]

The consumer revolution was here in the making. Within two more generations, after innovative technology and publicity had spread the spirit of consumption throughout the culture, no one could doubt, and many would complain, that the desire for goods and the psychological identification with promotional imagery had become a way of life.

By lending consumer products and their promotion economic preeminence, the consumer revolution ensured the alliance of art and commerce. Art, especially the techniques of modernism, offered marketing many advantages. The designing of consumer products according to modern aesthetic standards, as we shall see, grew into an immense enterprise engaging the energies of artists, manufacturers, publicists, and cultural critics alike. And the business of promotion enjoyed an even more influential career in partnership with art. Because advertising aspired both to mirror and to guide the interests of consumers through the use of psychologically subtle and historically apposite images, art became its natural ally. Like modern advertising—foreshadowed in part by R. H. Macy's chafing over the agate rule—modernist art trafficked in unconventional and ingenious appeals to the senses, aiming to tap and to shape frustrations, aspirations, and tastes born of modern life. Twentieth-century art and commerce thus shared a purpose that drew them inevitably together and made their influence over culture and character all but irresistible.

Advertising had, of course, made use of art in posters long before the consumer revolution. But only with the invention of color lithography in the 1860s did the advertising poster acquire the versatility and visual power required for the effective mass promotion of consumer wares. Although most nineteenth-century posters depicted their subjects with textbook literalness, the tendency inherent in poster advertising toward simplicity and directness of form and the integration of word and image (pioneered by Jules Chéret and perfected by Toulouse-Lautrec) turned the poster into art and made possible the visually compelling psychologically persuasive modern advertisement.

Both artists and advertisers urged this evolution forward. The Impressionist painters led the way, in the late 1860s and the 1870s, by reducing the constituents of painting to the shades of light that strike the eye. Although intended to capture the eye's perception of the world and thereby to heighten the realism and objectivity of painting, the supplanting of naturalistic detail by purely visual and aesthetic qualities fanned the flame of subjectivity that started the visual arts on the path to true abstraction—toward, as one early modernist put it, "the non-objective world."[9]

At the same time, by concentrating on subjective visual experience instead of objective fact, Impressionism taught people how to see anew. The eye now began learning to discern in art, as it often discerns in life, the subtlest hints of figure and form. This aesthetic education was bolstered by modernist, or protomodernist, theories of art and design, beginning with such works as Owen Jones's *Grammar of Ornament* (1857), the first to promote a new decorative style rooted in the psychology of perception, and Charles Blanc's *Grammaire des arts de dessin* (1867), which stressed *composition* over subject matter in painting, followed by artists like the Expressionists and the Bauhäusler, who aimed to reach the emotions or reflect the spirit of modernity through nonpictorial design. So keen a taste for abstraction was created that people came to expect abstraction in all art and to discover it in life.[10]

The rise of abstraction in art proved a boon to advertising. Not only did this art of imprecision and suggestiveness inspire poster artists to produce subtle and yet immediately comprehensible narrative images; it also served the advertiser's growing need to appeal to vague, subjective desires. The rationale for modernism, formulated, for example, by the symbolist painter Maurice Denis in the 1890s, could easily be adapted to advertising. The subject makes no difference, Denis wrote, for "it is through coloured surfaces, through the value of tones, through the harmony of lines, that I attempt to reach the mind and arouse the emotions."[11]

The adaptation began around the turn of the century. Writers in *Printers' Ink*, departing from their earlier preoccupations with a uniform rational human nature and with strictly informational advertising, began to encourage manipulative advertising directed at nonrational desires. From now on, the magazine's readers would grow increasingly familiar with such themes as "Advertising that Appeals to the Senses—the Coming Type," "Suggestion in Advertising," and "Applying 'New Thought' or Psychotherapy to the Dealer."[12] And exponents of the new advertising like Ernest Elmo Calkins started urging advertisers to enhance the "subtle, indefinable, but powerful force" in their hands by employing visual images that give "the opportunity of expressing the inexpressible, of suggesting not so much a motor car as speed, not so much a gown as style."[13]

Psychologists seeking clues to both advertising and the psyche spurred this movement on. Among the first of these, Walter Dill Scott of Northwestern University studied reactions to typeface and to the sizes, shapes, colors, and the associations of images and concluded that advertising could be scientific. He then induced the Chicago firm of Hart, Schaffner and Marx to launch an advertising campaign rooted in what he had determined to be the psychological attraction of their product (fine suits for men): masculinity and refinement. Translating this appeal into an advertising image, Scott produced a distinguished, well-dressed man sitting proudly astride a sturdy, distinguished horse. Suit sales soared. Scott had found the key to modern advertising: not products in themselves but their ties to the "self-image" of consumers.[14] A prominent conservative Chicago artist, Lorado Taft (who praised poster advertising as "a means of carrying art to the people"), acknowledged his own surrender as a consumer to the new advertising technique. Like numberless others after him, he identified himself with the advertisers' images: "Someone wrote that a person could not look at the Apollo Belvedere without straightening up a bit. By the same token, I cannot look at the advertisements of some of those clothing houses here without trying to appear a little more like the fellows in the pictures."[15]

Whether or not advertisers followed the advice of psychologists—and most advertisers well into the century believed they taught psychologists more than they learned from them—by the 1920s advertising had become the commercial laboratory of what was later to be known as "motivational research." John B. Watson, father of behavioral psychology, signaled the fact when he left his post at Johns Hopkins University in the early 1920s to join the prominent New York advertising agency of J. Walter Thompson. "We must face the fact," he told the nation's parents from his new position, that old modes of behavior and socialization are obsolete and that "standards of [child] training . . . must now conform to the dominant trends in our changing civilization." Those trends required, he insisted, less mothering and more instruction in the consumer culture's ways of "boundless activity" and constant "problem solving."[16]

The consumer's chief problem was what to buy; the advertiser's problem, amid the proliferation of goods, was how to forge consumers' identification with particular products. Brand names had arisen in the late nineteenth century to facilitate this identification—Singer sewing machines, Kodak cameras, Kellogg cereals, Heinz and Campbell soups, Pillsbury flour, Nabisco biscuits, and so forth. But now manufacturers and their advertisers laid siege to the consumer mind. "It is your job," announced a memo to the advertising department from the head of the Ralston Purina Company, "to shape the thoughts of your prospect and customer. . . . Make his thoughts simple, safe, conservative and so dynamic that they will lead to confidence and action."[17] A writer in *Printers' Ink* went farther, openly urging advertisers to address the emotions. "Emotions must be aroused," he said, "for only through an emotional mental picture do men experience empathy with conditions described. . . . The appeal to reason doesn't contain the elements that make a man want to do the thing you want him to do."[18]

This intensifying appeal to the emotions in hopes of forging identifications between personality and products took exemplary form in automobile advertising between about 1900 and 1925. The early ads show the car, always standing still and usually alone and at a distance, accompanied by a lengthy description of the car's attributes and merits. Then the pictures grow larger and the text smaller, now remarking the pleasures of driving. Finally text and car all but disappear in full-page illustrations conveying the impression of speed with just an outline of an automobile dashing past, or picturing only the driver's view of the world: a bit of steering wheel clutched by two hands, the car's front end piercing the air, the road whisking away under wheel—all, as Ernest Elmo Calkins had advised, communicating the experience of speed and announcing: This could be you.

Similarly bold psychological devices marked the promotion of all kinds of cosmetic articles in the 1920s. The goal, said *Printers' Ink,* was to make people "self-conscious about matter of course things such as enlarged nose pores, bad breath," etc.[19] Hence advertisements depicted forlorn individuals in the grips of anxiety or despair over their social or professional ruin from unknown causes. "He never knew why," the copy reads: "Remember—Nothing exceeds halitosis (bad breath) as a social offense";[20] or, "Suspect yourself first";[21] or, "A serious business handicap—these troubles that come from harsh toilet tissue."[22]

The new advertising, which elicited even "silent" Calvin Coolidge's commendation as "the most potent influence" in "changing the habits and modes of life" of the nation and in nurturing "new thoughts, new desires, and new actions," tightened its alliance with modernism as the century wore on.[23] The innovations in typography and graphic design of such artists as Jan Tschichold, El Lissitzky, Theo van Doesburg, László Moholy-Nagy, Herbert Bayer, and A. M. Cassandre provided the means for ever simpler and more dramatic imagery. While Cassandre's graceful, visually economical posters for aperitifs, railroads, and steamship lines set a new standard of modern graphic elegance, and raised to an artistic level never exceeded the advertisement intended to be seen from fast-moving vehicles, Moholy-Nagy's and Bayer's austere sans-serif type, lacking all flourishes as well as capital letters, established the "rational" Bauhaus style in an attempt to satisfy the modern need for what Moholy-Nagy described as "printing products . . . commensurate with the latest machines; that is, . . . based on clarity, conciseness, and precision."[24]

Modernist graphic designs soon became the chief models for the printing and advertising professions—well before modernism was admitted into American "high" art—largely through new publications dedicated to the best in graphics. The German journal *Gebrauchsgraphik* opened its influential career in 1924, publishing the latest and most effective graphic designs for manufacturers, printers, advertisers, and artists of all countries. Its French equivalent, *Arts et Métiers graphiques,* followed three years later, purveying mainly the *style moderne* or "art deco" style associated with the Exposition Internationale des Arts Décoratifs, held in Paris in 1925. And in the United States a leading paper and printing concern, the West Virginia Pulp and

Paper Company, or Westvaco, brought out a publication similar to these, if less ambitious and more insistently commercial, in 1925. One of the first issues of *Westvaco Inspirations for Printers* instructed readers in the rationale of modern commercial graphics, observing that the advertisement "must tell its story at a glance (or in a few words at most) to be effective. It must convey the idea even when viewed at a distance and without study; it must be striking and distinctive enough to be remembered."[25] Future issues fully spelled out the contract between modern art and commerce in illuminating detail.

Under such headings as "Modernism as an Inspiration for Printers,"[26] "This Dynamic Spirit Which We Call Modern," and "Modernism Turns Merchandiser,"[27] *Westvaco Inspirations* explained how the modernist style, better than any other, serves commerce. First, this style reflects the "modern spirit" of the product and the times, since "modern art is but one phase of an urge which expresses itself in all departments of life," in furniture, fabrics, gowns, and utensils no less than in the fine arts. Second, the modernist style can also influence the consumer, since the modernist way with "design, pattern, play of interlaced color, contrasts of light and shadow" yields graphics of such "high attention value" that they are able "to stimulate emotions which otherwise the graphic arts are well-nigh powerless to produce."[28] And these emotions could not fail to work to the advantage of commerce. For just as the consumer economy itself, as described by apologists like Hazel Kyrk in *A Theory of Consumption* (1923), frees people from binding habits, traditions, and customs by keeping them hungry for new goods, so the modernist style, as *Westvaco Inspirations* told its readers, "changes the fashions overnight. . . , writes a damning 'out of date' on yesterday's favorite . . . , and by boldly challenging the imagination, opens new avenues to the interest of the buying public—avenues which keen merchandisers are following apace."[29] And if products are to be modernistically designed, so they should be promoted through modernistic advertising: a stylish dress in an abstract print or modern tableware or a streamlined automobile could best be advertised through equally stylish and often abstract graphics. After all, as *Printers' Ink* asserted: by making use of the latest fashions in design, "advertising helps to keep the masses dissatisfied with their mode of life, discontented with the *ugly things* around them"—and thus perpetually buying new things.[30] It is no wonder that the advertising departments of retail stores made use of designs far more modernistic than those to be found in the "fine art" galleries in the same stores: for even while slow to conquer middle-class tastes in "fine art," modernism readily expressed and fostered the style-conscious, acquisitive temper of middle-class consumers who relish marginal differences among virtually identical products.

The packages enclosing the new modern goods (and traditional ones) also began conforming to the modern graphic style. Packaging was itself, of course, no older than the consumer revolution. Mass marketing had all but put an end to the days of open bins and barrels of foodstuffs, reams of yard goods, and raw merchandise of all kinds measured out and handwrapped by merchants. The requirements of transport and above all of mass display and self-service together with the proliferation of products made packaging indispensable to every manufacturer. Eventually, all products would be separately packaged by the producer, and many packaged in packages within packages, for the consumer's convenience, the transporter's necessity, the retailer's display—and sales.[31] And when packaging became indispensable to marketing, the package became more than a container: it became a form of advertising. And as advertising it soon came under the influence of modernist graphic design.

The German company Bahlsen Keks had led the way early in the century with a simple graphic design for its biscuit packages. By the mid-twenties, manufacturers could consult a growing literature on designing the modern package. Richard B. Franken and Carroll B. Larrabee's *Packages that Sell* (1928), for instance, gave as the "principles of package design" a list of rules for transforming the package into a modernist advertisement: simplicity, display value, harmony of design, memorable images, easy describability, and ability to make the person react favorably.[32] Such "principles" inspired companies, pressed by intensifying competition, to organize marketing strategies around the package bearing the brand name rather than around the product inside—like the Sunshine Biscuit Company, whose advertisements urged prospective buyers to look for the Sunshine "biscuit rack," not the biscuits.

So common in principle, if not in practice, had modernism become in product design, packaging, and advertising that traditionalists began recoiling. Two writers in *Advertising and Selling* complained in 1930 of pressures to be modernistic in everything and insisted that advertisements containing historical allusions and pictorial images could *still* sell products.[33] Another contributor complained in the same year—which also saw the magazine add a regular section devoted to "Advertising Arts"—of "the demise of quality" in goods caused "by Mrs. Style-Conscious Modern in conspiracy with Mr. Style-Conscious Manufacturer."[34]

But the alliance of the consumer economy and modernism was made. Modern life and modern art had demonstrated affinities not to be denied or dissolved. And these affinities helped install a culture in which personality would be increasingly shaped by public imagery, and the gulf between high and popular arts would virtually disappear. This culture was not only modern, or up-to-date; it was modernist, that is, impatient with traditional constraints, attuned to elemental realities and desires, responsive to abstract forms, and entranced by technological ingenuity.

In forging bonds between personality and public imagery and between commerce and the arts, this modernist culture also brought changes in the status of the capitalist or, as he was known from the late nineteenth century onward, the *businessman*. For as the consumer economy tightened its hold upon the culture, the businessman acquired new influence, and debate mounted over his cultural character and responsibilities.

The commercial middle class had long known the sting of adverse criticism. Aristocrats and workingmen, artists and intellectuals, conservatives and socialists of the nineteenth century had offered it little else—even when they endorsed middle-class ethics of work and success. They castigated this class for undermining traditional virtues and the social order; for the vulgarity of its tastes; for the banality of its morals; and for its most egregious sin, reducing all relations between people and things, people and ideas, people and people, to what Carlyle, in a phrase that rapidly became a cliché, called the "cash nexus." Among these critics, Karl Marx was not the most hostile, only the most theoretical. As Richard Hofstadter observed of the United States, ever "since the development of industrialism, . . . the values of business and intellect" have been "seen as eternally and inevitably at odds: on the one side, there is the money-centered or power-centered man, who cares only about bigness and the dollar, about boosting and hollow optimism; on the other side, there are the men of critical intellect, who distrust American civilization and concern themselves with quality and moral values."[35]

Even exemplars of the middle class itself, dedicated to self-help, achievement, and profit, experienced discomfort and sometimes guilt over their devotion to Mammon. These discomforts induced a duplicity and ambivalence toward the pursuit of wealth that were an undercurrent of late-nineteenth-century capitalism. "Money," remarks one historian of the Germany of this period, "was something one had but did not talk about," or, "if the subject was unavoidable," one spoke of it "with embarrassed pain."[36] Edith Wharton, the early-twentieth-century American novelist of manners, remembered her mother telling her unequivocally: "Never talk about money and think about it as little as possible."[37] The German novelist Theodor Fontane gave fictional expression to this duplicity in *Frau Jenny Treibel* (1893); his heroine knows full well that "gold is trump and nothing else," yet she conceals the fact under denunciations of materialism and paeans to the ideal.[38]

This ambivalence toward money arose from fears, some age-old, some recent, that the quest for wealth diminishes the spirit or stifles humanistic sensibilities. Henry James (whose brother William invented the angry phrase "the bitch-goddess success") wrote as a critic of capitalism in *The American Scene* (1907): "The business-man in the United States, may, with no matter what dim struggles, gropings, yearnings, never hope to be anything *but* a business-man."[39] And few people believed being *only* a businessman was enough. At age thirty-three, Andrew Carnegie lamented: "To continue much longer overwhelmed by business cares and with most of my thoughts wholly upon the way to make more money in the shortest time, must degrade me beyond the hope of permanent recovery. I will resign business at thirty-five."[40] A Chicago financier, Charles L. Hutchinson, asked in 1882: Awash as we are in money-making, "are we not losing sight of the being created in the image of God, with heart and intellect and soul?"[41]

Successful businessmen like Carnegie and Hutchinson were likely to try to redeem themselves by embracing cultural philanthropy. Carnegie did not resign at age thirty-five; instead he put his wealth into education, because, he said, "liberal education gives a man who really absorbs it higher tastes and aims than the acquisition of wealth, and a world to enjoy, into which the mere millionaire cannot enter."[42] Hutchinson threw himself into building up Chicago's cultural institutions, assuming the presidency of the Art Institute in its formative years (the 1880s) because he believed art could "discover and present the ideal" and thereby help save society from materialism.[43] The names Vanderbilt, Rockefeller, Guggenheim, Ford, Mellon, and others further punctuate this philanthropic tradition: if capitalist appetites could induce spiritlessness and philistinism, the capitalist would compensate by public generosity and cultural education (and his sons would likely devote themselves to culture instead of business).

But as the consumer economy installed the "business culture," criticism of the middle class and the businessman entered a new phase marked by bitter ridicule and lurid portrayals of spiritual ruin. Thorstein Veblen carried forward his assault on business as the corrupter of culture while H. L. Mencken, fired by the fulminations of Friedrich Nietzsche against bourgeois mediocrity and self-satisfaction, blasted the "booboisie" for its vulgar material appetites and mindless boosterism. The young critic Malcolm Cowley excoriated a society where "everything fitted into the business picture" and where the "consumption ethic" corrupted all sensibilities; and, like many others of his generation in the 1920s, Cowley followed the example, if not the motives, of Henry James and fled his native shores in search of culture—and cheap living.[44]

The businessman as philistine found his archetype in Sinclair Lewis's *Babbitt* (1922). An unabashed votary of the business culture, Babbitt builds his life around sales and consumer products and reveres the skyscraper (then a novelty and at its tallest in that monument to mass marketing, New York's Woolworth Building) as "a temple-spire of the religion of business, a faith passionate, exalted, surpassing common men." But for all his boosterism, Babbitt also suffers from the capitalist malaise—that pang of soullessness and want of culture; as he confesses at the end, "I've never done a single thing I've wanted to in my whole life."[45] F. Scott Fitzgerald infected Jay Gatsby with some of the same disease: although not lacking in refinement, Gatsby has sold his soul for riches and carries about him an atmosphere malevolent with ill-gotten gain.

When business made direct alliances with art, the critics of business bewailed the act as a debasement of art. Theodore Dreiser told a story of this debasement in *The Genius* (1909), through the life of a painter who deteriorates artistically and morally as he succeeds in advertising. True to the stereotype, success is the corrupter. Sherwood Anderson dramatized this theme and the conflict between the true artist and commerce by stomping out of his paint manufacturing business in 1912 to become a writer; he then drew upon his experience in both business and advertising to portray capitalist culture in literature as the enemy of art and spirit.

To counteract these images, both traditional and newly minted, advertisers, boosters, and public relations men sprang to the defense of the consumer economy. Success and business could be shown to be the allies of spirit and culture, they decided; profits and wealth would simply be represented as byproducts of social responsibility and spiritual growth. An ambitious book entitled *What Is Success?* (1923) explained that "success is a spiritual quality, an inward satisfaction, which cannot be measured by material things"—yet it could be achieved in the pursuit of them.[46] In 1930, Henry Luce, braced by the profits from *Time* magazine, inaugurated *Fortune,* a self-consciously sophisticated monthly publication addressed to the businessman for the purpose of sparking his intellect and identifying him with "the most beautiful magazine" in America and thereby raising his social status.[47] More extravagant were boosters like advertising innovator Ernest Elmo Calkins, who turned the tables on the critics with *Business the Civilizer* (1926), and Bruce Barton, who, in *The Man Nobody Knows* (1924), described Jesus as a businessman who knew "every one of the principles of modern salesmanship" and created in his parables some of the most persuasive of all advertisements. Had not Jesus himself, Barton asked, silenced his critics with the question: "Wist ye not that I must be about my father's *business?*"[48]

Corporations also joined the cause. As they had learned from public relations experts, beginning with Edward Bernays, the corporation must create a positive moral and cultural image of itself in everything it did, or lose sales to those who could. Instead of simply marketing a product, a package, and a brand, corporations thus started marketing benevolent impressions of themselves. A leading figure in the advertising of the twenties, Claude Hopkins, explained in *Scientific Advertising* (1923) how his agency served this higher end: "We try to give each advertiser a becoming style. He is given an individuality best suited to the people he addresses. That's why we have signed ads sometimes—to give them personal authority. A man is talking—a man who takes pride in his accomplishments—not a soulless corporation."[49] This idea produced such *soulful* advertisements as those of the Bell Telephone Company in 1928 proclaiming: "The biggest thing about your telephone is the spirit of thousands and thousands of people who make up the Bell system. The loyalty of these people to the ideals of their work is reflected in every phase of your telephone service."[50] No profits here, not even technology; the telephone company is all spirit and idealism.

Although the critics of business on the one side and the boosters, advertisers, and PR men on the other appraised the merits of consumer capitalism differently, they agreed that the business culture needed two things: an end to its stereotypically philistine, spiritless, and often puritanical mentality, and adoption of more urbane, commercially pragmatic, and "spiritually" satisfying ways of business, life, and mind. By satisfying these needs, the business culture would gain a status and influence greater than it had ever known before—and in a national culture more open to materialistic desires and popular pleasures than any America had yet seen.

This national culture was that first exemplified in the 1920s by members of the postwar generation who learned to shape themselves according to the mass images of advertising, films, publicity, and popular songs, and who provided the first market for the beauty parlor and scented toothpaste, and diverted themselves openly with automobiles, jazz, cigarettes, and sex. It was the culture mirrored and nourished by twenty-three-year-old F. Scott Fitzgerald in *This Side of Paradise* (1920) and by the glib, bittersweet poetry and stories of Dorothy Parker, who spoke so knowingly of intense and ephemeral adolescent experience. It was also the culture of Hemingway's bored café-goers in *The Sun Also Rises* (1926), and that which tore Hermann Hesse's Harry Haller apart with ambivalence in *Steppenwolf* (1927) and which Ortega y Gasset flailed in *The Revolt of the Masses* (1930). And it was the culture that saw modernist art and ideas assimilated, partly through the efforts of business, into the rhythms and atmosphere of everyday life.

Not all who helped create this modernist, consumer culture would approve of its every attribute. Some, detecting a decline of humanistic values, would try to hold back the decline through efforts at cultural regeneration. And nowhere were the unfolding of this culture and the struggle to improve it more pronounced than in Chicago and in the career of Walter Paul Paepcke, founder of the Container Corporation of America, patron and proponent of László Moholy-Nagy's New Bauhaus (later the Institute of Design), friend and advocate of Robert Maynard Hutchins and the Great Books movement, and developer of Aspen, Colorado, as a center of cultural reform and elite society.

Walter Paepcke was made by the consumer culture; and he knew it. He spoke often and warmly of the "packaging revolution" that had given his company life and had awakened his appreciation of modern art and design. And although he frequently referred to himself publicly, with the self-deprecation typical of the capitalist among artists and intellectuals, as "only a prosaic boxmaker," he rose by means of the Container Corporation to prominence as an exponent of modern design and of cultural reform in mid-twentieth-century America.

But before he became either a "prosaic boxmaker" or a cultural light, Paepcke enjoyed the benefits of wealth already made by his German immigrant father in the flourishing markets of late-nineteenth-century Chicago. The fire that destroyed that city in 1871, just after the transcontinental rail system had made Chicago the nation's transportation hub, proved an economic godsend. As the city rose from ashes, it materialized as the marketing capital of the Heartland. A mere twenty years later, it boasted a population of over a million (up from 50,000 in 1859) and some 4,000 retail establishments, including the great department stores and mail order houses that served the nation—Montgomery Ward (1872), Marshall Field (1881), Carson Pirie Scott (1891), Sears, Roebuck and Company (1893), and Spiegel Home Furnishers (1893).

Chicago was a boom town. Fortunes in consumer products and marketing and in the building trades begged to be made—Marshall Field's estate, for instance, at Field's death in 1906, was put at $125 million. One of those drawn to the city in search of opportunity and wealth was Hermann Paepcke, an immigrant by way of Texas from Menklenburg, Prussia. Arriving in Chicago in 1879, he set his sights on the lumber industry, which, fueled by construction after the fire and by escalating demand for all kinds of consumer goods from furniture to baseball bats, as well as by the need for wooden containers to transport those goods, made Chicago the nation's lumber distribution capital in the next decade. Hermann Paepcke and Company opened for business in 1887, and just a decade later Paepcke demonstrated his affluence by moving his family into a stately mansion on the newly fashionable Near North Side—the neighborhood of the social elite ever since the wealthy Potter Palmers, the Cyrus McCormicks, and the Marshall Fields had built their homes there after the fire.

In that house, on the corner of Michigan Avenue and Pearson Street, a few short blocks from Lake Michigan, Hermann Paepcke sheltered and ruled his family with all the intractable individualism, conspicuous consumption, and emotional constraint known to us in the stereotype of the old entrepreneurial capitalist. A family portrait captures the man's character and the mood of his household. Paepcke, the paterfamilias, sits rigidly upright in formal attire surrounded by his stiffly uncomfortable, blank-eyed adolescent children and submissive wife (his second, the children's stepmother). He looks like a man used to breakfasting on nails. And his children are the very image of steely obedience.

But Hermann Paepcke was no philistine. Touched by the cultural inse-curities over being "in trade" that infected so many capitalists, he clung to the Germanic *Kultur* of his youth and doggedly conveyed it to his children. The Paepcke household rang with the philosophic verses of Goethe and Schiller—regularly recited by the old German while shaving. Frequent fam-ily visits to the fledgling Chicago Symphony Orchestra gave the young Paepckes a concertmaster's familiarity with classical music. And friendships with professors at the University of Chicago (an institution born with the help of John D. Rockefeller's philanthropy in 1891) like William A. Nitze, chairman of the Romance Languages Department, gave the Paepcke family its desired ties to the world of learning. More a Buddenbrook than a Babbitt, the stolid, cultured burgher Paepcke spurned all vulgarity and unconstraint, the beer-drinking *Gemütlichkeit* of Chicago's immigrant community no less than idle diversions like golf (he denied Walter permission even to work as a caddy), and the emotionally free manners of contemporary American soci-ety. So determined was he to shield his home from such evils that he prohib-ited visits by his children's friends.

Isolated from young society and dominated by stern patriarchal author-ity, the Paepcke household knew no frivolity and seldom heard laughter or joy, especially after the children's gentle mother died, although it never lacked in earnest purposes and sibling affection. It was, like so many Victorian homes before it, a hothouse of repression. The daughters matured and married with-out high expectations of love, reserving some of their deepest feelings for each other and for their only brother, Walter. And Walter grew up to be a modern mirror image of his father.

Born in 1896, and thirteen years old when his mother died, Walter early acquired his father's demanding self-discipline and cultural sensibilities, as well as expectations of a life equal to his father's in economic prosperity and patriarchal authority. As a youth—and later as an adult—he did nothing without energy and purpose, and suffered never a reproach or punishment at home because, his closest sister said, "he never did anything wrong."[51] These industrious habits carried him from the Latin School in Chicago to a Phi Beta Kappa key at Yale. And they gave him an unquenchable appetite for *success*, an appetite whetted by a taste for risk and a distaste for idleness, contentment, emotional ease, and intimacy.

Here were the makings of a man driven by an ethics of action and achieve-ment and hostile to symptoms of weakness and indiscipline—in others and in himself. He would never cease racing from one bold accomplishment to another, growing bored when difficulties ended; and he would never get his

fill of property, buying one house after another in Chicago and finally own-
ing a sizable part of Aspen, Colorado, as if searching for a home to match his
father's. He would view those who succumbed to weakness of flesh or mind
and those who ministered to it as inadequate human beings, dismissing psychoanalysis as an agency of whimpering self-indulgence, and spurning medical care,
even when in the grips of the cancer that took his life, as an invitation to
infantile dependency.

Few emotions found release in him. And although friendships came easily,
they usually (with the exception, perhaps, of his friendship with Moholy-
Nagy) arose from common professional or cultural interests and were cir-
cumscribed by those interests. Even his marriage of nearly forty years was
marked, on his part, by emotional distance and suppressed feelings. Strained
by differences of temperament and nurture—manifested in Walter's desires
at once to control and to win the admiration of his beautiful, intelligent, and
cultured wife and in her desires both to serve him and to be independent—
it survived largely through a shared enjoyment of cultural and social life and
a deep, if erratic and unspoken, affection. Walter had been cheated, he frequently told his wife, by growing up in a home where the husband and father
ruled and then becoming a husband and father himself only to discover that
such authority was not to be his. The frustrations led him repeatedly to
endanger his marriage with ego-affirming infidelities, but then always to
repent at any intimation of divorce. Only in the last weeks of his life, knowing the end was near, did he voice a consuming love for his wife and regret
not having said so before. "I was afraid," he confessed with boyish vulnerabil-
ity, "of losing you."

To whom in all his sixty-four years did Walter Paepcke open his heart?
To whom was he truly close? His widow could only say, as if questioning her
memory: "He really was close to no one."[52]

Yet Walter Paepcke was anything but emotionless. And in him, as in
anyone, hidden feelings sought and found their escape. The obsessive will to
control and to succeed, the compulsive economic risk taking (including gam-
bling at cards no less than in business), the zeal to improve culture, as well as
incessant chain-smoking and periodic sexual conquests, gave those feelings
byways into the open. And all who knew Paepcke also detected a symptom of
repressed emotion in his handwriting—brittle, ragged, trembling with tension. Curious about the psyche behind it, a friend sent a sample to a handwriting analyst. "The handwriting of W.P. is one of the most unusual that
that I have ever analyzed," came back the German reply; an "individualist
held back by much self-control," he possesses "abnormal erotic capabilities"
and suffers "neurotic conflict" from a life "lived under constraint" (*Zwang*).[53]

Obsession, compulsion, constraint, repression, neurotic conflict, these
are the attributes of a man made distrustful of feelings by the stringent de-

mands of morality and culture and yet left unsatisfied after meeting those demands. They are attributes common among traditional entrepreneurial capitalists and familiar among the economic and cultural leaders of Paepcke's generation, as many of those who figure in this story confirm. These attributes also describe a personality type that late-twentieth-century psychotherapists, promising an end to psychic conflict and the advent of supreme self-fulfillment, would diagnose as unhealthy and vow to eliminate. But they also describe the personality type that Sigmund Freud had in mind when he observed the inevitable discontents of civilization, the discontents born of desires thwarted and energies diverted in the making of civilization itself. And no psychological portrait of Walter Paepcke (or the notables of his generation) would be complete without the attributes that enabled him to channel his desires and energies into the building up of his own civilization. These included capacious energy, high intelligence, fecund imagination, undauntable will, winning charm, a dedication to quality, and a generosity of mind and purse in causes he admired. Without such attributes, Paepcke would have been only a financially successful, emotionally repressed "boxmaker." Instead, he became a leader in commerce and culture.

Paepcke got his start in this direction in 1922. In that year, at the age of twenty-six, he married a woman destined to influence him, through conflict and persuasion, more than anyone after his father; and, in that same year, his father died, leaving him ownership of the family business.

It happened that the Chicago Mill and Lumber Company, as Hermann Paepcke's establishment was then known, fell into Walter's hands near the nadir of its fortunes. Having expanded with the consumer market and then with the demands of World War I, the company had stumbled into the recession of 1920–1921 (alongside many other businesses, most notably General Motors, saved only by Alfred P. Sloan's revolutionary decision to replace the company's centralized, entrepreneurial structure with a decentralized, professional management organization, thus creating the model of the modern corporation). Amid that recession, old Paepcke's health had broken; and Walter had begun preparing himself to take over.

Although Walter was only twenty-five at that time, he had already won his father's confidence by graduating summa cum laude from Yale and, above all, by demonstrating, while working as assistant treasurer of the family firm, a quick grasp of what Hermann Paepcke considered "a complicated business." "Ich bin ganz Stolz auf ihn"—"I am very proud of him"—the old man had written to his eldest daughter, Alice, in March 1920. A year later, the ailing capitalist conceded the inevitable, handing his company's reins to his son with the familiar injunction of the traditional entrepreneur: "You'll have to look after the business."[54] In another year he was dead, and Walter was on his own.

Fig. 1.1. Walter P. Paepcke at his desk in 1926, the year he formed the Container Corporation of America (CCA). Courtesy of CCA.

The young man proudly moved into his father's office and "looked after" the business with a constant eye to expansion. Sensing that the days of fortunes to be made in lumber were numbered (the world's first steel-frame skyscrapers had risen in Chicago in the 1890s), he looked elsewhere for riches. And he saw opportunities for obtaining them in a new industry, packaging—not in wood but in paperboard.

He nursed the company back to health and then made his move. In 1926, he split off the paperboard division (acquired during the war) and merged it with the Mid-West Box Company and then the Philadelphia Paper Manufacturing Company to form a new enterprise. Brashly naming it the Container Corporation of America (CCA), he confidently assured his modest and doubting advisers (as company legend had it): "We'll live up to the name" (see fig. 1.1).

Beginning with fourteen mills and fabricating plants located in Chicago, Philadelphia, and West Virginia, the company first produced "shipping containers" (the labeled boxes that bring goods to retailers) and then added small "folding boxes" (for individual products) and cardboard for "set-up boxes" (the kind displayed on store shelves). Eventually the company made cardboard and containers for every conceivable purpose. And the list of clients constitutes a catalogue of early-twentieth-century consumer products: Singer sewing machines, Campbell's soups, Hunt's foods, Post cereals, Sunbeam mixers, Scott tissues, Rheingold beer, and so on.

The early profits (over $1,000,000 in 1927) were great enough to permit the young Paepcke and his wife to live very well indeed. Served by seven servants at home, they were lionized by Chicago society and soon belonged to all of the "best Chicago clubs," as *Time* magazine noted in a short article on CCA in 1931.[55] And they made a striking couple. He stood strong and broad-shouldered, his dark hair combed straight back, his features bold and dignified yet graced with a touch of softness—a strong, even jaw, firm but expressive lips, and large intelligent eyes set beneath arching brows accentuating his proud, sharp nose. He exuded masculine strength and more than a hint of sensuality: women would easily be his.

The woman whom he made his wife was more stunning still. Seven years Walter's junior, Elizabeth Nitze, daughter of Professor and Mrs. William A. Nitze, was, according to one well-traveled journalist, "the most beautiful woman in America for a generation."[56] Her slight, graceful limbs and perfect figure cut the air with poise and assurance, while her face, set under a mantle of flowing blonde hair, was beauty itself: marble-smooth skin alive with warmth, finely drawn lips irresistibly given to infectious smiles, a delicately rounded nose, and irridescent blue eyes beaming light and affection all around. Socially (as well as intellectually) gifted, and lovable as a kitten, she was known from childhood on as "Pussy." No one could resist her—although, like many beautiful women, she made a certain emotional distance from the pressing affections of others a part of her nature, to her demanding husband's recurrent disappointment. As a couple, the young Paepckes discovered that society was theirs for the taking.

And it was a glorious time to be young, attractive, and affluent in Chicago. The ascendant consumer culture was booming and seemed only to gain in excitement from the inconveniences of Prohibition. The city reveled in speakeasies, festivity, and fun, while gangsters at war added a note of adventure, and the advent of mass publicity and celebrity lent new delight to social life. Paepcke registered his affinity with this culture (despite his emotional restraints) by plunking down several thousand dollars in cash for a flashy new Packard in 1928 and driving it proudly and speedily through the city streets. In the same year, he bought a large apartment at one of Chicago's most distinguished addresses, 999 Lake Shore Drive, on the edge of Lake Michigan and just a few blocks from the old Paepcke home.

But despite their social brilliance, Walter and Elizabeth lived very separate lives. Regarding her as suited mainly to social life—a mere "social butterfly," he often called her—and to the home (where they had begun a family and suffered the loss of their firstborn, a son), Walter left Elizabeth to her woman's world, suggesting she take courses at the Art Institute the better to occupy her leisure. For her part, Elizabeth had no use for business. Her father was a distinguished professor at the University of Chicago, and her mother an effervescent socialite with a taste for the arts; Elizabeth desired a life of culture and sociability and happily turned her back on the world of "trade." While Elizabeth cultivated the arts and socialized, Walter built the Container Corporation into a national enterprise.

This achievement came not without difficulty. Intense competition and the Depression changed black ink to red on the ledgers, producing a loss of $980,000 in 1931 and $1,380,362 in 1932. Meanwhile, a proxy fight waged by a vice-president accusing Paepcke of irresponsibly expansionist policies almost lost him control. Paepcke fended off the attack and then took measures to halt the slide. Always tight-fisted in business, like his friend the fabled conservative Sewell Avery of Montgomery Ward, Paepcke cut costs wherever possible. He requested rent reductions from landlords, reduced wages, hired the cheapest labor he could find (including a previously laid-off employee rehired because he promised to work for less than anyone else, and Paepcke thought "the attitude of mind is interesting"),[57] lengthened the work day to twelve hours, and curtailed the use of paper clips. True to his temperament and economic interests, Paepcke condemned the New Deal as a threat to both business and the nation. Like other conservatives, he hung his hopes for economic recovery on a balanced budget. A notice posted over his name throughout CCA plants in 1932 announced: "Every Nation and corporation within a Nation must balance its budget or come to disaster sooner or later. Our budget in Container Corporation at the present time is not in balance." And to Paepcke's mind, no expenditure was too small to affect the imbalance.

When a slow return of profits began in 1933, Paepcke started eliminating the standing debt, then in excess of $7 million, and embarked on a resolute search for new markets. A timely boost came with the repeal of Prohibition. Christmas of 1933 saw liquor stores agleam for the first time with varnished bound containers of Hiram Walker whiskey, introduced by CCA (although designed by Hiram Walker), which so impressed buyers that *Forbes* magazine later reported: "Never in the world had such containers been used on liquor bottles; hence there was no competition as regards price or as regards tender feelings."[58]

The recovery inched forward until by 1936 profits finally exceeded their pre-Depression high and hit $1,287,000. The Container Corporation was now "the dominant unit in its industry," according to *Barron's*,[59] or, in the words of *Time*, "the biggest maker of paperboard shipping containers and cartons in the U.S."[60]—although this still gave it only 10 percent of its fiercely competitive industry. But the company had more than recovered. As *Barron's* noted in 1937, "So successful were its merchandising policies as to create something approaching a packaging revolution."[61]

"Merchandising policies." Here was the secret of Container's success. Paepcke and his staff had hit upon a marketing device tuned exactly to the key of the modernist, consumer culture. This device was the "corporate image."

Corporations had already learned to market their wares through idealized images of themselves, as observed earlier. Brand names had hinted at this by promoting products under the aegis of a distinguished parent company; and the twenties had seen companies, growing ever larger and more impersonal on the pattern of Sloan's General Motors, project themselves as the embodiment of personality and idealism.

The economic reverses of the thirties, which cast business (instead of the individualistic businessman, now fading from the scene amid the rise of professional management and public ownership) in the role of villain, had forced a redoubling of efforts to sell "the corporation." The National Association of Manufacturers ran ads attacking those who "strive to pit class against class" by blaming business for the Depression;[62] and Walter Paepcke was among those capitalist critics of New Deal liberalism to complain that "the politicians have out-sold the businessmen with the public" and to cry: "Business has a job to do!"[63] Companies invested unprecedented amounts of money to promote an image of their humanity and honor (foreshadowing the campaigns of the 1970s by the publicly unpopular petroleum industry). And at the advertising firm of N. W. Ayer & Son this kind of promotion, known as "institutional advertising," now surpassed product advertising for the first time.[64]

The Container Corporation did not start this movement, but it soon emerged as a model of ingenuity and refinement by transforming a promotional tactic into a sophisticated and comprehensive corporate strategy. The company began by improving its standing with labor, returning workers to the eight-hour day and full wages after 1933 and granting an unprecedented two-week paid vacation to all employees of three-years tenure. In 1936, Paepcke ingratiated the corporation with its stockholders (who now received their first dividends in five years) by issuing what *Time* magazine called a "startling invitation" to Eastern stockholders to attend a stockholders' meeting in New York, should they be unable to attend the annual meeting in Chicago.[65] The invitation startled because corporate headquarters stood in Chicago, and no company had held stockholder meetings away from home simply for the convenience of its investors. The next year Container expanded upon this gesture with an innovative survey aimed at identifying its stockholders' income, education, interests, etc., in order to mold its image to theirs.

But the heart of the company's corporate image lay not in tactics such as these. It lay in Container's fashioning itself as the embodiment of commercial modernism or as the vogue phrase had it, "good design." This corporate image materialized methodically and rapidly, beginning in 1935. Before that, Container had done little more than go along with trends in package design; as the stockholder's report of August 1931 reported: "Our research laboratory is continually perfecting better designed and more attractive containers," attested by an unexceptional illustrated brochure entitled "Packaging Is both a Science and an Art." As late as 1932, Paepcke could see no reason to advance any distinctive commercial image of his corporation. In response to a stockholder's suggestion that CCA advertise more widely, he said that an "additional advertising effort is not quite as applicable to our business as it would be to many others . . . for the reason that we do not sell to the individual, but rather to the purchasing agents of the larger manufacturing corporations of the country who, generally speaking, know of us." And in a surprisingly nearsighted observation on the function of packaging, he concluded that no public gestures by CCA would help sales because CCA "cannot stimulate demand on the part of the individual user," since retail purchasers "are interested in the commodities [they] are buying and not the package in which the wholesaler, retailer or jobber has received them."[66] The corporate image came to the Container Corporation only when this state of mind had departed. And it left as Paepcke became gradually converted, mainly through the influence of his wife, to the commercial uses of modern art and design.

Nurtured in his youth on Goethe's poetry, Beethoven's music, Kant's philosophy, and pictorial representations of hearty Alpine scenes, Paepcke—like Hesse's Harry Haller—could at first see in modernism only triteness and self-indulgence; he equated culture with the substantial and enduring artifacts of the past. His wife was different. She had breathed the air of modernist culture since childhood. Through her mother and her mother's friend, Mrs. John Alden Carpenter, wife of the Chicago composer noted for employing jazz rhythms in orchestral music and one of the first collectors of modern paintings in Chicago, she encountered virtually all the modernism Chicago knew in the twenties and thirties. She went to the *Ballets Russes* and German Expressionist films. She heard the music of Hindemith and Stravinsky. She looked at the paintings of Rousseau, Picasso, Klee, and others, and joined the Arts Club and the arty Friday Club, where in 1934 she heard Mortimer J. Adler and Mrs. Robert M. Hutchins deliver a bizarre discourse on modernism under the heading "Diagrammatics." She became acquainted with Harriet Monroe, editor of the important modernist journal *Poetry: A Magazine of Verse*; she met painters like Matisse; and she formed friendships with classical musicians such as Artur Rubinstein and Isaac Stern.

For many years Elizabeth could share but few of these artistic interests with her husband. She pursued them instead with her mother or friends. And when she purchased paintings by modernists, like Paul Klee or Le Corbusier, she felt constrained to hide them in the apartment's shadowy corners until Walter could be put into an accepting mood—which in some instances occurred only years later. In time Walter learned to take his wife's artistic tastes and purchases in good humor and even to enjoy them, merely chuckling at a daring Picasso Minotaur she placed before him in 1944, presenting her with a Manet for her birthday, and even purchasing a Juan Gris because he liked it. But that acceptance came slowly. And it came not only as an education in taste but as an awakening to the affinities of modern design and business.

His teachers, besides his wife, were to include the immigrant artists from the German Bauhaus whom he drew into the circle of his life, especially László Moholy-Nagy, Herbert Bayer, and Walter Gropius. Another teacher was A. Conger Goodyear, the industrialist, art collector, and former army colonel who helped create the Museum of Modern Art in New York in 1929 and led it through its first decade as president. Soon after meeting Goodyear in the early thirties, Paepcke informed his wife one night: "I'm bringing a businessman to dinner—but he's your kind: he likes art."[67] Paepcke's friendship with this crusty art lover lasted nearly thirty years and was punctuated by a frequent correspondence of shared intelligence, taste, and nicely barbed wit. Although Goodyear evoked criticism for his authoritarian military manner among museum colleagues—who nicknamed him "Toughie"—his rough practicality helped sell Paepcke on modernism.[68]

But more important than modern painting and its partisans in awakening Paepcke to the modernist style and in leading him toward a corporate image shaped by that style was Elizabeth Paepcke's taste for the best in graphic and interior design. She had not studied art for diversion alone. She wanted good design to grace her home and all she touched, and she determined to teach her husband its practical uses.

In 1934—the year of the Museum of Modern Art's historic exhibition "Art in the Machine Age," and of Chicago's Century of Progress Exposition, which first popularized "streamlined" design—she accompanied Walter and his chief vice-presidents to a national paper box advertising exhibit at the Palmer House. To prove her often-repeated advice that the best advertising for a box maker is simple graphic design on his boxes, she asked the three men to submit to an elementary test. "Look at that revolving display of packages," she said. "Now turn your backs to it. Which package do you remember?" The response was unanimous: "Firestone." "Why that one?" she asked. When none could account for his reaction, she told them to look again. Now the reason was clear. The Firestone container bore only one word, "Firestone," emblazoned in red ink (albeit in Gothic script) and enclosed in a blue border. "Now that is good advertising," she went on confidently. "Barely a glance and you remember the name of the company. Never mind the product."[69]

To keep her victory alive, Elizabeth Paepcke began showing her husband how tasteless and cluttered the stationery and advertising of CCA appeared alongside the graphics published in the European journals *Graphis* and *Gebrauchsgraphik*. Here Paepcke could see the modernist aesthetic openly in the service of commerce: this was, after all, not fine art but *Gebrauchsgraphik*, i.e., "useful design," or "commercial art." Persistent wifely urging and the spirit of the times were too much to resist. Paepcke gave in. The Container Corporation, just rising from the Depression and searching for competitive advantage in a laggard economy and a positive public image in an antibusiness climate, would embrace "good design."

Not knowing how to introduce good design into his company, Paepcke asked his wife to set up an art department. Amazed at this about-face by her previously condescending husband, she modestly and prudently declined, advising him to hire a professional "art director"—one of a profession barely a generation old. Turning for suggestions to the large local printing firm of R. R. Donnelly, Paepcke discovered just the man: a former art director for the advertising agencies of J. Walter Thompson and N. W. Ayer, now a freelance designer and president of the Art Directors' Club of Chicago. His name was Egbert Jacobson.

At their first meeting, Paepcke told Jacobson of his uncertain needs, and Jacobson dashed off a few rough designs for improving the appearance of the company's trucks. Much impressed, Paepcke asked him to redesign the Annual Report for 1934. The result, one of the earliest annual reports in industry, a novel corporate device for winning public support, did the job. On April 1, 1935, Jacobson went on the payroll as head of the art department. He had an assistant, a year's time, and a free hand to work. The assignment: create a comprehensive design image for the Container Corporation of America.

This ingenious marketing strategy, undreamed of in the packaging industry and known elsewhere only in fragments or experiments (primarily in companies occupied with the design or sales of consumer products, such as the pioneering Allgemeine Elektrizitäts-Gesellschaft under designer Peter Behrens in Germany), carried far beyond the design of boxes. If CCA hoped to gain market advantage by tapping the growing popular taste for modern design, the company would have to exhibit good design in everything associated with it. In short, CCA would have to sell itself not as a boxmaker only but as a designer and as the embodiment of good taste.

Paepcke outlined the scope and early effects of this strategy a year after its inception in an address before the Art Directors' Club of Chicago. Since "eye value" had become indispensable to marketing, Paepcke reported, and since "almost every product has by its very nature either form, shape, color, design, composition, printing," the Container Corporation had decided it could turn the "eye value" of everything it touched to advantage by setting up an art department. This department not only would formulate design policies and fashion designs for clients; it would also decide what colors to paint the Container Corporation's factory walls, offices, and trucks, what printing to place on its vehicles, checks, letterheads, annual reports, visiting cards, and invoices, and what logo and advertising to set before the public.

The consequence, Paepcke proudly observed, was a uniform design image. Container's trucks hit the streets sporting fresh tan and dark brown paint, colors representing the company's product and shaded both for contrast and to cover surfaces easily marred. A new logo adorned the sides: the letters CCA in solid brown behind the abstract image of a box tilted toward the viewer to convey depth and to give the impression that it hovers over the country. Above the logo, solid white letters running the length of the trailer and one-third its height spelled out CONTAINER CORPORATION; between them and the logo in small white print came the words "of America." And, in a final touch of color contrast and style, the trucks rolled along on white wheels or white sidewall tires (see fig. 1.2).

No industrial vehicle had ever looked like this. And the remodeling had its desired effect: heads turned, eyebrows lifted, the words CONTAINER CORPORATION stuck in minds, and the company became publicly identified with good design. CCA stationery carried on the impression. All extraneous mat-

Fig. 1.2. Container Corporation truck displaying Egbert Jacobson's innovative design of 1936. Courtesy of CCA.

ter, like pictures and the officers' names, disappeared, and the company name appeared alone, or alongside the logo, printed in a simple sans serif type virtually the same for all documents. The annual reports became attractive booklets, typographically modern and catchily illustrated. Offices, lobbies, cafeterias, and restrooms assumed the clean, linear look of *style moderne* interiors, marked by strong yet welcoming colors, expanses of glazed tile, and functional metal furniture. And a permanent public exhibit of the best in modern package design opened in the New York office.

"These are some of the things," Paepcke concluded, "which our company is attempting to do in its struggle to prove to the great unwashed masses that we are thinking in terms of art." Paepcke had by this time come so to identify himself and his company with art that he felt compelled to ask his audience, "How can we tell an artist from an ordinary businessman?" and then to answer with a knowing smile: "Always address anybody as an artist and he will never object to the compliment."[70] When Noel Coward, whom Paepcke had met casually in the twenties, jocularly inquired of him in the year CCA's corporate image took form, "What is a container and what does it contain?"[71] Paepcke might have replied, "It is a box designed to be seen. It might contain nothing at all."

But improved artistic services and internal restyling did not alone create CCA's corporate image. The art department also initiated an ambitious advertising campaign geared to win recognition for the company as an eminent exponent of art in commerce. Paepcke's previous belief that CCA could gain nothing from mass institutional advertising had collapsed under the need to defend business against its critics in the Depression and had been extinguished by the desire to gain competitive advantage in a depressed economy by means of a distinctive corporate image. "We . . . have to sell our corporation . . . to the large public," he now announced. "Therefore, we are using advertising in an effort to educate the public as to what we are doing, what we manufacture, what our industry does, what sort of industry it is, what our position in that industry is, and all that sort of thing." And, he added, we "hope that our advertising will have some artistic value."

To insure this "artistic value," the art department would require advertisements marked by "simplicity, conciseness, unity of design and thought and line."[72] They would have very little text and, as Paepcke later explained, would give the observer "something interesting to look at which he could associate with us" and which would at the same time exemplify "the originality, imagination, and taste" of the entire organization. They would, of course, speak the visual language of modernism, for, as Paepcke said, "the techniques of modern artists would identify us with current developments in applied graphic art which were—and are—so important to packaging."[73]

The plan conceived, suitable artists had to be found. Jacobson sought help from Charles T. Coiner, art director of N. W. Ayer & Son, CCA's advertising agency. Coiner, an artist possessing a keen sense for modern advertising graphics and delighting in new ideas and the discovery of talent, suggested using semiabstract designs such as those common in European posters for a decade. When the American artists Coiner first turned to produced no acceptable sketches, he looked elsewhere. Discovering that the famous French poster artist A. M. Cassandre was on his way to the United States for a short visit, Coiner rushed to New York to meet him at the pier. Within minutes he walked away with a contract, Cassandre's first in this country, for twelve black and white drawings at a fee of $500.[74]

Cassandre combined the two qualities most desired by CCA: a knack for good design and the ability to strike the observer immediately and memorably. Each of the semiabstract drawings he produced (which appeared in *Fortune* from 1937 to 1939) illustrated a purported attribute of the corporation stated in bold print. A montage of goods announced "Diversification" (see fig. 1.3). A sketch of a battlement connected by the outline of a box to a classical figure bespoke "Strength and Beauty." An array of lines drawn together into a clenched fist illustrated "Unity." A disembodied eye gazing at a cube through interstellar space signaled "First in Development." Three partial profiles lining

Fig. 1.3. A. M. Cassandre, Container Corporation magazine advertisement, first modern art series, July 1937. Courtesy of CCA (Smithsonian American Art Museum).

Fig. 1.4. A. M. Cassandre, Container Corporation magazine advertisement, first modern art series, February 1938. Courtesy of CCA (Smithsonian American Art Museum).

the edge of a circle, their eyes focused on a box at the center, conveyed "Concentration" (see fig. 1.4). Beneath these well-integrated designs ran the company's name, accompanied in some instances by a dozen promotional words in small letters for anyone curious enough to look. The advertisements were wonderful—and surprising.

Impressed by Cassandre's first works, the art department hastened to recruit new artists both in the United States and abroad. Jacobson sailed to Europe to do this in August 1937 and there found a wire from Paepcke awaiting him:

TONI ZEPF GEBRAUCHSGRAPHIK MAY THIRTY-SEVEN
INTERESTING AS CASSANDRE ALTERNATIVE SUGGEST
YOU INVESTIGATE.[75]

Toni Zepf's designs—thanks to Elizabeth Paepcke, who in her common practice had placed the May 1937 issue of *Gebrauchsgraphik* under Paepcke's nose—soon joined Cassandre's in disseminating CCA's image. Then followed works of Jean Carlu, Leo Lionni, Herbert Bayer, Herbert Matter, Fernand Léger, Man Ray, Jean Hélion, Miguel Covarrubias, Richard Lindner, Henry Moore, Willem de Kooning, Xanti Schawinsky, and many more. From this time forward, through several successive series of ads—featuring wartime service and patriotism, the United Nations, the states of the Union, and finally, the most ambitious and successful of all, "The Great Ideas of Western Man" (see figs. 7.1 and 7.2)—CCA advertising grew ever more abstract in theme and more removed from explicit reference to the company's industrial identity.

Response to the modern art in advertising campaign was mixed. "Among some businessmen and some professional advertising people it evoked a reaction bordering on shock,"[76] Paepcke recalled. It also elicited some nasty letters. "It has been our misfortune to see your advertisement in the latest *Business Week* magazine," wrote a small corporation president to Paepcke in reference to Fernand Léger's poster of 1945 "France Reborn" (see fig. 1.5). "It would be far better if the rebirth had never taken place if this creation is symbolic of it."[77] "Not only is it punk art," wrote another critic of the same ad, "but it gives the impression of poor judgment on the part of your corporation."[78] Paepcke remained unruffled by such resistance. For "as the controversy continued," he reported gleefully, "the visibility and reader identification of the advertising increased out of all proportion to the dollars paid for it." Asked if he understood one or another of these ads, Paepcke would blithely reply: "No. But it stopped you, and you remembered it—that's all I ask." To justify this "education" by attention rather than understanding, of response rather than thought, Paepcke explained that "it is the dilemma and not the fault of advertising that it must appeal to each of us as if he were a hypothetical average. The trick is to do it without offense to the reader's taste and intelligence."[79] Container's novel advertisements turned the trick.

Fine art—by contrast to poster illustration—had of course appeared in American advertising before, dating back to the Currier and Ives prints for the Erie Railroad and P. T. Barnum in the mid-nineteenth century and the

FRANCE REBORN *New lifeblood—supplies in paper packages.*

CONTAINER CORPORATION OF AMERICA
SAVE WASTE PAPER

Fig. 1.5. Fernand Léger, Container Corporation magazine advertisement, United Nations series, June 1945. Courtesy of CCA (Smithsonian American Art Museum).

sophisticated Pierce Arrow and Steinway ads of the early twentieth century. It had already brought celebrity to one firm, the Abbott Laboratories, which spent millions on it.[80] And abstract design had become a familiar motif in the advertising of various consumer products. But the Container Corporation was the first company to engage modern artists in a systematic and enduring campaign of institutional advertising and of corporate identification with modern art. A year after the campaign began, and just after the company had published an abundantly illustrated geographic atlas for its friends and favored customers, *Gebrauchsgraphik* ran an article praising the "special character" of CCA for setting a standard in "the practical and at the same time artistic planning of the whole concern."[81] A vice-president of N. W. Ayer & Son remarked that "no other advertising in our experience has had so many requests to reproduce, to use in advertising art exhibits, and to demonstrate in schools and art classes as the work for Container Corporation of Cassandre, Zepf, and Bayer."[82] A few years later, the editor of *Harper's* magazine labeled CCA "the most daring of all" corporate advertisers because it alone "used abstract paintings in full color for their decorative and shock effect in magazines."[83]

This unique advertising campaign not only elevated the corporate image of CCA, it also helped prompt a wave of corporate courtships of art. It was no accident that several of the companies involved in these courtships—like Dole Pineapple, which utilized abstract art and gave Cassandre his second American commission, and De Beers Diamonds, which commissioned sentimental works and published them as "Painted for De Beers"—were clients of Charles Coiner.[84] But the idea soon caught on with other agencies as well, and before long it had become commonplace to promote products and corporations through an identification with "fine art." As a writer in *Printers' Ink* explained a decade after the CCA campaign began, "the association of *quality* art with merchandise tends to give the merchandise an air of quality that will appeal not only to a class audience but also to the dealers who cater to these customers."[85] Braced by such hopes, Lucky Strikes began pushing cigarettes by means of "paintings of the Tobacco country by America's foremost artists"; the United Brewers Foundation planned "a series of typical American scenes painted by America's foremost artists"; Pepsi Cola began in 1944 sponsoring an annual competition of artists, the 150 best paintings to be exhibited under the company's aegis at the Metropolitan Museum in New York; and corporations of all kinds started collecting art for display.[86] Thus when CCA exhibited its collection of "Modern Art in Advertising" (then numbering nearly one hundred works) at Chicago's Art Institute in April 1945 (see p. 75), Paepcke could boast of being at the leading edge of a cultural movement—one that has yet to abate. And he could be proud of heading the first industrial corporation to build a comprehensive image for itself upon the marriage of modern art and business. "Few consumer merchandisers and virtually no industrial manufacturers," remarked an author in *Industrial Marketing* in 1948, "can claim an advertising and public relations program that is integrated so thoroughly with the total management of production, sales, and finance."[87] It was therefore no accident that Paepcke became a familiar figure to readers of the nation's business magazines, and that although not himself an advertiser he was named "Advertising Man of the Year" by *Industrial Marketing* in 1955,[88] and that annual net profits at CCA reached a record of nearly $15 million soon after this. About this time, the company produced a promotional film celebrating its history and success titled "Design: Language of the Modern Market." The corporate image worked.

Yet Paepcke's commercial embrace of art served more than economic interests. Once converted to the principles of modern design, Paepcke drew upon his fervent moral energies, old-world cultural ideals, and American thirst for betterment to promote those principles. Sounding a theme growing common among the more visionary American advertisers and designers such as Ernest Elmo Calkins and his disciple Walter Dorwin Teague, Paepcke urged the complete integration of art and life. "Think of the various things all of us use every day," he told the Chicago Art Directors' Club, "the clothes we wear, the furnishings we buy for houses, automobiles, the presents we give to our friends, almost everything. They are all manufactured by some ordinary businessman who doesn't know much about art." But "they could all be made by companies that have their eyes on art," to the benefit of both the companies and the American sensibility.[89]

The art department of CCA thus reached beyond its immediate tasks to become a national center of design research. Jacobson, as president of the Association for Color Research, became an authority on color harmony. Rejecting the idea that color arrangement is an intuitive gift belonging to artists, he set out to make available to all designers a theory and a practical scheme for making the best color choices. "A harmony of colors," he wrote in his essay "The Science of Color," "is not a work of art but a scientific fact."[90] Drawing on the ideas of Wilhelm Ostwald, he set forth a simple system showing 680 gradations of twenty-four hues from white to black. By 1948, Jacobson's *Color Harmony Manual*, published by CCA, had become the standard in more than a thousand advertising agencies and printing plants.[91]

Meanwhile, Paepcke and CCA were carrying the message of good design abroad in disparate ways. Recognized by *Fortune* in 1941 as "the glamour unit of the paperboard industry,"[92] the corporation extended its manufacturing and marketing operations into Latin America during the war and into Europe during the next decade. Its growing art department added a specialty division and developed many artful and practical uses of paperboard, like cut-out dolls, children's books with pop-out figures called "Slotties," and cartons reusable as toys. A package design laboratory was created under Hungarian Albert Kner, who had come to Container from Europe, attracted, he said, by the advertising art. The lab's object was to study "all matters pertaining to the greater attractiveness of the good old everyday box."[93] In 1951, Paepcke and Jacobson founded the annual International Design Conference in Aspen, Colorado, an ambitious and influential organization of artists and businessmen, to promote "design as a function of management" that still continues. And the CCA advertising campaigns and the traveling exhibitions of advertising art grew ever more popular, culminating in "The Great Ideas of Western Man" series (see pp. 220–221, 223), as an eminent symbol of the modern alliance of commerce and culture.

Not only businessmen but educators and cultural leaders commended Container's achievements. The director of the San Francisco Museum of Art lauded CCA for its "consistently enlightened and distinguished use of art."[94] Art teachers and students from Chicago's schools tramped the company's halls and laboratories, inspired, said the Board of Education's director of art, by Container's "application of design principles to the problem of contemporary living."[95] Students of the Harvard Business School undertook to study CCA as a case history in "the public and design."[96] And young graduates of business schools and art institutes flooded the personnel files with applications for employment. "There was no place quite like Container," recalled Norman DeHaan, a member of the art department staff in the 1940s and later president of the American Institute of Designers; "It was an education in itself."[97] And the noted architect and apologist for modern design, Richard Neutra, extolled Paepcke's many missionary labors on behalf of good taste in a dedication scrawled on the fly leaf of his book *Survival through Design* (1954): "To Walter Paepcke: The great patron of Design in Time and Space—in all Dimensions."

Paepcke and the Container Corporation had made the corporate image a way of life.[98] And in doing this they helped make Chicago a vital center of commercial design in the country for twenty years. But they were not alone responsible for this vitality. Five months after Container's first modern art advertisement appeared, the New Bauhaus opened its doors to begin teaching designers the principles and practices of modernism as exemplified by the most famous art and design school of the century, the Bauhaus, closed by the Nazis in Germany a few years earlier. It was natural that the paths of the New Bauhaus and the Container Corporation should have crossed, and that the head of the school, László Moholy-Nagy, and Paepcke should have become friends; for the two men held many temperamental qualities and ideas in common—on art, industry, education, and cultural reform. But Paepcke and Moholy-Nagy shared more than a temperament and ideas. Together with the institutions they founded and led, they were both born of the marriage of art and consumer capitalism. And until Moholy-Nagy's death in 1946 they shared a history.

2

marketing modernism:

moholy-nagy and the bauhaus in america

The preeminent school of modern design, the Bauhaus, arrived in Chicago during the sweltering midsummer days of 1937 in the person and ideas of expatriate Hungarian László Moholy-Nagy. Almost a decade earlier, Moholy, as he was familiarly known, had left his teaching post at the parent Bauhaus in Dessau, Germany, along with his colleagues Walter Gropius, Herbert Bayer, and Marcel Breuer, in protest against moves to weaken the school's humanistic purpose and strengthen its vocational and political leanings; five years after Moholy's departure in 1928, Nazi harassment had shuttered the school for good. A zealous pedagogue and cultural reformer, as well as resolute modernist and experimental artist, Moholy had yearned for the teacher's influence while working during that next decade as an artist and commercial designer in Germany and England. When an invitation came from Chicago's Association of Arts and Industries to organize and head a school of industrial design modeled on the Bauhaus, he welcomed it—even though it meant beginning a new life in a land long derided by European artists and intellectuals as hopelessly vulgar, insatiably commercial, and entirely without art.

Moholy's first encounter with American culture, on board the S. S. *Manhattan* bound for New York, conformed to this stereotype while stirring hopes in the ever optimistic educator. "Today was my first meeting with the American mentality," Moholy wrote to his wife, Sibyl, who had remained in their London home. It was the Fourth of July, and, to his dismay, the passengers had fallen into raucous celebration. "We all got whistles and noisemakers and horns, just as if we were small children," and everyone began "singing and yelling into each other's faces. . . . This is America's highest national holiday," Moholy noted sadly, "but it seems to depend for success on a complete reversion to infantilism."[1] Yet Moholy soon discovered that this vulgar unconstraint had hidden virtues. For it yielded a "genuine friendliness" and "uninhibited curiosity" that won the teacher's heart within him. And, reporting with surprise that the Americans seem to "shrink from no inquiry—no matter how personal," he closed on a note of delighted expectation: "If this is a national characteristic, Americans will make wonderful students. They'll never be afraid to ask questions."[2]

Once in America, Moholy experienced new pleasures and renewed doubts. New York seemed to him an abstract artist's dream (just as it did later to his friend and fellow modernist, Piet Mondrian). Driving from the pier with his host, the author James Johnson Sweeney, Moholy "made the car stop several times to look down narrow streets they call 'alleys' to see the strange patterns made by . . . the beautiful fire escapes. This," he happily told Sibyl, "will make a fine film one day." And the buildings! From the terrace of Sweeney's apartment (a residence Moholy described as "the best—very best Europe: white walls, matting, very little furniture—a Picasso, a Miro"), where Moholy felt "so high I floated in the air," he cast his hungry eyes upon the vast abstract construction laid out before him: "Obelisks, menhirs, megaliths—every shape, historic and prehistoric—straightly perpendicular, or terraced like a pyramid; in solid formations, or single—pointing." Like the artworks he loved, this awesome scene contained "no detail." And when night fell, the city became for him a composition in light and form reminiscent of his own aesthetic creations: "A million lights perforated the huge masses—switching, flickering—a light-modulation dissolving the solid form . . . , an incredible symphony of shape and light." He confessed: "I got drunk—from seeing."[3]

But Moholy's intoxication didn't last. A few days later he informed Sibyl from Chicago that "the skyscraper illusion of my first night in New York has vanished." For "here I see [Chicago] from below with all the detail thrown into focus." Instead of modernist abstraction his eyes now beheld urban structures covered "with the facades of Trianon, Chartres, a mosque or a Doric colonnade" (the innovative modern buildings of Louis Sullivan and the Chicago school seem to have eluded him, just as they later eluded that other great Bauhaus alumnus in Chicago, Mies van der Rohe). Moholy quickly concluded that Chicago is a "strange town" with "no culture, just a million beginnings."[4]

Yet more disconcerting to Moholy than Chicago's eclectic traditional architecture was his discovery that the people who had brought him to the midwestern metropolis, the leaders of the Association of Arts and Industries, exhibited no taste for modernism at all. "They called me here—knowing what I stand for," he wrote, disappointed and confused. "They wouldn't have gone to all that trouble otherwise. But their homes, the style of furniture, their architectural preferences, the pictures they hang on their walls, show not the slightest influence of any modern taste." One member of the association, a printer and book designer, showed Moholy two books he had designed. "He must know about Bauhaus typography?" Moholy puzzled; but here were glowing "imitations of Gothic prayer books. Why," Moholy wondered, "would he join this whole venture?" Even in the home of Walter Paepcke, the association member whom Moholy deemed "the most charming of them all," the modernist recoiled at seeing "madonnas all over the place, strange draperies, and imitation Louis Quinze furniture" (mostly family heirlooms; the few modern paintings still hung in the shadows). "What am I to believe?" he asked his wife. "Shall I be an optimist and say: Everyone is a potential student; or shall I be a pessimist and say, 'Forgive them for they know not what they're doing'?" Disheartened, he laid down his pen with the words: "I am bewildered, Darling. Do they know what they're doing?"[5]

They thought they knew. The letter inviting Moholy to Chicago had even confidently assured him that the Association of Arts and Industries had "always subscribed to the plan of the Bauhaus" and intended "to establish much the type of school you had at Dessau."[6] The story of the Bauhaus in America is the story of how the association and the Bauhaus saw their fates entwine, and then how Moholy-Nagy, deserted by the association but backed by Walter Paepcke, kept the Bauhaus idea alive and helped put Chicago for a time in the vanguard of modernist culture and cultural reform.

The Association of Arts and Industries invited Moholy-Nagy to Chicago in the summer of 1937 to cap its efforts, which had begun in 1922, to encourage better design in industry by bringing designers and industrialists together and demonstrating their common interests.[7] These aspirations were not, to be sure, the exclusive property of the association. They belonged as thoroughly to the modern consumer culture as did, say, modern advertising and packaging. And, like modern advertising and packaging, they had grown from a whetted public appetite for art and from a widening commercial recognition that artful designs sell products.

That appetite had been roused in the first place by the British, who had seen the economic advantages of art at the very dawn of industrialization.

The London Society of Arts had awarded prizes for well-designed manufactured products in the 1750s; Britain's Royal Academy had been formed in 1768 "for promoting the Arts of Design" and to provide a competitive edge to English artists and designers over their foreign counterparts;[8] and, at the same time, the pioneering industrialist Josiah Wedgwood had searched England for artists capable of giving marketable fashion to factory-produced stoneware. With the spread of industry in the early nineteenth century, the uses of design in economic competition had begun to absorb the energies of industrialists, designers, educators, and politicians alike. Sir Robert Peel stood in the British House of Commons in 1832 to complain, as the official record reported, that while British "manufacturers were, in all matters connected with machinery, superior to all their foreign competitors . . . , in the pictorial designs, . . . so important in recommending the production of industry to the taste of the consumer," the British "were, unfortunately, not equally successful; and hence they had found themselves unequal to cope with their rivals."[9] Peel's listeners seem to have agreed, particularly those mindful, as one of them said, of "the superiority of the French in this respect to our manufacturers." The Ecole des Beaux Arts had long stimulated "improvement in patterns and articles of taste"[10] (albeit in the fine arts and architecture, not directly in manufactured products). Within two decades of Peel's observations—and recommendation for the creation of a National Gallery of Art—Britain's place in industrial design had improved sufficiently, through political pressures, the creation of schools of design, and the labors of advocates like Henry Cole, Owen Jones, and Matthew Wyatt, that the nation could stage an international exhibition (in 1851) to demonstrate the excellence of British arts and industry to the world—although the only semblance of *modern* industrial design at the exhibition was the iron and glass "Crystal Palace" that housed it.

Britain benefited most from the industrial uses of art until near the end of the century when, as the historian of modern design Nicholas Pevsner says, "the initiative now passed to the continent and the United States, and after a short intermediate period, Germany became the center of progress."[11] The passage to America came in the same years of the late nineteenth century that came to see painting, the graphic arts, and advertising move toward visual abstraction and psychological persuasion and a vogue of "aestheticism" spread a craving for artistry throughout the culture. This craving readily infected Americans yearning for self-improvement, and it became something of an epidemic thanks in part to the flamboyant and popular proselytizing of Oscar Wilde.

Later famous for his clever plays debunking Victorian manners, Wilde had first made a name for himself as a witty and eccentric aesthete bearing a lily in his hand and the doctrines of "art for art's sake"—or, more accurately, art for Life's sake—on his tongue. His sensational lecture tours of America in 1882 exemplified his astonishing appeal, which aroused even in frontier mining towns (see Chapter 4) a taste for art, beauty, and good design. "As regards my practical influence," Wilde wrote from Chicago (where he pontificated on "house decoration" and prophetically asked residents, "Why don't you get some good public dwellings?"), "I have succeeded beyond my wildest hope. In every city they start schools of decorative art after my visit and set on foot public museums, getting my advice about the choice of objects and the nature of the building. . . . They really are beginning to love and know beautiful art."[12]

Wilde overstated his importance in awakening Americans to art and the artistic, but the two decades following his visits indisputably brought a flowering of publications and organizations dedicated to purging America's aesthetic tastes in domestic things of ignorance and retrograde eclecticism. Interior decoration flourished as never before, prodded by new magazines, some of which survive today, like *Ladies Home Journal* (1884, and especially after 1889, when Edward Bok became editor), *Good Housekeeping* (1885), *The House Beautiful* (1896; it had adopted the title of a collection of articles by Clarence Book published in 1878), *House and Garden* (1901); and books of protomodernist advice like *The Decoration of Houses* (1897) by Edith Wharton and Ogden Codman, Jr.[13] At the same time, artists themselves began organizing to improve the appearances of manufactured goods. Most of these organizations took their immediate inspiration not from Oscar Wilde but from the arts and crafts movement of the 1880s in England led by William Morris. Devoted to "elevating . . . by art . . . all the details of daily life,"[14] the movement spawned arts and crafts societies everywhere, bent on restoring handicraft, reforming art education, and curtailing, or at least upgrading, the machine manufacture of everyday articles.

One of the first of these societies in the United States appeared in Chicago under the guidance of some design-conscious citizens, including Frank Lloyd Wright and Jane Addams. But Wright soon sensed folly in the antimachine bias of the arts and crafts mentality; designers, he decided, risked thwarting their influence by rejecting industrial production. And in a famous essay of 1901, "The Art and Craft of the Machine," he dissociated himself from Morris's philosophy, professing his "gradually deepening conviction that in the machine lies the only future of art and craft."

Wright had not lost sight of the imperatives of art for the "articles of everyday use"; he had simply seen the need to adapt those imperatives to the demands of modern production; he even hoped "to prove that the machine is capable of carrying to fruition high ideals in art—higher than the world has yet seen."[15] This recognition—shared by others and prefigured notably by the career of the energetic Englishman Henry Cole, editor of the *Journal of Design* (1848–1852), promoter of the Crystal Palace Exhibition of 1851, and founder of the British Department of Practical Art in 1852—gave rise to the "industrial arts" movement with its Chicago branch, the Industrial Arts League, formed by Wright, Louis Sullivan, and associates in 1899. Although less ideologically zealous than the arts and crafts societies, the industrial arts movement exercised more lasting influence by urging the unity of art and industrial production and training designers to achieve this unity. Both the Bauhaus in Germany and the Association of Arts and Industries in Chicago were to take life from these same motives.

It was not long after the turn of the century that leadership in industrial design began swinging to Germany. It did so as heated economic competition pushed industrialists toward a union with the modernist aesthetics that called for relatively unornamented functional forms easily mass-produced. As this alliance materialized, many organizations sprang up in Europe and the United States to foster it. But the Germans were the first actively to forge and exploit it, in their hope of vanquishing their chief industrial rivals, the British. Their successful campaign even bore traces of diplomatic intrigue.

Troubled by British prestige in industrial design, the Germans assigned a man to their embassy in London to report on the causes of that prestige and recommend ways for Germany to eclipse it. Between 1896 and 1903, Hermann Muthesius, in the role of an attaché, scrutinized British culture and economics and detected the clue to Britain's competitive market advantage in the modern functional style of recent English architecture and interior decoration—especially the work of Charles F. A. Voysey. Returning to Germany, he published his observations in a three-volume study, *The English House* (1904–1905), which praised the absence of aesthetic affectation, the calm rationality, and the taste for "forms developed purely from purpose" typical of contemporary British design. In the future, he concluded, this functional style "will be seen as the most eloquent expression of our age."[16]

But Muthesius did not stop there. He began polemicizing against the backwardness of Germany in industrial design and against the arts and crafts mentality of the leading German design association, the Kunstgewerbe. And he predicted "a sharp economic recession if the motifs used in the shaping of [German] products continued to be thoughtlessly borrowed from the form-treasury of the previous century."[17] To give his ideas greater impact, Muthesius established the Deutsche Werkbund in 1907, an association of "the best representatives of art, industry, crafts, and trades," which he hoped would serve as "a rallying point for all those who are able and willing to work for high quality" and thus enhance "the future status of Germany in the world."[18] And high quality meant for Muthesius not handicraft but the best in standardized machine production. "It is not the machines" that cause low quality, insisted Muthesius's colleague Theodor Fischer in the Werkbund's first inaugural address, "but our inability to use them properly."[19]

Learning the *proper* use of machines, or how to lend modern, not imitative, artistry to manufactured articles, now became a recognized exigency of the design profession. German art schools soon "deserted the routine of the nineteenth century and adopted the new course" embodying the "ideals of the Modern Movement."[20] At the same time, organizations similar to the Werkbund appeared in many countries—Austria and Sweden in 1910, Switzerland in 1913, and Britian in 1915. The most important of these, the British Design and Industries Association, openly conceded the leadership of the Germans. "The remarkable expansion of German trade, achieved largely at the expense of our own," wrote one of the association's founders, "has resulted not simply from the energetic exploitation of markets, but from . . . the intelligent cooperation of artists, educationalists, and manufacturers (assisted by such organizations as the Deutsche Werkbund) with the object of freeing their products from the stigma of 'cheap and nasty.'" The association vowed to regain the lost trade by following the Werkbund's example and fostering "the cooperation of the manufacturer, the designer and the distributor."[21]

By the time World War I ended, not only the industrial uses of art but the rationale of modern industrial design was sweeping Europe, propelled by both aesthetics and profits. As the young architect Walter Gropius had written in 1913, "leading big business has proved—and this is decisive—that in the long run it pays to care about the artistic value of its products."[22] Now Germany, although defeated in war, raised the curtain on a new phase in the competition for profitable modern designs and, even more, in the education of designers to produce them, with the opening of the Bauhaus under Gropius's direction in April 1919.

As a professional school of design, the Bauhaus had its conceptual origins in Walter Gropius's early career as apprentice to the pathbreaking industrial designer Peter Behrens. A capacious worker, adroit artist, and cautious modernist, Behrens had initiated a revolutionary program in corporate and product design for Emile Rathenau's Allgemeine Elektrizitäts-Gesellschaft, Germany's largest manufacturer of electrical equipment, in 1907 (the same year Muthesius founded the Werkbund). As artistic adviser, Behrens had redesigned everything associated with the company, buildings and products alike. And in 1908, he had hired Gropius, who took inspiration, as he said, from Behrens's "comprehensive and thoroughgoing interest in shaping the whole environment, an interest that extended beyond architecture to painting, the stage, industrial products, and typography."[23] By the time Gropius left Behrens's firm three years later, he was a dedicated and versatile modernist, attentive to the benefits of mass production and prefabrication, and particularly adept at designing functional industrial buildings employing interior steel structural supports and glass exterior walls—exemplified by his seminal Fagus Shoe Last Factory of 1911 in Alfeld, Germany, and later by the Werkbund Exhibition Hall of 1914 and the Bauhaus building of 1925–1926 in Dessau.

Then, after working as an independent architect and serving in the military, Gropius had seen his career take its most momentous turn. Offered the leadership of the Weimar School of Arts and Crafts and the Weimar Academy of Fine Arts at the war's end, Gropius united the two institutions to create the Staatliches Bauhaus. For the next ten years, first in Weimar and then, after 1925, in Dessau, Gropius and his colleagues would expand the alliance of modernism and industry to embrace virtually every artifact of the consumer culture; and they would develop the first comprehensive modern style and program of art education, which would eventually extend the reach of the Bauhaus across the landscape of twentieth-century design, consumer commerce, and art education. But this influence was still years away when the Bauhaus opened. And while Gropius and his colleagues began building their reputation, industrialists and designers in the United States started looking for ways to imitate and excel their now-predominant European competitors.

From this search came the Chicago Association of Arts and Industries, founded in 1922 as an offshoot of the American Arts and Industries Society, founded the previous year. "The Association of Arts and Industries has recently been organized," announced its president, William Nelson Pelouze, in May 1922, "for the purpose of impressing upon the industries of the central west the great importance of improved artistic design as a national asset in world competition." And the better to serve this national cause, he said—foreshadowing the later invitation to Moholy-Nagy—the association planned to establish a school in Chicago to train artists and designers for work in industry. Pelouze underscored the need for such a school by observing that because America lagged behind Europe in providing such training, the "art centers of Europe take millions of dollars from Americans who want . . . manufactured articles of great variety and artistic design." If this country "were fortified by having its own industrial art schools . . . , much of this great loss could be saved."[24]

Despite the need for such a school, however, the association did not soon create one. Instead, it largely restricted itself to fostering relations between artists and industrialists and encouraging potential industrial designers to enroll in classes at the Art Institute of Chicago. Fifteen years would pass before the association and Chicago would see truly modernist industrial design education in their midst. Meanwhile, the Bauhaus would become the international model of this education, and the widening gyre of artistic modernism would draw in Chicago, preparing there a home for the Bauhaus in America.

Modernism came to Chicago in waves, ebbing and rising again. Architecture rode the first wave. In the wake of the Great Fire and amid the commercial flowering of the 1880s and 1890s, a handful of architects created the first "skyscrapers," erected on interior steel frames and sporting the handsome broad-paned windows later known as "Chicago windows." These Chicagoans (D. H. Burnham, John Root, William Le Baron Jenney, Dankmar Adler, Louis Sullivan, Frank Lloyd Wright, and others) were also the first American ar-chitects to influence their European counterparts; the sight of Chicago's relatively unornamented commercial buildings gave the Austrian Adolf Loos inspiration to launch his famous assault on "ornament as crime"; and Wright's domestic architecture aroused extensive interest in Germany, where Wright's writings on architecture were first published and won acclaim long before they gained recognition in the United States.

But this early rise of architectural modernism waned under the sway of antimodernist tastes. The World's Columbian Exposition of 1893 in Chi-cago turned back the clock of modern design in that city by shunning (as Moholy-Nagy, for one, later noted) commercial architectural modernism in favor of grandiose beaux-arts classicism, and by spurning the honest sim-plicity of American patent furniture in favor of the ornamental elegance of ersatz aristocratic designs. "The damage wrought by the World's Fair will last for half a century from its date, if not longer,"[25] Louis Sullivan wrote. And, abandoning Chicago to this fate, Sullivan, an intractable, often arro-gant individualist, let his career there founder after the turn of the century (his famous design for the department store Carson Pirie Scott, constructed in 1899, being one of his last local commissions). Although other members of the Chicago school continued to work in Chicago, and Wright designed some important houses in the suburbs, a decline in Chicago's architectural vitality started that was to last until the arrival of the Bauhaus alumni in the late thirties—almost fifty years after the exposition, just as Sullivan had said. This decline produced a nice irony in the architectural competition for the Chicago Tribune building in 1922. From the Bauhaus, Walter Gropius submitted a striking plan for a tall, austere, modernist skyscraper somewhat reminiscent of the best of the Chicago school. The judges set this aside, choosing instead the neo-Gothic design of Raymond M. Hood and J. M. Howells. Chicago lost its chance to erect a pioneering modernist landmark— almost thirty years before Mies van der Rohe's steel and glass apartment towers a few blocks away won that distinction. But the incident was not without benefits to the partisans of modernism. For a controversy erupted over the relation of style and purpose in contemporary commercial build-ings that gave the ideology of modern architecture its first public airing in Chicago.[26]

While the tide of modern architecture was ebbing away from Chicago, modernism visited, if sometimes briefly, in other forms. The literary journal *Poetry: A Magazine of Verse*, founded there in 1912, became the most important American journal of modern verse. It was followed by Margaret Anderson's *The Little Review*, established in Chicago three years later, which gained even greater distinction as publisher of James Joyce's *Ulysses* and, in Ezra Pound's words, as the "official organ" of English-language modernism[27]—although local provincialism eventually drove the magazine to a sequence of more hospitable cities, and it finally settled in Paris.

Modern painting also came to Chicago as something of a curiosity received with ambivalence. The first American exhibition of European modernists, originally installed in New York's Sixty-ninth Regiment Armory in February 1913, traveled to Chicago's Art Institute later that spring, attracting some 200,000 curious Chicagoans during its three-week stay. The Art Institute itself, founded in 1866 with a handful of works by European masters, took its first modest steps toward a permanent collection of "modern art" in 1926, when it received the Birch-Bartlett collection. This included several postimpressionist paintings, such as Seurat's famous *Sunday Afternoon on the Island of La Grande Jatte*, but nothing close to twentieth-century abstraction.

More nearly modernist in artistic taste than the Art Institute were the private clubs, such as the Arts Club (established 1916), which gave many modernists their first Chicago showings, mainly in the 1930s, and the private galleries (e.g., Roullier's, Chester Johnson's, and Gaulois's), which gave at least casual early recognition to modernists. But neither art exhibits nor a few connoisseurs would make Chicago a center of modernism in the fine arts. The social order remained too cohesive, a few commercial interests possessed too much power, and conservative midwestern tastes and sensibilities held too firm to show much hospitality to cosmopolitan modernist painters. Even in the late 1950s, one resident art critic and modernist gallery owner, Katharine Kuh, would flee the city for good, complaining that artistic modernism would never find a home there;[28] and only in the late 1960s would Chicago finally get a modern art museum, the Museum of Contemporary Art.

While modernism met resistance in the fine arts in Chicago, it thrived in the commercial arts, for Chicago had made itself the inland capital of the consumer economy. Visual forms unappealing in fine art proved to have unmistakable and acceptable uses in commerce. As the local art critic Clarence Joseph Bulliet observed in January 1931: although the art galleries in Chicago department stores would purvey only "soft and soothing" art works "to rest the 'tired businessman'. . . , the advertising departments know better, . . . eagerly adapting for their own purposes the discoveries of Matisse and Picasso."[29]

And again, two months later, reviewing a Léger exhibition, Bulliet remarked that whether or not the public liked modernism, "the practical decorators and architects" were "helping themselves to the discoveries of Picasso, Braque, and Léger for practical purposes."[30] Spurred on by its hearty commercial spirit and aided by the consumer economy, Chicago was certain to invest more in the modernism of commercial design than in that of fine art.

A nudge in this direction came from that most influential postwar exhibition of modern design, the Exposition Internationale des Arts Décoratifs et Industriels Modernes (1924–1925). Viewed from America as not only "the first international exposition to be confined to works conceived in the modern spirit"[31] but as an attempt by the French to exploit modernist design "to capture the trade of the world in this field,"[32] the exhibition had unequivocally modernist requirements for participation: "Works admitted to the Exposition must show new inspiration and real originality. . . . Reproductions, imitations and counterfeits of ancient styles will be strictly prohibited."[33] More ornamental and thus commercially adaptable than the austere functional modernism associated with the Bauhaus, the "new style in decoration" that typified the exhibition, aspiring "to meet new conditions of living with frankness and understanding,"[34] became the first commercially popular modern style, loosely known then as *style moderne* or *art moderne* and nowadays as art deco.

The American government, recognizing that "American manufacturers and craftsmen had almost nothing to exhibit conceived in the modern spirit,"[35] declined to participate, although the official who made the decision, Secretary of Commerce Herbert Hoover, sent a commission of observers from American trade and manufacturing associations. The report of this commission was as unequivocal as had been the French requirements for participation: "As a nation, we now live artistically on warmed over dishes," but "the nation which most successfully rationalizes the [modern] movement and brings its expression into terms acceptable and appropriate to modern living conditions and modern taste will possess a distinct advantage both as to its domestic and foreign trade."[36]

After some 400 objects from the exhibition went on display in Boston, New York, and Chicago in 1926, exposing the American public to something "utterly and astoundingly new," American "decoration was at last unloosed from the bonds of period slavery."[37] And in answer to the French, the Association of Arts and Industries, together with the Art Director's Club of America, staged a large-scale "Modern American Decorative and Industrial Art Exposition" in January 1929. The show's sponsors planned "to muster the forces of modern designers and craftsmen and to bring them into contact with the forces of industry" by demonstrating "the advance of the modern movement in America."[38]

By this time, modernist design was acquiring numerous supporters in Chicago. The Society of Typographic Arts, created in 1927, fed the modernist flame by holding public lectures and exhibitions devoted to modern graphic design. One of the society's leaders, Douglas C. McMurtrie, set forth the modernist case in *Modern Typography and Layout* (1929), exploring "the true nature of the modern movement as applied to typography."[39] Although the book—illustrated by examples from Moholy-Nagy, Herbert Bayer, Jan Tschichold, and many others—could not be called innovative, since modernist graphics had been promoted for several years by graphics magazines, it helped introduce not only the principles of modern graphic design but also the Bauhaus ("an institution which is exerting a profound influence for modernity in a number of the applied arts")[40] to Chicago and the nation.

Interior design also gained professional status. Drawing together practitioners from Chicago, like members of the short-lived, modernistic Designer's League, and other cities, the first national association of interior designers, the American Institute of Interior Decorators (now the American Society of Interior Designers) was formed in 1931 under President William R. Moore (a Chicagoan) to certify the credentials, in Moore's words, of those "qualified to plan, design and execute interiors and their furnishings."[41] Half a century after Oscar Wilde's public appeal in Chicago for more artistic "home decoration," good design, judged too sophisticated and potentially lucrative to be left to amateurs, would now enter homes and offices through the studied sensibilities and organizational prestige of nationally certified professionals.

Most important in awakening public awareness of modern design in Chicago and elsewhere was the World's Fair of 1933–1934, heralded as the Century of Progress Exposition. Much had changed in popular and professional taste since the Columbian Exposition forty years earlier. Modern architecture, while not yet widely accepted in the United States, had been canonized as the "International Style" in an exhibit mounted at the Museum of Modern Art in 1931 and in the influential catalogue written by Philip Johnson and H.-R. Hitchcock. And the "bogus antique"[42] (as Sullivan had called it) of beaux-arts design had given way, at least in advanced opinion, to a modernism mingling the commercial ornamentation of art deco and the standardized functionalism of the Bauhaus.

The fair reflected the changes, if only cautiously. Exemplifying, as H.-R. Hitchcock said, "a consistent, if not especially distinguished, standard of modern design throughout,"[43] it did not so much exhibit stylistic novelty as stimulate a popular desire for domestic modernism. From the 1933–1934 exposition onward, the modern commercial style it represented began to sweep the country under the shibboleth "streamlining," bringing mass-produced and often flimsy artifacts and novel uses of interior and architectural details like mirrors, chrome, and corner windows to every city and town.

By the late thirties, modern design had thus established itself not only among designers but among the public in Chicago and the country at large. Adaptations of *art moderne* were reshaping interiors; the international style was growing familiar as a set of architectural principles, if not yet as practice; modern graphics were dressing up advertising; gifted designers such as Walter Dorwin Teague, Raymond Loewy, Norman Bel Geddes, and Henry Dreyfuss, spurred on by companies hungry for sales in the Depression economy, were introducing numerous artfully fashioned commodities into the marketplace; and many lesser designers were making "streamlining" the dominant style of all kinds of products—autos, vacuum cleaners, refrigerators, and drinking glasses alike.[44] The original mission of the Chicago Arts and Industries Association, although not accomplished, had at least lost its novelty. But now the association found an opportunity to bring to life the school it had long desired.

For several years the association had sent prospective designers to the school of the Art Institute. Then, suddenly, long-festering tensions between the two institutions over pedagogy and style erupted. The association broke with the Institute and resolved to set up a school of its own. An informal steering committee, headed by Norma K. Stahle and including Walter Paepcke and the architect George Fred Keck, quickly decided to take the Bauhaus as their model.

The committee could hardly have failed to look to the Bauhaus for inspiration. For despite its relatively short life and only marginal influence in America, the Bauhaus was by this time widely recognized as the preeminent twentieth-century venture in the teaching of modern industrial and graphic design. The critic Bulliet had informed Chicagoans in 1927 that "of late the eyes of the world have been turned on the little city of Weimar, where there have been in progress some intensely interesting experiments in abstraction, looking toward a fusion of art and the machine."[45] During the next decade, this kind of sketchy information stressing aesthetics had become a swelling current stressing the practical applications of this aesthetics. The much-publicized Barcelona Pavilion of 1929 featuring Mies van der Rohe's elegant building and numerous creations, followed by the traveling exhibitions of Bauhaus work in 1931–1932 and the Museum of Modern Art's machine art exhibit in 1934, had made the Bauhaus commercial style familiar. Bauhaus graphics had gained notice in magazines and in Douglas C. McMurtrie's *Modern Typography and Layout* (1929), and Bauhaus architecture had been recognized in books like H.-R. Hitchcock's *Modern Architecture* (1930), Sheldon Cheney's *The New World of Architecture* (1930), and of course the Hitchcock-Johnson Museum of Modern Art catalogue of 1932. And shortly after the Bauhaus closed in 1933, its many accomplishments in design had been set in historical perspective by Herbert Read in his seminal lectures published as *Art and Industry* (1934), followed two years later by Sheldon and Martha Cheney's *Art and the Machine* and, most influentially, Pevsner's *Pioneers of Modern Design from William Morris to Walter Gropius*, which gave the Bauhaus pride of place in a far-reaching artistic revolution. The Bauhäusler had also added to the publicity. The year before the Bauhaus folded, Moholy-Nagy's elaborate description of the first-year curriculum had appeared in English under the title *The New Vision* (first published in 1928); and in 1935 Gropius brought out his own version of the Bauhaus program and philosophy, *The New Architecture and the Bauhaus*. Finally, the Bauhäusler had started exporting their experience and ideas in person as they fled Nazi oppression to take up new lives in foreign lands.

Consequently, when an author writing in the *American Magazine of Art* proclaimed in 1934, "Wanted: An American Bauhaus,"[46] the opportunity to have one was near at hand. And when the steering committee of the Association of Arts and Industries decided to grasp that opportunity in the spring of 1937, they could easily promise, as one of them later said, "to establish in Chicago a school which would be based upon the philosophy"[47] contained in Moholy's *The New Vision*. Yet for all they had learned of the Bauhaus, it is doubtful that they knew much of that philosophy.

The call for an American Bauhaus came from people who knew the German institution primarily as a professional school of modernist aesthetics and design. But the Bauhaus had been much more than that.

In organizing the school amid the collapse of imperial Germany and the hot winds of revolution, Walter Gropius had envisioned the teaching of modern industrial and graphic design, painting, and architecture as serving not only or even primarily the practical ends of artists and industrialists, much less the economic interests of the Fatherland, but the universal, humanistic ends of culture as viewed through his vaguely socialist eyes. Like artists and intellectuals all over Western Europe in the late nineteenth and early twentieth centuries, especially in Germany, Gropius had painfully sensed a deepening disintegration of culture, and with it humanity, into disparate pursuits, bloodless categories, and spiritless labors. And like Muthesius before him, who had avowedly formed the Werkbund not only to improve German industrial design but "to restore to the world and our age the lost benefits of an architectonic culture,"[48] Gropius had set out to satisfy his "hunger for wholeness" by launching the Bauhaus on a heady course of cultural integration.[49]

He had spelled out his cultural criticism and reformist aspirations in grandiloquent manifestos and apocalyptic addresses to the students during the Bauhaus's early days. "Together let us desire, conceive, and create the new structure of the future," Gropius had effused, "which will embrace architecture and sculpture and painting in one unity which will one day rise toward heaven from the hands of a million workers like the crystal symbol of a new faith" beaming "its abundance of light into the smallest objects of everyday life."[50] Embodying a "dawning recognition of the essential oneness of all things,"[51] the Bauhaus had thus represented for Gropius nothing less than the "transformation of the whole life and the whole of inner man" and "the building of a new concept of the world"[52] by "the architects of a new civilization."[53]

When Gropius spoke of architects here, he had had in mind those who would at once design products and buildings for the new technological civilization *and* give a metaphysical architectonic order to that civilization. Not for nothing had he named the school the Bauhaus (House of Construction), for it had existed to advance architecture in the broadest sense, "an architectonic art, which, like human nature, should be all embracing in its scope,"[54] uniting "all the disciplines of practical art" under "men of kindred spirit."[55]

The school's curriculum had carried out these precepts, deploying generally pragmatic, modernist means to achieve transcendent cultural ends. Beginning with a Preliminary Course (Vorkurs) in elementary principles of forms and materials, it had proceeded, under the guidance of an exceptional faculty of artist-teachers (see fig. 2.1), to Practical Instruction in the use of hand and then machine tools and design methods (ranging from printing and weaving to painting and stage direction), and had culminated, for gifted students, in Structural Studies in the comprehensive design and construction of buildings and their contents. Appropriate to this curriculum and its aims, the book that had first publicized them, written by Moholy-Nagy, bore the German title: *Von Material zu Architektur* (*From Material to Architecture,* published in 1928, given the English title *The New Vision,* 1932).

But if comprehensive architecture had been the end of the Bauhaus education, and if the practical courses and workshops had made the Bauhaus style of "clear and crisply simplified forms" familiar to the consumer economy, the pedagogical heart of the Bauhaus had been the Preliminary Course. First taught by Johannes Itten and after 1922 jointly by Moholy-Nagy and Josef Albers, the Vorkurs had taken as its purpose "to liberate the pupil's individuality from the dead weight of conventions" through direct experience with "the physical nature of materials and the basic laws of design."[56] As conceived and executed by Itten, along the lines of a previous course in Vienna and consistent with his mystical sensibility and with what he took to be the Bauhaus's mystical bent, the Vorkurs had first concentrated on the student's intuitive understanding of materials and forms and the development of his "whole personality" through states of feeling. Itten had so encouraged learning by subjectivity and had found members of the postwar generation—who also made a popular sensation of Hermann Hesse's inward-

Fig. 2.1. The Bauhaus faculty, Dessau, 1926. Left to right: Josef Albers, Hinnerk Scheper, Georg Muche, László Moholy-Nagy, Herbert Bayer, Joost Schmidt, Walter Gropius, Marcel Breuer, Wassily Kandinsky, Paul Klee, Lyonel Feininger, Gunta Stölzl, Oskar Schlemmer. Courtesy of the Museum of Modern Art, New York.

looking novel *Demian* (1919)—so susceptible to his methods, that subjectivity had become for him an end in itself. The Bauhaus had then started acquiring a reputation for emotional indulgence in the vein of the then prevalent Expressionism in the arts. Compelled to restrain this pedagogical drift lest it compromise the school's more practical ends, Gropius had reminded Itten and his followers in 1922 that "what is important is to combine the creative activity of the individual with the broad practical work of the world!"[57] This reassertion of objectivity, practicality, and communal work (strengthened by the presence in Weimar of the antisubjective artist and teacher Theo van Doesburg, as well as by the rise in German artistic circles of the tendency labeled *die neue Sachlichkeit,* "the new objectivity") had driven Itten and eventually Expressionism from the Bauhaus. And with their departure the dominant figure in the Bauhaus, next to Gropius himself, had become László Moholy-Nagy.

Moholy-Nagy had been just twenty-eight when he took over the Preliminary Course from Itten in 1923, a generation younger than the other major painters on the faculty, who were all identified with Expressionism—Wassily Kandinsky, Lyonel Feininger, and Paul Klee. A Hungarian by birth and an energetic, unself-conscious extrovert, both teachable and an inspiriting teacher, and captivated by objective "constructivist" painting, optics, and the arts of technology, Moholy had come to the Bauhaus from the vital international artists' community in Berlin (where he had met and learned from formalists El Lissitzky and Theo van Doesburg and the collage artist Kurt Schwitters). Far from bohemian by nature despite an early period of poverty and mystical exercise, Moholy always bore the very look of a professor, or a football player turned professor—hefty, tight-lipped, bespectacled, invariably besuited—and he had the temperament of a Puritan: driven by self-discipline and ethical purposes, he disdained emotion and remained unstintingly serious in work and undauntingly optimistic in life.

Energized by teaching and enthralled by the act of creation, Moholy had quickly established himself as a popular instructor and influential member of the Bauhaus faculty. Under his guidance—along with that of Albers—the Preliminary Course had become a technical rather than intuitive introduction to the complete language of the modern visual arts. And after the Bauhaus moved from Weimar to its own buildings in Dessau in 1925–1926, Moholy's authority had grown so pronounced that the more Expressionistic painters on the staff had begun to chafe.

Feininger (whom Moholy replaced as head of the print workshop and whose Expressionistic graphics in Bauhaus publications had then given way to those reflecting Moholy's rational, geometric Constructivism) told his wife during the move to Dessau that "the trend of the Bauhaus" was "stated more precisely" than anywhere else "in an essay . . . written by Moholy." It "makes me cringe!" Feininger cried, repelled by Moholy's technological aesthetics; "Nothing but optics, mechanics, taking the 'old' static painting out of service. . . . We can say to ourselves that this is terrifying and the end of all art—but actually it is a question of mass production, technically very interesting—but why attach the name art to the mechanization of all visual things, why call it the only art of our age, and moreover, of the future?"[58]

But Moholy had had the ascending historic tide of objectivity on his side. And he had had Gropius's confidence in his teaching, technological imagination, and pragmatism. "Moholy was one of my most active colleagues in building up the Bauhaus," Gropius later said; "much that it accomplished stands to his credit."[59] And although it is exaggeration to say that "it was above all Moholy-Nagy's personal interpretation of Constructivist attitudes that contributed to the emergence of a recognizable Bauhaus style,"[60] no one besides Gropius did more than Moholy to make the Bauhaus idea thrive.

As teacher of the Preliminary Course, head of the metal and printing workshops, and as publisher of the Bauhaus books, Moholy had been in an ideal position to develop and publicize the pedagogical theory and the linear, unornamented, rational style of design that typified the Bauhaus. The lighting fixtures he fashioned remain models of uncluttered, mass-produced attractiveness today. And the typography developed in the print workshop under his direction, particularly by Herbert Bayer, utilizing uniform sans serif typeface, no capital letters, and bold figures, enhanced, just as Moholy said, "the optical effectiveness of the page" with a new "clarity, brevity, and precision."[61] Perfectly suited to the needs of modern publishers and advertisers, as intended, this Bauhaus graphic style (drawing on innovations by El Lissitzky and Theo van Doesburg) is still the most characteristic modern print form. And the fourteen Bauhaus books Moholy produced (designing twelve himself), along with the journal *bauhaus*, also set standards in layout, print, and illustration—some of the cover designs becoming modernist classics of composition, communication, and beauty.

Like his pedagogical practice, Moholy's artwork during the Bauhaus years had also carried forward a search for a "standard language of optical expression."[62] Moving toward ever greater abstraction in painting, photography, constructions, and light-and-motion technology, Moholy had produced paintings of appealing, if emotionless, composition, and devices, like his light-space modulator, of arresting aesthetic ingenuity. And while his technological aesthetics offended colleagues like Feininger, they proved Moholy to be the supreme devotee of technology among modern visual artists and made him a pioneer in abstract photography and kinetic art.[63]

Yet novel aesthetic and technological pursuits did not dim Moholy's firm Bauhäusler conviction that art exists not for its own sake or for the edification of a few votaries but for the enhancement of humanity and the advancement of cultural reform. Even his pre-Bauhaus celebrations of light had told of its metaphysical powers: "Light, total light," he had poetized in 1917, "creates the total man."[64] And in *The New Vision* he had proclaimed, "The future needs the whole man," asserting that "the true function of art is to be the graph of our time, an intuitive search for the missing equilibrium among our emotional, intellectual, and social lives."[65] Later, shortly before he came to the United States, in an essay reaffirming the socialist uses of modern art that had animated his youth, he had insisted that "painting, photography, film, and light display" are not just the playthings of artists but "weapons in the struggle for a new and more purposive human reality" or, again, for the "whole man."[66]

The cultural mission Moholy consistently assigned to art echoes not only Gropius and other Bauhäusler but most of the social critics, educators, artists, and designers of Central Europe (and many elsewhere) in the early twentieth century. All had believed a truly *modern* art and design would express with honesty the character of modern culture and help bridge the divisions between aesthetics and technology, art and industry, feeling and intellect, universality and specialization, community and individuality.

So many artists and social critics have in fact shared this vision of modern culture that the intellectual history of the past two hundred years would be unrecognizable without it. But nowhere was this vision more insistently held than in the Bauhaus and among those close to it, like Gyorgy Kepes, Alexander Dorner, and Sigfried Giedion,[67] and by no one more unequivocally than by Moholy-Nagy himself. It was this vision that had prompted Moholy, following Gropius, and along with Bayer, Marcel Breuer, and Xanti Schawinsky, to leave the Bauhaus in 1928 when internal and external pressures had threatened to turn it into a school of specialized and political education: "We are in danger of becoming what we as revolutionaries opposed," Moholy had written in his letter of resignation, "a vocational training school which evaluates only the final achievement and overlooks the development of the whole man."[68] And it was this vision that Moholy was to take with him to Chicago in hopes not only of reinstating the Bauhaus pedagogy but of giving the Bauhaus philosophy a new crack at transforming mankind.

When the Association of Arts and Industries set its sights on the Bauhaus as a model for its school, the Bauhäusler had all long dispersed (the Bauhaus had been dissolved in 1933, not long after resettling in Berlin). The painters were carrying on their work in diverse places, Kandinsky in France, Klee in Switzerland, Feininger in the United States; Josef Albers and Xanti Schawinsky were reviving some of the Bauhaus practices at Black Mountain College in North Carolina; Mies van der Rohe and Bayer were engaged in private design work in Berlin; and Marcel Breuer, Moholy, and Gropius, after a period in Berlin, had gone to London, from which Gropius and Breuer had moved on to Harvard's Graduate School of Design. With Gropius's reputation now beginning to soar, stimulated by expanding public knowledge of the Bauhaus's work and by publications praising the Bauhaus, the association naturally invited the founder of the Bauhaus to head an American incarnation of the school.

Having no desire to leave Harvard, Gropius recommended his "nearest collaborator in the Bauhaus" and "the best man you can get,"[69] László Moholy-Nagy. The recommendation came at a good time for Moholy. Growing restless and dissatisfied with his steady diet of commercial work and private painting in London, he hungered for more in art than merely its creation. "Painting is not enough," he told his wife after a successful show of his works in London in early 1937, "not even exhibitions are enough." For the finished work, he said, "reaches so few and reaches them in such a completed, rarified form that the living problem gets obscured by the finish." That "living problem" was the act of creation with its vital unification of thought, feeling, and form, and its potential for giving birth to "the whole man." Moholy had now decided that "no money one makes in industry and no satisfaction of shows and public recognition can equal teaching."[70]

This was Moholy's mood when Norma Stahle of the association cabled in early June 1937:

PLAN DESIGN SCHOOL ON BAUHAUS LINES TO OPEN IN FALL. MARSHALL FIELD OFFERS FAMILY MANSION PRAIRIE AVENUE. STABLES TO BE CONVERTED INTO WORKSHOPS. DR. GROPIUS SUGGESTS YOUR NAME AS DIRECTOR. ARE YOU INTERESTED?[71]

Moholy was in Paris at the time, and his wife, protective of his interests, fearful of Nazis, and ignorant of Chicago, sent it on to him with a stiff warning:

URGE YOU TO DECLINE. GERMAN EXAMPLE SHOWS FASCIST RESULTS WHEN FIELD MARSHALS TAKE OVER EDUCATION. STABLES AND PRAIRIE SOUND JUST LIKE IT.[72]

Moholy knew nothing of Chicago either but doubted that field marshals posed much of a threat there. He was indeed interested and soon won assurance from Stahle that Marshall Field was no swagger-stick-swinging general but a safe "philanthropist and businessman"[73] who had simply donated his father's aging mansion to the association for its school. And Stahle also assured him that since the association had "always subscribed to the plan of the Bauhaus," and now saw "an opportunity to establish much the type of school you had at Dessau,"[74] Moholy was the perfect man to head it.

Six weeks later, Moholy was in Chicago struggling with his ambivalence toward his friendly, if unmodern, hosts. By early August, he had decided to stay. And on the eve of receiving a five-year contract, backed by a $100,000 endowment for a school to be known as the New Bauhaus, he explained to his wife: "You ask whether I want to remain here? There's something incomplete about this city and its people that fascinates me; it seems to urge one on to completion. Everything seems still possible. . . . I love the air of newness, of expectation around me. Yes, I want to stay."[75]

This was a historic moment not only for modern design in Chicago, but for marking the passage of Bauhaus modernism to America. Albers and Schawinsky had arrived in this country three years earlier, and now the immigration and assimilation would soon be complete. Only months before Moholy's arrival, Gropius and Breuer had assumed their teaching positions at Harvard (where Gropius was soon to become chairman of the department of architecture). The next year would bring Herbert Bayer who, with Walter and Ise Gropius, would organize the first full-scale exhibition, complete with catalogue, of the Bauhaus's career from 1919 to 1928 at the Museum of Modern Art. Although this exhibition was to elicit criticism from journalists,[76] it nonetheless furthered the Bauhaus's reputation in this country as an institution identified with modernist design and unconventional pedagogy. At about the same time as this exhibition in 1938, Sigfried Giedion would commence his influential Eliot Norton Lectures at Harvard (later published as *Space, Time, and Architecture*) containing high praise for the

Bauhaus's contribution to the rise of abstraction and formalism in architecture—and to the reintegration of culture. And in that same year the assimilation of Bauhaus teachings and personnel into American culture was to win its final victory with the settling in Chicago of Mies van der Rohe as head of the Armour Institute, later the Illinois Institute of Technology (IIT). The Bauhaus could now confidently claim recognition not just as an episode in the history of modern design and the teaching of it but as the leading edge of that history, its characteristic aesthetic style and innovative pedagogy almost universally celebrated and many of its chief personnel installed in important positions in American culture. Both formally and colloquially, the Bauhaus had arrived.

The settling in Chicago of two of the prominent Bauhäusler in 1937–1938 as directors of educational institutions constituted a particularly important prize. Moholy and Mies, together with their respective professional and financial allies, Walter Paepcke and the architectural firm of Skidmore, Owings, and Merrill (established in 1935–1936 by Skidmore and Owings, riding on the success of their modernist work at the Century of Progress Exposition), would put Chicago ineffaceably on the map of twentieth-century design and architecture. But the prize was not as rich as it might have been. For notwithstanding their ties to the Bauhaus, the two artists repelled each other like mismatched magnets. This repulsion resulted from dissimilarities in professional interests and from an impassable gulf of temperament.

An architect above all, Mies disdained the title "designer" and never used it. He, as much as anyone, raised architecture to preeminence in the world of design and made a cultural hero of the architect. From his first architectural drawings (executed under the influence of the classical architect Karl Friedrich Schinkel and Peter Behrens, in whose firm he worked alongside Gropius and also Le Corbusier) onward, he evinced the tastes and temperament of a magisterial classicist. And his elegant works of the 1920s—including his stunning projects for glass and steel skyscrapers in 1919 and 1920–1921, the fully realized Barcelona Pavilion of 1929, and the Tugendhat House of 1930—had earned him the directorship of the Bauhaus, at Gropius's recommendation, in August 1930, followed three years later by the sad responsibility of closing the school after the Nazis came to power.

In the United States, Mies's severe architectural style gave rise through his long and prolific career and the work of colleagues and imitators to the most common form of modern urban architecture, the "glass box" known to every large city (and a principal cause of the reaction against modernist architecture that gained ascendancy in the late 1970s). Mies's classicist tastes and imperious manner also led him to draw inspiration mainly from his own sense of architectural order rather than from pragmatic functions or the examples of others. His absorption in questions of form was total. When asked if the architecture of the Chicago school with its innovative uses of steel and glass had influenced him, he replied without hesitation: "No; living in Chicago has had no effect on me. When I first arrived, I immediately went to the campus of the then Armour Institute" and returned home. "I really don't know the Chicago School," and "I rarely see the city."[77] And when advising Katharine Kuh on the layout of her Gallery of Art Interpre- tation at the Art Institute, Mies would sit locked in silence for great lengths of time pondering a change of line here, an angle there, and spending one entire day adjusting a partition three inches.[78] Even Mies's teaching bore traces of this insistent classicist composure; his restrained and laconic classroom performance, with his halting English, prompted the joke that his famed motto, "Less is more," described not only his aesthetics but his pedagogy.[79]

To the high-minded, self-absorbed Mies, the enterprising extroverted Moholy stood in stark contrast. Mies thought him little more than an artistic dabbler, a huckster, a self-aggrandizing charlatan. Nor was Mies alone. Josef Albers became by his own admission the chief "Moholy hater,"[80] convinced as he was that Moholy had greedily seized credit for pedagogical techniques in the Preliminary Course that Albers had developed. Similarly, the avant-garde artist and photographer Man Ray criticized Moholy for dishonestly claiming priority in the invention of the technique of abstract photography that Moholy called the photogram and Ray named the Rayogram. Even Moholy's long-time friend Gyorgy Kepes fell out with him over purportedly misclaimed credit for optical and aesthetic experiments.

These blights on Moholy's reputation arose not so much from a competitive streak in Moholy's nature as from the near absence of it. Moholy—more than any other Bauhäusler, even Gropius—had rejected the cult of the individual artist and embraced the Bauhaus ideal uniting art and craft, community and individuality, aesthetics and technology, education and cultural reform. Whatever his passion for abstract painting, optical experiments, and machines, as Sibyl said, his "distaste for working in solitude never changed,"[81] and he believed artistic self-interest should be subordinated to the common cause of art education. "The meaning of 'art' has changed since the industrial revolution," he liked to say. Art has entered everyday life; it has attached itself to human, not just aesthetic, ends. Hence "the esotery [sic] of art must disappear; its limitation to specialists; the mysticism surrounding it; the looking for geniuses only." "Art," he continued with emphasis, "is a community matter"[82] whose purpose is cultural and anthropological and whose rallying cry must be: "Everyone is talented."[83]

This egalitarian, social conception of art set Moholy at odds with many of his fellow artists, who saw in it merely an excuse for Moholy to plunder their work. But it suited him perfectly to the American industrial arts mentality, which could easily ignore his philosophical anthropology. Thus Moholy's decision to accept the Chicago assignment delighted his supporters. And they eagerly announced that "the hopes of many years" were now to be realized in "a school of design" that will "meet the needs of industry and reintegrate the artist into the life of the nation."[84]

Moholy's first public act as head of the New Bauhaus occurred on September 23, 1937. Before a crowd of nearly a thousand people in the Knickerbocker Hotel, he summarized his principles and outlined his plans. The speech bore the familiar marks of Moholy's exuberance and philosophical zeal; but as an introduction to the New Bauhaus for an audience of wealthy, naive, and practical-minded sponsors, it was intellectual chaos. Industrial arts education had never seemed like this. "For more than two hours," his wife recalled, Moholy "poured a stream of analysis and suggestion over their unprepared heads, presented in a language that shrank from nothing to be explicit, and omitted definite articles to save time."[85]

"Everybody is talented," he announced, because everybody possesses five senses and the ability to awaken them to all experience. The purpose of art education must therefore be not to train specialists or, as in the beaux arts tradition, to teach the imitation of the masters, but to "extend the sensorial directness you had as a child—remember the red toys—into creative work with materials and relationships"; only then can "you feel for the first time that you are a supreme individual." Thus at the New Bauhaus, he explained, underscoring his anti-elitist conception of art, "we don't teach what is called 'pure art,' but we train what you might call the art engineer. . . . If our students become artists—this is their own job." In deference to the economic interests of his listeners, Moholy also gave assurances of the benefits to industry of this kind of education. "To you—the industrialists," he said, "we offer our services for research. We shall work on your problems";[86] and he listed dozens of the problems to be explored, ranging from the fabrication of synthetic fibers to packaging and architecture.

The more practical of Moholy's proposals could find ready resonance in the audience, but the grandiose promises of a universal education in the natural and social sciences, in philosophy and the arts and crafts, born of Moholy's claim that "in the future we can never speak about a single thing without relating it to the whole,"[87] could elicit only puzzlement and skepticism. For, besides the intellectual and rhetorical difficulties of the presentation, the curriculum and aspirations outlined by Moholy were not merely impressive, they were unrealizable. The finances then available, although great by Moholy's standards, could never sustain such a program. When warned of these impossibilities by Walter Gropius, who got a summary of the plan from Moholy while the two vacationed together, Moholy responded with characteristic innocence and pluck: "Thank you so much, Pius. All you said has made everything so much clearer to me. Thank God, the program is already in print."[88]

The New Bauhaus opened its doors in October to some thirty-five students and a faculty including former Bauhäusler Archipenko and Schawinsky. Herbert Bayer had also been listed in the course catalogue but, like Jean Hélion, did not appear when his visa failed to come through. The curriculum, less ambitious than Moholy had wished, contained a few departures from the original Bauhaus, but all were consistent with its philosophical principles and pedagogical practice. The chief of these departures was the inclusion of academic courses, taught by members of the University of Chicago faculty. Incorporated to carry forward the pedagogical synthesis of art and craft, aesthetics and mechanics, and so on, these courses fell under the aegis of "Intellectual Integration." And they demonstrated an open affinity between the Bauhaus and another eminent organization of cultural reformers in the second quarter of the twentieth century—the Unity of Science movement.

The professors chosen to teach Intellectual Integration all belonged to this movement, an organization in the philosophy of science analogous to the Bauhaus in the arts. An extension of the Viennese philosophical school of logical positivism in the 1920s, this organization (led by Otto Neurath, Rudolf Carnap, Philipp Frank, and Herbert Feigl) sought the unity of language, axioms, method, and analytical dialogue that its members believed to underlie all quests for knowledge, especially in science. Once discovered and articulated, this unity would dispel clouds of intellectual confusion by providing a reliable pragmatic form of scientific discourse free of all deceptive, nonempirical terms. And recognizing that the Bauhaus had a kindred ambition in its desire for a functional, pragmatic language of pedagogy and design free of specialized interests, useless appearances, and deceptive historical allusions, the Viennese positivists had sent Herbert Feigl there in 1929 to lecture and learn. Feigl had found the Bauhaus imbued with the healthy "fact-minded, sober attitude"[89] that he and his colleagues espoused as indispensable to knowledge and as an antidote to that intellectual boondoggle, metaphysics—he did not, it seems, run across the metaphysical pronouncements of Bauhäusler like Gropius and Moholy who had departed the previous year.

When these philosophers came to America during the thirties, they, like the immigrant Bauhäusler, had assumed academic posts from which they were able to disseminate their ideas anew. Philipp Frank went to Harvard, where he headed the Foundation for the Unity of the Sciences; Neurath stayed for a time, and Feigl permanently, at the University of Minnesota; and Carnap joined the University of Chicago, where he and a colleague, Charles

Morris, helped Neurath plan an International Encyclopedia of Unified Science to be published by the University of Chicago Press.

A thread of instructive irony lies in the settling of part of this movement at the University of Chicago and in the forming of ties between the movement and the New Bauhaus. For in those same years, under President Robert M. Hutchins and his philosophical companion Mortimer J. Adler, the administration of the University of Chicago was more publicly committed to the humanities and to metaphysics and critical of positivism than that of any other university in the country (see chapter 3). In an early battle between humanists and positivists over an appointment in the philosophy department, the humanist Adler had even lost his job to none other than the positivist Charles Morris, who could claim more supporters in this department, which still honored its tradition of pragmatism going back to the tenure of John Dewey. And although Adler and Hutchins stood closer to Moholy in metaphysics and humanistic vision—they also believed in the fundamental unity of Western culture, albeit as manifested in the Great Books—it was not Adler but his old nemesis Charles Morris who carried a philosophical banner from the University of Chicago to the New Bauhaus.

The presence of Morris on the staff of the New Bauhaus—and later John Dewey's strong support of the school—signified that the humanistic cultural criticism of the New Bauhaus had more evident, if not more elemental, affinities to science and pragmatism than to the bookish and inevitably elitist cultural ideals of Hutchins and Adler. For no matter how drawn Moholy-Nagy was to metaphysical imagery, the reunification of culture, and a "new humanity," he was also a devotee of the present. And for him the present meant abstract art, technology, and practicality, not the Great Books.

Charles Morris defined the philosophical kinship between the Unity of Science movement and the Bauhaus in the catalogue of the new school. "Certain it is," he wrote, "that the integration and interpenetration of the characteristic human activities of the artist, scientist, and technologist is a crying need of our time." And because, he continued, evoking one of the cardinal tenets of his philosophy, "we need desperately a simplified and purified language in which to talk about art . . . , the New Bauhaus shows deep wisdom in using contemporary science and philosophy in its educational task of reintegrating the artist into the common life."[90] The theme of cultural unity had already given Morris the philosopher and Moholy the artist a common language.

While the ideal of cultural integration animated the faculty, some students and backers decried it in practice as a roundabout road to art. Moholy had heard the complaint before, and it was common to all critics of general education: insufficient vocational training. At the New Bauhaus, this criticism came mainly from those who mistook the institution for a conventional art or design school and felt dissatisfied with the disparate and un-usual offerings or with the ambiguous place held in the curriculum by the fine arts, painting and sculpture. Within a month, Moholy was chiding "unoriented members of the Board"[91] for meddling in the school and under-mining his work. The Bauhaus philosophy did not win converts as easily as Moholy had thought.

Still, enrollments increased in the first year to more than a hundred, and Moholy hatched plans to expand the school as "a cultural working center" for the "synthesis of all specialized knowledge." He also hoped to add to the faculty such notables as Herbert Bayer, Jean Hélion, Hans Arp, Piet Mondrian, and Sigfried Giedion. A circular advertising the expansion set forth the vital importance of extending the Bauhaus's ambitions to the unifica-tion of *all* human experience, not only aesthetic, technological, and commercial but imaginative and intellectual as well. "Since the Industrial Revolution," Moholy wrote, in terms almost identical to those used by Hutchins and Adler in advancing their educational reforms, "we have been overrun with scientific discoveries and technical inventions without number; but we have lost access to their entirety because we have learned to concentrate on parts alone." There is therefore, he emphasized again, "an urgent necessity to . . . restore the basic unity of all human experience which could restore balance to our lives." And, anticipating critics like Bruno Bettelheim, who later con-demned modern architecture and design for psychologically damaging people through its cold impersonality, Moholy concluded that designers could fur-ther this "basic unity" by improving man's relation to his environment: "When we design we must relate technical inventions and scientific discov-eries to our psychological and physiological needs with a view to social im-plications," including "work, recreation and leisure, group response and per-sonality growth."[92]

Moholy's expanded vision completed the original Bauhaus idea of an institution wholly dedicated to building an architectonic culture. Now all fields of learning would be represented, and the New Bauhaus would become *the* universal agent of cultural unification—suggesting the polymathic, if ethe-real, intellectual community of Herman Hesse's novel *The Glass Bead Game* (1943), then taking form under Hesse's pen.[93]

While his big ideas were getting bigger, Moholy did not know that his spon-sors, the board of the Association of Arts and Industries, were faltering in their pledge to raise the annual $90,000 needed for the school's current operating expenses. In the summer of 1938, amid a deep slump in the na-tional economy and with potential benefactors rapidly vanishing, one board member, Walter Paepcke, warned Moholy that all possible sources of funds were drying up.

Foreseeing disaster, Moholy took to the road to raise the money himself. Traveling from corporation to corporation, foundation to foundation, he spent the summer mobilizing all of the resources of salesmanship for which people like Mies van der Rohe so derided him. He returned to Chicago in August with several grants of materials (from Kodak, among others), pledges of packaging and graphics contracts, and the interest of the Carnegie Foundation, whose director, Frederick Keppel, became a lasting friend. But he brought no money. And the board of the association, which, as its president said in an apologetic letter to Walter Gropius, had been "forced to sell securities to operate the school, at 50% to 60% of their former value,"[94] had already decided to close the school. The sudden and irreversible decision shook the faculty and students. And it summoned from the faculty a strong statement of support for Moholy, spiced with criticism of the association.

The association never recovered from the debacle and soon, its resources depleted, faded out of existence. But Moholy, armed with the loyalty of his teachers and a $10,000 contract to design graphics and products for the Spiegel mail-order house, decided to try again. This time he would remain independent of any outside organization and of the Chicago businessmen whose understanding of his work he now doubted more than ever. In the place of a board of trustees to whom he would have to be responsible, he recruited the formal moral sponsorship of a group of distinguished people friendly to the Bauhaus idea: his old mentor, Walter Gropius; John Dewey, who had met Moholy through Charles Morris and admired Moholy's theories of education; Joseph Hudnut, dean of the Graduate School of Design at Harvard; Julian Huxley, with whom Moholy had collaborated on a film about the London zoo; W. W. Norton, publisher of the first American edition of *The New Vision*; William Bacharach, chairman of the Committee on Education of the Chicago Association of Commerce; Alfred Barr, director of the Museum of Modern Art. An admirable roster, but not likely to yield much of the money needed for the school to survive.

Only one businessman and former member of the association's board stuck by Moholy, offering him hope of financial support. This was Walter Paepcke. As the next incarnation of the Bauhaus took shape, Moholy turned to Paepcke. "Knowing your public spirit and your invaluable activities in cultural matters," he wrote, "I dare to ask you to help us in the opening of a new school of design," adding, "I will be ever thankful for any amount which you find right to give for our purposes."[95] In response, Paepcke invited Moholy and his wife to dinner to learn more; having seen the early rewards of modern design at the Container Corporation, Paepcke did not want the world's most famous school of modern design to breathe its last breath in Chicago. But economic recession and his company's large capital investment in a pulp-making plant had cut into Paepcke's resources, too. His only available funds, he confessed, were some $8,000 tucked away for a crisis. Hearing this, Moholy looked at Sibyl and said in his heavy Hungarian accent: "Howw muuch haff vee in der bank fromm Spiegel?" "About $8,000," she replied. "Vee kann liff on four t'ousand, yess?" "Yes," she said, with little hesitation. "Vee vill put za ott'er four t'ousand in zis school. Valter, kann you help uss?" Paepcke paused. Then he said, "All right, Moholy. If you can give up half your income and float the school on a pittance, I guess I can give up some savings."[96]

Yet even Paepcke's $8,000 added to Moholy's $4,000 would fall far short of the $100,000 that had established the New Bauhaus in the first place. Nevertheless, Moholy's determination, aided by Paepcke's friendship and assistance (including the donation of a vacant house in Somonauk, Illinois, for a summer school) and the good faith of a faculty who agreed to teach for a semester for nothing (Gyorgy Kepes, George Fred Keck, Robert Jay Wolff, Andi Schiltz, Charles Morris, Carl Eckart, and Ralph Gerard), enabled the Bauhaus to revive.

Renamed the School of Design, in a gesture of Americanization and in deference to Moholy's true vocation, the new institution opened in February 1939 to forty students on the second floor of an old building on East Ontario Street under the tapping feet from the floor above of rehearsing dancers from the Chez Paree night club. The stated purposes of this "American Bauhaus," as the first prospectus referred to it, were again the "integration and inter-penetration of art, science, and technology."[97] But those purposes also began to reflect Moholy's enlarging conception of the Whole Man, stressing the unity not only of the senses and of art and life, but of all learning, and of man and his environment. Hence the courses and workshops moved toward a more fundamental pedagogy. The Preliminary Course would consist of a full year rather than one semester of "unifying experiences" with light, color, photography, tools, volume, space, tactile constructions, and art history.

Building upon these experiences, the workshops would then produce ingenious finished objects, such as dripless coffee cups and thumb-indented glasses. The regular curriculum culminated, as before, in the study of archi-tecture—although never as important to Moholy as to Gropius or Mies— now supplemented by town planning.

Besides the regular curriculum, the catalogues—splendidly illustrated works of photography and graphics typical of Moholy (see fig. 2.2)—also listed offerings in contemporary art, music appreciation, and gymnastics, lec-tures by Sigfried Giedion on the mechanization of the modern household (part of the book published in 1948 as *Mechanization Takes Command*), as well as evening courses for professional designers in advertising art, product design, and interior design. One of Moholy's favorite additions was a children's class on Saturdays labeled the "Find Yourself" course, where children from six to

Fig. 2.2. László Moholy-Nagy, School of Design catalogue cover, not dated.

twelve would translate their native experiences into artistic forms.[98] Here, in the children's responses to abstract paintings, Moholy found confirmation of his deeply felt intuition that abstraction in modern art reflects abstraction in modern life: "Oh, it's speed, it's airplane speed," the children cried, or "This picture isn't empty, it's painted air," or again, "It's a picture of tumbling." Best of all was his daughter's retort to someone's praise of a realistic landscape as a good "picture": "This is no picture," she insisted. "This is a story. A picture is what my Daddy does."[99]

Like many of Moholy's pedagogical programs, much that he advertised at the School of Design never came to pass. But Moholy, in characteristic disregard of convention, waved away criticism with the remark that the school catalogue was not a contract but a statement of intention as to what the comprehensive designer *should be*—a complete human being. It summoned students to the School of Design to become designers of the universal type, not mere technicians or egocentric artists. And, lest students forget their true purpose (and in striking contrast to Mies van der Rohe at the Armour Institute), Moholy virtually banished the term *art* from the school, supplanting it with Mies's detested *design,* and caused individualism to be frowned upon.[100] Although its financial fate hung in doubt, one thing was certain: the School of Design would remain loyal to the Bauhaus ideals of modernism, pragmatism, community, and cultural reform.

The pitch worked. The school took hold. Next to Moholy, "the key figure"[101] in enabling it to do so, as Sibyl recalled, was Walter Paepcke, who had come to see in Moholy not only an inspired educator and an adroit designer but a man of kindred humanistic and practical interests, a reliable friend, and a challenging competitor at chess. During the next seven and a half years, the artist and the industrialist kept the school alive, raising funds, proselytizing, hoping, and exchanging encouraging words over the chessboard.

The friendship was sealed two weeks after the semester began, when the Paepckes and the Moholy-Nagys visited the recently built Paepcke country estate at Sandwich, Illinois, and the farm in nearby Somonauk to be used by the school in summer. The rural setting and nascent camaraderie fired the artist and his wife with fresh enthusiasm. "My head is humming with figures and projects for the school," Sibyl wrote to Paepcke on their return, "and I only tremble that this cold heartless thing called reality might thwart all these daydreams."[102] For his part, Moholy looked at the country summer school with a predictable glint in his eye. Here, he said, he would have "a chance to carry cooperation and integration to a point that can never be reached within a city group." Before the summer session began, he was thanking the Paepckes again for giving him that opportunity by being "so generous with our school, . . . not alone giving the farm house and land but also money for it."[103]

Buoyed by the cooperation of his new friend and benefactor, Moholy's fund-raising energies went into high gear. He traveled the country again, addressing amateur artists in Idaho and school children in Brooklyn, bearing news of his school and soliciting contributions. "Since we can't afford to advertise," he explained to Sibyl from the Northwest, "I have to be the advertisement."[104] And he eyed every new acquaintance as a prospective donor. In the company of businessmen, his mind worked like a calculator. He was known to pull Paepcke aside and inquire all too audibly: "Tell me Valter, howw muuch ar' zey vert'?"[105] And despite his intimacy with Paepcke, Moholy never entirely escaped the solicitor's brashness and the modernist's condescension toward these men of money; he, after all, lived to serve culture, they existed to make that service possible.

Just as Moholy's personal warmth, earnestness, and aggressive promotional manner prompted mixed responses from observers and prospective supporters, his formal intellectual performances often disappointed those who bought his promotional line. When Sears, Roebuck, for example, sent some seventy top executives to attend a series of lectures by Moholy, "they were all open-minded," according to the Sears chief executive, but "none got anything out of it."[106] Moholy's words and ideas had flowed but to no identifiable end. Paepcke subsequently advised Moholy to talk less and paint more. And another friendly critic bluntly said Moholy should "stop talking about education and concentrate on design construction."[107]

Moholy's eccentricities notwithstanding, the school was staying alive, if only just alive. Lacking a board of trustees to keep it financially stable, it lived from hand to mouth. One student recalled that "nobody on the faculty ever knew when he was going to get paid. And when there weren't many students, things would get terribly gloomy and everyone would know there wasn't any money in the bank; and then Moholy would go out and persuade someone to buy one of his paintings. He would come back with a thousand dollars and it would be fine for a while. Then it would happen all over again."[108]

With the onset of World War II, the difficulties deepened. Both materials and potential funds began to be diverted to the war effort, followed by students and faculty. To keep the school afloat and insure its future, Paepcke began seeking a home for it under an established educational institution. In 1942, he asked his friend Robert M. Hutchins, whom he had met through the Nitzes years earlier, to draw it under the wing of the University of Chicago (where its cultural aims if not its methods would have been comfortable). He also put out feelers to the Illinois Institute of Technology (IIT), formerly the Armour Institute, where Mies still reigned, and to Northwestern University. None was interested. Moholy and his unique school could not be easily absorbed.

Meanwhile, the pragmatic, resourceful, ever optimistic Moholy turned his practical imagination to the war effort itself. He would demonstrate how indispensable the Bauhaus could be to a nation struggling under constrained economic and material circumstances. Two weeks after Pearl Harbor, Moholy was appointed to the mayor's committee on ways of camouflaging Chicago from the air. He flew over the city in all kinds of weather, conjuring up such inventions as a system of floating islands and a false shoreline. He also had Gropius open the spring semester with a lecture, "Site and Shelter: A Contemporary Problem," and had Kepes, a master of optics, head a camouflage workshop where visual forms would be explored for the ambiguities of configuration, contrast, movement, surface, etc. The results of these efforts, like the wooden bed springs created in the wood workshop to replace those of now-scarce metal, brought the Bauhaus idea new publicity, including a story in the *Saturday Evening Post* praising its ingenious synthesis of art and practicality. [109]

Moholy also devised a course in occupational therapy for those handicapped by injury. Under the instruction of Moholy's long-time friend, the psychoanalyst Franz Alexander, director of the Institute for Psychoanalysis in Chicago, Moholy adapted the principles of Bauhaus education to the rehabilitation of damaged bodies and minds. The nurses and social workers who took the course—all too few—learned to employ art, psychology, and technology to help patients explore all of their sensory and intellectual faculties, thereby to regain self-confidence and acquire new skills. Although the program met professional opposition for its unconventional methods (described by Moholy in his essay of 1943, "Better than Before"), it anticipated courses now common in occupational therapy.[110]

These novel ideas, together with Moholy's salesmanship, won for the school in 1942 a Carnegie Corporation grant of $5,000, followed by another from the Rockefeller Foundation of $7,500, obtained through the intervention of Walter Paepcke—to whom the foundation's director explained, "I knew you had your heart in this project, and that was one reason why the grant was made with little question."[111] In gratitude for this and other contributions, Moholy confessed to Paepcke how much he had come to depend on him: "I have said it so often, and I know that with words such things cannot be expressed adequately enough, that without you we could not have gotten so far."[112]

Paepcke's constant support of the School of Design softened—without dispelling—the distrust of businessmen that Moholy had felt so intensely after the New Bauhaus died. "Valter iss so nice," he said again and again;[113] and it was Paepcke more than anyone else he had in mind when he told his wife that "the genuine businessman is actually quite a romantic. He's the dreamer and I'm the realist," for the businessman, he said, believes he can do anything with enough effort.[114]

Paepcke had so strengthened Moholy's confidence in business that at the beginning of 1944 he convinced Moholy to appoint a board of directors to shoulder the school's financial burden. His purpose, he explained, was to liberate Moholy from the economic and managerial tasks that threatened to drain his energies and divert him from his true vocation. "Everybody expects you to be a leader, educator, and creative artist," Paepcke told him, "and not an individual doer of a thousand and one miscellaneous relatively unimportant mechanical duties which now others can be found to do but which in the past you very understandably had to do yourself. . . . Even if worse came to worst," he added, "I have not the least fear but what we could raise in one hour's time the $1,000 or $2,000 that you might save by watching everything like a mother hen."[115]

To rally sufficient backing for the new institutional arrangement, Paepcke had to sell the Bauhaus idea with renewed determination to industrialists. "You have no idea," he wrote to G. F. Keck, "how uninformed important business executives are about the school in the first place and design in the second place."[116] To help inform them he wired Walter Gropius, whom he had met through Moholy, for extra copies of the Museum of Modern Art's Bauhaus exhibition catalogue of 1938, which, he said, was "invaluable" in his efforts to assemble "a rather distinguished board of directors . . . and additional industrial financial support for Moholy and the School of Design."[117] He pressed the catalogue into every willing hand, showing men of business that the Bauhaus was their ally and coaxing them to lend their influence and time to the vital cause of modern design. And he succeeded. In March 1944, the board of directors—composed of executives from Marshall Field; United Airlines; Sears, Roebuck; the Harris Bank; the Chicago Association of Commerce; and others, under Paepcke as chairman—raised the curtain on yet another Bauhaus in America, rechristened, in a step toward higher professional status, the Institute of Design.

Paepcke began at once urging measures to bring the institute in line with this new status. The school, he said, needed a full-time administrative staff in place of the virtually one-person performance of Sibyl; and, he insisted, it also needed to cultivate an image of propriety, cleanliness, efficiency, and responsibility, lest prospective industrial clients and donors dismiss it as bohemian and uncommercial. Finally, to exploit and maintain this image, the institute required a permanent publicity and fund-raising system to be implemented through private "contacts," mail, public lectures, channels to the press, and a printed prospectus designed, as Paepcke said, "to do some selling."[118] So important was publicity in the plan of survival for the institute that a public relations officer went on the payroll at the same salary as Moholy—$6,000. To ease the way to professionalization, Paepcke also made new contributions of his own. He provided office space at the Container Corporation, complete with secretarial help; and, loosening his purse strings once more, he gave the institute $10,000 in Container Corporation capital stock and $5,000 in cash.

These improvements and benefactions brought Moholy's school greater security than it had had since the first days of the New Bauhaus. But the new image and the public identification with Paepcke had their drawbacks. Many Chicago businessmen looked askance at the institute and resisted donating to it because they wondered, in the words of a memo circulated at the Chicago Association of Commerce, "Does this organization have an active Board of Directors, or is it . . . mainly the project of Mr. Moholy-Nagy" and "primarily the personal hobby of Mr. Paepcke?"[119]

To placate such critics, Paepcke publicized the cultural and educational benefits of the institute to Chicago, emphasizing the professional and practical character of the school and, above all, its uses to industry. Over and over he repeated the refrain (unwittingly echoing those who exploited design as a mechanism of planned obsolescence to ensure perpetual consumer desires) that no manufacturer of consumer goods could afford to ignore the commercial uses of modern design. "There is no question in anyone's mind," he wrote to a donor, "that in the postwar era practically all civilian products, whether they are refrigerators, automobiles, Mixmasters, or cooking utensils, are going to be redesigned in an attractive and streamlined way." And "to do this functionally, practically, and artistically, men and women must be trained and educated" with the "combination of craftsmanship, artistry, and science that the Institute teaches."[120] A once-grudging convert to modern design, Paepcke had become its missionary and marketing agent, urging its benefits to commerce on the manufacturers and retailers of Chicago.

To adapt itself still further to the professional demands of the marketplace, the institute began to attenuate its grandiose claims. As written no longer by Moholy but by his administrative staff, the publicity issued by the institute shed the visionary promises of cultural regeneration and a "new humanity" and assumed a matter-of-fact professional tone. The first publicity release stated simply that the objectives of the institute were "to develop a new type of designer for today's new needs," that is, a designer "able to face every requirement, scientific and technical, social, aesthetic and economic." The idea of integration appeared here only as the last in a long list of objectives: "To integrate art, science, and technology."[121] The school catalogues, once works of art boldly illustrated and resounding with Moholy's cultural and metaphysical credo, were also recast, becoming conventional pamphlets describing the "course of study," listing classes, and leaving the idea of integration a mere shadow of its former self, implicit in the interrelation of subjects.

The curriculum still started out with a preliminary course, renamed Foundation Course (which now wholly absorbed "Intellectual Integration"), but the rest of it was divided into four specialized divisions: industrial design, advertising arts, textile design, and photography. These divisions fell in line with the Bauhaus tradition, but they encompassed a broader range of subjects than any previous incarnation of the Bauhaus had known—history, sociology, literature, mathematics, and physics. And although architecture still held pride of place, required in all specialties as "the unifying agent for all branches of the Arts,"[122] it no longer stood out as the unifying goal of design education. Only students specializing in industrial design could go on as graduates to concentrate in architecture alone; others could take an advanced degree in visual arts. For all the resemblances to its predecessors, and its expanded offerings, the curriculum of the institute looked suspiciously like a standard liberal arts program. And it very nearly was, satisfying as it did, for the first time in the career of the Bauhaus, state requirements for a college degree.

Imbued with its new professional image, espousing modest educational aims, and offering a relatively conventional course of study, the Institute of Design was unmistakably loosening its ties to the early-twentieth-century Bauhaus and joining mid-century American culture.

Not even these concessions to practicality, however, could spare the institute financial troubles. Within a year it again faced imminent extinction. With full-time enrollment still at only thirty in March 1945, some members of the board began doubting the school would live up to its promises, and they blamed Moholy for persisting in bad managerial habits. An executive of United Airlines reported to the company president, who was a member of the institute's board, that the merits of the institute were engulfed by disorganization. The "apparently unorganized" method of teaching there, he said, should either be justified or expunged "to prevent its falling into the class of a cult advocating a pet idea and expecting its followers to gather at the feet of the master and accept everything on faith."[123] Paepcke shared some of these doubts and informed Walter Gropius of his worries about the future of the institute. Gropius, with a friendly nod to Bauhaus tradition, replied that "to stimulate the inventiveness of the designer a certain amount of indefinite by-chance procedure has to be accepted I am afraid. I had to suffer from this myself in the Bauhaus." But "I am confident," he concluded, "after my lengthy talk with Moholy that he will try to change some of the debatable features which seem to hurt his prestige"[124]—presumably his inclination to dominate the institution with his intrusive personality and unconstrained energies.

What Moholy would not change, despite all criticism and public concessions, was the priority of comprehensive fundamental education over quick vocational training. "We refuse to promise a two-semester training for a breadwinning job," he told an audience in Milwaukee in May. "And we won't give a thought to fashionable trends in design unless they're sound and functional. Visual fundamentals are a slow-acting ferment. They have to be absorbed and applied in a hundred different ways before they produce an integrated vision and mature results. I shall keep on considering the process of education more important than the finished result."[125] Moholy had fled the original Bauhaus largely over this issue; he would not give in to vocationalists and opportunists now.

The financial situation grew worse. As the war in Europe drew to a close, money and students still failed to flow through the institute's doors. This, compounded by unrest within the school among those who, summoning up an old complaint, accused Moholy of abandoning the true artistic purposes of the Bauhaus for the sake of commercial success (a controversy prompting the departure of Moholy's old friend Kepes), led the directors again to consider closing down the school. Enraged at the very hint of the directors' inclinations, Moholy declared he would carry on without them, as he had done before; and in an unexpectedly ill-tempered allusion to Paepcke, he told Sibyl that the board would let the school die as indifferently as if "we were just an unsuccessful box factory."[126]

But Paepcke took the institute's fate to heart, now as before. He cajoled fellow businessmen; he scheduled meetings to discuss the problems with Gropius, Bayer, and Giedion; and with Moholy's consent he opened new negotiations with neighboring colleges (Northwestern and IIT) about affiliation, provided "the autonomy of the Institute could be maintained."[127] But Paepcke's involvement in Moholy's cause went far deeper than the loyalty of a friend and obligations of the chairman of the board. Paepcke's professional identity had by this time become thoroughly and publicly entwined with the principles of design that the institute embodied. The corporate image and the modern art in advertising campaigns of the Container Corporation had made the company known as a purveyor of modern design for nearly a decade. And no less an authority than Gropius judged Paepcke the perfect exemplar of what the Bauhaus had stood for. After mutual respect between Gropius and Paepcke had grown through their support of Moholy and through Gropius's work as architectural consultant for CCA (producing sketches for a plant in Colombia, South America, and later designing the company's most attractive factory, at Greensboro, North Carolina), Gropius wrote to Paepcke: "You represent for me the rare exception of a man in power and leadership who seriously tries to fuse business with cultural progress. I certainly know how difficult a task this is and you can hardly imagine how much reassurance and confidence your attitude gives me for my own outlook."[128]

Paepcke's reputation as a businessman among artists and as a man of artistic tastes in business gained new prestige when the Container Corporation's unprecedented "Modern Art in Advertising" exhibit opened at the Art Institute on April 27, 1945, in the midst of the struggle to keep Moholy's institute going. Although not the first exhibition of modern advertising art (Katharine Kuh, for example, had mounted a small show at her gallery in 1941, featuring the "advance guard of advertising artists"),[129] no other single company could display a collection of modern advertising art like this.

As laid out by former Bauhäusler Herbert Bayer in complex patterns of panels, wires, and painted lines of traffic direction, the exhibition of eighty-nine pictures by forty-four artists from Cassandre and Carlu to Ben Shawn, Richard Lindner, and Willem de Kooning led visitors through a dramatic maze of mostly abstract images and subtle propaganda. Bayer—the artist responsible for several of the advertisements but not previously acquainted with Paepcke—had come to the job through the recommendation of Gropius, who had assured Paepcke that Bayer was "versatile, full of ideas, and has learned the American vocabulary of propaganda."[130] And even before Gropius's intervention, Bayer had suggested such an exhibition to the Museum of Modern Art. But when Alfred Barr, director of that museum, hesitated to turn his galleries over to the advertising art of a single company, Daniel Catton Rich, director of the Art Institute, seized the idea and acted on it.

The opening on April 27 (see fig. 2.3) brought together more leaders of modernism in the visual arts than Chicago was likely to see together again: Moholy, Bayer, Man Ray, Léger, even the then-unknown de Kooning—poor, partially toothless, and shy, still working his way (as in the faintly expressionistic Dutch scene done for CCA—see frontispiece) toward the explosive abstract expressionism that would make him famous. Delighting in their artistic achievements and encouraged by the promise, as Paepcke wrote in the exhibition catalogue, of a "remunerative and agreeable" alliance between "the artist and the businessman,"[131] they all toasted the Container Corporation for making that alliance work in the name of modernism. Sigfried Giedion (slated to write the introduction to the catalogue until the curator of the Print Gallery vetoed the choice) praised Paepcke's rare courage in promoting genuine modernism instead of the "streamlined nonsense" typical of most advertising art. "As far as I can see," Giedion wrote to Paepcke, "you are the only one in the U.S.A. who is able to utilize the creative forces" of modernism in advertising.[132]

But the artists and their supporters were not alone in judging the show a success. Attendance records at the Print Gallery of the Art Institute fell before the surprising numbers of people—several thousand a day—curious about this union of abstract art and industry. Writing in *Art News* magazine, Rosamund Frost lauded the Container Corporation's use of modern art as

Fig. 2.3. Man Ray, Katharine Kuh, and László Moholy-Nagy (right) at opening of the Container Corporation's Modern Art in Advertising exhibit, April 1945. Advertising designs by Man Ray (left) and Leo Lionni appear in the background. Photo by Gordon Coster.

marking an epoch: "The painter has proved his economic worth in the world of industry. Art has come out of the studio and entered the lives of 131,000,000 people."[133]

The ascending reputation of CCA in its "unique role as patron" and "benefi-ciary. . . of art and design" (as *Industrial Marketing* later put it)[134] recharged Paepcke's determination to defend Moholy's cause. Nor did Paepcke shrink from badgering friends or employing pressure tactics. "As a graduate of the Great Books Course" (the Adler-Hutchins seminar for Chicago executives, established in 1943), he wrote to the president of Marshall Field, who had declined to renew his company's grant to the Institute of Design, "you can well imagine what would have happened' to Christianity if there had been a defection in the ranks of some of the original Twelve Apostles."[135] And he varied the jocular tone with the serious. To the same correspondent: "It would be too discouraging and almost fatal [for the institute] if firms such as yours dropped out!!! For the good of the country, the city, design education, and even Marshall Field & Co., this must not happen, and I warn you I am going to do everything I can, short of being a nuisance, to dissuade you."[136]

Marshall Field finally relented and contributed again, although in a smaller amount than before.

Sometimes Paepcke's reputation alone was enough to win support for the institute. The Rockefeller Foundation, having previously acknowledged Paepcke's role in winning a grant for Moholy, told Paepcke that they would never have become interested in the institute had he not headed its board of directors. "The school is important," an executive of the foundation explained, "but we . . . think that the fact of your connection with it is of the utmost importance," for "you are, to put it mildly, a key figure for whatever is to be done in bettering the relation of art to industry."[137] The foundation then gave Moholy a $5,000 grant that resulted in Moholy's last and most comprehensive statement of his modernist and Bauhaus ideals, *Vision in Motion* (1947).

Yet, even with Paepcke's efforts, the institute might not have survived had not a large and unexpected influx of veterans, subsidized by the G.I. bill, raised enrollment from under a hundred to nearly four hundred in the next academic year, 1945–1946. The future looked brighter than it had in years—the school solvent, Moholy financially free to pour fresh energies into his art and writings, and a Christmas visit planned, along with the Herbert Bayers, to Paepcke's idyllic new vacation spot "discovered" the previous summer at Aspen, Colorado. But then came a stunning reverse: Moholy fell seriously ill. The vacation was cancelled. The future was again clouded in doubt.

Diagnosed as leukemia, the disease forced Moholy into the hospital, where after eight weeks of X-ray treatments, it seemed to abate. Moholy was back at the institute in January, fervently working on new paintings and the manuscript of *Vision*. To commemorate his victory over the illness, he painted a large abstract canvas entitled *Leu I, 1945*. And he rushed with revived enthusiasm into the organization of a one-man show in Cincinnati and a new photographic seminar at the institute.

But the disease recurred in the spring and began again to drain Moholy's strength—just as the school was preparing a massive fund-raising campaign and a move into renovated quarters in the old Historical Society building on North Dearborn Street. By midsummer, Moholy was thinking of possible successors: first Marcel Breuer, then José Luis Sert, Kepes, Ralph Rapson, and Charles Eames. Whoever the successor, Moholy told Paepcke, he would have to be not only an educator but an artist, because "the idea of integrating art, science, and technology will always require a greater emphasis on the arts since the other two are usually accepted as a matter of course," and Moholy didn't want the institute to be "turned into just another engineering school."[138] Yet neither Moholy nor anyone else then knew how soon Moholy's concerns would have to be dealt with.

The fall semester brought nearly a thousand students and an atmosphere of postwar political fervor into the institute. The conservative Paepcke cautioned Moholy against the leftists, but Moholy brushed off their ideological zeal as the high-spirited radicalism and curiosity of youth, and he vowed to put it to "creative" uses by harnessing it, he told Paepcke, to "a full understanding of the traditions and achievements of our civilization." For Moholy, now perhaps more than ever, the purpose of education was "helping the young generation to acquire a philosophy of life."[139] And to improve the chances of doing this, he had added some appropriate courses: John U. Nef of the University of Chicago, then working in the movement for world government and conducting the university's ambitious Committee on Social Thought, which he had set up, agreed to give a series of lectures, "The Foundations of Modern Man." Moholy's wife, as the first step in a distinguished academic career, would teach a course on the history of modern education as "man's post-Renaissance struggle for inner freedom and civic responsibility."[140] Moholy was dying, but the Bauhaus idea of cultural reform, however attenuated, was still alive.

Although failing physically, Moholy continued to paint, construct, and put the finishing touches on *Vision in Motion*. In mid-November he went with Paepcke to the Museum of Modern Art's "Conference on Industrial Design as a New Profession," where he reiterated his long-held belief in the importance of comprehensive art education not only for industry but for culture and human character. It is only by integrating the "creative abilities" with the emotions and knowledge, he said, that a "higher level of personality is achieved." And to the specialists in attendance who represented industry, not art, and who accused him of merely "dabbling" in design, he replied: "I love to dabble," adding that all creation and education originate in dabbling. "Design," he went on, reasserting the antivocational bias that had earned him criticism before, "is not a profession; it is an attitude"—a way of experiencing the world that everyone should learn.[141]

Standing between the industrialists who saw design as merely a tool of profits and the designers who wanted good design irrespective of profits, Moholy was vulnerable to attack from both sides. But he never doubted his mission to bring the two together and to improve culture in the act. And just before he left New York, he told his old colleague from the School of Design, Robert Jay Wolff, then at Brooklyn College, "I don't know yet about my paintings, but I'm proud of my life."[142]

That life and its work, as Wolff observed during that last visit, were unrelentingly energized, even as Moholy neared death, by Moholy's "refusal to be motivated by conflict and tragedy, fear and disbelief," and by "his great faith in himself and the power of his own optimism."[143] "I have never been, strictly speaking, deeply unhappy," Moholy had written in response to a questionnaire sent to many modern artists by the *Little Review* in 1929.[144] Probably he never was. This spirit of affirmation characterized Moholy's life, temperament, art, pedagogy, and ideas as much as anything—even as much as the wariness of emotions that nourished his attraction to technological rather than expressionistic art and to communal rather than individual creation and that held him at an emotional distance from other people, at least until shortly before his death when he learned "to see emotion as the great adhesive"[145] that could facilitate instead of thwarting human unity. For it was this spirit that led Moholy to embrace rather than deny the modernity of cities and machines, to delight in abstraction, to honor craft and design, and to disseminate his message of cultural integration through untiring teaching and writing.

Moholy's last book, *Vision in Motion*, consummated this affirming life, just as it stands as the final statement of the Bauhaus vision of culture and aesthetics. Surveying the history of modern culture's disintegration through specialization, vocational education, shallow information, and the war between art and science, it outlines a remedy in the Bauhaus ideology of good design—"thinking in relationships"[146] with the aim of wresting unity from diversity. It illustrates the makings of this unity in works of Moholy and others, and, expressing Moholy's fully developed conception of cultural integration, it analyzes the modern movement in various arts (painting, sculpture, "space-time problems," motion pictures, literature, and "group poetry") to disclose the underlying bond among them. Moholy finds this bond in a "moving field of mutual relationships," which the modern artist grasps through "vision in motion," or by "seeing, feeling and thinking in relationships and not in a series of isolated phenomena."[147] The artistic manifestation of "vision in motion" is thus the abstract, integrated rendering of space and time, light and shadow, line and volume, rest and motion, and multiple images—as in all great modern art and especially in Moholy's own optical and kinetic inventions.

However opaque in phrasing, no stronger expression of the yea-saying voice of modernism exists than *Vision in Motion*. And to crown his celebratory message, Moholy closed the book with a proposal for "an international cultural working assembly . . . composed of outstanding scientists, sociologists, artists, writers, musicians, technicians and craftsmen," to "investigate the roots of our intellectual and emotional heritage," and lend order to every pursuit of modern life, from the relation of art and industry to city planning and the organization of government. The Bauhaus idea here achieved its most exalted formulation. No more the program of a single institution, it would draw together a nucleus of world government that, Moholy concluded, "could translate Utopia into action."[148] The Bauhaus as ideal educator of a disintegrated culture had become the Bauhaus as ideal governor of an architectonic culture.

Before sending this summation of his intellectual life's work and his loftiest aspirations to the printers, Moholy added a final note. He wanted the book formally dedicated to his most enduring and efficacious champions. Taking a pen in hand for one of the last times, he instructed the publisher to include the inscription: "To Elizabeth and Walter Paepcke."

A few days later, on November 24, 1946, Moholy died. When the news reached Paepcke in his Lake Shore Drive apartment, he received it in silence. Then turning away from his wife he walked slowly to the windows and stood looking out over the mists rising from Lake Michigan. It was the only time in forty years of marriage that Elizabeth Paepcke saw her husband cry.[149]

With Moholy's death the Institute of Design entered a time of troubles less economic than political. Paepcke's devotion to the school could never be the same without Moholy at its head. Paepcke told Gropius he wanted to give up the chairmanship and asked Gropius to take over the school himself. But Gropius insisted that "they need you badly" and suggested as Moholy's successor "a younger man, still in the prime of his years."[150] Paepcke stayed on to help find such a man, and after failing to get Kepes or José Luis Sert, he won acceptance, at Gropius's suggestion and with Sibyl's assent, from Serge Chermayeff of Brooklyn College.

Unfortunately, as Gropius and Paepcke had feared, friction quickly grew among the faculty, especially between Chermayeff and Sibyl, who had now joined the faculty as head of the humanities department and whose inflexible attachment to Moholy and his ideas made it difficult for her to work under anyone else. Her relations with Paepcke also became strained as he came to seem to her insufficiently loyal to Moholy's memory and too concerned about matters of administration and finance.

Before long Sibyl was gone, embarking on a career as a scholar and educator in her own right, and producing the moving biography *Moholy-Nagy: Experiment in Totality* in 1950, in which she sanctified her husband and vengefully portrayed the businessmen of Chicago as almost uniformly philistine and insensitive. She also represented Moholy's attitude toward them as most often critical, marked by condemnations of the "insidious paternalism" of "industry as the great white father of the arts" that "strangles creative independence."[151] Paepcke alone occasionally escaped the blanket censures but, even then, only as an occasional exception to the rule.

By the time the biography appeared in print, Sibyl was reeling from further disenchantment. For the Institute of Design as an autonomous school had itself disappeared, absorbed in December 1949 by IIT in the culmination of Paepcke's long efforts, previously sanctioned by Moholy, to find it a permanent, financially secure home. Despite Paepcke's good intentions, without Moholy to guide it the Institute of Design was bound to lose its identity to the larger institution. Thus while the institute maintained its reputation as a leading school of industrial and interior design, and many of its faculty remained loyal to Moholy's pedagogical principles, it drifted farther and far-ther from Moholy's impassioned experimentation and cultural vision and toward the more strictly commercial and vocational preoccupations he ab-horred.[152] This drift provoked something of a rebellion among the Moholy loyalists in 1954 with the appointment of nondesigner Jay Doblin as direc-tor, an upheaval that drew in Gropius and Mies van der Rohe on the side of the traditional Bauhaus idea.[153]

But the movement away from the Bauhaus idea could not have been stemmed amid the growing acceptance of modern design by business and the inexorable professionalization of design education, already marked by the evolution of the New Bauhaus into the Institute of Design. This movement did not in itself mean that the Bauhaus idea had failed. Far from it. It more nearly meant that the campaign for modern design and design education that had once assumed the character of a cultural battle between modernists and traditionalists was actually terminating in a victory of the modernists—albeit a victory more in the form of consumer tastes and capitalism than in that of cultural regeneration. Substantial victory had meant partial defeat. Having embraced the aesthetic and economic benefits of modern design, what need had consumer commerce of the modernists' metaphysics and cul-tural anthropology? What need had it even of the Bauhaus's elementary art education for professional designers? "Who needs to go to a Bauhaus any more," asked prominent Chicago architect Harry Weese some years later, "to learn about space and volume by waving your hand around in a paper bag? Kids do that in first grade."[154] Even the old Bauhäusler Marcel Breuer, who Moholy had hoped would succeed him, had declined to carry on the peda-gogical tradition, seeing no need or possibility for the Bauhaus to thrive in America. "The Bauhaus ideal," he said, "was starting from zero" in a devas-tated society of a previous age. And although the "basic design course . . . changed visual education . . . , the Bauhaus idea as it really existed could not be transplanted."[155]

Moholy's Bauhaus did not achieve the cultural integration Moholy had dreamed of (although the mass technological consumer culture that he served grows more integrated all the time); nor could it be said to have itself changed the course of industrial design, since the proliferation of commercially suc-cessful styles by professional designers in every industry constituted too strong and unwieldy a current for any one institution to steer. But through those who taught and studied there, and through others who learned of it by repu-tation, the school did leave a mark on American commerce, art, and educa-tion and won a place for the Bauhaus idea in American culture.

At the same time, Moholy's Bauhaus helped bring a golden age of culture to Chicago. And while it had a powerful ally in the person of Walter Paepcke, it also had another in a second educational institution that Paepcke championed—one even more dedicated than the Bauhaus to educational reform and cultural unity, if unity of a different order. This was the University of Chicago under the regime of Robert Maynard Hutchins. Although Hutchins and Moholy took no opportunity to join forces openly (and were in some respects philosophically at odds), the reforms and ideals associated with Hutchins at the university complemented Moholy's and—also in part through the efforts of Walter Paepcke—excelled them in making Chicago the center of educational and cultural reform in America for a generation.

3

great books and cultural reform:

the chicago bildungsideal

Three months after Moholy-Nagy died, Walter Paepcke found himself drawn again into strategies for curing the spiritual ills of modern civilization. Invited to lunch by Robert M. Hutchins on February 21, Paepcke learned of some curative plans then on the minds of Hutchins and a few colleagues. One plan called for the creation of a private foundation to stimulate and administer Great Books classes throughout the nation. Another proposed an international festival to celebrate the two-hundredth anniversary of the birth of the great humanist Johann Wolfgang von Goethe. Academic as these projects seemed, they were to far surpass the seemings, forging a lasting partnership in cultural reform between Hutchins and Paepcke, giving birth to both the most ambitious program of adult education ever and the premier cultural event of postwar America, and leaving in their wake a nationwide network of Great Books reading groups and the Aspen Institute for Humanistic Studies.

When Robert Hutchins drew Paepcke into plans for the Great Books Foundation and the Goethe Bicentennial Celebration, he was cashing in on an association that went back nearly twenty years to Hutchins's early days as the *Wunderkind* president of the University of Chicago. The two men had met through Paepcke's parents-in-law, Mr. and Mrs. William A. Nitze. From the time of Hutchins's arrival on the campus in 1929, Anina Nitze had courted the young president and his wife, Maude, with an aplomb well known in the university—generous attentions, gracious introductions, convivial sociability. Mrs. Nitze could hardly have resisted launching such a courtship. For no university had seen a president like this before—thirty years old, well over six feet tall, with the even features, soft eyes, and black wavy hair of a matinee idol, and gifted with a lightning-quick intellect, irrepressible wit, and rhetorical flair. Hutchins and his wife—equally handsome, stately, and dark, impressively intelligent and artistically talented as well—brought an unprecedented glamour to the Midway campus (see figs. 3.1 and 3.2). They also brought an occasionally supercilious and willful manner that could and did rankle the stolid professors. But while Hutchins would often offend traditional academicians, his public performance earned him many friends and allies among students, cultural reformers, and men of affairs—among them, Walter Paepcke.

Like Paepcke's friendship with Moholy-Nagy, his relationship with Hutchins grew from both common interests and affinities of temperament. Four years apart in age, molded by severely moralistic Protestant fathers, and honor graduates of Yale, Paepcke and Hutchins were driven by a desire to elevate the common run of mankind to the demanding standards of culture and morality that they themselves possessed—although the atheistic Paepcke divorced these standards from religion. And their every labor to accomplish this elevation, separately or together, demonstrated the stringent self-discipline and passion for work, lightened by beguiling wit and seductive social charm, that distinguished both men. Unproductive and mere emotional indulgences had little place in either man's life. Hutchins remarked in his last years: "I've never overcome the notion that having fun is a form of indolence."[1] More adept and confident in public pursuits than in private feelings, they both took their keenest satisfactions from cultural enterprises requiring earnest energies and persuasive public relations.

That Paepcke and Hutchins should have seen their social relationship lead into common cultural enterprises was to be expected. Individually they had already contributed in a substantial way to Chicago's cultural life during the 1930s and early 1940s. They had also worked together on wartime labor relations and nutrition commissions and on the University of Chicago's board of trustees (which Paepcke joined in 1945); and they had enjoyed the pleasures of philosophical argument in the ongoing Great Books class created for businessmen by Hutchins and Mortimer Adler in 1943. Now that Paepcke no longer had Moholy-Nagy to summon him to the cause of reforming culture through the Bauhaus, he was

Fig. 3.1. The young Mr. And Mrs. Robert M. Hutchins in 1929, the year Hutchins became president of the University of Chicago. From the University of Chicago Archives.

prepared to take up Hutchins's cause of reforming culture through the University of Chicago.

The University of Chicago had been a prestigious institution almost since its founding under the endowment of John D. Rockefeller in 1891, featuring an illustrious faculty and determined administrators. During Hutchins's tenure the university acquired another reputation as well. It became the epicenter of educational reforms that attracted the eyes of the nation and sent shock nation and sent shock waves across the landscape of higher learning, stirring a revival of traditional humanism and achieving a triumph in public relations. One historian long on the faculty, Daniel J. Boorstin, has called Hutchins "the great public relations genius of American higher education in this century."[2] Like Paepcke—with whom Boorstin linked Hutchins as an adroit manipulator of public attitudes through images[3]—the university president successfully promoted a distinctive institutional image through displays of highbrow taste, self-confident intelligence, well-chosen phrases, and razzle-dazzle. Hutchins's deft public statements about the university even had the ring of advertising copy, like the words quoted beneath his picture on the cover of *Time* magazine in 1949: "It is not a very good university. It is simply the best there is."[4]

But Hutchins's reputation in the reform of education came not from public relations alone. The ideals that Hutchins and his colleagues espoused constituted a systematic and powerful indictment of the evils of modern culture and a persuasive prescription for cure. These ideals formed so definite a pattern of humanistic pedagogy and psychology that they warrant the label *Bildungsideal,* the German term coined in the eighteenth century to denote the ideal of a fully developed and whole human being. And they were so thoroughly identified with the University of Chicago during Hutchins's reign that they can be called the Chicago Bildungsideal.

No body of educational principles and practices in higher learning was to become better known and more enthusiastically implemented in this century than those of the Chicago Bildungsideal—by dint of academic and public controversy, the many institutions shaped by them, and the dissemination of the Great Books program. Yet, curiously enough, those principles and practices had played no part in Robert Hutchins's coming to Chicago in the first place. For when Hutchins assumed the presidency of the university in the summer of 1929, the Chicago Bildungsideal was not so much as a whisper in the wind: neither Hutchins nor the trustees who hired him had any plan of educational reform in mind.

"I was chosen," he said later with characteristic mock self-deprecation, "because of a prevailing euphoria and the lack of general discrimination. The feeling was 'we got to have a president, and it doesn't matter how old he is.' I couldn't have been elected two years earlier or a year later."[5] Hutchins told a commencement audience in the spring of 1930 that he believed the university president's role consisted mainly in ensuring that the university put no "insuperable obstacles"[6] in the path of learning.

This innocent remark held the germ of a revolution in higher education. For Hutchins discovered many such obstacles in the university in the form of entrenched habits, organizations, and ideas. And, impelled by the brashness

Fig. 3.2. Robert M. Hutchins and adoring students at an informal lunch, circa 1949. From the University of Chicago Archives.

of youth, a will to reform, and an expanding theory of education and culture, he and his younger confrere, Mortimer J. Adler, soon set about smashing those obstacles.

On an October evening in 1929, Hutchins and the twenty-seven-year-old Adler (a friend since the year before when the two had prepared a paper together on legal reasoning while Hutchins was dean of the Yale Law School) started talking about a subject quite foreign to them both: undergraduate education. Hutchins said his own education then consisted only of a little knowledge of the Bible, Plato, Shakespeare, Goethe, and the opinions of some judges; Adler chuckled and told him that if he didn't do "something drastic" fast, the university president would likely "close his educational career a wholly uneducated man."[7] But when Hutchins asked Adler to describe a proper education, Adler could offer nothing but recollections of the best part of his own schooling, the General Honors course of Professor John Erskine at Columbia.

A brilliant, brazen, diminutive Jewish native of New York, driven, as he later confessed, by "an analerotic compulsion toward orderliness that insists upon classifying things and putting everything into its proper place and keeping it there,"[8] Adler had not been an easy student to please. Most of his classes at Columbia had aroused in him only boredom or contempt—particularly the philosophy classes of John Dewey, which had provoked an early antipathy to pragmatism, often expressed in long, argumentative letters slipped under Dewey's office door. "I was an objectionable student," Adler was to admit, "in some respects perhaps repulsive."[9] But Erskine's course differed from the rest. More than any other, it opened Adler's eyes to books and ideas he could love—and would later classify. For this was the first course in the country devoted to what would come to be known as the "Great Books."

Erskine had conceived the course during World War I as a corrective to what he judged the deliberate and evil trends at Columbia toward specialized learning, the imitation of pseudoscientific German scholarship, and the abandonment of the liberal arts tradition. First proposed in 1917, the idea met rebuff; but, after Erskine had implemented it briefly at a college established for American servicemen after the war in Beaune, France, he submitted it again at Columbia. This time it won acceptance, and the class went into the schedule for 1921–1922 under the title General Honors.

The change of heart at Columbia reflected a new estimation of general education caused in part by the war. A general course designed to instruct future soldiers in the complexities of modern politics had already entered the Columbia curriculum while the war raged. Entitled "War Issues," it had won such a following that it survived the armistice and continues today in revised form as Contemporary Civilization. A new pattern of undergraduate learning was here in the making; the class on what Erskine called the Classics of Western Thought filled that pattern out. Contemporary Civilization and General Honors were destined to become the model of general education nationally. For as the postwar years saw colleges attract an ever larger and more diverse, relatively uneducated population (between 1910 and 1930, college enrollments rose from 355,000, 4.8 percent of college-age youth, to 1,100,000, or 12.2 percent, many of these immigrants),[10] the need that Erskine had recognized for nonspecialized humanistic learning became even more compelling.

Erskine organized his own course to mirror that need as closely as possible. Believing most of his students would come from homes where the classics went unread, he insisted that they encounter the books directly rather than through the secondary works that can crush the desire to learn under a surfeit of scholarship.

The first class assembled with Erskine in the fall of 1921, the intellectually energetic Adler in attendance. Adler's keen mind reveled in the rich variety of readings (fifty-two titles beginning with Homer and ending with William James) and in Erskine's way of conducting "highly civil conversations about important themes and in a spirit of inquiry," as Erskine had promised in an essay of 1915 entitled "The Moral Obligation to Be Intelligent."[11] Two years later, Adler was leading his own section of the course alongside another future cultural luminary, Mark Van Doren.

These early experiences in studying and teaching the Great Books were, Adler subsequently observed, the most important "among all the educative influences that good fortune has conferred on me."[12] For in those experiences Adler discovered the idea that was to shape his life, taking him from Columbia to the University of Chicago, and onto leadership of the Great Books movement and preparation of the *Great Books of the Western World* with its unique *Syntopicon*, then to creation of the Institute for Philosophical Research, the Paedeia Group, and finally the Center for the Study of Great Ideas.

After Adler had told Hutchins his one definite idea of education, Hutchins agreed: reading and discussing the classics of Western thought, the Great Books, would make for a perfect education—his own as well as that of students at the University of Chicago. But Adler added a caveat. The program would meet resistance because "organized departments and departmentally minded individuals don't understand it, resent it, distrust it," and "specialized scholars think that it is pretentious, and that the work must be sloppy because it isn't their type of scholarship." But he encouraged Hutchins to push ahead because "it is one of the strongest attacks upon specialism and departmentalism; it is the best education for the faculty as well as for the students; . . . and it constitutes by itself, if properly conducted, the backbone of a liberal education."[13]

Hutchins first hinted publicly at his inclinations toward general education in his inaugural speech of November 1929, with the suggestion that the undergraduate curriculum be divided between large lectures and small discussion groups for honors students. Then, after installing Adler as a member of the philosophy department in a coup that irritated members of the faculty and produced lasting conflicts with the department, culminating in Adler's expulsion, he stunned Adler and everyone else by offering to conduct at Adler's side the first Honors course introduced into the curriculum for the fall of 1930. The prospect of a university president leading freshmen through the rigors of classroom discussion was novel enough. That he should do so with books known in little more than name to most people—and to Hutchins himself—made the experiment a thoroughgoing curiosity both in the university and outside.

Under the heading "General Honors Course" ("limited to twenty by invitation"), the class offered "Readings in the Classics of Western European Literature"[14] from Homer to Freud, requiring two years to complete and granting credit only at the end. Adler, in a characteristically presumptuous gesture, insisted on setting aside a special room for the exclusive use of the class, whose elect members could then study there at their convenience. Against the opposition of the College (that is, the undergraduate school) dean, who disliked the very idea of the course, Hutchins maneuvered the space, assuring Adler that "we are going to move the library of the Art Department to bring this about" and adding in his typical tone of jocular mockery: "If there are any other little changes that you would like to have made in the structure of this University in order to accommodate your whims, just let me know."[15]

The seminar quickly became a star attraction on the University of Chicago campus, even drawing visitors passing through Chicago, like Gertrude Stein, who led a discussion of the *Odyssey* with all of the rhetorical obscurity for which she was famed and who clashed with Adler over what she judged the foolishness of reading translations. Students loved it. The remarkable intellectual stringency of discussion and the dramatic contrast in style between the dashing, poised, witty, viciously cutting Hutchins and the more common-looking, intellectually persistent Adler gave the class an electricity like no other and helped win the student body to the cause of educational reform.

But the General Honors seminar was only the first step in Hutchins and Adler's program to establish a general education curriculum for undergraduates. By the time the class assembled, Hutchins had already prepared the reorganization of the university itself as part of what would be known as the Chicago Plan. Instead of the seventy-two departments, the university was divided into four upper-level divisions (Biological Science, Physical Science, Social Science, and Humanities) and a preparatory two-year "College." Students could specialize in one of these divisions only after fulfilling the course requirements of the College, which Hutchins and Adler hoped to make autonomous and totally committed to general education—although this didn't come for another ten years, largely because, as Adler later conceded, Hutchins's willfulness and Adler's abrasive manner set too much opposition against them. Still, progress was made in those early years toward general education. In addition to the administrative reorganization and the creation of General Honors, the College instituted year-long lecture courses supplemented by discussion groups concentrating on the broad conceptual issues fundamental to the four divisions. Hutchins added to the public appeal of these innovations by recruiting his old friend Thornton Wilder to help execute them with lectures and seminars. In another bold move, he pushed through a plan to make class attendance in the College optional and to have achievement measured only by comprehensive examinations at the end of the two years.

From these beginnings Hutchins and Adler went on to expand the theory and practice of general education and the place of the Great Books in it through a series of experiments that repeatedly engulfed the campus in controversy and made the University of Chicago known throughout the country for pedagogical adventures and intellectual ferment. In 1933, the College incorporated (on paper only, never wholly in fact) the last two years of the University High School to give the general education program the four years desired for it. Hutchins and Adler conducted a Great Books course for high school students that same year, and became more convinced than ever that the Great Books could be taught to anyone—although Adler's analytical lectures on the liberal arts, or the Trivium (grammar, rhetoric, logic), sailed over most students' heads.[16]

The next year Adler put his ideas on the Trivium to better use. By this time he had long since bidden farewell to the philosophy department, after his and Hutchins's unrelenting opposition to the appointment of the pragmatist Charles Morris had brought Adler's expulsion in 1931. Having become, through Hutchins's unstinting administrative ingenuity, associate professor of the philosophy of law or, as his detractors put it, "Professor of the Blue Sky,"[17] Adler now inaugurated a series of courses for pre-law students dwelling entirely on the Trivium. Taught by Adler and two young tutors hired for the purpose, William Gorman and James Martin, these courses were the closest thing yet to the full-scale Great Books curriculum implemented for the first time at St. John's College in Annapolis, Maryland, in 1937 and finally, albeit temporarily, at Chicago in 1942.

The introduction of this curriculum at St. John's, to widespread publicity and lasting success, stemmed from the work of the Committee on the Liberal Arts established at the University of Chicago in 1936 under an unrestricted gift of $25,000 from a wealthy Hutchins devotee, Marion Stern. This committee—consisting of Adler, Richard McKeon (Adler's fellow Aristotelian recruited from Columbia in 1934–1935), two of McKeon's most promising students, Paul Goodman and William Barrett, Stringfellow Barr and Scott Buchanan (both from the University of Virginia), Arthur Rubin, and William Gorman—had the assignment of devising a new curriculum for the undergraduate College of the university based on the elements of the classical curriculum, the Trivium and the Quadrivium (geometry, arithmetic, astronomy, music), and consisting of studies in the Great Books. To Hutchins's deep disappointment, the group, beset by criticism from the outside as being another of Hutchins's efforts to impose his will on the university, and vexed by internal dissension over what books should be read and how much freedom should be allowed in conducting classes, eventually abandoned its task.

While the committee failed to create a complete Great Books curriculum for the University of Chicago, its discussions did result in the "New Program" at St. John's. This happened when, in the spring of 1937, Stringfellow

Barr learned that the two-hundred-year-old St. John's College had consumed its financial resources and was about to close. Moving fast, he obtained sufficient funds and faculty to try an experiment. In the fall of that year the new St. John's opened with Barr as president (Hutchins having declined the post), Scott Buchanan as dean, and a curriculum consisting entirely of courses in the Great Books—although, in consequence mainly of Buchanan's influence, these would include theoretical works on science and mathematics previously omitted at Chicago. Hutchins and Adler, who had both toyed with the idea of leaving Chicago as early as 1933 to try a similar experiment at Cornwall College, Connecticut, affirmed their support of the college by close affiliation with it: Hutchins became chairman of the board of visitors-governors and Adler became visiting lecturer, offering monthly addresses there for several years and carrying the banner of the New Program elsewhere, introducing it to the public at large in his first popular book, *How to Read a Book* (1940), helping to install versions of it at Notre Dame and at St. Mary's of California, and later serving as the impetus for its adaptation to institutions as disparate as the University of Kansas in Lawrence and the Manhattan School of Music in New York City. The Chicago Bildungsideal was proving its appeal and practicability (see fig. 3.3).

The passage of the Great Books idea from John Erskine's General Honors to this comprehensive curriculum formulated at the University of Chicago and adopted elsewhere led far beyond a set of educational principles and practices. For Hutchins and Adler had transformed a technique of general education into a vision of salvation: they believed their Bildungsideal could save mankind and the modern world from moral decay and physical destruction. Hence they promoted it with religious zeal as both pedagogy and philosophy.

True to its origins, the Chicago Bildungsideal took its first principle from the general education program at Columbia: to hold back the tide of vocationalism and scholarship that threatened to turn all university education into an apprenticeship for professional scholars. "The object" of the Chicago Plan, Hutchins explained in 1933, "was to give a general education and to eliminate, wherever possible, courses with a professional aim."[18] "The tricks of the trade," he later said, "cannot be learned in a university, and if they can they should not be. All that can be learned in a university is the general principles, and the fundamental propositions, the theory of any discipline. If education is properly understood, it will be understood as the cultivation of the intellect."[19]

"The cultivation of the intellect": this was the second principle and the heart of the Chicago Bildungsideal—and it was a rallying cry. For beyond their affirmation of general by contrast to specialized knowledge, Hutchins

Fig. 3.3. Mortimer J. Adler (right center) and Milton Mayer conducting a Great Books seminar at the University of Chicago, April 1945. Myron Davis, *Life* magazine, © Time Inc.

and Adler asserted the superiority of philosophical to factual or pragmatic truth.

There was nothing novel in this assertion. It had been an abiding principle of humanistic education and culture since the Greeks; and it had many times compelled its partisans to clash with advocates of technical, vocational, or merely contemporary fashions in learning. Socrates' disputes with the Sophists had been such a conflict, as were the Battle of the Books in the seventeenth century and Matthew Arnold's struggle in the 1860s against the growth of the anarchic and vulgar notions of the popular mind and the philistines. Yet the many predecessors served not to weaken but to strengthen the authority of Hutchins and Adler's ideas as well as to prepare for their acceptance. For this humanistic tradition held that the intellect could best be cultivated by studying traditional classics, "the best that has been thought and known in the world,"[20] as Matthew Arnold had put it, rather than attending to every contemporary experience and fad. Thus the cultivation of intellect would ensure both the attainment of excellence and the survival of culture.

Although this humanistic doctrine had been a part of Robert Hutchins's life since childhood (as the son of William James Hutchins, a Presbyterian pastor, professor of religion at Oberlin College, author of *A Preacher's Inspiration and Ideals* [1917], and later president of Berea College), the younger Hutchins threw in his lot with it only as the Chicago Bildungsideal took form. While furthering his own education and rejuvenating the humanities at the University of Chicago, amid the social and political ferment of the 1930s, Hutchins detected, so he believed, the greatest threat to humanistic and democratic culture in the fact-finding ethos of science. Rising before the College convocation of December 1933, he addressed this threat in a speech entitled "The Issue in the Higher Learning" (deliberately echoing *The Higher Learning in America* [1918] by Thorstein Veblen, a former member of the faculty and an equally outspoken cultural critic).

"Since we have confused science with information," Hutchins said, "ideas with facts, and knowledge with miscellaneous data, and since information, facts, and data have not lived up to our high hopes of them, we are witnessing today a revulsion against science, ideas, and knowledge . . . exemplified by a fashion to be bewildered" and the fierce irrationalism of D. H. Lawrence and Adolf Hitler. The fault, Hutchins went on, lay not in any overpraise of intellect or any proof of its fallibility but in a misuse so egregious that men have come to reject intellect without knowing its true powers. He blamed that misuse on "the nineteenth century's anti-intellectual account of empirical science, which placed primary emphasis upon the accumulation of observed facts," and overlooked the need for "understanding them." That understanding could only be achieved, he claimed, by supplanting "the gadgeteers and the data-collectors" with the true thinkers (including some scientists) who "grapple with fundamentals." Those "fundamentals" are the modes of analysis from which inquiry proceeds and upon which explanation rests. And they are best learned and taught through works of the great thinkers "who clarified and developed them." But most important of all, Hutchins concluded, whatever the rewards it yields in knowledge, this comprehending humanistic intellect gives the only hope of restoring confidence to mind and saving culture from the amoral and irrationalist cult of "passion" and "personality."[21]

Hutchins's words, reminiscent of the many enemies of science since romanticism, were taken as a battle cry by both supporters and opponents. Controversy raged for months on the university campus and beyond, fed by Hutchins's unapologetic reiterations, by the pro-Hutchins student newspaper, by Adler's forensics, and by vocal opponents on the faculty such as Anton J. Carlson, Charles Morris, and Harry Gideonse. Never before—and it was probably never to happen again—had quarrels over the purpose, form, and content of education so stirred a college campus, affecting everybody, Adler said, "from the President down to the janitors—the students as well as the faculty."[22] Nor was the controversy all academic politics and showmanship. At its heart lay disagreement over the very character of knowledge and especially of scientific knowledge. Hutchins's opponents condemned him for attacking the very essence of science, and in particular the theory of science associated with the philosophy department at Chicago and its ties to the positivistic Unity of Science movement and to the tradition of pragmatism going back to John Dewey, James H. Tufts, George H. Mead, and Addison W. Moore. They ridiculed his attack as obscurantist and reactionary dogmatism: he defended old ways of thinking against new ways, traditional ideas against modern research, books against experience. As one of the opposition's leaders, Anton J. Carlson never tired of retorting to the glib and bookish pronouncements of the humanists (at least in their caricature of him): "Vat iss the ef-fidence?"[23]

But this preoccupation with evidence was exactly what Hutchins and his allies opposed: rules of scientific evidence do not apply to questions of meaning and value. And on these, not on questions of fact, hinge the quality and the fate of civilization. Hence the only hope of answering them lies in the nonscientific humanistic disciplines. "The crucial issue of our day," Adler baldly declared, is this: "*Whether science is enough, theoretically or practically;* whether a culture can be healthy, whether democracy can be defended, if theology and metaphysics, ethics and politics are either despised or, what is the same, degraded to topics about which laboratory scientists pontificate after they have won the Nobel Prize."[24] As the chief philosophical spokesman for the Chicago Bildungsideal, Adler was the one to spell out in the greatest detail the humanists' assumptions and inferences about mind, knowledge, and learning.

Since "the basic problems of education are normative,"[25] not empirical, Adler said—that is, occupied with standards of value, not just facts—they can only be resolved by the normative disciplines, notably metaphysics and logic. Drawing inspiration from his favorite philosophers, Aristotle and Thomas Aquinas, and never one to go in for intellectual understatement, Adler went on to detail the "absolute and universal principles on which education should be founded."[26] These principles require the cultivation, through good habits of mind and behavior, of the attitudes and needs that Aristotle had defined as *natural* and *unique* to human beings. These inherent attributes include those of the flesh and feeling, but they have their fullest expression in the needs and potentialities of intellect. The oft-quoted words that open Aristotle's treatise on metaphysics (and which put skeptical wrinkles on many a teacher's brow, if not on Adler's) announced Aristotle's and Adler's conviction: "All men by nature have the desire to know."

For Adler, this desire meant chiefly logic and metaphysics as applied to the great questions of meaning and value in morality, politics, theology, and the like. He encouraged this desire through books, articles, and lectures, many modeled in form and content on the meticulously organized and argued system of St. Thomas Aquinas's *Summa Theologica* and *Summa Contra Gentiles* (also the model of Adler's early scheme for a philosophical encyclopedia to be named *Summa Dialectica*). And as he did so he identified himself ever more with the spirit of metaphysical and cultural unity typical of the High Middle Ages. "The intellectual anarchy and confusion of the twentieth century," he wrote in an unpublished eighty-page "Outline of Knowledge" in 1935, "are caused by the degradation of the medieval world, but more essentially by the *sin of pride* in modern man. Thus philosophy in the modern world is individualistic rather than scholastic or traditional," and this "makes the story of modern times conform to the pattern of *tragedy*."[27] How similar are these historical, communal, and metaphysical yearnings to those of the Bauhäusler, and how similar the hopes of satisfying them: the votaries of the Great Books and the Bauhaus modernists had more in common than they knew.

Adler's tightening alliance with medieval scholasticism invited renewed criticism of the Chicago Bildungsideal as backward-looking and obscurantist. But Adler was not alone in inviting this criticism. The principles uniting the Great Books with a plea for metaphysical and intellectual order received their fullest and most provocative public expression in Hutchins's remarkable Storrs lectures delivered at Yale in 1935 and published the next year as *The Higher Learning in America*. Condemned by critics at the University of Chicago and elsewhere as a defiantly reactionary, medievalist, and antidemocratic tract, the book quickly sold nearly ten thousand copies and made Hutchins and the Chicago Bildungsideal more famous—and infamous—than ever.

Some of the blame for the hostile response belonged to Hutchins's rhetoric, which did nothing to deflect accusations of arrogance, authoritarianism, and medievalism. Repeating his previous denunciations of vocational and specialized learning and of the scientistic misuse of mind, and reaffirming his certainty that a humanistic course of study rooted in the Great Books must provide the foundation of the Higher Learning, Hutchins went on with characteristic pugnacity and lack of equivocation to declare that the Higher Learning must be organized according to a systematic ordering of truths—not *re*organized, since no organization exists within the reigning "chaos" of competing disciplines and anti-intellectually empirical methods.[28] This ordering principle could be found, he said, in the intellectual hierarchy of the medieval university, although the supreme place held there by theology would be occupied by metaphysics.

Taking his cue from Aristotle and Adler, Hutchins defined metaphysics as that inquiry into the "first principles" of knowledge and reality (explanation, existence, relation, function, value, etc.) that could lead students into the foundations of every subject. But more important even than this pedagogical use, metaphysics would also show the way out of the intellectual and moral relativism that threatens to destroy civilization because metaphysics can disclose truths of principle or value, which science cannot do. ("Anyone who denies that there is knowledge which is not scientific knowledge," Adler liked to remind Hutchins, "denies all your educational proposals.")[29] In the absence of metaphysics, Hutchins insisted, no "intelligible basis for the study of man in his relations with other men" can exist, since "the truths of ethics" must then degenerate into "merely commonsense teachings about how to get along in the world." Amid this intellectual degeneration, even science itself must succumb. For "if the world has no meaning, if it presents itself to us as a mass of equivalent data, then the pursuit of truth for its own sake consists of the indiscriminate accumulation of data" and "the moral consequences are an immoral morality."[30] In short, the hegemony of fact induces the deterioration of mind and the disintegration and ultimately the death of culture.

And the death of culture will come, Hutchins said, in a variation on earlier accusations, not simply because human beings have banished all metaphysical and moral truths from their lives and learned to live without them. It will come because, having abandoned traditional standards of thought and action, they embrace evil substitutes. "We are, as a matter of fact," he complained, "living today by the haphazard, accidental, shifting shreds of a theology and metaphysics to which we cling because we must cling to something."[31] Those shreds include "the love of money, a misconception of democracy, an erroneous notion of progress, a distorted idea of utility,"[32] as well as antiintellectualism, fascism, and Marxism, all of them ugly icons of false gods.

Finally, in quasireligious phrases, Hutchins—ever the Presbyterian pastor's son—urged the sweeping reform of education with the explicit purpose of redeeming this depraved culture. "The times call," he cried, "for the establishment of a new college or for an evangelistic movement in some old ones which shall have for its object the conversion of individuals and finally of the teaching profession to a true conception of general education." For "unless some such demonstration or some such evangelistic movement can take place, we shall remain in our confusion; we shall have neither general education nor universities."[33] But, he concluded, if we can reform general education, and "if we can revitalize metaphysics and restore it to its place in the higher learning, we may be able to establish rational order in the modern world as well as in the universities."[34]

Cast in these tones and terms, mingling Presbyterian moralism with medieval scholasticism—both expressing a hunger for certainty, unity, and metaphysical and moral truth—Hutchins's lectures were sure to raise hackles in the academic world. The joke soon circulated that the University of Chicago was a good Baptist school (in reference to its founder) where Jewish boys and girls went to learn Catholicism; and it was no joke that Hutchins and Adler found some of their staunchest supporters among Catholics, like Father John Cavanaugh, president of Notre Dame, and his successor, Theodore Hesburgh. But the witticism put no smiles on the faces of most professors. One of them, Harry Gideonse, an economist and later president of Brooklyn College, issued a fierce rejoinder to Hutchins's pronouncements in a pamphlet entitled *The Higher Learning in Democracy*. Charging Hutchins with an authoritarian will to impose his own system of values on the university, he argued that the methods of science, not the assertions of philosophy, supply unity to the various disciplines while preserving the democracy of different intellectual interests. Hutchins replied in numerous addresses reiterating his and Adler's distinction between science, as the study of fact, and philosophy, or metaphysics, as the comprehension of value, insisting that without philosophical guidance science and the university and culture must lack direction and moral purpose. Yet Hutchins could not escape the implication of his words, whatever his disavowals, that this guidance should be provided by a single set of doctrines, those of Aristotle and Thomas Aquinas as interpreted by Robert M. Hutchins and Mortimer J. Adler.

Even the father of the Great Books idea, John Erskine, got no pleasure from the fate of his idea in the hands of his Chicago disciples. "This course of mine," he wrote a few years after the Chicago program had spread to other universities, "has been adopted in many colleges, but not always as I intended it. Many teachers have turned it into a course on philosophy, on some specific philosophy, and others have tried to expand it into an educational method for teaching all subjects. With these aberrations I have no sympathy whatever. . . . I was concerned with no philosophy and no method for a total education; I merely hoped to teach how to read."[35] At the University of Chicago under Hutchins's visionary guidance, reading was not enough.

Hutchins's exalted educational program also drew fire from Alfred North Whitehead of Harvard, who derided its medievalism and antivocational bias as detrimental to students living in the modern world. Appealing to the constancy of human nature, the imperatives of intellect, and the democracy of mind, Hutchins's criticism of vocational learning inevitably bore traces—inherent in most programs of humanistic education, Erskine's not excepted—of the elitist desire to elevate the common man to heights of pure understanding, with scant regard to the exigencies of modern economic life. This desire gave the Chicago reformers a certain idealistic appeal, but it caused them plenty of trouble in securing support for their ideas—just as it had troubled Moholy-Nagy at the School of Design, and as it would trouble Walter Paepcke at the Aspen Institute for Humanistic Studies.

The most challenging and persistent criticism came from Hutchins and Adler's chief philosophical adversary, John Dewey. Beginning with a scorching review of *The Higher Learning* that denounced Hutchins's "authoritarianism," his "contempt for science," his faith in "fixed and eternal truths," and his withdrawal from the real world,[36] Dewey issued several articles over the next few years setting forth the defects of the Chicago Bildungsideal and the virtues of an education and culture governed by the open-minded and this-worldly precepts of empirical science. The conflict between Dewey and Hutchins had one of its fullest airings in the pages of *Fortune* in 1943–1944, prompted by the publicity surrounding the "New Program" at St. John's.

In response to this expanding institutional career of the Great Books idea, and specifically to Hutchins's restatement of his ideas in *Fortune* in November 1943, Dewey summed up his antagonism in an essay, "Challenge to Liberal Thought." That challenge, he wrote, lies in "the present campaign of assault upon what is modern and new in education" in the name of what is fixed and eternal in both human nature and education. Yet no such eternal verities can be found to exist, he said, for human beings and societies change with changing conditions. Hence just as the "liberal" ideal of Greek education suited the needs of the aristocratic city-state, and the medieval hierarchy of learning with theology as its crown suited the feudal and Christian era, so an empirical and pragmatic education fits the age of democracy, technology, and science. In this light, the Chicago Bildungsideal appeared to Dewey as illiberal, elitist, antimodern, authoritarian, blind to the pressing vocational and intellectual needs of most people, and subservient to an archaic theological standard of morality. By contrast, "a truly liberal, and liberating, education" concentrates on what is growing and vital in the present, and with deliberate omission of that which has served its time"; to do otherwise, as the Chicago idealists proposed, is to remove intellect from actuality and "to perpetuate the confusion and conflicts of the world in which we now live."[37] Only the ethos of science can lead us from confusion, he maintained, for science studies the world as it is in all of its variety and seeks provisional pragmatic understanding of it, unlike the traditionalists and metaphysicians who perceive the world through lenses clouded by antiquated prejudices and simplistic, untestable certainties.

The quarrel between the Dewey and Hutchins forces—a "cleft that now marks every phase and aspect of Philosophy," according to Dewey—was thus not, so Dewey had said many times, between science and philosophy as such, but between those who grounded philosophy in everyday experience and those who removed philosophy from such experience. It was between "an outlook that goes to the past for instruction and for guidance, and one that holds that philosophy . . . must pay supreme heed to movements, needs, problems, and resources that are distinctly modern."[38]

Yet for all the distance between them in rhetoric and philosophical disposition, the pragmatists and idealists quarreled here and elsewhere more over misunderstandings than irreconcilable differences. Neither side seems to have granted the other's ideas sufficient respect to try to understand them fully—the facile Hutchins being perhaps the more guilty, provoking Dewey at one point to a contemptuous dismissal: "I must ask his forgiveness," Dewey lashed out, "if I took his book too seriously"[39]—and they exchanged more blows over rhetoric and implications than over issues of substance. For in truth, although at odds in rhetoric and means, both the pragmatists and the idealists desired a humanistic society open to ideas, values, democracy, and the growth of human personality. Thus while Hutchins and Adler could see their brand of humanism advancing through the Great Books curriculum at Chicago, St. John's, and elsewhere, Dewey could see his advanced through institutions dedicated to education by experience, not only the so-called progressive elementary schools but Moholy-Nagy's School of Design and John A. Rice's Black Mountain College, both of which he endorsed. And it was to the credit of the two contrasting "philosophies" that these several institutions and their exponents made educational principles and reforms a subject of spirited public and professional concern during the 1930s and 1940s.

If any one person could take credit for igniting this concern and keeping it alive, it was Robert M. Hutchins. His unequivocal pronouncements, love of polemics, and personal flair gave educational reform a new cachet. Backed by Adler's intellectual energies and aided by the appeal of the Great Books idea, Hutchins couldn't fail to attract public attention to what, in one of his early combative addresses, he had labeled the "issues in the higher learning." One of his more notable triumphs as publicist for these issues was to thwart a threatened political investigation of the university in 1935 initiated by drug magnate Charles Walgreen, who had been shocked by his niece's enthusiastic reports of Marxist readings and discussions in her Great Books class. Charging the university with spreading "Communistic influences" and "seditious propaganda under the guise of academic freedom,"[40] Walgreen determined to root out the evil. "U. of C. Radicals under Fire" blared the front-page headline of the *Chicago Tribune* in a prelude to what became weeks of stories on the controversy.[41] But Hutchins, with the help of his Yale classmate William Benton, whom Hutchins brought to the university from a phenomenally successful career in New York as a pioneer in advertising to help defuse the crisis, impressed upon Walgreen the purpose behind such readings and finally converted him to the university's cause. And not only did they win his acquiescence. So convinced was he of the university's stability that he put up a handsome endowment to create there the Walgreen Foundation for the Study of American Institutions.

Hutchins also succeeded, in 1937 amidst the furor following his Storrs lectures, in persuading the university trustees to implement his plan (accepted on paper since 1933–1934) of incorporating two years of the university's high school into the College program to make a four-year program terminating with the traditional sophomore year. While this innovation lasted only until postwar enrollment pressures forced its lapse, another feat of Hutchins's persuasions at that time has persisted since then. In a move that brought Hutchins both much satisfaction and heated criticism, he managed to get intercollegiate football dropped from the university in 1939, justifying the revolutionary act with instinctive aplomb: "There are two ways to have a great university—it must either have a great football team or a great president."[42]

Notwithstanding these accomplishments at the university and the widening acceptance of the Great Books idea elsewhere, the late 1930s brought deepening discouragement to Hutchins and Adler. Their limited success felt like failure. "The letters . . . that passed between us in the summer of 1938 and 1939," Adler later wrote, "contained repeated expressions of unrelieved despair. Bob's hopelessness led him to write me that he ought to be looking for another job";[43] yet the position with the Roosevelt administration that Hutchins desired and discussed during visits to the White House never came.

Adler gave voice to this disconsolate mood in an intemperate address of 1940 to members of the conservative academic profession gathered at the Jewish Theological Seminary in New York entitled "God and the Professors." "The glorious, Quixotic failure of President Hutchins to accomplish any of the essential reforms that education so badly needs," he announced, demonstrates that professors refuse to examine "the relationship of science, philosophy, and religion in our education and in our culture." Hutchins had failed not because he was proved wrong; "he failed because he was asking the professors to change their minds," for "what Hutchins proposed ran counter to every prejudice that constitutes the modern frame of mind and its temper."[44]

While the professors recoiled and a new round of controversy over the Chicago ideas and manners raged—stirred by the nationwide distribution of the speech in newspapers and by Sidney Hook's sharp rebuttal in *The New Republic*—both Adler and Hutchins marshaled their principles for a new attack on the culture at large. With the tide of fascism spreading across Europe, and world war imminent, the contest between the value-charged idealists and the value-free empiricists would cease to be an academic tussle over philosophical conceptions of knowledge and education. It would become an existential conflict over war and peace, destruction and survival. And the Chicago Bildungsideal would now move more assuredly and combatively than ever from the academy into the world.

"The present generation has been immunized against anyone who might really try to argue for democracy in terms of justice," Adler wrote not long after France surrendered to the Nazis in June 1940. Bred on a cult of fact or "scientism" that dismisses all moral judgments as mere opinions or preferences by contrast to the empirical truths of science, how could the young avoid conceiving of justice as "nothing but the will of the stronger?"[45] Yet at the same time, how could they sustain such a moral nihilism in the face of the Nazi conquest of Europe? Are the Nazis no less just or right than we? Adler asked. And he answered: No one nurtured on "scientism" could know.

Hutchins had played upon this same theme with dramatic clarity in an address during the very month that France fell:

> In order to believe in democracy we must believe that there is a difference between truth and falsity, good and bad, right and wrong, and that truth, goodness, and right are objective standards even though they cannot be experimentally verified. . . . Political organization must be tested by conformity to ideals. Its basis is moral. Its end is the good for man. . . . These are the principles which we must defend if we are to defend democracy.
>
> Are we prepared to defend these principles? Of course not. For forty years and more our intellectual leaders have been telling us they are not true. They have been telling us in fact that nothing is true which cannot be subject to experimental verification. In the whole realm of social thought there can, therefore, be nothing but opinion. Since there is nothing but opinion, everybody is entitled to his own opinion. . . . If everything is a matter of opinion, force becomes the only way of settling differences of opinion. And, of course, if success is the test of rightness, right is on the side of the heavier battalions.[46]

The world war was thus exactly the kind of cultural crisis—not just a political crisis—that Hutchins and Adler had predicted for a world dominated by value-free fact-finding, moral relativism, and the distrust of intellect. Hadn't Mussolini actually delighted in the pragmatism of William James, and hadn't Hitler found a variant of it to his liking in Nietzsche? Here was a nihilism in events mirroring a nihilism in the soul.

But Hutchins and Adler's opponents, the defenders of science, did not simply turn their cheeks. They countered by reversing the argument. John

Dewey blamed the world crisis on the persistence in Europe of a philosophical dogmatism and worship of tradition similar to that of the Chicago humanists. If Europe, especially Germany, had truly embraced the open-minded, liberal, scientific spirit, objective in its methods, and modest and flexible in its claims to truth, the moral arrogance and authoritarianism that had led to the war could not have arisen. And the divorce of fact from value that Hutchins and Adler insisted upon could, Dewey said, only weaken the defense of democracy. For there exists an "intrinsic kinship of democracy with the methods of directing change that have revolutionized science."[47] To deny this kinship, Dewey insisted, is to open the door to arbitrary authority.

Unpersuaded by the pragmatists' arguments—for reasons of temperament and reformist passion as much as of logical necessity, since pragmatism is in itself no more or less conducive to war than is philosophical idealism—Hutchins and Adler continued to press the political implications of their educational ideals throughout the war, although at the outset they disagreed on the actions to be taken. Hutchins, the cosmopolitan Protestant humanist, translated his principled defense of democracy into support of the pacifist "America First" movement, resisting war with Germany for the sake of American and Western culture as a whole. Adler became a vigorous interventionist (along with his philosophical foes, Dewey and President James Bryant Conant of Harvard), urging military support of Britain for the sake of freedom and democracy.

After Pearl Harbor, Hutchins rallied to the American cause, and in 1942 he even allowed the Manhattan Project to settle at the University of Chicago, which resulted in the first nuclear chain reaction being set off by Enrico Fermi under the weather-beaten stands of the long silent Stagg football stadium. Yet Hutchins never lost his conviction that military conflict between nations is both wrong and preventable; and as hostilities widened and persisted, he directed this conviction into the movement for world government. He had Adler's support in this, for Adler had also come to see a logical and metaphysical connection between democracy and a universal political order, a connection he elaborated upon in his wartime book *How to Think about War and Peace* (1944). But Hutchins had found an even more determined and impassioned ally in a man destined to play an important, if brief, role in directing Hutchins's cultural ideals into politics and then directing their political expression into a mass public relations event. This was Giuseppe Antonio Borgese.

An intense, eloquent, hot-blooded Sicilian, short and stooped, with burning, deep-set eyes and fiercely emphatic opinions, Borgese had joined the Romance languages department at the University of Chicago in 1936 at the invitation of William A. Nitze. Less a scholar than a poet and critic by nature, Borgese had won youthful recognition in Italy as an opponent, like many of his generation—including Mussolini, born in 1883, one year after Borgese—of the complacent democracy, intellectual positivism, cultural timidity, and moral indiscipline that he had believed held Italy in their deathly grip. After founding the literary periodical *Hermes* (1904–1906) to propagate a cultural idealism uniting rich emotionality and aestheticism, he had gone on to join the rising chorus in Italy urging war as a step toward cultural renewal. Italy's defeat in World War I had renewed Borgese's preoccupation with reform through art, but this had been gradually consumed by a deepening disapproval of the philistine and authoritarian regime imposed by Mussolini in 1922. When disapproval turned to loathing by the 1930s and erupted in open denunciations, Borgese had been forced out of Italy. Five years of temporary stints at several American universities had culminated in his appointment at the University of Chicago.

A year after settling in Chicago, Borgese had published his powerful and sweeping indictment of fascism, *Goliath: The March of Fascism*. Typical of Borgese's moralism and subjectivity, if freed of some youthful emotionality, *Goliath* blamed Italian fascism on the influence of an intellectual tradition that had so consistently esteemed the spiritual over the material that it had prepared the way for fascist appeals to irrationality as a defense against Marxist materialism. "Fascism," he wrote, "remains what it is: an outburst of emotionalism and pseudo-intellectualism, thoroughly irrational in its nature. . . . The Italian mind, this saddest instance in a world-wide abdication of culture," he lamented, "had few if any reserves of force against the disease which itself had bred."[48]

But Borgese did not limit his attack on fascism to his effusive, powerful, unsubtle book. Once in Chicago he pressed for the creation of a "Council of Wisdom" to draw together great minds and issue papers on the condition of the world. His proposal had such affinities with the idealism of Hutchins and his allies that one of the outsiders invited to join the council, Lewis Mumford, decried "the atmosphere of Chicago" for inflating the original idea to such "grandiose proportions" that it "scared the necessary financial backers away."[49]

Although this first conception came to nothing, a second and less ambitious proposition bore fruit in 1940, bringing together a remarkable assembly: Borgese, Hutchins, Mumford, Thomas Mann (Borgese's father-in-law), Herman Broch, Reinhold Niebuhr, William Benton, and several others. Borgese and Hutchins represented two extremes in manner and political strategy. Borgese, swarthy and coarse, advocated the immediate military defense of democracy. Hutchins, "tall, urbane, boyish-looking" (as Mumford, who sided with Borgese, observed), was "keen but supercilious, rational, and outwardly reasonable, but shallow," and still "an unawakened isolationist."[50] Mumford's opinion of Hutchins was not improved by Hutchins's friend William Benton, who had been invited mainly as a source of financial support and advice on publicity, and who snappishly dismissed Borgese's outline for a joint statement of principles by saying that such an announcement should be produced by advertisers not by a group of stuffy intellectuals. But after the committee published its work, in a book entitled *The City of Man*, largely written by Borgese, to the tepid reception of "a minute number of the already awakened," Mumford conceded that "the Chicago advertising magnate's estimate proved correct."[51] The lofty intellectual labors had availed next to nothing.

The committee members had nevertheless learned something from the experience, something Hutchins should have known better than most: even good ideas must be properly promoted to prevail. Hutchins would not soon make the same mistake again. And as the political relationship between Hutchins and Borgese grew—once Hutchins had abandoned his isolationism and both men had become convinced that the only hope for eliminating war lay in creation of a world republic—they jointly searched for more effective means of pursuing their common ends. After the war they would find these means, for a time, in political proselytizing and in a widely publicized cultural event uniting the Chicago Bildungsideal and the quest for world government. But before these postwar pursuits could be launched, the Chicago Bildungsideal, in the form of the Great Books program would consolidate its hold, if only temporarily, on the University of Chicago and begin its momentous passage out of academe into the mainstream of American life.

While Hutchins and Adler were applying their philosophical principles to politics, their educational theories and practices were making gains both within the university and without. In 1942, some ten years after Hutchins had pushed through the first phase of the Chicago Plan, the College finally accepted—by virtue of Hutchins's tie-breaking vote—a completely prescribed general education curriculum independent of the upper divisions and organized around the Great Books. Students could enroll without a high school diploma after an entrance exam and could finish at their own pace or follow the standard pattern of four years. Under its strong early deans, Clarence Faust and F. Champion Ward, the College flourished as never before, attracting rising numbers of inquisitive, self-motivated students (enrollment went from 1,700 to 2,700 in four years). Although the postwar influx of returning students and faculty disrupted and undermined these innovations, inducing their virtual abandonment after Hutchins left the university in 1951 ("The problem," he quipped, "was that my successors didn't have the courage of my convictions"),[52] at last the Chicago Plan had run its full course.

But by the days of these wartime victories and postwar reverses, Hutchins and Adler were tiring of the triumphs and tribulations of the academy. Not only had the problems of political culture seized their imaginations, they had also hit upon new and potentially more effective uses of the Great Books outside the university: they had discovered adult education and the prospect of putting a collection of the Great Books in every American home.

The idea of employing the Great Books in the education of adults was not new. Mortimer Adler and several Columbia colleagues had tried it in the late 1920s at the People's Institute in New York, and Adler had moderated Great Books discussions for some university alumni in Highland Park, Illinois, during the 1930s. The extension division of the University of Chicago had also offered a Great Books seminar beginning in 1939. But the spark that ignited what was to become the country's most popular program of adult education came with a remark to Hutchins in 1943 from a vice-president of the university and former executive of Marshall Field, Wilbur Munnecke.

Hutchins had asked Munnecke what he thought of setting up an executive training program for business students at the university. "Sounds all right," Munnecke replied, "but what we really need is a program to help people after they become executives. Take me, for example. I'm supposed to be an executive, but the truth is that I cannot read or write properly—and neither can a lot of other executives you and I could name."[53] "What the businessmen of this town need to learn," he later added, "is not accounting and financing. They're experts in their own businesses already, and they can hire experts in other lines, but they can't hire anybody to read and understand for them."[54]

Hutchins jumped at the idea. Here was the perfect way to communicate his message of cultural reform directly to those responsible for conducting the affairs of the nation and the culture. And it had the added advantage of providing an opportunity to draw into the Great Books program important Chicagoans and university trustees whose sympathies could be a valuable asset in furthering Hutchins's reforms.

Some thirty prominent executives and their wives received invitations to attend the first meeting of a class scheduled for October 27, 1943, at the University Club in downtown Chicago with Hutchins and Adler moderating. Among them: Hughston McBain, president of Marshall Field; Harold Swift, head of Swift Packing and chairman of the university's board of trustees; Meyer Kestnbaum, president of Hart, Schaffner, and Marx; Lynn Williams, vice-president of the Stewart Warner Company; William Benton; and Walter Paepcke. Paepcke struck the tone of good spirits and earnestness that was to mark the seminar—and that always distinguished his correspondence with Hutchins—in responding to Hutchin's invitation. Unable to attend the first session, he nevertheless enclosed the full fee of "150 bucks so that the University won't fail prior to the time you have accomplished this great good work of educating the businessmen of Chicago—God knows they need it."[55] When Paepcke failed to appear not for one but for three sessions, Hutchins fired off a note of encouragement: "I love to take money away from you," he said, "but I like to do it subtly. . . . If you are not going to [attend the class], I'd like to send back the $150."[56] Paepcke and his wife finally came and kept coming. Thus began an intellectual companionship that molded Paepcke into a powerful proponent of the Chicago Bildungsideal, and altered his life.

Meeting every two weeks, the class proved a public relations coup for Hutchins, converting the capitalists to the Great Books and nourishing a friendship between town and gown. It also acquired a unique title that helped the publicity along. Alluding to the nickname of the undergraduate program, "The Great Men's Fat Book Course," and with a nod to the affluence of the executives enrolled, Milton Mayer, author and occasional moderator, dubbed it "The Fat Man's Great Books Class."[57] Most of the "fat men" liked the name and loved the class. "Everyone participated for all he was worth," Adler said. "They tried to read the books from the outset and tried to talk and talk about them." And "that's the way it's been," Adler could say fifteen years after the first session, "each year leading to another. The class will go on forever."[58] He was still leading it, with a new philosophical colleague, Charles Van Doren, well into the 1980s.

But the Fat Man's class was destined to have reverberations far beyond the lives of its members and beyond the expectations of Hutchins and Adler. For it gave birth to the most ambitious and effective adult education program ever attempted, the Great Books movement, and gave impetus to a publishing venture without precedent, the *Great Books of the Western World*.

The notion of publishing a set of the Great Books came up at about the same time as the idea of the Fat Man's class. And like the class, it had its origins not in the musings of an intellectual but in the practical imagination of a former executive from the world of business. William Benton, founding partner in 1929 with his friend Chester Bowles of an advertising firm that was among the first to exploit the selling potential of radio, and now the university's vice-president for public relations (where he produced the much-respected academic radio programs "University of Chicago Round Table" and "The Human Adventure"), had acquired the Encyclopaedia Britannica for the university in early 1943 from its publishers of twenty years, General Wood and Sears, Roebuck. But when the university trustees declined to back so commercial a venture, Benton made a gift of the Encyclopaedia to the university and then suggested publishing a companion set of volumes to consist of great books, most of them out of print and difficult to obtain in those days before the paperback revolution. In June 1943, he enlisted Hutchins's assistance in answering three decisive questions: how many volumes would be required? what should the set be called? and, most important, could he come up with some "special idea to add to the books themselves" to enhance their appeal in the market?[59] The first two questions posed no difficulty. The third was trickier; but Hutchins and Adler agreed that without some "special idea" the set would either not sell or would merely ornament people's shelves. Thus the "special idea" became the key to the entire undertaking.

Searching for a "special idea" through the summer, Adler finally hit upon the notion of an index of ideas—such as "war" and "peace," then occupying him while preparing *How to Think about War and Peace*. Such an index, he said, could "provide a map or chart of the conversation about fundamental subjects in which the authors of the Great Books engaged with one another across the centuries."[60] The conception was not altogether new to Adler; as early as 1927 he had outlined with Scott Buchanan his plan for a *Summa Dialectica* to encompass contrasting ideas on all philosophical themes. But the index would be far less expansive than this; it was to be merely a practical, commercial device, or, so Adler later said, "a gimmick."[61]

Adler proposed his gimmick in October, just as the Fat Man's class was beginning—for which publication of the Great Books was deemed a boon. Hutchins and Benton bought it on behalf of the university and allotted a budget of $60,000 for a labor of two and a half years, with Adler at a salary of $5,000 per year, and each member of an advisory board to receive $1,200.[62] Adler would prepare the index, and the advisory board, consisting of old and new devotees of the Great Books, like John Erskine, Scott Buchanan, Stringfellow Barr, Mark Van Doren, and Clarence Faust, had the job of selecting the works to be indexed.[63] The Great Books idea had brought forth a formidable intellectual and commercial enterprise, as well as a new band of book lovers, soon to be jocularly known across the country as "great bookies."

The project took more than eight years of mind-bending labor,[64] dogged by costs soaring to $2.5 million, erratic financing, and criticism of "Benton's Folly" from trustees and academicians (including Daniel J. Boorstin and John U. Nef), defectors (Scott Buchanan), and the skeptical, who feared the project would lead—as one wrote to Hutchins—to "ancestor worship" and a "retreat from reality into mysticism and obscurantism."[65] The *Great Books of the Western World* finally appeared in 54 volumes, comprising 443 works by 74 authors, from Homer to Freud. It also included an introductory volume entitled *The Great Conversation* by Hutchins, the formal editor of the set, laying out the intellectual rationale for the collection, and Adler's "gimmick," the two-volume *Syntopicon*.

Not simply an index of words as originally conceived, the *Syntopicon* indexed nearly 3,000 *topics* found throughout the 443 works organized under 102 headings from Angel to World. And more than a device to get readers into the books, the *Syntopicon* (a word invented by staff researcher and long-time "great bookie" William Gorman) proved to be an ingenious instrument for demonstrating the "topical unity" of Western thought, presupposed by Hutchins and Adler's educational and cultural theory. Adler and Hutchins weren't merely dabbling in rhetoric when they referred to this unity as "The Great Conversation" (a phrase taken from Erskine). For they believed that despite variations of time, place, and language, the thinkers of the Western tradition shared a common human experience that they have debated by means of common themes—topics or ideas, not words—across the ages. Adler was so convinced of this cultural unity of ideas that he never bothered to learn a foreign language. And in the *Syntopicon* he set about showing this unity in action. Here Plato can be heard speaking to Freud, Aristotle to Shakespeare, St. Thomas to William James, Homer to Kant, among the many possible combinations—and all in English.

Reviewers and critics found much to criticize in the conception and execution of the *Great Books of the Western World*. Many judged the project too reminiscent of medieval scholasticism and lacking in historical understanding; others said it compounded the folly of relying on translations by relying on bad ones; still others complained that it included too many scientific, mathematical, and philosophical authors to the exclusion of humanists such as Cicero, Voltaire, and Dickens, and that it omitted all but one truly twentieth-century writer, Freud. Yet on the whole the work received more admiration than censure, and only Dwight MacDonald, biting critic of mass culture, saw unmitigated evil in it—a clumsy prostitution of intellect, he wrote, in the service of the "religion of culture" that infects American life.[66]

But no harsh words from critics, no matter how numerous or severe, were likely to dim the pride of Hutchins and Adler now. For they believed the *Great Books of the Western World* to be more than a conventional publication subject to the casual judgments of reviewers. And at the inaugural banquet for friends and subscribers (who had paid $500 each for a first edition) at the Waldorf Astoria in April 1952, they basked in the confidence that they had wrought nothing less than an instrument of redemption for civilization itself. "This is more than a set of books," Hutchins told the sympathetic audience. "It is a liberal education." And since "the fate of our country and hence of the world depends on the degree to which the American people achieve liberal education," the *Great Books* will place in their hands "the means of continuing and revitalizing Western civilization for the sake of the West and for the sake of all mankind."[67]

For about $250 per set (soon raised to $300 and later much more), Americans could now bring the Chicago Bildungsideal into their homes. And over the next ten years, aided by a slick marketing campaign utilizing a high-brow image, door-to-door selling, and credit purchasing, more than 150,000 Americans did just that. Adler would later claim that a million copies of the set had been sold, and he would bring out a second edition in 1990, including six new volumes, to keep the sales going.

There is no knowing how effective the *Great Books of the Western World* have been in advancing the cultural ideals that inspired their publication. The *Syntopicon*, intended to draw readers into and guide them through the books, has probably made actual reading of the books seem unnecessary more often than not, and possibly reduced the set in some hands to a glorified *Bartlett's Quotations*. But the successful extension of the Great Books idea outside of the university convinced Hutchins and Adler that they had made progress and that the future of their ideals lay not with academicians and undergraduates but with nonacademic adults. "I can hardly remember," Adler said in a lecture the year the *Great Books* were published, "what I used to think when I had the mistaken notion that the schools were the most important part of the educational process; for I now think exactly the reverse. I am now convinced that it is adult education which is the substantial and major part of the educational process." Arriving at this conclusion had required, he went on, abandoning the common view of "adult education as something for the underprivileged." For he had learned by teaching undergraduates, returning GI's, and adults that the ability to appreciate the Great Books depends not on high intelligence or prior education but on an openness of mind to the perennial intellectual questions raised by life experience. He had also discovered in the Fat Man's seminar that even the most educated and privileged people benefit more from reading the Great Books as mature adults than they had as students. And he had found during preparation of the *Great Books* that even his own ability to learn grew with every passing year and every book read and reread. "Only in mature soil," Adler concluded, "soil rich with experience—the soul in the mature person—can ideas really take root."[68] And best of all, unlike undergraduate schooling, the education of adults need never end.

Thus adult education gave Adler and Hutchins something their reformist ambitions had long desired: a truly continuous, universal form of learning. And, offering the added benefit of freedom from tradition-bound institutions and entrenched academic prejudices, adult education, as represented by the Fat Man's class, provided the perfect setting for the Great Books idea to thrive.

The Fat Man's class sparked the Great Books movement in more than idea. The publicity surrounding the class caused an avalanche of applications for the Great Books courses given by the university's extension division (then called University College), and within a year the governing committee of

University College had to begin training nonprofessional teachers to lead them. In early 1945, Adler started conducting demonstrations and training sessions for prospective seminar leaders through both University College and the Chicago Public Library. Later that year, these newly trained leaders opened thirty-four discussion groups throughout the Chicago area. By early 1946, the Chicago classes had become part of a network reaching coast to coast and involving over 5,000 people.

Spurred on by the missionary efforts of Adler and his colleagues at University College and by national publicity, enrollment jumped to 20,000 by the end of 1946, overwhelming the capacity of University College to administer the program. So, early in 1947, Hutchins (who had taken a leave of absence from his duties as chancellor of the university, having left the office of president in 1945 to help with the Great Books movement) started planning for an independent organization to take over the responsibilities from the university. On February 21, he invited Walter Paepcke to lunch to enlist his support for the plan. And before February ended, Hutchins, Paepcke, Adler, and several others had created the Great Books Foundation, at least on paper.

The foundation opened for business on July 1 in offices at the Container Corporation with Hutchins as chairman, Lynn Williams, Jr., president, Walter Paepcke, vice-president, and Wilbur Munnecke, secretary and treasurer. Taking over the entire Great Books program of University College (although the university supplied early operating expenses), the foundation assigned itself a host of tasks. It would help organize the reading groups and train their leaders, as well as publicize available editions of the Great Books in print and provide low-cost reprints of those otherwise unobtainable. (The responsibility for recruiting, conducting, and sustaining the groups would rest with the local participants.) It would also conduct a campaign of "careful publicity" to win converts to the Great Books idea. This meant arranging contacts with editors and publishers, staging press conferences, issuing press releases, and broadcasting the educational principles behind the program.

Although the foundation hoped to recruit as many as possible of the estimated fifteen million American adults capable of reading the Great Books, it addressed itself (inspired by the Fat Man's class and foreshadowing the Aspen Institute for Humanistic Studies) chiefly to professional and business people. Referring to members of the Fat Man's class, the first publicity release, in June 1947, proudly announced that "all of these men have become interested in the Great Books educational program through their own participation in it." Not only had they benefited from the books and discussions, they had purportedly adopted the Hutchins-Adler philosophy. "As practical businessmen," the release went on, "they have come to believe that the need for today is not more specialization, more science, or more technologists. The greatest need in business is a broad understanding and right purposes."[69] To strengthen this humanistic appeal to men of affairs, the foundation also mobilized a mass publicity campaign equipped with testimonials from prominent Fat Man's class alumni, like Walter Paepcke, who proclaimed the need "in these turbulent days of international crises" and of "vastly expanded" and "highly perfected mechanical and physical processes" to "develop a more philosophical attitude of mind" and turn to the "fundamental principles affecting government and the life of individuals which have not varied substantially"[70] over time. Having summoned to its flag a cadre of accomplished executives, the Chicago Bildungsideal was now making its way not only into the political world, but into the world of business and the professions.

Fortunately for the organizers, the times invited such an experiment. The aftermath of war had again breathed new life into educational idealism. Just as the end of World War I had seen the rise of General Education— including the Great Books idea—the end of World War II had brought a resurgence of similar curricular reforms, embodied most formally in the so-called Harvard Red Book (1946), which outlined a general education program (far less ambitious than Chicago's, requiring only a sampling of various disciplines) that rapidly became the model used in dozens of universities. This postwar flowering of humanistic education gave the Great Books Foundation a ready-made clientele. And in its first year the foundation enrolled nearly 10,000 new participants in Chicago alone, prompting its president, Lynn Williams, to aim for 100,000 more across the country during the next year. Although the foundation achieved only about half of this goal, so much public attention was stirred that in September 1948 the city of Chicago officially celebrated "Great Books Week." It featured Adler lecturing to crowds in a downtown department store and Adler and Hutchins together conducting a discussion of Plato's Apology before a capacity audience of 3,000 in Orchestra Hall (another 1,500 were turned away at the door), and it elicited tributes from the governor of Illinois and the president of the United States. Similar triumphs followed as Adler toured the country with Great Books under his arm and philosophical certainties on his tongue. Milwaukee even emblazoned a Great Books advertisement in lights on the City Hall. The Great Books idea was no longer just a prescription for academic and cultural reform; it was show business.[71] Conceived as the core of a general education curriculum, having endured years of struggles and gained only limited victories in academe, it now swept the country as a cultural fashion attractive to people with no academic pretensions or aspirations but with much desire to be cultivated "great bookies." It looked as though, having left the university through the corridors of adult education and mass publicity, quite apart from the excursion into politics, the Chicago Bildungsideal might renovate culture after all.

While Adler and the Great Books movement were carrying the Chicago Bildungsideal far beyond the University of Chicago, Robert Hutchins continued disseminating it, too. Called by President Truman to direct a commission on the freedom of the press in 1945, Hutchins and his associates produced a document the following year accusing the mass media of failing to nourish the public mind and of distorting the portrayal of reality for commercial purposes. (Hutchins would, of course, have exempted his own uses of publicity from such an indictment.) The media thus threaten freedom by promoting ignorance, the commission argued, for only an alert and knowing populace can preserve democracy and free speech from the encroachments, however benign in intention, of public authority. To further these ends, the commission, among its other contributions to the understanding of mass media, articulated a rationale for educational television that yielded historic results in the years ahead.[72] Yet the labors Hutchins devoted to this historic document in the criticism of mass culture arose less from love than from duty. For his keenest public energies during the early postwar years went into the movement for international peace and world unification.

As the war ended, Hutchins returned to the antiwar, cosmopolitan humanism that had animated him before Pearl Harbor. Speaking at the university graduation in June 1945, he denounced the "moral confusion" that had led Americans to dehumanize their enemies as "fanatics, . . . murderers," even "apes," and to seek greater armaments for the postwar era. Such a brutish "new realism" signified to him "the conquest of the United States by Hitler": not unlike the Nazis before them, the Americans now viewed themselves as the superior race, self-righteously condemning their enemies and encouraging world tensions and disunity. America's true interests lay, he said, not in a vaunted national superiority or American hegemony but in a "world community" comprising friends and former enemies alike.[73]

The nuclear devastation of Japanese cities two months later deepened Hutchins's fears for the survival of civilization and strengthened his certainty that this survival depended upon global unity. To advance this conviction, Hutchins joined with Adler, Borgese, and Richard McKeon in November 1945 to form the Committee to Frame a World Constitution. The committee solicited the cooperation of scholars and intellectuals from across the country and published their argumentative papers against atomic warfare and for world government—including the *Preliminary Draft of a World Constitution* (1948)—in the committee's magazine *Common Cause*, edited by Borgese. (*Common Cause* had been the title of a wartime book by Borgese.) Hutchins was also involved with world federalist John U. Nef in forming the Committee on Social Thought at the University of Chicago. An early postwar manifesto of this committee spelled out the assumptions and the dreams of Hutchins and his fellow unificationists: "Humanity is greater than any nation, any doctrine, any interest. Let us try to form a world parliament with the help of governments if they respond to our appeal, without them if they fail us."[74] This theme issued repeatedly from Hutchins in the early postwar years, at home and abroad. Frequently setting himself against the confederationist United Nations, he always stood alongside those who believed world peace could only be achieved by a sovereign world federation superior to nation states.

Because this campaign for world peace presupposed an elemental kinship of human cultures, Hutchins had no difficulty describing the lines of force between this campaign and the Great Books educational and publishing enterprises. He told a gathering at the university in December 1945, in a speech entitled "Science and Wisdom in the Atomic Age," that the perils of the atomic age had their roots in the divorce of factual knowledge and the power it gives from the wisdom to use them: we know the *how* and we know the *what* of things but not the *why* and the *ought*. Needed, he said, echoing words he had often used in other contexts, was the wisdom to direct actions and judgment toward mankind's *best* ends, given the limits of human nature and historical circumstances. Previous ages had intellectual systems for this purpose, he went on, and now the world requires "a philosophical synthesis for the atomic age." This synthesis, grounded in the unity of the Western tradition and the moral objectivity afforded by logical analysis and synthesis, was, he announced, taking form at that very hour in Mortimer Adler's index to the Great Books. To carry Adler's vital work forward, Hutchins said, "a continuing Philosophical Conference" should be established to draw upon the "raw materials of the Index" and clarify the purport, interconnections, and logical consequences of the ideas common to the Western tradition. Introduced into the culture at large through liberal education, Hutchins concluded, this comprehensive intellectual clarity would provide "the new wisdom man needs for the guidance of his life and the conduct of society in the atomic age."[75]

Thus did the Chicago Bildungsideal show its political face anew: the Great Conversation at once expressed the coherence of Western culture and clinched the case for humanism, democracy, world peace, and global unification in a world threatened with destruction by the atom bomb. This political vision led Hutchins into his next and one of his most ambitious ventures in the quest for cultural reform.

The idea for this latest venture came to Hutchins from an unlikely source. A group of scholars of the Modern Language Association—Victor Lange of Cornell University, Carl Schreiber of Yale, and Arnold Bergstraesser of the University of Chicago—hatched the notion of holding a conference in 1949 to celebrate the two-hundredth anniversary of the birth of Johann Wolfgang von Goethe. Conceived as a conventional academic celebration featuring learned lectures and a new edition of Goethe's works in English, the celebration began undergoing a change of plan when Bergstraesser broached the subject to his colleague Giuseppe Borgese. The fiery and politically impassioned Borgese immediately saw in the Goethe Bicentennial an opportunity not only to commemorate the great German author of *Faust* and other literary works but to honor Goethe the cosmopolitan humanist and universal man—poet, philosopher, scientist, administrator, and exponent of the cultural unity of mankind—and thereby to help heal the wounds of war and to promote world government. And when he put the proposal to Hutchins, the chancellor, a long-time devotee of Goethe who had addressed a university convocation honoring the one-hundredth anniversary of Goethe's death in 1932, also saw here a chance to dramatize the unifying powers of the Chicago humanism in a war-torn and science-dominated age.

But neither Borgese nor Hutchins could have foreseen how far removed from the customary academic ritual of honoring great writers the Goethe festival would become. No one had yet decided exactly how or where the celebration would be held. And these decisions were eventually to take the festival almost completely out of the hands of the Modern Language Association and place it firmly in the hands of cultural entrepreneurs and public relations experts.

The first step along this path came with the agreement of Hutchins, Borgese, and Bergstraesser that the celebration should not be held at a university or in a large city but in an out-of-the-way place unconnected to any particular group of people and demanding some special effort to visit. Hutchins soon had a place in mind. He invited Walter Paepcke to lunch on February 21, 1947. "We discussed at some length quite a few exciting ideas," Paepcke told a friend, the publisher James Laughlin, in enthusiastic, tumbling prose:

> One was a foundation which might more properly run the Great Books courses throughout the United States. Another and very intriguing idea was to think about and plan for a Bicentennial Goethe Celebration commemorating his birth in 1749 and having a week's festivities—lectures, plays, opera, etc.—to familiarize more adequately the American public with a great writer, poet, philosopher, scientist, musician of German origin and attempt in some modest way to reestablish a cultural relationship between the Teutonic peoples and the rest of the world, following the natural hatred, misunderstanding, and dislocation caused by the last war.

And, he went on, barely concealing his gleeful self-interest, "the men who are behind this, like Bob, thought it could be of considerable international importance, and, oddly enough, thought that an appropriate location might conceivably be Aspen."[76] The Goethe Bicentennial was about to say goodbye to academe and become a world cultural event—in the unlikely location of the moribund alpine mining town of Aspen, Colorado, just then reviving as Walter Paepcke's Magic Mountain.

II

healing

the wounds of war

4

the magic mountain:

discovering aspen

May 1945. The war in Europe was over. Hutchins and Adler were translating the Chicago Bildungsideal into a publishing enterprise and a program of world politics. Paepcke and Moholy-Nagy were struggling to keep the Institute of Design alive and lead it into the postwar world. Record crowds were flowing into the Art Institute to see the Container Corporation advertising exhibit, while the company itself was reaping unprecedented profits ($7 million per year), thanks to its ingenious corporate image campaign and courageous expansion at home and abroad. It was a time of transition and uncertainty. Paepcke, growing restless for new adventures, decided to embark on another one. Why not, he thought, buy a few properties as a vacation spot for family and friends and as an investment, in a remote former mining boom town of the Rockies—Aspen, Colorado, now languishing in fading memories and physical decay. That almost offhand decision was to result in another series of triumphs for the Chicago Bildungsideal and the most ambitious cultural enterprise of Paepcke's career.

Paepcke had "discovered" Aspen by no mere happenstance. For many years, he and his family had vacationed with the William Nitzes in Estes Park, Colorado, and Paepcke had long wanted to please his nature-loving wife by buying property in the region. Failure to find suitable Colorado real estate had prompted him to build a substantial summer house complete with swimming pool on the working farm he owned in Sandwich, Illinois, in 1935–1936. But his desire for a mountain retreat did not die. And no sooner had the Sandwich residence risen from the ground than an opportunity presented itself.

In the summer of 1936, Paepcke purchased a 7,500-acre ranch, known as Perry Park, sixty-five miles south of Denver, for $250,000. As usual, he had in mind both pleasure and business, hoping to raise cattle and ship them to Chicago markets. But Perry Park was to see not only cattle on its land. At one time or another during the next decade, Paepcke tried half a dozen ways of turning a profit: dude ranching; the breeding of pedigree hounds, thoroughbred stallions, and Clydesdale mares; and in 1945, he announced the supreme stroke: he was "going into the raising of turkeys in a big way."[1] These ventures paid off only in inconvenience, headaches, and red ink; and the last ended during the summer of 1946 in the swift death from Black Leg disease of two thousand turkeys.

An economic failure, the ranch looked to Paepcke's business friends like an instance of Paepcke's tireless, entrepreneurial imagination gone astray. "He made a lot of *soft* deals,"[2] they would say, conceding that in truth he seldom set profit as his only object; the ranch was only among the more conspicuous of these deals. But Paepcke knew what he was doing: for if he couldn't turn a profit, he could turn losses to his advantage. Uncle Sam would subsidize, through tax write-offs, the costs of this ideal vacation home for the Paepcke family and friends.

The friends came often, in both summer and winter, and one of these visits left the name of Aspen resounding for the first time in the Paepcke home. It was the winter of 1939 and Mr. and Mrs. Curtis Munson were greeted at Perry Park by temperatures so frigid that the water pipes froze solid and an escape from the disaster had to be made. While Walter Paepcke nursed the crippled house, his wife and the houseguests set out on a weekend skiing expedition. Recalling the praise of a Colorado friend for the slopes up across the Continental Divide to the west looking down upon the little town of Aspen, Elizabeth Paepcke pointed to these as their goal.

The trip to Aspen around the mountains by train took most of the day, and then the travelers had only reached Glenwood Springs, where the railroad ended, twenty miles from Aspen. But having called ahead to the management of Aspen's lone hotel, the Jerome, they were met at the train and chauffeured the rest of the way by a man who identified himself as Laurence Elisha. Night had fallen by the time they entered the sleepy valley of the Roaring Fork River where Aspen lay. Along the road snow crested to the points of the fence posts, and mountains rising on three sides held the valley air almost still. The town, home for some eight hundred people, seemed virtually abandoned; all around stood the dark, snow-laden forms of buildings and houses long vacant. As the travelers approached the hotel, they could see a single lightbulb, swaying eerily from the portico, playing light and shadows across the snow. They climbed from the car surrounded by silence that only winter knows, and entered the lobby. Welcomed by a menagerie of ineptly stuffed animals peering down at them from the somber walls, they looked around in puzzlement for a living person to sign them in. Then their chauffeur stepped behind the registration desk and smiled. "Oh," he said, "I own the place."[3] The three skiers settled into two of the Jerome's ten inhabitable rooms—others had long been closed. Room and board cost a mere three dollars per person. Meals, so a weathered sign informed them, were served at 6 A.M., 12 P.M., and 6 P.M. Resigned to eating breakfast before dawn, they slept.

After breakfast, the hotel guests—five in all, counting two earlier arrivals—set out for the slopes. There was only one way of getting there: packed into the back of a truck with sixteen miners, a remnant of Aspen's former flourishing industry, on their way to work at the Midnight Mine on Aspen Mountain. From the mine they hiked on to the top for the slide down. But before the descent, they cast their eyes upon an awesome sight. Virgin land and mountain peaks under a blanket of snow glinting in the morning sun and stretching in all directions. It was the most breathtaking landscape of natural wilderness Elizabeth Paepcke would ever see. And as she looked down toward the slumbering town, she thought to herself: if ever a place looked like Sleeping Beauty awaiting Prince Charming's kiss, this was it.[4]

Aspen was no mere shanty town of tumbledown huts and shuttered saloons. It was a city of stately, if unused and ill-repaired, Victorian houses and public buildings—a central business district, several churches, a courthouse, a grand hotel, and an opera house. Now providing shelter and uncertain livelihood to only a few hundred inhabitants, Aspen had once been the "Crystal City of the Rockies," a boom town where fortunes had been won and lost and nearly 15,000 people had made their homes (see fig. 4.1). All that was long ago in a time honored in memory, which Aspen's remaining residents had faint hopes of reviving.

That age had lasted little more than a dozen years, from the first concerted exploitation of the valley's silver mines in 1880 to the decision by Congress to demonitize, or go off, silver as a base of U.S. currency in 1893. Those years, however, had brought an affluence and civilized grandeur to Aspen rarely surpassed in any mining town of the West.

Fig. 4.1. Aspen, Colorado, 1887. Composite photo by William H. Jackson looking toward Aspen Mountain. Courtesy of Colorado Historical Society.

It is unlikely that anyone besides the Ute Indians, in whose territory it lay, had set foot in the Roaring Fork Valley before 1879. But after F. V. Hayden's Geological Survey of the region in 1873 located rich mineral deposits in neighboring mountains, it was only a matter of time before the prospectors arrived. The stage for their arrival was set in 1877, when silver strikes in Leadville—just twenty-five miles northeast of Aspen across the Continental Divide—sparked a boom. Miners and investors became millionaires overnight, speculators and vagabonds poured in, and Leadville quickly became known for possessing the richest lode of carbonate lead and silver in the country—and for hosting one of the roughest societies in the West.

So famed was Leadville that it attracted Oscar Wilde on his American tour of 1882, hoping to convert the grizzled miners and uncultivated nouveaux riches to his gospel of aestheticism. "I spoke to them of the early Florentines," Wilde reported to a friend,

> and they slept as though no crime had ever stained the ravines of their mountain home. I described to them the pictures of Botticelli, and the name, which seemed to them like a new drink, roused them from their dreams, but when I told them in my boyish eloquence of the "secret of Botticelli" the strong men wept like children. Their sympathy touched me and I approached modern art and had almost won them over to a real reverence for what is beautiful when unluckily I described one of Jimmy Whistler's "nocturnes in blue and gold." Then they leaped to their feet and in their grand simple way swore that such things should not be. Some of the younger ones pulled their revolvers out and left hurriedly to see if

Jimmy was "prowling about the saloons" or "wrastling a hash" at any eating shop. Had he been there I fear he would have been killed, their feeling was so bitter.

Despite the pistols brandished in contempt of Whistler's modernism—the same works that had provoked John Ruskin's famous jibe: a "bucket of paint thrown at the canvas"—the miners seem to have taken to Wilde himself, inviting him to open a fresh vein of ore in the eminent "Matchless" mine and naming the vein "The Oscar," and showering him with "artless and spontaneous praises" that, he said, "touched me more than the pompous panegyrics of literary critics ever did."[5]

Legend has it that Wilde also visited Aspen at this time; but he did not. For Aspen, in the early 1880s, was still a remote settlement barely starting on its way to fame and fortune as the Crystal City—although it never produced the quantities of ore or attained the population of its rowdier neighbor to the east.

Aspen's rise to prominence began when prospectors, frustrated at finding no new land to stake in Leadville, dared to venture west across the Divide into unknown Ute land. The first of two parties made their way across on the Fourth of July, 1879, leaving as a monument to their expedition the name of the 12,000-foot-high pass that put them over onto the Western Slope—Independence Pass. As they descended to the flat land where the Roaring Fork River and Castle Creek meet—at 8,000 feet—they detected ready traces of ore. Here they staked claims, built cabins, and called their settlement, in deference to its supposed owners, Ute City. But the Utes were not accommodating to trespassers, and, three months later, when a courier raced up the valley from towns to the west warning all prospectors on the Western Slope that the Indians had gone on the warpath, the thirty Ute City settlers packed their goods and fled to the safety of Leadville, leaving two stubborn prospectors to guard the claims.

The news these frightened settlers carried of silver in the Roaring Fork quickly roused a flurry of would-be seekers. And as soon as an Indian truce was signed, the seekers began to move. One of them, an unlikely adventurer named Henry B. Gillespie, a bookkeeper and mining broker (whose company helped finance prospectors) with a dream of riches, arrived with more than prospecting on his mind. After buying some claims, he determined to develop the town itself, and departed for Washington, D.C., to obtain support for a telegraph and adequate roads into the settlement.

While Gillespie was gone, another promoter got wind of events in Ute City and decided to act. With money provided by an eastern investor, the entrepreneurial B. Clark Wheeler bought, from two of the original settlers and sight unseen, eight mining claims and two ranch claims at a promised

$160,000, with $5,000 down. He then set out on snowshoes in the dead of winter from Leadville for the ten-day trek to study his purchases. Aggressive, enterprising, and well-educated, known as "the Professor" for his knowledge of geology, he also came equipped with an order from the surveyor general of Colorado to survey a town site where the settlement lay.[6] Soon after greeting the thirteen wintertime inhabitants of Ute City, he surveyed the land, resolved to make it his home, and, not one to live in an Indian town, changed its name to Aspen—after the prevalence of the quaking trees in the surrounding mountains.[7] Then, like Gillespie before him, he went off to find investors in Eastern cities—from Leadville on to his home state of Pennsylvania. Before long he had a standard speech, "Aspen over the Range," which he delivered hundreds of times across the country as he solicited investments for saw mills, merchandise, and a smelter.[8]

By the time Gillespie and Wheeler returned the next summer, Aspen was alive with activity generated by scores of new prospectors and ore pouring from the mines. But Aspen still had no serviceable roadways for the transportation of ore to outside smelters. And the trail across Independence Pass was so treacherous that, as one of the pioneers observed, "even for the patient burro" it was "pretty rough" and "literally covered with freight which has been thrown off and temporarily abandoned."[9] So, while the Aspen mines proved rich and the population grew to about seven hundred over the next two years, the high costs and inconvenience of transporting ore limited the town's development. Settlements down the valley, Highland and Ashcroft, closer to transportation routes, soon surpassed in size the future Crystal City.

But Aspen's very isolation had its benefits—then and later. Removed from thoroughfares, Aspen was relatively free of transient rowdies and developed a social stability and local culture remarkable for a frontier mining town. Led by civic leaders Gillespie and Wheeler, who cooperated congenially, Aspen soon sported a literary society, a glee club, a Sunday school, an elementary school, a post office, and a newspaper. The *Aspen Times* was founded by three enterprising early settlers with presses laboriously hauled across the pass. Its first issue appeared on April 18, 1881, with stories of Aspen's first election, first birth, and first death (the quiet end, months earlier, of a man eulogized before the Literary Society for having once honored frontier justice: "Frenzied by another's wrong, he had slain the slayer who had struck his father down").[10] Purchased and expanded within a year by Wheeler, the *Aspen Times* has continued to publish ever since.

But Aspen's growing prosperity did not become a true "boom," nor did Aspen gain its status as a city of elegance, until after the arrival in 1883 of another man named Wheeler. Jerome B. Wheeler (no relation to B. Clark), co-owner since 1879 of Macy's Department Store in New York, was "taking the waters" at Manitou near Colorado Springs when an Aspenite, probably Gillespie, learned of his presence. Always on the lookout for money to invest in Aspen's future, Gillespie dashed off to sell the easterner on the young silver city's prospects. A few days later, Jerome Wheeler, dignified, refined, impeccably dressed, and noted for his finely barbered beard, was in Aspen and its environs investing in mines and ranch lands and envisioning smelters, railroad lines, and cultural and economic institutions to make the Roaring Fork Valley the economic and social hub of Colorado. This astute and careful entrepreneur rapidly became the major developer in the area, holding vast mining interests, importing large numbers of employees, building a smelter, running a bank, and eventually pushing the Colorado Midland Railway into the valley. Coincidentally, the fortunes of Macy's, having risen consistently during the reign of founder Rowland Macy, went into a decline in 1883 and did not pull out of it until after 1888, the year Wheeler's partner bought him out. During that time "the store," according to its historian, "was suffering from some sort of managerial weakness."[11] Whatever else had gone wrong, one of its managers had simply found something more inviting to do with his time.

Macy's loss was Aspen's gain. When Jerome Wheeler arrived, Aspen was a town of a few dozen merchants, nearly 2,500 residents, and a bullion output running at about $5 million a year. Within another year the population had doubled and the boom had begun, ignited by Wheeler's smelter and a telegraph and telephone system installed in 1884, and fueled by the state's first complete electric light and power system, switched on in 1885. Finally, the Denver & Rio Grande Western and Midland Railroads were run in on spurs from Glenwood Springs in late 1887 and early 1888.

By 1892, Aspen was a bustling city of 12,000 to 14,000 people. The mines, especially the Aspen, the Smuggler, and the Mollie Gibson, were producing at a rate well above $10 million a year and yielding some of the largest silver nuggets ever mined—1,600 pounds, 1,765 pounds, 2,150 pounds, and the record holder, 2,330 pounds, taken from the Smuggler and trimmed to 1,840 pounds of 93 percent pure silver. The business district blossomed with dozens of retail and service establishments—including thirty saloons—laid out in handsome two-story, block-long offices and storefronts constructed of red sandstone and granite. The demand for housing was so great that contractors and realtors had to compile waiting lists.[12]

While Aspen was rising from the ground almost overnight, it was rising not as a shanty town but as a fashionable, well-built, Victorian city. The homes of its affluent new citizens, utilizing all the devices of the "gingerbread style" (multiple levees, bay windows, porches, gables, turrets, finials, iron trim, irregular rooflines or mansard roofs) and marked inside by a cluttered cosiness of carved oak woodwork, curtained walls, soft lights, and abundant furniture, were not the transient homes of grubstakers but monuments to the middle-class tastes and stability of Aspen society.

Yet the chief landmarks of the prosperity and building boom were not shops or houses but the hotel and the opera house built by Jerome B. Wheeler. The $90,000 Wheeler Opera House, a sturdy, three-story, red stone building that also housed the Jerome B. Wheeler Bank, had its debut in 1889. Glowing under a frescoed dome and a thirty-six branch brass chandelier trimmed with silver, the gilt and red velvet boxes with their brown morocco leather chairs regularly welcomed six hundred Aspenites and visitors to performances of plays, concerts, and opera.

Six months after the opera house curtain went up for the first time, the Hotel Jerome opened its doors to a throng of celebrants invited—as the second Aspen newspaper, the *Daily Chronicle,* put it—to feast and dance the "Handsomest Hotel on the Western Slope" into life. At a cost of over $100,000, Wheeler had tried to create a hotel to match any in the country. The three-story brick structure with a stately covered portal featured electric lights, a hydraulic passenger elevator (then unusual) in carved red birch, steam heat, hot and cold running water, a carved oak bar, a first-class dining room, uniformed bellboys, a French chef, and a German gardener. The opening night guests pronounced its sixty-nine rooms—priced at three to four dollars a day—"magical, superb," and the celebration unparalleled. "History records such feasts, fiction fables such a treat," hymned one celebrant, "but never before, and probably never again in the pages which register the events of the silver metropolis will such an epoch be noted."[13]

Equipped with money, vision, and style, Jerome Wheeler was enabling Aspen to live up to its nickname as the Crystal City of the Rockies. And with new and richer lodes of silver opening almost every day, it looked as though Aspen would remain the Crystal City for years to come—provided the U.S. Treasury retained silver as a backing for American currency.

But the position of silver was insecure. The Treasury had stopped minting the silver dollar in 1873, in deference to gold, an action that gave rise to the Free Silver movement, which advocated the policy of "bimetalism," the minting of both metals, as economically sound and socially just. The movement succeeded in getting Congress to rectify the "Crime of '73" by requiring the Treasury to buy up to $4 million worth of silver each month beginning in 1878. Then the Sherman Act of 1890 superseded the previous rule, increasing the monthly purchase by half. Things looked good for silver. But critics of bimetalism, mainly eastern industrialists arguing the greater strength of a currency based solely on gold, continued to be heard.

To dramatize their support of the two-metal policy, Aspen mining interests, near the peak of their productivity, decided in 1892 to send a lavish exhibit to the World's Columbian Exposition scheduled for the next year in

Chicago. At a cost of $10,000 they constructed "The Silver Queen"—the nickname of Aspen Mountain—a statue of a woman, with a head carved from a single silver nugget surmounted by an eagle also of solid silver, drawn in a chariot by two winged gods each carrying a cornucopia, one pouring gold, one silver. The statue stood eighteen feet high, and at its base in bold script was inscribed the name: "Aspen."[14]

The Silver Queen went on view in the exposition's Hall of Mines in June 1893. Less than a month later the Treasury, preparing for the impending repeal of the Sherman Act in consequence of pressure from the new president, Grover Cleveland, ceased ordering silver. Mining stopped dead; the Silver Panic of '93 was on—setting the Free Silver populist William Jennings Bryan to tuning up the oratory that would lead him to victory at the Democratic Convention of 1896 with his famous "Cross of Gold" speech. The price of silver plummeted, reaching less than one-half cent per ounce after repeal in November. Aspen's days of glory were over. The Silver Queen now stood in silent mockery of Aspen's fate.

Close to $100 million in silver and other ores had come from Aspen's mines in just over a dozen years. Now those mines closed down, the miners drifted off to the gold fields, merchants and banks failed, and once-proud home owners left their houses to molder and to lapse onto the tax rolls. Jerome Wheeler, who in that very year had completed his fine new brick residence, took out bankruptcy in New York with debts three times greater than his assets (those assets had been placed at $1.5 million when he left Macy's). Gillespie, stripped of his possessions, departed for South America in a futile search for new fortune. B. Clark Wheeler held on to his newspaper and became Aspen's first "hard times" mayor.

The Hotel Jerome slowly settled into disrepair, its top floor ravaged by a leaky roof, its inhabitable rooms dwindling in number. It languished until one of its bartenders, Mansor Elisha, leased it for one dollar a year around 1910 and then bought it for taxes in 1911. Charging one dollar a night, Elisha operated it until he died in 1935, to be succeeded by his son Laurence, who kept it alive mainly by serving cheap meals to locals in the dining hall and turning its public rooms into something of a town social club.

The Opera House suffered even greater indignities. Disused and neglected, it fell victim in 1912 to a succession of fires—widely believed to have been set for the insurance payoff—that left it charred and unusable. The population of Aspen had by this time sunk to one thousand, and continued edging downward. All that remained were the families of small merchants and a few die-hard miners still picking away at any unmined ore and dreaming of a return to fortune for the Crystal City. Aspen settled into her deepening sleep.[15]

Elizabeth Paepcke returned to Perry Park from Aspen in that winter of 1939 full of idyllic memories and hopes of returning. "Walter," she cried. "You simply must see it. It's the most beautifully untouched place in the world." "Sometime," he replied, unattracted to skiing and weary of winter's inhospitality. "Perhaps in summer."[16] But summer came and went and then came the war, and Paepcke, involved with Moholy-Nagy at the School of Design and conjuring up plans of expansion for the Container Corporation, had other things on his mind than Rocky Mountain excursions. Sleeping Beauty was not to be disturbed on his account in those years.

But what Elizabeth Paepcke did not know was that Aspen had fed the hungry eyes and roused the imaginations of people like her before, and would again before Prince Charming arrived. For Aspen had inspired visions in others of turning its majestic setting into a center for America's newest popular sport, which had brought Elizabeth Paepcke and her friends there in 1939: skiing.

Skiing had hardly existed in this country before the Winter Olympics of 1932 in Lake Placid, New York (the third meeting of the Winter Games). And even at those games the skiing was pretty modest. This was not the Lake Placid of the Winter Olympics held there in 1980, with its masterfully engineered seventy- and ninety-meter jumps, capacious snow-making equipment, and exciting downhill and slalom runs. "They had no mountains there, really," a participant remembered, "worthy at that time of the ski jump." And "there was nothing, really, in the way of downhill skiing."[17] Thus the ski competitions in the Olympics were confined, as they had been before and would be until 1948, to Nordic, or cross-country, events and a single jump.

No other American winter resort at that time could offer more than this. Skis in those days were little more than long flat boards suitable only for traversing snow in straight lines. And the binding was nothing but a strap across the toe to keep the ski in place during forward movement. With this apparatus, maneuvers must be few and always awkward—high speeds under firm control or graceful parallel turns were not only impossible but unthinkable. Lacking grace and thrills, skiing was done mainly by those who needed it for transportation—like the miners in Aspen—and a few energetic New England collegians.

But the Lake Placid Games were followed by an influx of Europeans, fleeing fascism or invited by enterprising Americans and bringing with them their recently developed techniques of ski instruction. This influx, together with improved equipment, caused a rapid change. Almost overnight Austrian and Scandinavian ski instructors could be found at every winter resort, contributing technical help to aspirant skiers and the image of the romantic foreign ski teacher to American folk culture. Skis became lighter, shorter, and sharper-edged, and bindings more secure, all of which brought greater speed and more control and glamour to the sport. And with the new skiing came new resorts, constructed less for everyday snow-lovers than for skiers. Stowe, Vermont, once a minor winter retreat for undergraduates, grew into a major resort under the inspiration of owner Cornelius Starr after he took ski lessons from an Austrian instructor. Fred Pabst translated his enthusiasm for skiing, acquired on a visit to Switzerland, into a chain of ski resorts in New England crowned by Big Bromley. In the West, Alex Cushing began developing Squaw Valley, California. And, most celebrated of all, Averell Harriman's Sun Valley, sporting the world's first chair lifts, opened in 1936.

Like so many others, Harriman had become captivated by skiing in Europe, and in 1935 he induced an Austrian skier, Count Felix Schaffgotsch, to return to the United States with him and go searching for a location in the western states suitable for a ski resort. Harriman planned to use the resort not only for his own pleasure but, following the practice of many corporations in the 1930s, to lift the public image of his Union Pacific Railroad and at the same time to give an economic boost to the western states during those lingering Depression years. After visiting many locations, including Aspen, Count Schaffgotsch settled on Sun Valley, Idaho, for it had gentle, undemanding slopes and a mild climate; the town rested at a relatively low altitude (6,000 feet, compared to Aspen's 7,944 feet); and, not least, it was near the Union Pacific line (Aspen was not). The very ease of its skiing and its ready accessibility perfectly suited Sun Valley to the state of skiing in the thirties, when many of those making their way to the slopes were beginners, and unrefined equipment limited the movements even of experts. Aided by its elaborate new lodge and its appeal to celebrities, Sun Valley immediately became the American Saint Moritz, thrusting skiing into the public eye in this country as a glamorous recreation.[18]

But at the very time of Sun Valley's grand opening to much fanfare at Christmas 1936, another, rather less ambitious resort opened in Colorado. This was Aspen's first, the Highland-Bavarian Lodge, just west of town at the base of the Aspen Highlands Mountain. It was the work of a zealous group of ski enthusiasts led by Billy Fiske, who had carried the flag for the American team into the Lake Placid Olympics and gone on to win a gold medal in the bobsled races, together with an old-time Aspenite, Thomas J. Flynn. Flynn had given Fiske his first look at Aspen a few years earlier after a conversation between Fiske and Flynn's son had turned to the subject of the perfect ski slope. Fiske had conceived great ideas for Aspen at once, and he had hired European Andre Roch to survey the hills and lay out the runs, and had then set builders to work on the lodge.[19]

The Highland-Bavarian Lodge accommodated only sixteen persons and provided skiers no tows—they would have to rely on the traditional Aspen methods of ascent: trucks, miners' ore cars, and hiking. But Fiske and Flynn hoped this would be just the beginning. The *Aspen Times* heralded the project as "the greatest news that the residents of Aspen have ever heard in the past thirty years"; for the new lodge and its presumed successors, capitalizing on "the fastest growing recreation in the world today will make Aspen the leading winter sports city in America."[20] Then as the lodge neared completion, the newspaper solemnly announced: "Sunday, December 27, 1936, will go down in the history of Aspen as the day in which the fortunes of this community were reborn, for on that day, next Sunday at one o'clock, the Highland-Bavarian Winter Sports Club up Castle Creek formally opens with flag raising and dedication ceremonies and the influx of winter sports enthusiasts from all corners of the world begins."[21] This high-blown optimism in the economically depressed little town mingled hopes for an affluent future with nostalgia for a fabled past; at last, the *Times* speculated, Aspen "may again rise to the glories that were hers as the 'Crystal City of the Rockies' during the boom days of the early Nineties."[22]

These hopes proved premature. Although Aspen gained some national publicity over the next few years in ski publications and films, and acquired another ski run—laid out by Andre Roch on Aspen Mountain—with a rope tow in 1938, and played host to the championship races of the Southern Rocky Mountain Ski Association in 1939 and the National Association races in 1941, it proved impossible to obtain sufficient investment and clientele to keep developments growing. Unlike Sun Valley, where the skiing was easy and a beginner's paradise, the runs at Aspen were steep and barely manageable. Roch Run on Aspen Mountain formed a troublesome corkscrew, and another run, Silver Queen, had one turn with a five-hundred-foot drop, making Aspen inappropriate to the fledgling sport. The management of Sun Valley even showed films to its patrons of the treacherous Aspen slopes for laughs.

But Aspen's potential still beckoned a few would-be developers. When Elizabeth Paepcke was rhapsodizing over Aspen in 1939, she did not know that her brother, Paul H. Nitze, a colleague of Billy Fiske's at Dillon Read investment house in New York, had discussed Fiske's project with him at the beginning, and had since followed Harriman's example and tried to get another railroad, the D. & R.G.W., to expand the skiing at Aspen. In the same prewar years, the journalist Lowell Thomas had visited Aspen with Sepp Rusch, instructor and part owner of Stowe, where, awed by the scenery and recreation possibilities, Thomas spoke of transforming the town into "one of the gay spots of the West."[23] The war, however, put an end to all these prospects as well as snuffing out the imaginings of Fiske and Flynn. Investment finances dried up; Fiske went off to join the RAF (becoming the last fighter pilot killed in the Battle of Britain); and finally Flynn lost his faith in the grand design. Sleeping Beauty, barely aroused, went back to sleep.

Yet even before the war ended, another band of discoverers wandered into Aspen. Members of the army's Tenth Division Mountain Infantry, all collegiate or professional skiers stationed for training at nearby Camp Hale in Pando, Colorado, came over to Aspen for weekend skiing expeditions. Several of them fell in love with the place and vowed to return to live there in peacetime. One of them, Friedl Pfeifer, even went to the town council during the war to stir interest in building up the ski industry. "I want to start a ski school here," he explained, "and I'll give the local children free lessons so that we can develop a real skiing community. People will be interested in expanding commercial possibilities, and we'll get enough money to build more adequate tows and lifts. The War won't last foreever."[24]

True to their vows, the Tenth Division skiers returned after the war. Among them were men destined to influence Aspen's future: Fritz Benedict, an architect; Leonard Woods, who married one of Paepcke's daughters; John Litchfield; Percy Rideout; and Pfeifer, who organized the Aspen Ski School. But before they had a chance to return, Aspen had begun to awaken.

On an April evening in 1945, Paepcke and his wife entertained a good friend of recent years, Eugene Lilly, visiting Chicago from Colorado Springs, Colorado, one hundred miles east of Aspen. A vice-president of Bellows and Co., liquor distributors, and an independent producer of gourmet foods at his High Valley Farms, Lilly was a soft-spoken, unassuming, homey charmer with a wit bespeaking cultivation and intelligence and the tastes of a connoisseur. When talk turned to the subject of Colorado, Lilly and Elizabeth Paepcke sang the praises of Aspen, and Paepcke, riding the crest of his business triumphs and hungry for fresh adventures now that the war was ending, seemed idly curious.

A month later, Paepcke wrote to Lilly: "Pussy and I have been thinking seriously of making a trip to Aspen," and "I was wondering what the disposition of the Lillys' would be to joining us."[25] The Lillys—and Elizabeth Paepcke, then at Perry Park—were delighted. At last Paepcke would know at first hand the beauties and charms of the old mining town in the Roaring Fork Valley, and all would enjoy a diverting holiday. The trip was scheduled for the Memorial Day weekend.

But unknown to his wife and friends, Paepcke was thinking of something more than diversion. In recent weeks, he had been nurturing through research and financial calculations a new enterprise slated to have Aspen as its home. This was the development of Aspen itself.

Shortly after the April dinner with Lilly—and just as the Container Corporation exhibit was about to open at the Art Institute—Paepcke had started to move. He first asked his secretary to look into Aspen's vital statistics. She came up with a sketchy sheet of facts "as of about 1936" obtained from the D. & R.G.W. Railroad, listing such items as: Alt.—7944; Trading Area Pop.—1000; Rivers—Roaring Fork, Hunter; Bank—Aspen State; Newspaper—*Aspen Times*; Hotel—Jerome; Raw Materials—ore, silver, lead, zinc; Special inducement—tourist resort.[26]

This wasn't much, but it was a start. Next Paepcke told her to make direct inquiries, concealing the source of her referral, for more details from institutions in Aspen and Denver. "I have some friends who are interested in skiing and winter sports and particularly at Aspen, Colorado,"[27] she began her letter of April 30 to the *Rocky Mountain Winter Sports News* (dictated no doubt by Paepcke). Could the newspaper supply information about facilities and accommodations? The same day she wrote to the editor of the *Aspen Times* for facts about advertising and circulation, to assist "some friends who are somewhat interested in possibly buying an old, very cheap but well-located vacant house, if there is such a thing in Aspen."[28] And she queried the Aspen Bank (the Pitkin County State Bank). "Attention—President: Some friends of mine were wondering whether it would be possible to buy very, very cheaply an old house with some ground around it, which could be fixed up not too expensively for a few families who might want to come out to Aspen for skiing in future years and if so, what the approximate price would be."[29] If such a place existed, could the bank provide pictures?

Paepcke got into the act himself that day, also in the name of "friends." He put through a call to a Denver real estate acquaintance, asking for general information about Aspen—real estate values, desirable locations, names of possible contacts. The realtor replied the next day, May 1, enclosing an Aspen Lions Club brochure, and suggesting that "your friends" come see the town for themselves in early summer after the spring mud dries. He also recommended that they "beware" of certain malevolent characters, like a particular "disbarred Texas attorney practicing his bad habits at Aspen, . . . into whose clutches visitors are likely to fall," and that they consult one "Judge Shaw" (William R. Shaw of the Pitkin County Court), a "reputable gentleman."[30]

Paepcke thanked his source for the tips immediately and included an urgent and mildly deceitful caution of his own: "I meant to tell you, but fear I neglected to, that I would like if possible to keep our name out of any inquiries, because if we are going to try to pick up anything for our friends, I think their purposes will be better served if the population around Aspen does not know that we have anything either directly or indirectly to do with it." Nor did Paepcke think one caveat enough. He repeated in closing: "Please remember not to mention our name in connection therewith."[31] Paepcke was not a dishonest man, but he was never blind to the ways of the marketplace. An investment like that he envisioned in Aspen would, he thought, require "discretion" in the disclosure of intentions, and he would preserve discretion as long as possible.

Another letter went out from Paepcke on May 3 outlining his aspirations for Aspen to a young public relations expert, Albin Dearing, who had ably publicized the opening of the Container Corporation Fernandina pulp-processing plant in 1938 and who, now awaiting release from the army, might be helpful in promoting Aspen developments. Appealing to young Dearing's passion for skiing, Paepcke told him that some "top Austrian ski instructors" (veterans of the Tenth Division of whom Paepcke had probably learned from his realtor acquaintance) intended to establish a ski school and village at Aspen, where snow conditions are "the most reliable and perfect" in the country. And, he went on, besides its winter sports potential, the area "is excellent as a year-round vacation spot," and so "some of us have been toying with the idea of buying two or three houses dirt cheap and fixing them up for either ski stores, gift shops, restaurants, boarding houses or what not." But, Paepcke indicated, economic gain was not the only purpose. Stressing his determination to bring in people with ability and "reasonably good taste," he disclosed his ambition to restore Aspen physically and rejuvenate it as an economically vibrant, culturally alive community. "If in this general way," he wrote, "the whole tone of Aspen and Ashcroft [the neighboring town] could be revivified and made more alert and aggressive and the town built up in a very simple yet attractive way, as was done with Williamsburg in the east, the result might be extremely attractive, novel, and pleasant."[32] Paepcke the commercial and high-minded entrepreneur was now plainly bent not only on a casual visit or even the purchase of a vacation home but on sparking the renaissance of an entire town in the spirit of cultural idealism that so animated his life in Chicago.

While Paepcke engaged in a discreet and indirect correspondence with Aspenites—particularly with the banker W. Lucas Woodall, who informed Paepcke's secretary in mid-May that a reasonably well-maintained house, without hot water, could be purchased for four hundred dollars, a figure Paepcke thought a little high[33]—Paepcke began prodding a hotelier acquaintance from Illinois, Floyd N. Gibbs, to consider Aspen as a future home. On May 17, while vacationing in the West, Gibbs and his wife stayed overnight at the Hotel Jerome, eyeing its economic prospects, while soliciting information from Judge Shaw and relaying details—and photographs—to Paepcke. When Shaw failed to deliver the facts Gibbs wanted about the hotel, Gibbs thought of having Paepcke intervene but discarded the idea because, as he acknowledged, that would not be possible without bringing Paepcke into the picture.[34] The secret held fast.

Paepcke was now ready to see Aspen for himself. But just before leaving Chicago he invited Gibbs to follow him, saying that although he wouldn't be in Aspen long enough to "conclude anything," he could arrange accommodations for the Gibbs family if they wanted to go "out there" in hopes of "making some hotel or other deal."[35] Gibbs took the bait.

Paepcke also sent off an enticing invitation to another associate, Herbert Bayer, whose life would change course because of it. Paepcke had known Bayer only since March, when preparations for the advertising art exhibit at the Art Institute were getting underway, but the two men and their wives had hit it off at once. Bayer had recently married the radiant Joella Loy Levy, daughter of the avant-garde poet Mina Loy and ex-wife of Julien Levy, the modernist gallery owner in New York. It was through Levy's gallery that she had met Bayer, and it was through Elizabeth Paepcke, sent to New York to convince Bayer to do the Container Corporation exhibit, that the two couples got together. The Paepcke style had worked its charm immediately. "How I admire you," Joella Bayer wrote, "and your way of living."[36]

But for Walter Paepcke the friendship offered much more than convivial pleasures. For, even more than Moholy-Nagy, Bayer was the kind of artist, if not quite so much the kind of man, that Paepcke appreciated. Darkly handsome, deep-voiced, contemplative, and familiar with the ways of commerce, Bayer, despite his frequent melancholy, was the one artist who caused Paepcke no discomfort in the shared company of businessmen. Lacking Moholy's heady ambitions as teacher and cultural reformer (Bayer disliked teaching and shunned metaphysical claims for art) and possessing a gift for integrating abstract visual form and practical communication, Bayer could quickly grasp commercial imperatives and translate them into powerful yet elegant layouts and graphics; as Gropius had said, with complimentary intent, Bayer had mastered "the language of propaganda."[37] Not for nothing—although with some exaggeration—would Alexander Dorner proclaim Bayer the artist who led "the way beyond art" toward the unity of art and life; or, as a newspaper put it: "New Style of Artist: Herbert Bayer Is Real Cog in Industry."[38]

Bayer was, of course, living up to the practical Bauhaus principles of his youth, but while these principles helped change the face of product and graphic design, they also tended to bind Bauhaus artists so closely to the demands of technology and communication that the private artworks of these artists were often more technical than inspired, however pleasing to the eye. Bayer had suffered from this seeming bondage to technique by being largely ignored as a painter and admired only as a graphic designer—a label he welcomed most of the time, but not always. And in the spring of 1945, Bayer was depressed and thinking of giving up his commercial work in New York and making a new start in postwar Europe.

Paepcke saw here a chance to help both himself and his new friend. Why not, he thought, get Bayer, a lover of nature and a skier homesick for his native Austrian Alps, to take a look at Aspen? Maybe he would find there

what he was seeking; and then Paepcke would have a good start in the making of his cultural community, his Magic Mountain.

"Before you definitely move with bag and baggage and select a somewhat
permanent residence in the Bavarian Alps or Tyrol," Paepcke wrote Bayer in
late May, "you ought to consider the American Rockies." To strengthen the
incentive, Paepcke disclosed that he was "seriously thinking of buying two or
three cheap little pieces of property which I think over a period of time
would be fun to renovate and might even be a very interesting investment."
And, reminding Bayer of Bayer's promise to visit Perry Park along with Gropius
later that summer to discuss the future of Moholy's Institute of Design, he
added that this would be the perfect time to "make the trip over to Aspen
and look around."[39] The seed planted, Paepcke would nourish it with cajoling
and further enticements until it flowered. Meanwhile, he had to explore
Aspen himself.

Two routes lead travelers from Colorado Springs through the junction at Granite
to Aspen. One goes over one hundred miles around the mountains from
Granite on Highway 24 to Glenwood Springs and up the Roaring Fork Valley
to Aspen on Highway 82 from the west. The other cuts three-quarters off
that distance by rising twelve thousand feet across the Continental Divide
at Independence Pass, near the highest peaks of the state, to descend into
Aspen on the same highway from the east. Even in late May, Independence
Pass is often blocked by snow. And a road sign so warned the party of four
traveling from the Lillys' home in Paepcke's Buick. Yet, enraptured by the
warm temperatures and blue skies, enjoying the company, and enthralled by
the adventure, Paepcke scoffed and headed for the pass. Patches of thawing
snow drifts appeared here and there along the gravel road ascending the
Rockies. Paepcke forged onward. Suddenly the car jolted to a stop. Before it
stood a wall of snow that had tumbled from the mountain above and now
impenetrably blocked the path. Grudgingly conceding defeat, Paepcke inched
the car backward until he could turn it around. Their spirits undampened,
the foursome took advantage of the detour for lunch along the shores of
glistening Twin Lakes. There, moved by the majestic landscape and nervous
at having talked her husband into an out-of-the-way vacation, Elizabeth
Paepcke embraced him innocently and said with her warmest smile: "Oh,
Walter, I hope you like Aspen." "I'm sure I will," he replied affectionately.[40]
Little did she know that he knew more of the place than she did.

They arrived in Aspen to the quiet greeting of a seemingly sleeping,
largely forsaken village. Taking rooms in the Hotel Jerome, they began to
explore the town, Elizabeth Paepcke with an eye to natural beauties and rustic
charm, Walter Paepcke with an eye to investment. What they found captivated
them both, and set ideas of development dancing anew in Walter's head.

The sudden end to Aspen's mining industry, while snuffing out the town's early glory and driving away its inhabitants, had not been without consolation. The very speed and duration of the Crystal City's decline had left much of the town just as it was before the lethal blow fell, untouched by new industries and population, and damaged only by weather and neglect. Walter Paepcke lost no time in exploiting these circumstances. While his companions still slept at the hotel the following morning, he was out negotiating with Judge Shaw over properties, deeds, owners, and prices, jotting down in his broken handwriting on a sheet of Jerome stationery the probable prices of several desirable residential and commercial properties—including the Stallard house built for Jerome Wheeler and completed in the fateful year of 1893, available for "1500 tops."[41]

After leaving Shaw, Paepcke made two quick calls to Chicago. In one, he requested his lawyer to wire Floyd Gibbs in Wisconsin with the news that Paepcke had residential and hotel possibilities in hand.[42] The other call went to his secretary with instructions to wire Aspen realtor E. E. Jackson expressing *her* interest in one of Jackson's properties and one of Aspen's finest Victorian houses, Pioneer Park, requesting details of its location in town (Paepcke's ruse), the number of adjoining lots, price, and date of possible occupancy. Jackson replied that all five lots west of the house were available on tax title for two hundred fifty dollars, and the house was ready for occupancy and at a reasonable price.[43]

This was just the news Paepcke wanted to hear: good properties available cheap and many for nothing more than back taxes. He then made a stop at the county treasurer's office, noting on a list labeled "delinquent taxes" the names and addresses of several owners and the back taxes due. Before long he put Judge Shaw on retainer to negotiate and carry through real estate deals for him, with the instructions that Paepcke was "perfectly willing to spend up to $5,000 or $6,000 at the rate of about $25 a lot" in the county tax auctions, in addition to the cost of developed properties purchased individually. But Paepcke did not want to be reckless, and he cautioned Shaw that "$250 for four or five lots is pretty high"[44]—which would raise a laugh in future decades (see Chapter 10).

By the end of his first full day in Aspen, Paepcke had his sights on half a dozen homes and hundreds of lots. He had also agreed to buy a block-long, two-story commercial and office building (the Collins block) for $7,500 from young Tom Sardy, who ran both a hardware shop and mortician's business, which he casually separated by a curtain.[45] Thus began a close business and friendly relationship between Sardy and Paepcke that persisted until Paepcke's death.

The second day Paepcke was again on the street in pursuit of deals before the others got up. And at lunchtime he walked proudly into the Jerome dining room with news of his activities and a surprise gift for his wife. "What is it?" she asked, startled. He sat down, visibly pleased with himself, and replied, "A house." Instead of the delighted cheers he had expected, Elizabeth Paepcke burst into tears. "Not another house to run!"[46] she cried. Managing the Sandwich estate and the Perry Park ranch while her husband disdained domestic responsibilities had already driven her more than once to a sickbed with exhaustion. Now she saw Walter setting off on another real estate adventure leading where she dared not think. The happiest days of her life, spent in the open air and occasional idyllic leisures of Perry Park, were likely to be gone. Walter, not one to trouble himself over a mere woman's worries, brushed them aside. Aspen would be great fun, he said. The new house would bring plenty of pleasure, and maybe a little profit.

His gift was the Lamb House, a well-maintained frame dwelling of eight rooms on the west side of town, once the elegant Victorian home of Aspen's prosperous druggist, Alfred Lamb. Although it had been vacant for four or five years, the taxes were paid up, and Paepcke had paid five hundred dollars more for it than the three thousand he had expected. The Aspen renaissance had begun.

When the sale was made public two weeks later, it made news. The *Aspen Times* ran a story on page one headlined: "Lamb Property Sold."[47] But while the story identified the new owner as Walter Paepcke, it contained no hint of Paepcke's other doings or future ambitions. The only person in Aspen who knew of these was Judge Shaw, who, true to his honorable reputation, was keeping quiet. And, convinced of Paepcke's good intentions and ability to get, as Paepcke assured him, "more and more people interested in Aspen,"[48] Shaw was being more than honorable; he was, as he told Paepcke, delighted "for all the residents of Aspen that they have fallen heir to an angel."[49]

Returning to Chicago, "the angel" kept his schemes multiplying. He offered the Lamb House free of rent to Floyd Gibbs if Gibbs would put it in shape and look after "such other properties as we might pick up,"[50] including the Jerome, through purchase or rent, or some other building that could serve as a hotel. And he began putting a buzz in the ear of "potential fellow Aspenites." One of them, a Colorado friend and ski enthusiast, Robert Collins, as Paepcke reported, grew "very excited about organizing a group to put in a ski tow because . . . some of his friends have done it in various parts of the U.S. and Canada and . . . he thinks that would be a very profitable investment." Another friend, the Chicago architect Walter Frazier, who had designed Paepcke's neo-Victorian Sandwich estate, became "terribly enthusiastic about the whole idea" of doing "some city planning, rehabilitation, tearing down shacks, dressing up other buildings, etc.,"[51] as well as creating a vacation

home for himself. Paepcke also informed Herbert Bayer, as a further inducement to settle in the West, that not only Paepcke himself but "several very
nice friends" were thinking of "building up the old ghost town of Aspen, in
its material, social, and commercial aspects and making that a life's work."[52]
Wouldn't Bayer like to join them?

While drawing in a few outsiders, Paepcke still cloaked his activities in
caution, if not secrecy. He didn't want the development of Aspen to become
a land-grab affair for vulgar people. He wanted it to be an activity among
people "from various parts of the country who we knew might be interested
and would keep the matter quiet."[53] And quiet it remained—for a while.

The first of these people to arrive was Floyd Gibbs, who with his family
liberated the Lamb House from years of shuttered darkness on June 15. Gibbs
immediately saw signs of change in the town, reporting to Paepcke that
there seemed to be much more economic activity than there had been a
month earlier, several buildings now being repaired and painted and some
properties even changing hands.[54] Paepcke would have to move faster than
he had wanted. He repeated to Gibbs the cautions previously given to Judge
Shaw against saying "anything about our ideas of purchasing property, building up Aspen, etc., because we do not want to stir up more excitement than
is necessary. Otherwise," he added, "the whole plan will be slowed up indefi-
nitely"[55]—that is, the plan of controlled growth at the right prices for the
right people.

In another few days, Paepcke had further instructions for Gibbs. It was
time for the nascent development to start turning a profit, or at least covering costs. He told Gibbs to start preparing for paying guests in the newly
purchased houses; and, calculating the number of rooms and good beds, food
and help, Paepcke ticked off projected receipts at eight to ten dollars per
person per day for board and lodging, totaling eight hundred dollars for a
house of five people for twenty days.[56] A tidy profit, he thought. Next he sent
an urgent request for installation of a phone in the Lamb House to facilitate
his "associates'" efforts "to build up the commercial and business life of
Aspen over a period of years."[57] The "prosaic boxmaker" was happily don-
ning a hotelier's hat.

Paepcke was in Aspen again at the beginning of July 1945 for three and a half
days, accompanied by his wife and the architect Walter Frazier. Now events
picked up speed. New properties were scouted and plans laid for restoring
Aspen as a "Victorian frontier mining town."[58] Amid the rising national
interest in America's architectural heritage (Williamsburg, 1933; Henry Ford's
"reconstruction" of a nineteenth-century town, Greenfield Village, 1932;
the founding of the National Society for Historic Preservation, 1947), the
restoration seemed to promise benefits to Aspen in both appearance and

economics. But what seemed like an irreproachable idea to the outsiders aroused suspicions among the locals. Many old-timers, holding fast to their hopes of a revival of mining in the Aspen hills, would hear nothing of commercial strategies for reviving the town's economy. In response to the old-timers, the *Aspen Times,* as usual on the side of economic expansion, printed an editorial on July 5 declaring that "the town would be better off if those who cannot see a future for the Crystal City would move out or keep as quiet as the proverbial mouse" and advising that "if newcomers come in and take over the town for development in any way the residents will need to go along with those plans whole-heartedly or propose a better one and support it."[59] Some of Paepcke's supporters, like Dorothy Shaw, the Judge's wife, showed sympathy to the townspeople and urged Paepcke to have patience. The people of Aspen, she said, have "suddenly awakened from a long Rip van Winkle nap and are rubbing their eyes but fail to see anything they can understand."[60]

Then the *Times,* in its first story devoted to Paepcke—following his first public relations visit to its offices—gave reassurance that Paepcke wanted to cooperate with the residents and desired no more than they did "to build up a strictly resort town." What is more, the paper said, Paepcke had demonstrated his generous and congenial spirit "by paying fair prices for the property he has acquired to date. He has one price, a fair one, no more, no less."[61]

The same issue of the *Times* announced that Paepcke had now purchased three more houses, among them, Pioneer Park. Built by a mayor of Aspen, Henry Webber, at the height of Aspen's glory, this graceful two-story, mansard-roofed brick house in the town's west end, containing nine rooms and boasting a fine brick stable-carriage house out behind, had been, as the *Times* said, "the show place on the Western Slope."[62] Later, spruced up with new hardwood floors, a coat of surprising but pleasing pink paint, an enlarged half-acre yard, and with the stable converted into a guest house, Pioneer Park became the manor house of Aspen (popularly known as "Pussy's Pink Palace"), where for nearly ten years the Paepckes enjoyed summer, fall, and winter vacations, entertained guests of all kinds, including such figures as Albert Schweitzer, José Ortega y Gasset, Dimitri Mitropoulos, Artur Rubinstein, Walter Gropius, Robert M. Hutchins, and Thornton Wilder, and played host to the earliest seminars of the Aspen Institute. Most of these events were still years away. But now Paepcke proceeded on the conviction that Aspen was his Magic Mountain.

He started at once steering vacationers from the Perry Park ranch, which he closed to paying guests, to Aspen, through some sixty letters to former clients mailed in early July. He told Gibbs to prepare publicity pictures for mailing and encouraged him to write directly to prospective visitors. "It is important," the experienced advertiser explained, "to have quite a few people see Aspen so that they in turn will spread the word; it is the best advertising there is."[63]

But this heightened activity in purchasing properties for himself and friends and in promoting Aspen among an expanding transient clientele soon brought complications worse than the sporadic complaints of Aspenites. It also had one of the effects Paepcke feared most: pushing real estate prices up. Paepcke felt compelled to repeat yet again, and with renewed emphasis, to all those around him that his Aspen ambitions must be kept quiet. He urged Sardy, Shaw, and Jackson "for the good of us all and particularly for the good of the town . . . to say as little about . . . deals that I have made or may make in the future as possible. If there is too much excitement in the air, I will simply have to regrettably back away from any additional new transactions, because as prices and values get out of sight it would be foolish of me to do anything further."[64]

To cool the market, he told Sardy that rising prices had already scared off some of his friends, and he informed or, rather, *mis*informed Jackson in mid-July that "to all intents and purposes I think we are just about through with house purchases . . . not only for ourselves but for some of our friends."[65] The ploy worked. "Well, the news is rapidly 'grapevining' its way around our fair city," Shaw happily reported, "that you have all the property that you need and I think you will be able to buy quietly now." But he added a disquieting note: "It is surprising, however, the number of strangers that are finding their way into Aspen looking for cabin sites."[66] The postwar expansion of recreation was creeping into the Roaring Fork Valley, both because of Paepcke and despite him.

Paepcke's next step, while exchanging promotional ideas with PR man Albin Dearing and trying to establish ties with Friedl Pfeifer, was to send out a legal representative to handle his real estate affairs in Aspen. He chose young Samuel Mitchell from Paepcke's Chicago law firm of Bell, Boyd, and Marshall, because Mitchell, Paepcke said, was "a very modest and quiet appearing chap" who, besides being a good lawyer, "will not cause any excitement in the already turbulent waters."[67] That was an overstatement. Small and pale in appearance, retiring and meticulous to a fault, given to averted eyes, soft studied speech, and a nervous rubbing of his hands, Mitchell possessed discretion in his very bones, yet he had a lawyer's agility and toughness of mind. And because his bosses, who had handled Paepcke's legal matters for years, thought Paepcke's Aspen enterprise sheer "folly,"[68] Mitchell brought a certain skepticism toward his assignment with him when he arrived July 23.

Within a week Mitchell had closed eight house deals. By early August he had purchased another sixty-five lots from a tax sale, and in early September he added thirty more. By the summer's end, discreet Sam Mitchell was convinced: the Aspen adventure was not mere folly, and not even he could now hold the cloak of discretion over it. Paepcke's investments had grown too numerous, and word of them had even begun filtering out of Aspen, prompting an article in the *Denver Post* of August 26. The Aspen renaissance was becoming more than local news.

But this renaissance meant much more than real estate changing hands. True to his ambitions, Paepcke had also been preparing Aspen's cultural future. And since he had neither the resources nor the desire to own the entire town himself, he wanted it to be populated, as he so often said, by a "high type" of person, interested not in commercial exploitation but in tasteful restoration, gracious sociability, and cultural life. With this aim in mind, he asked Sam Mitchell to contemplate whom they should promote for local political offices[69]—a move wisely not carried through, since it would have alienated rather than persuaded townspeople. More to the point of his ambitions, Paepcke invited his friend Walter Gropius to look the town over with the idea of designing a master plan for its controlled restoration and growth.

Gropius had arrived at the Perry Park ranch in late August, after spending a few weeks at Black Mountain College with his old Bauhaus colleague Josef Albers to talk with Paepcke and Bayer about ways of ensuring the survival of Moholy-Nagy's Institute of Design. But Paepcke obviously had other intentions as well. When Bayer cabled from his Mexican vacation that illness would prevent him from joining them, the Paepckes packed Walter and Ise Gropius in their car and, followed by fellow vacationers Mr. and Mrs. William Nitze, set out for Aspen.

Once in Aspen, the Nitzes wandered the deserted streets, whose somnolence they found belied at night by brawls in the bar below their room at the Jerome. Gropius also encountered another side of Aspen. Studying the town's careful geometrical layout (the legacy of Henry Gillespie), its many vacant Victorian houses, its worn but sturdy public buildings, he then met, at Paepcke's instigation, with the citizens at a town meeting on August 29. Addressing the group, alongside Paepcke and Walter Frazier (now an Aspen homeowner himself), Gropius told his listeners that if Aspen desired to grow properly, a long-range plan would have to be devised, taking fully into account the town's traditions, social composition, institutions, geography, and climate, and the interests of its residents.

Gropius's attentiveness to local needs and traditions surprised many, including Paepcke, who had expected the pioneering modernist to "be horrified by the Victorian aspect of [Aspen's] architecture."[70] Was Gropius not the historic figure who had recoiled at the imitative, styleless jumble of nineteenth-century architecture and had made programmatic efforts through education, writing, and his own designs to create "a new . . . architecture corresponding to the technical civilization of the age we live in"?[71] But Gropius was not the doctrinaire modernist of his reputation, especially as that reputation had been fostered by his uninspired imitators. Architecture and design should always, he believed, serve *human* purposes, not the purposes of aesthetics alone. He had put himself in the vanguard of modern "functional" architecture in the first place from opposition to what he judged the dehumanizing ornamentation and aestheticism of much nineteenth-century design. And the modern style he devised, shorn of useless ornamental and historical accretions, was intended to be both humane and artful, reflecting the human spirit of our times, not merely echoing the spirit of former times. But Gropius had respect for the styles of former times, too. Thus Paepcke discovered he was "not annoyed, but rather pleasantly amused by the thought of reviving and recapturing the typical Victorian spirit"[72] in Aspen.

Gropius did add one qualification to his approval: restore the best of the old, but if you build, build modern. Otherwise, he said, Aspen would become an antiquarian museum of tacky, nonsensical, historical imitations, unworthy of the name good design or the high tastes of its sponsor. From this suggestion, welcomed by Paepcke and his wife, as well as by Frazier and later Bayer, came the best in the architectural appearance of modern Aspen: authentically restored Victorian buildings standing beside boldly modern ones. And only with the real estate boom of the 1960s and 1970s did ersatz Victorian houses begin cropping up together with the pseudo-Tyrolean lodges that threatened to make Aspen look like just another sham cute-mountain-village resort.

Gropius left Aspen the gift of his experience and good advice. He took something away with him, too. For the awesome natural landscape of Colorado had affected him to the heart. "I felt elated like a boy coming to your miraculous place," he wrote to Paepcke, "and could not get enough of roaming about." The experience had also touched his imagination. "I had a curious experience facing these great American scenes," he went on. "First it makes one very humble standing on Buckskin Pass and looking from the mighty horizon to the flowers at one's feet; then these beautiful sensations transform into an incessant stimulus of which I hope to make good use."[73]

What use he made of it one can only guess. Perhaps the traces in Gropius's later works of decorative elegance and freedom from the factory as an architectural model owe something to his experience in the Rockies. But one thing is quite likely: the trip helped assure his permanent expatriation—just as a similar trip was to do for Bayer. "I have always been very susceptible to the greatness of Nature and to climatic glories," Gropius wrote, but America, good as it had been to him, had not played to that susceptibility before. Now Gropius could warmly confess: "My love for this country has noticeably grown in Colorado." This love also got a boost from a chance observation of some children's artwork surprisingly displayed in a Denver store window. "These exhibits are right up my alley," he told Paepcke, "as they introduce the children into all sorts of knowledge by letting them create and re-create themselves. I wonder who is responsible for this very promising approach, in which Moholy would be greatly interested."[74] American ingenuousness and ingenuity held the same irresistible appeal for Gropius as for Moholy. Little wonder that the Bauhäusler and the American pragmatists had learned to work together.

Back in Aspen, the desire of Gropius and Paepcke to create, as Paepcke put it, "a master plan, not only as far as general layout is concerned but also as to architecture, social and communal matters, etc.,"[75] was gaining ground. Citizens' committees were formed to report on the town's character and needs. Paepcke began circulating an article from the *Reader's Digest* about Taxco, Mexico, which, under the inspiration of Bill Spratling, whom Paepcke knew and had visited, had become a jewel of coherent historical restoration and planning.[76] Gropius offered to serve as consultant for the overall city plan and zoning but suggested that the city hire one of his former students, Charles Wiley, then working with Eero Saarinen, to design and execute the job in Aspen.[77]

When Wiley's fee of $2,000 struck Paepcke as too high, hopes for a master plan collapsed into piecemeal, if sometimes effective, efforts at zoning and rehabilitation. Enlightened local residents were known to go out at night on vigilante raids to cut down offending billboards along the highway. And in 1947 the first zoning regulations went into effect, against some sharp civic opposition, limiting the size of the commercial part of town, prohibiting neon signs and billboards, and restricting building size and population. Although Aspen continued to keep its tradition of stiff zoning very much alive—with the ironic result that Paepcke's own Aspen Institute would eventually clash with the city over municipal resistance to its growth—Paepcke's dream of a controlled community akin to Williamsburg or Taxco was not to be realized.

Just as Paepcke's hopes for a master plan were fading, other events began edging Aspen out into the open, setting it on the path to becoming a major resort. In November 1945, *Business Week* hinted at things to come with a photograph of Aspen over the caption "Readying for Another Rush"[78] and a few words crediting Paepcke with instigating the rush by purchasing twenty houses. At about the same time, the Tenth Division veterans were making good their promises to return to Aspen at the end of the war. Friedl Pfeifer, wounded in the last days of the European campaign, was among the first to arrive. He quickly established a ski school with two of the others, Percy Rideout and John Litchfield, while another, Fritz Benedict (later to be a prominent Aspen architect and the husband of Joella Bayer's sister), bought six hundred acres of farmland for $12,000, across the valley from the ski slopes on Red Mountain, where for a time he ran a dude ranch.

Meanwhile, Paepcke had become a partner of Tom Sardy in the Aspen Lumber and Supply Company and was negotiating with Pfeifer to get a ski lift built. And he continued promoting Aspen among, as he liked to say, "a whole lot of very carefully selected individuals,"[79] holding off general promotion in national magazines like *Reader's Digest* and *Harper's Bazaar,* now seeking articles, until the ski lifts were ready. Among those "carefully selected individuals" was Aspen's most celebrated native, Harold W. Ross, the rustic and rough founder and infamously hairsplitting editor of the nation's archsophisticated magazine, the *New Yorker.* Born in Aspen's heyday, 1892, the son of a building and mining technician, Ross had moved to Salt Lake City with his parents after the home town economy collapsed. In World War I his editorial genius and passions had produced the military newspaper *Stars and Stripes,* followed in 1925 by the *New Yorker.* Approached by Paepcke's budding public relations assistant, Albin Dearing, Ross was eager to meet Paepcke in order to learn whether the developer had bought the house of Ross's birth.[80] Paepcke hadn't, but, pleased at the news of Ross's curiosity, he pledged to meet the editor on his next trip to New York.

Before Paepcke could make that trip, Aspen welcomed, at the end of 1945, another carefully selected individual, one who was to become far more strongly identified with Aspen's future than Harold Ross had ever been with its past. This was Herbert Bayer.

After illness had forced Bayer to cancel his August visit to Colorado, the enthusiastic reports of the Gropiuses, followed by Paepcke's insistent encouragement, finally brought him and his wife to Aspen just after Christmas. So determined had Paepcke been to get Bayer there that he had arranged for the travel expenses to be paid by the newly formed Aspen Company (which managed Paepcke's real estate) in exchange for design advice. Paepcke had also held out to Bayer the promise of a retainer from both the Aspen Company and the Container Corporation should he decide to settle in Aspen and serve as a consultant. Bayer was simply too good a prospect for Aspen to lose, and Paepcke was not about to lose him for lack of trying.

Enticed by Paepcke, prodded by his wife, Joella, and seduced by the opportunity to ski, Bayer could not have resisted. Unfortunately, the vacation began on a somber note. The Bayers and the Paepckes were to have enjoyed the company of the Moholy-Nagys in Aspen as well. But in late November Sibyl had wired her sad regrets: they could not come: "MOHOLY HAD ATTACK OF LEUKEMIA."[81] One year later, almost to the day, Moholy died.

Bayer was not so well himself when he reached Aspen. Still suffering the lingering effects of his Mexican illness and touched more markedly than usual by weltschmerz, he fell under Paepcke's skeptical eye as a hypochondriac. Paepcke took the morose Austrian off to a local pub, where he plied him with steak and conversation. When Bayer returned to the house, he seemed slightly energized; and within days his spirits had lifted. The alpine air and setting, aided by the Paepcke charm, had won his heart. He decided to make Aspen his home.

Bayer wanted to buy one of Paepcke's houses on the ridge above lovely little Hallam Lake at the northwest corner of town, but Paepcke refused, pleading the need for such well-selected and thoroughly converted people as the Bayers to purchase unredeemed properties. So Bayer bought a modest Victorian residence a few yards from the Lamb House. This was home for the Bayers until 1955, when they moved to a new house of Bayer's own design in the Bauhaus style high on barren Red Mountain overlooking the town.

To insure Bayer's future in Aspen, Paepcke arranged for the designer to receive $6,000 a year in consulting fees from the Container Corporation and $2,500 from the Aspen Company for designing publicity pamphlets and assisting with renovations. "For the remaining half of Herbert's time," Paepcke remarked in a mock sales pitch to the new Aspenite couple, the artist would be able to "paint, write books, ski, fully regain his health, and all the rest of it, which I estimate to be worth roughly a million dollars a year."[82] And lest Bayer think that design work in Aspen would be scarce, Paepcke kept up a steady flow of news about his own purchases and plans. First, he disclosed his hopes for a "new hotel on the mountainside."[83] Next, he announced the purchase of two more block-long, downtown storefront and office buildings (known as the Brown Block and the Aspen Block); and then he reported taking a lease on the Hotel Jerome, adding that now "at least three of the major buildings can be painted in cheerful, eye-pleasing colors and alleviate to that extent at least the monotonous reddish brown."[84] Yes, Bayer would have more than enough challenging design work to do. "The old town is buzzing," Paepcke assured him, "and there seems to be enough momentum so that it is beginning to carry me along with it, sometimes a little sooner than fits entirely with my own time schedule."[85]

In early April 1946, the Bayers took up temporary residence in the Lamb House while awaiting renovation of their own house and assisting in the alterations of other buildings, particularly the Jerome, on which Elizabeth Paepcke, now reconciled to her unfolding Aspen life and fast learning to enjoy it, and Walter Frazier had already begun work. Paepcke had taken over the dreary and decaying hotel in mid-March under the aegis of the Aspen Company on a twenty-five-year lease at $5,000 a year and had immediately closed the doors to begin recreating the Jerome's former glory as a first-rate hotel, attractive to the "high type" of person he wanted to draw to Aspen. By the time the hotel reopened in June, $100,000 had been spent renovating everything from the lobby, the elevator, and the guest rooms to the bar, the dining room, and the kitchen—soon to boast two chefs imported from Switzerland and a European menu that struck locals as pretentious, with its foreign names for dishes like trout. Paepcke was now a hotelier in earnest. But profits would not come to the Jerome for its stylishness alone. The hotel needed paying guests. And they would come only for satisfying recreation, which in this remote mountain setting most likely meant skiing.

Having learned from Friedl Pfeifer that the cost of substantially improving the ski facilities would be great, Paepcke sought help from his own brother-in-law, Paul H. Nitze, an avid skier, former investment banker, future statesman, and a man of means by marriage. "Let's divide Aspen three ways," Paepcke said lightheartedly: "Pussy will be in charge of taste and culture; I'll be in charge of business and mind; and you be in charge of the body, i.e. skiing."[86] Nitze had already come within a hair of investing in Aspen skiing during the days of Billy Fiske, and now he snapped at this second chance. Of the total $300,000 Paepcke told him would be required to capitalize the "Aspen Skiing Corporation" and run a lift up the face of Aspen Mountain, Nitze put up $75,000, making him the major investor—at more than double Paepcke's outlay—which he was to remain until Twentieth Century Fox bought the Aspen Skiing Corporation in 1978. But Paepcke, no skier himself, cautioned Nitze that the purpose of the Skiing Corporation, like the entire Aspen development, was to create not so much a financially enriching resort as a refined and somewhat exclusive vacation community that could nonetheless turn a profit. "We don't want to make Aspen a mass skiing center," he explained in soliciting Nitze's resources, "but rather have it fairly selective and just large enough to make it entirely profitable, but not overrun, especially on weekends."[87] With a projected gross income of $75,000 to $100,000 against operating expenses of $50,000 per season, the Aspen Skiing Corporation was not likely to make anyone rich soon—and it didn't.

With the Skiing Corporation organized (in February 1946 under a board of trustees consisting of Paepcke, Nitze, Pfeifer, George Berger, and Robert Collins) and new investors joining almost every day, with springtime construction underway on what would become the world's longest ski lift, and with the Hotel Jerome shaping up for the opening in June 1946, Paepcke turned his energies to other parts of the Aspen renaissance. First, he made use of a business trip to the east to establish ties with Harold Ross. "I am the man who has gotten perniciously active about Aspen,"[88] he wired Ross in setting up a meeting. And over lunch at New York's posh "21" Club, the two talked about Paepcke's economic and cultural ambitions for the Crystal City of Ross's birth. "I'll do anything I can to promote the old town,"[89] Ross assured Paepcke. But while Ross could refer Paepcke to some people interested in building a restaurant and casino in Aspen, Ross balked at putting up money himself: "As for me," he said, "I have no money at the present time, and haven't had for a long time," adding, "I'm not interested in Aspen from a profit motive; I've always thought I'd do right by the home town if I got a chance."[90] Although Paepcke failed to elicit an investment from Ross, he and the colorful editor entered into a friendship that continued over the remaining years of Ross's life, bringing Ross back to Aspen more than once for recreation and to enjoy the hospitality of Aspen's new leading citizen.

Meanwhile, Paepcke pursued his development projects unabated. And in doing so he provoked increasing local opposition. A seemingly disinterested and generous offer to supply paint free of charge to anyone who would paint his house during the annual town cleanup in 1946 turned into a public relations gaffe when Paepcke added the proviso that Herbert Bayer must choose the color values. Not a single taker came forward, and the patronizing gesture had ill reverberations for years.

Paepcke also aroused suspicions and resentment when he took a twenty-five-year lease, starting June 1, 1946 (at one dollar a year for the first six years), on the burned-out opera house, pledging himself to spend $20,000 to restore it. Some citizens saw this as a sure sign that Paepcke was turning their town into his own private kingdom. In a stinging rejoinder to his critics, Paepcke threatened to take his investments elsewhere if Aspen didn't want them and to leave the town to those "who would have in mind turning the whole thing into a mammoth amusement park, full of bars, liquor stores, honky-tonks, tourist cabins, motels, shooting galleries, etc., in which, as you know, I have not the least interest but which might actually pay promoters well in hard cash while ruining, to my way of thinking, the entire charm of a potentially most beautiful community."[91]

The argument worked, as it was to work many times again. But a year later it almost backfired. Failing to secure a top-flight restaurateur from the outside for Aspen, Paepcke took it upon himself to create a social gathering and dining place. He bought and remodeled two large houses in the hills southwest of Aspen to serve as a private country club, equipped with a fine restaurant, bar, tennis courts, and a clear lake for swimming. It also occurred to Paepcke that the club, called the Four Seasons, would benefit from exclusive fishing rights for members in nearby Castle Creek, and he petitioned the State Fish and Game Commission to obtain the rights. Now, his critics said, who could doubt Paepcke was building a kingdom in blatant disregard of local interests? Hostility against him erupted not only in pressures to have his request denied by the state—and it was—but also in resistance of the local authorities to issue a liquor license for the club. If they persisted and the club was refused a license, Paepcke threatened again, he would pack up his investments and go. This time more than one Aspenite was heard to grumble: "If that's all it takes to make him leave, let's do it."[92] Paepcke finally got his license, but the experience chastened him and thereafter he tried to avoid open confrontations with the town and to restrain his impatient entrepreneurial will. As for the Four Seasons, it proved an elegant failure, constantly in the red and passing through numerous changes of management while Paepcke continually tried to sell it. Eventually he closed it down—and later it became the home of the Music Associates of Aspen.

While Paepcke's grand designs and peremptory methods were rousing occasional opposition against him in Aspen, they were winning recognition for the town on the outside. By the autumn of 1946, enough "high-minded" and influential people knew of Aspen through Paepcke's diligent proselytizing and the hosting there of friends—which had netted another distinguished homeowner, Mrs. John P. Marquand—to give it national recognition as a fashionable vacation spot. *Life* magazine, *Vogue*, *Town and Country*, *Reader's Digest*, and *Harper's Bazaar* all wanted stories—which Paepcke still managed to delay until the formal opening of the ski lift the following January. The department store Carson Pirie Scott in Chicago did a fall fashion show with Aspen as its setting; and Marshall Field showed an Aspen ski film that winter.[93] Then Paepcke readied for the grand opening by inviting the governor-elect of Colorado, Lee Knous, to cut the ribbon and Lowell Thomas to broadcast the proceedings on his national radio show.

As 1946 ended, Paepcke could count over $200,000 spent building up Aspen as a home for a select and cultivated populace; and he had yet to see any net economic gain from his investments (notwithstanding profits from the Aspen Lumber and Supply Company, as would be expected with all the construction going on). But now the Aspen renaissance would be caught in a paradox. The beginnings of a refined culture were about to be surpassed by the ascendancy of popular recreation. For with the grand opening in January, Aspen would open its doors forever to anyone with money. And from then on the ski industry and the economic development of Aspen would grow ever farther out of Paepcke's control and away from his cultural aspirations. The time would come when he would regret his failure at least to have harnessed his unprofitable cultural programs to the profits of recreation. But by then it would be too late. Aspen would go its own schizophrenic way.

Fourteen thousand feet long, with a vertical rise of over three thousand feet, the world's longest ski lift—albeit with few competitors in those early days of skiing—was dedicated in Aspen on January 11, 1947. A special train had brought visitors and journalists in from Denver, to be greeted by a crowd bearing torches and escorted through the newly fallen snow by sleigh to the Jerome for the opening reception and dinner. On the morning of the eleventh, two thousand people heard the governor-elect, the mayor, and Paepcke praise Aspen and Colorado as the new winter sports capital of the country—despite the unusually mild winter that had so far dumped only a foot of snow in the town and had threatened to spoil the opening. Then the spectators watched races, frolicked on the slopes, and rode the giant chair lift that made the spectacular distant runs of Aspen Mountain accessible and promised to become a boon to summer tourism as well.

Amid all the hoopla, the proud officials of the Skiing Corporation had one fear: would anyone notice that the skiing on those high runs could be handled only by experienced skiers? Albin Dearing's publicity for the opening had studiously ignored this fact, and no film of skiers at the festivities was made for fear of scaring off potential customers with shots only of experts. Aspen was still no place for beginners; and in those days, most skiers were beginners still.

Thus partly from its lack of adequate facilities for the inexperienced, and despite the fanfare of the opening, Aspen did not become a winter sports capital all at once. In its first two years, the corporation did far worse than projected, losing $15,000 a year, and it showed a respectable profit only in 1951, after completion of several new trails and a couple of beginners' hills (the first, called Little Nell, cut at the base of Aspen Mountain in the summer of 1947) and following the national and international publicity occasioned by the Goethe Festival in 1949 and the world championship races sponsored by the Fédération Internationale de Ski in Aspen in 1950.

While skiing grew relatively slowly, the public opening of Aspen put the once Crystal City on the road to economic revival and to its reputation as a place where fashionable people would congregate for diversion. A story in *Time* magazine emphasizing Aspen's stylish, cosmopolitan ambiance even prompted mail hostile to Paepcke for importing foreign chefs and trying to create a European resort on American soil.[94] Another journalistic tribute to Aspen incensed Paepcke himself. A film prepared by the "March of Time" portrayed, he thought, too much of the revelry surrounding the three-day grand opening celebration and elicited from him a communication to the Skiing Corporation stockholders apologizing for the vulgarly recreational image in the film of what was a quaint and beautiful mountain town.[95] Reviving the economic and cultural life of Aspen had thrown Paepcke up against a stubborn problem: recreation and culture do not mix smoothly.

To counteract the possible ill effects of the public opening, Paepcke redoubled his efforts to insure Aspen's cultural vitality. He heated up his search for "select people" to buy real estate or at least to vacation in Aspen. Lowell Thomas, unavailable to broadcast the events of the opening, came out with Harold Ross later that winter in the first of a succession of visits that made Aspen a familiar name to his listeners. A few friends of the Paepckes from

Chicago bought houses that same year. And Paepcke marshaled his energies and charm to try winning over a distant acquaintance, Noel Coward. Offering the famed playwright, actor, and pundit a cottage in Aspen practically free of charge during the peak winter season, and lauding the beauties and pleasures of the setting, Paepcke enclosed a publicity pamphlet and concluded on a note of mock warning and encouragement:

> I warn you again that Aspenites are very wholesome and God-fearing folk so probably would not know you, and as a result you would not be lionized, and God only knows what you would do for a salon, sycophants, and admirers in general. Of course the result of all this, novel as it might be, would in the end do you and your work an awful lot of good; instead of sophisticated drawing-room comedy, you would probably find yourself writing an appendix to the Bible.[96]

But Paepcke had misjudged his man. Coward had no use for winter sports and declined the invitation with his typical panache and untypical inelegance: "Thank you for your fascinating little letter and the brochure with all those people on skis. Me personally am not so hot on skis on account of them going up my nose rather." But, he concluded, "snow or no snow, if I can manage to get to Aspen I will."[97]

Coward never made it, but Paepcke had better luck with another show business figure on whom he set his sights about this same time. While surveying the facilities of Sun Valley in 1947 for clues to the Idaho resort's popularity, he met movie actor Gary Cooper, a skillful skier and then near the height of his popularity. When Paepcke broadly hinted that Cooper might enjoy Aspen's remarkable scenery and challenging slopes even more than Sun Valley, Cooper took Paepcke up, and in 1948 not only skied in Aspen but bought thirty acres of land and started building a house there. Cooper's presence with his wife, Rocky, and daughter, frequently pictured together in national magazines skiing or fishing or strolling the rustic streets and exploring the abandoned houses, furthered Aspen's image as a place of stylish and unworn diversions. And his modest manner and unaffected warmth won Cooper many friends in Aspen—"he was truly a saint," Elizabeth Paepcke said of him.[98] He vacationed there regularly for several years until his marriage broke up and he sold the house.

Paepcke envisioned still more for Aspen than a vacation retreat or home for "select people." He wanted to make Aspen something of a *Kulturstaat*, a civilized state organized around culture and thriving on it. As early as 1946, he had been unequivocal on this point to publisher James Laughlin, whom he had recently met when Laughlin was in Aspen to try the skiing. "The phase of Aspen development that interests me most," he said, is "the cultural, educational and architectural."[99] And shortly after this he fantasized to Gene Lilly: "I can't wait to see the time when we may have a Theatre Inc., Glyndebourne Opera, Schnabel, and Joseph Szigeti, and other internationally famous people at Aspen."[100]

To breathe life into this "phase" of his ambitions, Paepcke discussed with Laughlin setting up a center for young writers. Then, drawing upon his most abiding love, he started working up a summer music festival. Replying to a request from the musically ambitious neighboring town of Red Rocks for assistance in making that a music center, he politely refused, confessing his own hopes of turning Aspen into the "American Salzburg, Glyndebourne, etc.,"[101] and remarking his attempts already to get Wilhelm Furtwängler as music director. When Furtwängler declined, Paepcke brought John Christie, director of England's Glyndebourne Festival, to Aspen with the thought of persuading him to schedule performances by the Glyndebourne Orchestra there; but nothing came of this either.

So, for the time being, Paepcke had to settle for lesser attractions, like Burl Ives, who in May 1947 gave the first performance heard in almost four decades at the cleaned but still unrenovated opera house. "We sat on cushions, blankets, and benches," Paepcke reported to Lowell Thomas, "and the audience was not too depressed by the burnt out embers, or even a pigeon flying around which we had been unable to shoo out."[102] It was hardly high culture, but, together with a similar program a few nights later by the minstrel team of Richard and Mel Dyer-Bennet, it pleased Paepcke enough to have him put the Dyer-Bennets on salary to run a minstrel school, which they did until the early fifties. Meanwhile, the opera house provided a stage and partial shelter for concerts by highbrow performers, too, such as the harpsichordist Dorothy Lane, the violinist Oscar Chausow, and flautist David von Vactor. Yet the rebirth of the opera house as the true home of Aspen culture would come only after renovations in 1950 that gave it a new roof and, under the guiding hand of Herbert Bayer, a clean, bright, colorful, modern interior. There, over the years, Aspenites and visitors were to enjoy many kinds of entertainments, musical and otherwise—as well as the early lectures and debates of the Aspen Institute.

Culture was returning to the Crystal City at considerable cost to the chief patron. To be sure, there was money to be made in the Aspen renaissance, but not yet, and not ever through the kinds of cultural pursuits Paepcke hoped would flourish. In an early concession to this fact, in the spring of 1947, Paepcke sold his estate at Sandwich, Illinois. His every spare dollar and minute now flowing into Aspen, the Sandwich house had become dispensable.

At the same time, to promote what he judged the best in Aspen, Paepcke had the Aspen Company establish a publicity office and begin issuing a glossy, illustrated monthly newsletter, the *Aspen Leaf*—designed by Bayer—

describing cultural events, social and economic developments, and important visitors in and around town. If Aspen was to be a community of refinement and style, so Paepcke thought, it had better become conscious of itself
and project the appropriate image. And since refinement and style defined
an image Paepcke knew how to project very well, how could Aspen fail?

Once properly publicized, the Aspen style of life, uniting recreation,
social prestige, and culture, was bound to attract adherents—desirable and
undesirable—in the postwar decades. And as a winter resort, of course, Aspen couldn't miss, even without Paepcke. But for all of Paepcke's imagination and energies, Aspen could never have gained eminence as a cultural
center without the historic event that Paepcke and Robert M. Hutchins
began putting together over lunch on February 21, 1947, just six weeks after
the Aspen grand opening.

5

selling

the postwar goethe

The idea of celebrating Goethe in Aspen came to Paepcke from Hutchins like the answer to a prayer. Aspen's cultural life would get a shot in the arm from the gathering of intellectuals while the stagnant summer economy would pick up some extra dollars. And, besides its direct benefits to the town, the Goethe Festival appealed to Paepcke because it would honor the poet-philosopher whose verses extolling will and energy and individuality had echoed in his boyhood home and had given him, like so many Germans before him, a kind of spiritual nourishment unknown to those bred on English and American literature. Now that nourishment, prepared anew in the message of cultural unity, would be dispensed to the postwar world from Aspen, Paepcke's own nascent Kulturstaat, the heir of Goethe's Weimar.

"According to Bob and the other educators," Paepcke told James Laughlin, in tones mingling irony and earnestness, "Goethe was specifically an international figure who rose above the nationalistic tendencies which Mr. Hitler had promulgated." Commemorating the great internationalist would therefore help "reestablish at least cultural relations between the Teutonic peoples and the rest of the world."[1] And since the sponsors wanted a location befitting their noble purpose, they had taken to Hutchins's suggestion of Aspen. "Aspen seems to appeal to them," Paepcke went on,

> even though I described faithfully the tumble-down condition of some of the houses, the charred interior of the Opera House, the somewhat out of the way location, and the relatively small surrounding population. However, it seems that they want, and I think correctly so, a location which people would have to go some little trouble to get to and which would be in a scenically and climatically attractive spot, rather than to have it outside of New York, Chicago, or what not, where people who are about to see "Abie's Irish Rose" and couldn't find seats could decide to go to the Goethe Festival instead.[2]

Aspen was far from the distractions of Broadway and State Street, to be sure. More than this, it suited the solemnity of the event. Carl F. Schreiber, curator of Yale's famed Goethe collection and one of the originators of the festival, told Paepcke he saw a "glorious symbol" in taking "Goethe up into the mountains on the two-hundredth anniversary of his birth," just as "Moses brought the Tables of the Law down from the mountains so many years ago."[3] Schreiber let symbolism get the better of him here, but he accurately reflected the mood of heady expectations that grew as preparations proceeded.

The program as first outlined, however, hardly conjured up images of Moses and the burning bush. It called for a few "European professors" to "give some lectures," followed by performances of "one or two of Goethe's shorter plays, some Mozart or other small opera," and accompanied perhaps by "some little exhibit of Goethe's works."[4] Little resemblance to the Moses saga here, nor much prospect of cultural reform. The Goethe Festival still had a long way to go.

It started on this way in earnest during the spring of 1947 when Paepcke and Arnold Bergstraesser took the reins while Hutchins was in Europe— Giuseppe Borgese having stepped to the sidelines with his work on *Common Cause* and readying his repatriation to Italy, and Mortimer Adler, unable to read German and in any case never able "to figure out why all the fuss about Goethe,"[5] was steeped in work on the *Syntopicon*. Although Bergstraesser lacked the political passions of Borgese and had been on the faculty of the University of Chicago only since 1944, he possessed reasons for embracing the festival similar to those of his idealistic colleagues. A native German, Bergstraesser had fled his homeland during the thirties and now believed, along with many other Germans, that their aberrant and fallen land could be redeemed only by reaffirming its great humanistic tradition or, as some German intellectuals put it, by a *Heimkehr des Geistes*, a return home of the spirit, and especially through the study of Goethe and his age.[6] Bergstraesser had already joined with Borgese in aiding this return and reviving German-

American friendship by participating in an exchange of lectures between the University of Chicago and the Goethe University in Frankfurt. A long-time devotee of Goethe's humanism, he was now completing a book, *Goethe's Image of Man and Society*, in hopes that those ideas, marked for him by tough-minded realism and humanistic idealism, would serve as an antidote to post-war insecurity and disillusionment everywhere. Thus, like Hutchins and Borgese, Bergstraesser saw in Goethe a figure who might lead modern culture out of tragedy and despair and into hope and redemption.

Bergstraesser had already laid some of the groundwork for a new translation of Goethe's selected works, and now he recommended to Paepcke that they begin thinking about the festival program and establishing a fund-raising committee. Leaving the program to Bergstraesser, Paepcke set to work on organization and publicity. He spread the word among his many professional and cultural associates that something big was in the offing. And he requested William Benton, then serving as assistant secretary of state in Washington, D.C., to look into the "international implications and problems"[7] posed by the festival. He received the dry response that Benton saw no connection between diplomacy and the Goethe celebration but would inquire further to find out "if any one in the State Department knows more than I do, which you must admit is unlikely."[8] Paepcke also arranged to meet with Benton and Hutchins in New York upon Hutchins's return from England to discuss the political ramifications of the festival and a public relations strategy. In agreeing to the meeting, Hutchins wryly conceded Paepcke's assumption of command: "I feel sure that in my absence you have been able to make great progress and that in the years to come people will not be able to remember whether it was Goethe or Paepcke who was being celebrated."[9] Whoever the chief beneficiary, it was decided to create a nonprofit foundation to finance the festival, and Hutchins then recruited the most prominent public figure available, former president Herbert Hoover, to serve as the foundation's honorary chairman.

The Goethe Bicentennial Foundation became a legal entity at the beginning of October 1947 with its incorporation for five years as a nonprofit organization under the three-man directorate of Hutchins, Paepcke, and Wilbur Munnecke. Certain to be assured of tax exemption for contributions, the festival could now be launched publicly.

A month later, after preliminary publicity luncheons in Chicago and Philadelphia and after Hutchins had made his first trip to Aspen, the festival sponsors increased the directorate to twelve, including Marshall Field, Alfred P. Sloan, Jr., and Hutchins's long-time friend Thornton Wilder. Although the friendship of Hutchins and Wilder had cooled in recent years, mainly because of strong differences over wartime politics—notably Hutchins's isolationism—and would never again be what it had been, the two always remained friends, and near the end of his life Wilder would honor this friendship by dedicating his last book, the autobiographical *Theophilus North* (1973), to Hutchins. Now, at the beginning of 1948, Wilder accepted Hutchins's invitation to join the Goethe Bicentennial Foundation in a friendly cable: "GLAD TO ENDORSE YOU OR GOETHE AT ANY TIME."[10] As the principal literary man among the foundation's directors, Wilder also agreed to manage the presentation of drama.

Other major tasks fell to Paepcke and Bergstraesser. Paepcke, known for his love and knowledge of music, accepted responsibility for the music program, as well as for accommodations and other practical arrangements in Aspen, in addition to his work as publicist and fund-raiser. Bergstraesser continued his work on the Goethe edition and the academic program, shortly producing some definite requests: the projected ten volumes of Goethe's writings would, he said, cost $50,000 to $60,000; and the academic program needed a budget of $40,000 to pay twenty European scholars and writers at an average rate of $2,000. Such generous fees, he remarked, would make it possible to obtain distinguished speakers like those on his "tentative list," including Albert Schweitzer, Ortega y Gasset, Karl Jaspers, Werner Heisenberg, Jules Romains, Carl Jung, T. S. Eliot, and Arnold Toynbee, and insure the festival's eminence.[11] Bergstraesser's proposals sounded good, but realizing them wouldn't be easy, since financing the festival posed problems.

Those problems now played in discordant counterpoint to the foundation's idealistic aspirations. And with Hutchins occupied in other pursuits—such as delivering addresses on politics and humanism before the German National Assembly and the Rector's Conference in Frankfurt in the spring of 1948—the principal burden of hustling up funds rested with Paepcke, and he found it a burden not easily borne. He told Carl Schreiber in March that the total cost of the festival looked as if it might exceed $300,000, and he doubted such a sum could be raised because "so far, Bob Hutchins and I have not found it all that easy to persuade people to convert their enthusiasm [for the festival] into financial support. Unless this condition changes," he lamented, "we may have to modify our plans very substantially."[12]

It only slowly dawned on the festival organizers that theirs was not an ordinary fund-raising task. They had neither a permanent institution to support nor an immediate crisis to subdue. To obtain finances for a memorial celebration in a remote mountain town and budding ski resort honoring a foreign poet dead over a hundred years and little read in this country, surely no casual solicitation would do. The Goethe Festival would have to be sold on a mass scale in a concerted publicity campaign: cultural reform could not go forward without the engine of commerce behind it.

But advances made to public relations and fund-raising organizations only deepened the directors' discouragement. Two such organizations doubted that the money necessary to finance the campaign—estimated at about $200,000—could be raised, at least not without great expense.

Then an assistant of Hutchins at the university, Sims Carter, made a decisive contact. He presented the festival idea to Mitchell McKeown of the Mitchell McKeown Organization in Chicago and heard what he and the foundation directors wanted to hear: publicizing and raising money for the Goethe Bicentennial could be done, but it could not follow the traditional practice of simply disseminating information and touching philanthropic organizations for support. It would require selling the American public on the idea of the festival and thus sweeping potential givers up in a movement of cultural conscience.

At once a creature and a master of public relations—and a self-confessed "fan" of Hutchins, to whom he often referred, in the show business parlance that Hutchins readily evoked, as a "star"—McKeown knew just what was needed: people "must be made acutely aware of the contributions Goethe has made to the culture of the modern world"[13] before they will underwrite a festival honoring him. In short, Goethe must be given the proper *image* before he will sell.

"The telling of the Goethe story," McKeown went on, will require "a full-scale public relations activity, over and above and entirely apart from the specialized technique of practical fund raising," because the "machinery of giving" only goes to work after the incentive for giving has been aroused. Thus Goethe's ideas and the cultural aims of the festival must not be left to the festival itself but must be made popular fare for a mid-twentieth-century audience in advance. As McKeown put it in his proposal:

Goethe must be familiarized and humanized to the public. His life and experiences need to be retold in entertaining, news-worthy style. The philosophy of life underlying "Faust," for example, must be interpreted and shown to be a contribution to the world that no other modern poet has ever rivaled. That Goethe's was a universal mind, and his achievements were not limited to his literature, similarly must be related to the public. Goethe's work as a statesman, and practical political economist, his modern outlook on the changing social conditions of his age, and his sympathetic understanding of the dynamics of modern industry, have to be told in highly meaningful form, to a mass audience in this country.

Nor did McKeown conceive of this "public relations task" as merely a means of getting the festival's fund-raising off the ground; in "scope and importance" the publicizing of Goethe would be "an integrated part of this entire Bicentennial program."[14] If McKeown had his way, commerce and culture would join hands in a lively alliance of education and hype, and the Goethe Bicentennial, born in quiet academic chambers and nourished on

Chicago's idealism, would become not only a cultural event but a triumph of mass culture.

Yet appropriate as was McKeown's proposal, the directors hesitated to commit themselves to the nearly $20,000 asked by McKeown for a year's work, at least not until the foundation had "consolidated" its own organization and widened the "geographic distribution" of the directorate.[15] The directors decided to delay a national campaign for the time being and limit publicity for the summer of 1948 to Colorado, where it could be readily handled by the Denver firm of Galen F. Broyles.

Summer then brought a lull in activity while the leading organizers occupied themselves with other interests. Hutchins at last extricated himself from a marriage that had been deteriorating for years and moved out of his home. After his official visit to Germany, he stayed at the University Club in Chicago, and then welcomed an invitation from Paepcke to spend the rest of the summer with him on Lake Shore Drive while Paepcke's wife and children vacationed in the West.

As it happened, Hutchins found himself living alone in the Paepcke residence. "Hardly had he accepted the invitation," Paepcke reported to his friend Gene Lilly, "when I had to tell him that the day before he moves in I am going to go away for five or six weeks." Paepcke had decided to take a trip with his wife to Hawaii, with a stop in Colorado and a visit with the Lillys on the way back. "You see," he said in a characteristic jest at Hutchins's expense, "this is just the reverse of the way we treat the Lillys, where we fly back from 3,000 miles away just in the hope that they may be on the ranch, while with Bob Hutchins we immediately put 3,000 miles between us! I've always preferred the physical, earthy type to the intellectual."[16]

While Hutchins remained in Chicago on leave from the university and working in the offices of the Encyclopaedia Britannica, of which he was now formal editor, in addition to holding the same post for the Great Books (and where he met the woman who became his second wife the next year), Paepcke put the cares of the Goethe Bicentennial behind him and took to Hawaii's beaches for a bask in the sun—his one accepted form of indolence. But these Hawaiian days turned out to have an unpredictably important effect on the Goethe Festival. For one afternoon while Paepcke reposed in the sun, his wife returned from a shopping venture with a book of essays on Goethe by an author known to her mainly for his study of Johann Sebastian Bach. "This looks like the kind of thing you've been talking about for the festival,"[17] she said, handing her husband Albert Schweitzer's *Two Studies of Goethe*. Paepcke thumbed through the book, glancing at Schweitzer's Goethe Prize address of 1928 and another given in Frankfurt at the centennial of Goethe's death in 1932, both registering Schweitzer's deep affinity for Goethe's humanism and philosophy of nature, the second closing with lines that caught Paepcke's eye:

> Before two decades have come to an end, Frankfurt will celebrate the two hundredth anniversary of the birthday of its greatest son. May it be that he who gives the memorial address at that new festival be able to state . . . that a race with a true feeling for reality . . . is beginning to achieve a mastery over material and social needs, united in its resolve to remain loyal to the one true ideal of human personality.[18]

Yes, Paepcke contemplated, this is the kind of thinker we want. He scrawled a note reminding himself to ask Hutchins what he knew of Albert Schweitzer. The Goethe Bicentennial, although to be celebrated most resoundingly far from Schweitzer's war-ravaged Frankfurt, had found its living symbol—but no one, not even Paepcke, sensed this at the time.

When work on the festival resumed in the fall, Paepcke disclosed his Hawaiian discovery to Hutchins. The chancellor's response took him aback: Hutchins sighed and said he had tried for years to get Albert Schweitzer to visit the University of Chicago. The Good Doctor would not leave Africa, except for occasional lectures in Europe. Not even the American Schweitzer Foundation, which raised money for Schweitzer's hospital in Lambaréné, French Equatorial Africa, had been able to persuade him to come across the Atlantic. Paepcke dropped the subject for the moment, but he was not one to abandon a challenge, and he let the idea simmer.

While it did, Paepcke and Hutchins disseminated word of their cherished forthcoming events and cajoled the wealthy and influential for support. They even made sport of the task, quickened by friendly competition and the teasing that typified their relationship. "THROUGH PINKERTON AGENCY FINALLY FOUND YOUR WHEREABOUTS," Paepcke wired Hutchins in October at New York's Ritz-Carlton Hotel. "UNDERSTAND THERE IS TO BE AN EISENHOWER DINNER TONIGHT WHICH YOU ARE ATTENDING. PLEASE DO YOUR STUFF."[19] Hutchins spiced his cable reply with the familiar sarcasm. Disclaiming knowledge of such a dinner, he rapped his friend's skullduggery in tracking him down: "PLEASE DO NOT WIRE ME TO THIS HOTEL. MY SOCIAL STANDING HERE IS ONLY A LITTLE LOWER THAN THAT OF A FRENCH COUNT. I WOULD NOT WANT THEM TO KNOW I KNOW YOU."[20]

But Paepcke's wire gave Hutchins more than an opportunity for a witty rejoinder. It had also brought news of the first large contribution to the foundation—a check for $10,000 from philanthropist D. S. Gottesman. It was the largest single donation the festival would receive. And in a letter of gratitude, Paepcke thanked the donor profusely, underscoring their common cause under that well-worn Hutchins-Adler shibboleth: the humanities versus "the scientific and material aspects of our present day civilization."[21]

The Gottesman gift was a boon, but it was not enough. And by mid-October the Goethe Foundation directors, in Paepcke's words, "finally came to the conclusion that we had better engage the Mitchell McKeown Organization to help us."[22] The task of organizing and administering an integrated national fund-raising and publicity campaign was too great for the foundation to handle alone. Sims Carter gave a sigh of relief and delight at this "gratifying news,"[23] and he quickly turned responsibilities for publicity over to the professionals. The selling of the postwar Goethe was on.

———

A "Program of Public Relations Action for the Goethe Bicentennial Foundation" expanded upon McKeown's earlier statement with specific strategy and tactics. To raise the $275,000 he estimated the festival would require, McKeown recommended a national campaign directed especially toward people and organizations attuned to humanistic ideas and sensitive to the festival's purposes. The campaign would extend from the foundation headquarters to regional organizations and on down to local soliciting committees in cities carefully chosen by "culture pattern, ethnological composition, and geographic location." Volunteers, he said, should be selected for three qualifications: "devotion to the spirit of Goethe," leadership in their respective fields, and the sine qua non, "personal sales ability to convey the story of the Foundation to potential donors, excite their interest, and stimulate the final action of giving."

But solicitations would not depend on the volunteers' abilities alone. Each volunteer would go equipped with a "Goethe Bicentennial sales package," including "a tastefully written and designed brochure" stating Goethe's historic importance and contemporary relevance, the purposes of the observance and who sponsors it, why it needs funds, and how to contribute. And believing the campaign could only succeed by awakening "potential donors' appreciation of the contributions Goethe has made to the thought and philosophical standards of the Western World" and his "anticipation, by almost a century and a half, of the problems of our time," McKeown insisted that "the Goethe story" be "carefully researched and processed into editorial form suitable for the appropriate media of mass communication." Thereafter the "press, magazines, radio, television, movies, newsreels, exhibits, displays, pamphlets, special events, and personal contacts all must be utilized in the dissemination of 'the Goethe Story' in humanized, newsworthy style." Against this onslaught, the public's resistance could never hold.

True to the idealistic purposes of the festival, McKeown promised even more than publicity and funds. Properly promoted, he said, the festival would make its mark as a mass educator, teaching "precisely how the great body of American people and people of the world can set about to readjust their lives in accordance with the Goethe spirit."[24] The modern advertiser's ploy of inducing people to fashion themselves in the image of products here found its way into cultural reform. If McKeown's scheme worked, people would begin fashioning themselves in the image of Goethe.

It is not entirely a coincidence that while McKeown in downtown Chicago was formulating these ways of selling Goethe to a mass audience, a young social scientist on the faculty of the University of Chicago, David Riesman, was preparing his landmark study, *The Lonely Crowd,* describing in part how Americans were turning everything, ideas and tastes no less than popular songs and automobiles, into products of the marketplace to be consumed, largely for the sake of self-improvement and social acceptance.[25] McKeown knew his public: sell the "Goethe spirit" as a classy product and the Goethe Bicentennial would be a triumph of the consumer culture.

To set McKeown's machine in motion, the foundation called its first press conference on November 9, 1948. Some three dozen journalists crowded into the University Club's Green Room to learn of Hutchins's latest device for promoting his cultural ideals. A "fact sheet" prepared by the McKeown organization stated the purpose of the festival: to "reexamine and reinterpret" Goethe's principal conviction, that is, "his faith in human beings," for the twentieth century in hopes of revitalizing the "will for decency, ethical conduct, and morality." The festival would not, therefore, "merely investigate and analyze Goethe" but, being an exercise in what would later be known as advocacy advertising, would encourage "our society to *act* in the spirit of Goethe."[26]

Speaking for the foundation, Hutchins underscored this program in terms taken from his battles on behalf of the Chicago Bildungsideal. The celebration had two overriding purposes, he said: "to dramatize the fundamental nature of humanistic studies at a time when science and technology are on the crest of such a high wave," and to advance the cause of "world community." These two aims, he went on, had a natural ally in Goethe, whose universal humanism could lend moral direction to the awesome powers of modern science and whose cultural internationalism could help unite mankind. Restating a theme much on his mind in those days, Hutchins reminded his listeners of Goethe's German blood and remarked that "at a time when we are concerned about the fate and future of Germany, it is well to remember the values that Germany has contributed to our civilization." Celebrating a good German would thus help heal the wounds of war, an end the foundation meant to emphasize, Hutchins pointed out, by holding its inaugural press conference on Armistice Day.

The location of the festival also called for a few words. The sponsors had chosen Aspen, Hutchins explained, because, situated in a beautiful mountain setting distant from large cities and between the two coasts, it should draw a diverse and serious-minded audience. And, he added, Aspen also offered the benefits of an emergent cultural vitality betokening "an incipient American Salzburg."[27]

There the press conference ended. The Goethe Bicentennial had made news. But it was not left to the participating journalists to spread that news. McKeown's organization blanketed the media: a news release went out to all of Chicago's radio and TV stations, to all of Colorado's fifty newspapers, to over fifty national news syndicates, and to every newspaper in 120 cities representing every state; the same release with fact sheets went to forty magazines; another forty-five magazines received fact sheets and personal letters; and seventy-five periodicals received fact sheets alone. No opportunity would be lost for exploiting the free publicity of *news*. If the gambit worked—and the 150 lines given the story in the *New York Times* indicated it was working—publicity would generate publicity, and Goethe would at least become a posthumous celebrity, that is, in Daniel Boorstin's phrase, one known for being known.

To follow up this opening, the PR advisers called for a sweeping campaign to keep Goethe and the festival in the public eye. And to the resourceful McKeown organization, the possibilities for doing this seemed unlimited: magazines could print articles on Goethe; bookstores, libraries, and schools could offer Goethe exhibits and encourage Goethe readings; the Post Office Department could issue a postage stamp bearing Goethe's image and the Bicentennial date; radio networks could carry panel shows and public interest programs on Goethe, and present dramatizations of his works and of the music influenced by him; music companies could issue special records and printed scores of the same music; film companies could make short subjects; and, most inventive, a leading designer and manufacturer of women's apparel might be induced to create "special printed fabrics bearing a unique pattern of Goethe's profile" accompanied by an advertising campaign tied to the Goethe Festival in women's magazines and retail stores promoting what else but "Philosophic Fashions."[28] The romance of commerce and culture had produced few marvels of ingenuity to top this.

The first step in this unprecedented "educational" onslaught was the creation of a pamphlet as part of the festival "sales package." The text by Ronald Goodman (McKeown's man assigned to the Goethe Foundation), with help from Bergstraesser, Hutchins, and Paepcke, restated Hutchins's now-familiar appraisal of Goethe's importance for humanism and cultural unity and added a *coup de chapeau* to the Cold War politics then swirling around the festival preparations in an emphasis on Goethe's healthy, noncommunist "efforts to reconcile the liberty of the individual with his service to society."[29] Its appealing graphic design by Herbert Bayer expressed the cosmopolitan spirit of the event by combining traditional and modern styles—a distinguished classical profile of the old Goethe on the cover, bold modernist layout and typography within. As Goodman explained to the printer, "Anything we do in the way of graphic arts must be a blend of antiquity and modernism,"[30] because while Goethe belonged to the past, his relevance to modernity had given rise to the celebration. No one was better able than Bayer, the pioneering modernist at home in Victorian Aspen, to unite the two.

As 1948 ended, ten thousand copies of the pamphlet were being readied for mailing to newspapers, colleges, radio stations, publishers, and cultural leaders, to be followed in March by a more substantial and detailed booklet. And in recognition of the dominant place of publicity in the Bicentennial, Ronald Goodman now took over the burden of the foundation's everyday operations, coordinating the directors' activities, communicating with philanthrophic and cultural organizations, publicists, and interested citizens, drawing individuals and committees into the promotion, and trying, albeit unsuccessfully, to interest MGM and Movietone News in making a short film on Goethe.

Paepcke had also tried to get Hollywood into the act by inviting new Aspenite Gary Cooper to participate in a film biography of Goethe, which he said would be written in consultation with Thomas Mann (who had joined the foundation's directorate) and would feature the singing voices of Lotte Lehmann and Lauritz Melchior.[31] But neither Cooper nor the rest of Hollywood could see profits in a movie musical about a long-dead German poet.

Hollywood might turn its back on Goethe, but Colorado could not afford to. Or so Paepcke believed as he started, in the fall of 1948, rallying support among his fellow Coloradans. Characterizing the festival as "a tremendous opportunity to obtain nation-wide and in fact international free publicity" for the region, and deceptively hinting that the festival might go elsewhere if sufficient local cooperation did not materialize, he urged his neighbors to "make every effort possible consistent with good business to secure this celebration for our territory."[32] He also recommended, with the hasty assertiveness that sometimes made him enemies, that all of the cultural activities of central Colorado—e.g., the operas at Red Rocks and Central City and the concerts of the Denver Symphony—fall in line with the Aspen events and become observances of "a Goethe year."[33]

Then, while Paepcke continued rousing Coloradans to his cause, scouting means of transportation and the like (the shortage of hotel rooms and railroad seats for the Labor Day weekend, on which the anniversary of Goethe's birth—August 28—was to fall that year, had already necessitated rescheduling the festival in late June), Aspen took a decisive step in opening its doors to the outside world, for the Goethe Festival and after. On December 19, 1948, jubilant fanfare greeted the inauguration of the Aspen Airport. This event completed months of work, beginning with the purchase in May by Paepcke and his deputy at Container Corporation, Jack Spachner, of property for an airfield lying two miles northwest of town. Construction had begun in October on a 4,500-foot unpaved runway, and the first planes had landed to test the strip on November 9 (the day of the Goethe Festival's unveiling in Chicago), prompting the local newspaper to declare, now "Aspen is really getting on the map"—thanks again "to the farsighted vision of Mr. Walter Paepcke."[34] Paepcke had then formed the Aspen Airport Company (with Spachner and William Hodges) in late November and leased the facilities to the Aspen Air Service, which was to supply charter service from Glenwood Springs, Grand Junction, and Denver.

As it happened, the announcement of the airport's formal opening date had come at an epoch in Aspen's history. For the same issue of the *Aspen Times*, November 18, that had printed this had also carried front-page stories about two other portentous forthcoming events. One story had reported that the Goethe Bicentennial celebration would take place in Aspen the next summer. The other had broken the news that the world skiing championships, sponsored by the Fédération Internationale de Ski (FIS), would be held in Aspen in February 1950. These simultaneous proclamations marked the dawning of Aspen's international reputation; but they also symbolized the Janus-faced character and future of a town divided between the cultural riches of summer festivals and the recreational and commercial boon of winter sports. The division, however, was easily lost in soaring expectations. For the first time in half a century the future of Aspen looked indisputably bright.

For Paepcke, that future held out mainly the prospect of cultural activities attractive to the "high type" of person he liked. He had not spent all his time soliciting cooperation and preparing for the festival guests physically. He had also been putting together a musical program, with Mrs. Jack Spachner, a prominent musical organizer in Chicago, and working out ways of staging it. While Mrs. Spachner communicated with management agencies about artists and fees, Paepcke set about securing a symphony orchestra. After rejecting the Denver Symphony as overpriced for its worth, at $8,800 for five days, Paepcke turned to the Minneapolis Symphony, largely because of its famed conductor, Dimitri Mitropoulos, and went to Minneapolis to negotiate a deal directly. Bent on getting his prize, Paepcke, as usual, let costs take a back seat to quality; and on December 10 he succeeded: the orchestra signed a contract for ten concerts at a sum of $32,500 covering the transportation and fees of seventy-five musicians plus $2,500 for Mitropoulos.

Within another month most of the principal performers were also signed. And it was a roster certain to make the Goethe Festival a first-rate musical event if nothing else. Besides Mitropoulos and the Minneapolis Symphony, there were Metropolitan Opera stars Mack Harrell, Jerome Hines, Herta Glaz; noted black soprano Dorothy Maynor; pianist Artur Rubinstein; dual pianists Victor Babin and Vitya Vronsky; cellist Gregor Piatigorsky; and violinists Nathan Milstein and Erica Morini. Paepcke's vision of an American Salzburg was coming true.

The price tag for the music alone now exceeded $50,000. Paepcke's only hope of recouping such an expense lay in high gate receipts. But here was a problem. Aspen's largest hall, the Opera House, could seat only 650, far fewer than the 1,500 to 2,000 people needed to cover costs without overpricing tickets. Besides this drawback, the Opera House had no roof, and Aspen's fierce summer thundershowers could not be relied upon to respect the claims of culture. A suitable hall could be built, of course, but that seemed a foolish investment for a one-shot affair. So Paepcke began seeking alternatives, both cheap and temporary.

He turned for advice to the first place that came to mind: the Institute of Design. Paepcke was, after all, still chairman of the board and had reaffirmed his commitment to the school in its prospectus of 1948, where, noting the increasing importance of the institute's program "in this postwar era, when practically every product is being redesigned," he had invited industries to submit "special problems and projects involving any of the various elements of design."[35] Now Paepcke accepted this invitation himself and submitted his unique problem in design to the institute's director, Serge Chermayeff.

Chermayeff informed Paepcke in November of two main architectural options. They could build a conventional structure that could be draped with sheets of war-surplus canvas used in airplane hangars as a cover; this would cost about $40,000. Or they could try something much more ingenious, and much riskier—an experimental domelike structure of the type recently designed by a friend of the institute, R. Buckminster Fuller. This novel invention, a lightweight dome supported by a self-reinforcing structure of triangular or polygonal facets rather than by mass—later known as the "geodesic dome"—would, Chermayeff said, perfectly suit the festival's needs; and it could be constructed for a mere $24,000.[36] It had only to be fully tested first. This was the catch. The only attempt to erect a large model so far, at Black Mountain College the previous summer, had ended in disarray. And the first successful effort on a similar scale, at the Institute of Design itself, was still months away—the first functional geodesic building to be constructed, the Harvard Observatory on Mount Climax, Colorado, was not yet on the drawing boards. So, in the light of their joint wariness,

Chermayeff and Fuller recommended that Paepcke play it safe for the time being by putting up a simple canvas tent at a cost of $5,000 and then construct the Fuller dome when it proved ready—probably not until after the Goethe Festival.[37]

A tent was all right with Paepcke. It would be convenient and inexpensive. It would also embody one of the first principles of educational institutions as set forth by Robert Hutchins, the only such principle Hutchins shared with the president of Black Mountain College, John Rice, who liked to quote it: "Colleges should be made of tents, and when they fold, they fold."[38] When the Goethe Festival had finished its work, it too could fold up and go away.

Of course, not any tent would do. It had to be acoustically right for music, suited to the location, and inexpensive. A tent of the kind Paepcke had in mind, he told Herbert Bayer, could be rented, together with chairs, for $3,000, with an equal sum for construction. If they should opt for a more lasting structure, he added, "we might be willing to go to $10,000 or $12,000 more or less. . . . However, I don't think we should envision $50,000 or $60,000." And he remarked that he had been thinking of "using [Eero] Saarinen as a consultant, simply because he did design and build Tanglewood five or six years ago and that is uniformly considered good."[39]

This intimation of Saarinen's involvement set off a chain of events that resulted in the enduring public emblem of the Goethe Festival and of Aspen culture for years to come: Eero Saarinen's specially designed amphitheater-tent. When Saarinen visited Aspen in January 1949, he was not widely known and had yet to design the buildings of swooping and lyrical forms that would bring him fame as an architect. But with his father, Eliel, he had established an architectural firm of rising reputation. After persuading Paepcke to build a temporary amphitheater using a rented canvas top, and after Paepcke failed to locate a suitable canvas, Saarinen readily took on the task of designing the whole thing.

The Aspen amphitheater, or "the tent," as it quickly became known, that Saarinen designed—one of his first domed structures, foreshadowing the many he was to create with such inventiveness in the twelve short years left to him—measured 147 feet in diameter. The top would rise some eighty feet at the center pole from an excavated bowl, leaving about seven feet of open space around the sides near the ground and providing covered seating for two thousand people, with one-quarter of the interior space provided for the orchestra. Paepcke had reason to be pleased: everything fitted his specifications. Except the expense. Before the ground was even broken, the cost—including tent, stage benches, poles, lights, excavation, toilets, and architects' fees—totaled $57,000. And other incidentals had yet to come in, such as seat pads and orchestra chairs as well as the revisions required by

Mitropoulos for expanding the orchestra space and the backstage area and supplying restrooms and water for exclusive use of the artists. By the time the tent began rising from the ground at the end of May, Paepcke's wildest estimates of the amphitheater's cost had long been surpassed. But then the scale of the festival was expanding, too.

While the music program and other parts of the festival were taking impressive shape, and growing ever more costly, the academic program was becoming equally expansive, although not quite so expensive. As names of possible lecturers were tossed around, virtually no thinker of public or scholarly repute failed to be mentioned. Some, like Jean-Paul Sartre, were eliminated as unsuited to the occasion. Others, like Albert Schweitzer, first suggested in early 1948, fell aside as impossible to obtain. Others still, including T. S. Eliot, André Gide, Thomas Mann, and Arnold Toynbee, declined invitations, pleading other obligations. And at least one, George Bernard Shaw, dismissed the festival as a futile tribute to genius; Shaw's assistant shot back a laconic rejection in the form of Shaw's response to a Viennese publisher in 1947:

> Who dares write about Goethe?
> Insects will buzz around the colossus, but not I.
> I take my hat off, and hold my tongue.[40]

Then Paepcke, persuaded of the humanistic preeminence of Albert Schweitzer and tantalized by the challenge of achieving the impossible, persuaded Hutchins to try once more to entice Schweitzer to these shores. After all, if Schweitzer could be enlisted, the festival and Aspen would be assured of international recognition. A telegram went out in late October 1948, from Hutchins to Schweitzer's hospital in Lambaréné, offering a $5,000 fee—the same offered to Eliot and Toynbee—in return for an address on Goethe. No reply. Two weeks later (November 12), Paepcke urged Hutchins to send another. Still no reply. Then Hutchins discovered that Schweitzer was not in Lambaréné at all but residing temporarily at home in Gunsbach, Alsace, France. Another cable. Finally a letter came back with the word, as Paepcke reported to a friend, that Schweitzer "simply had to go back from Europe to Africa, that his sick and ailing natives needed him."[41]

But Paepcke got a hunch for one last try. If Schweitzer wouldn't come to America to receive dollars or bestow honor on his beloved Goethe, perhaps he would come for a sum made directly available to his hospital. Rather than $5,000, why not offer Schweitzer a nice round figure in Swiss francs—worth somewhat more than the dollar amount—payable as a donation to his hospital. Hutchins agreed to try. He sent off a final appeal January 19:

RE EARLIER CORRESPONDENCE, GOETHE FOUNDATION INVITES YOU TO PARTICIPATE IN
INTERNATIONAL CONVOCATION TO RECEIVE GOETHE PRIZE OF 1949 IN THE AMOUNT OF TWO
MILLION FRANCS WHICH WE CAN PAY TO YOUR HOSPITAL AT LAMBARENE. FOUNDATION WILL
ALSO PAY TRAVEL EXPENSES. WE HOPE YOU CAN BE WITH US JULY 2–12 OR FOR PART OF
THIS TIME AND THAT YOU WILL GIVE PRINCIPAL ADDRESS ON GOETHE. PLEASE INDICATE
FURTHER FORMULATION OF YOUR THEME IF INVITATION IS ACCEPTABLE.[42]

Now they could only wait—again.

Invitations were wired that same day to several other prospective speakers. José Ortega y Gasset, the influential Spanish philosopher and eminent cultural critic, was informed that the convocation would "discuss the bearing of Goethe's conception of literature and Humanität on the contemporary crisis in civilization," and he was invited to "promote understanding among all nations by giving a leading address on a topic that you think appropriate." (He would receive travel expenses and a "five thousand dollar Goethe prize.")[43] Another, the scholar Ernst R. Curtius, offered $1,000, was asked to help "clarify Goethe's conception of world literature and its significance today."[44] And Thornton Wilder, then in Paris, received Hutchins's informal cable:

GOETHE CELEBRATION CANNOT GO ON WITHOUT YOU. WE COUNT ON YOUR PRESENCE JULY
2–12. WE HOPE YOU WILL DELIVER A TALK, PARTICIPATE IN DISCUSSIONS, AND MOST OF ALL BE
THERE. TO MAKE IT FINANCIALLY POSSIBLE WE HAVE VOTED YOU TWENTY-FIVE HUNDRED
DOLLARS AND TRAVEL EXPENSES.[45]

By the end of January, acceptances had come from Ortega, Curtius, and Wilder, as well as from the theologian Martin Buber, the Swiss scholar and diplomat Charles Burckhardt, Norway's Ambassador Halvdan Koht, and the Dutch historian Gerardus van der Leeuw. But nothing from Schweitzer. Hopes of obtaining the star attraction were fading. Then, on February 2, Hutchins received a wire: "VIENDRAI JUILLET. LETTRE EN ROUTE. SCHWEITZER"[46] ("Will come July. Letter on the way"). The Goethe Foundation had achieved the impossible.

Sims Carter fired off a copy of the "precious document"[47] to the foundation's directors, and at Paepcke's suggestion passed the word on to a few chosen persons. Melvin Arnold, for one, editor-in-chief of the Beacon Press, the publisher of Schweitzer's *Two Studies of Goethe* and *The Africa of Albert Schweitzer*, exulted in Carter's "electrifying news." Having returned from Lambaréné eighteen months earlier after a failed attempt to induce Schweitzer to visit the United States, he pledged every support for Schweitzer's visit—money, publicity, etc. And, knowing that Schweitzer would be deluged with honors and offers to speak, he was certain the festival organizers would need all the help they could get. "No one needs to tell you," he wrote Carter, "that you have something immense on your hands."[48]

But Schweitzer's letter of acceptance threw cold water on many of Arnold's buoyant expectations. "After spending five sleepless nights trying to make a decision,"[49] he had agreed to come only because, as Paepcke later reported, "he thought the grant would enable him to buy all types of medical supplies, surgical instruments, etc., but that he could only spare three or four days at the most and make one or at the very most two speeches and then would have to go right back to Africa."[50] Hence he requested that no other engagements be made for him. The Goethe Foundation was more than glad to respect this request, since they feared the pressures of public attention might force him to withdraw his acceptance; and, of course, the exclusive booking (broken only by a brief stop in Chicago to receive an honorary degree from the University of Chicago) could do the festival publicity campaign no harm.

The master of that campaign, Ronald Goodman, seized upon the Schweitzer engagement as a promotional godsend: now he could sell Goethe and Schweitzer as a single package. And he discovered the sales gimmick for doing this ready-made on the dust jacket prepared for the Beacon Press's forthcoming bicentennial edition of Schweitzer's *Goethe: Four Studies* (the two previously published essays and two later ones). Schweitzer, it read, "is the man who is acknowledged to be more like Goethe than is any other living man."[51] From this time on, Goodman was to repeat the statement whenever he could—understandably omitting the source and neglecting the significant differences between the two thinkers remarked in Schweitzer's text and in the editor's introduction. Schweitzer would now go forth as the modern Goethe; and the festival could celebrate not one but two world-historical figures.

With the festival's roster of luminous performers in place, the publicity campaign entered its second phase. A spate of press releases went out in mid-February 1949 reiterating the festival's purpose and publishing parts of the program and the names of its participants. "Many of the nation's foremost artists," one release announced, would perform compositions illustrating "Goethe's tremendous effect on the world of music" and expressing "in music Goethe's sweeping faith in a common humanity."[52] Other releases carried word of scheduled appearances by Thornton Wilder, Halvdan Koht, Charles Burckhardt, and "Spain's greatest living philosopher and staunch anti-Franco oppositionist," José Ortega y Gasset, whose book *The Revolt of the Masses* was here praised, in Hutchins's words, as "an essential contribution to our consciousness of our own times."[53]

Then on February 22 came the major announcement. Goodman had prepared it from material supplied mainly by the Beacon Press, which stood to gain from any publicity of Schweitzer. Beacon's promotional director, Edward Darling, had sent Goodman numerous books and photos, as well as information obtained by the American translator of Schweitzer's works,

Charles Joy, during his long visits with Schweitzer in France and Lambaréné. Goodman had learned from these documents not only the pertinent facts of Schweitzer's career but, much to his delight, that Schweitzer had never been to the United States. He saw here a good angle for publicizing the affinity of Schweitzer to Goethe (although Edward Darling's explanation that Schweitzer's previous refusals to visit this country arose from his inability to speak English could not have pleased the PR man).[54] Summarizing Schweitzer's manifold accomplishments in scholarship, thought, and music, and his saintlike sacrifice of worldly rewards for medicine and for his jungle hospital, Goodman's press release pointed to this first trip to the United States by "one of the great men of our times" as testimony to Schweitzer's spiritual kinship with Goethe. Like the Beacon Press jacket blurb, the release continued: philosopher, humanist, universal man, Schweitzer "is acknowledged to be more like Goethe than is any other living man."[55]

The selling of Schweitzer had begun. Although conceived as a way of selling Goethe and the Bicentennial celebration, it would do more for Schweitzer than for Goethe. For if Goethe and the Goethe Festival won passing popular notice from their identification with Schweitzer as the living exemplar of the "Goethe spirit," Schweitzer saw his reputation among the American public at large virtually created by his much-publicized identification with all that the festival represented.

Difficult as it is to imagine today, few Americans knew much of Schweitzer before the Goethe Festival, even though he was almost seventy-five years old at that time and had virtually completed his life's work as a scholar and thinker. The man most responsible for bringing him here, Walter Paepcke, had not even heard his name (or had forgotten it) before the summer of 1948. And the man responsible for promoting Schweitzer as the living symbol of the Goethe Festival, Ronald Goodman, had known little if anything of the man before turning to Schweitzer's dedicated followers for information.

To know much of Schweitzer in the United States prior to 1949 was to have a specialized interest in one of Schweitzer's principal occupations: the performance and study of Bach's music, to which his critical biography of 1905 remains a monument; the study of Christianity, to which he had made many contributions, beginning with his influential book *The Quest of the Historical Jesus* (1906); and humanistic philosophy, explored in Schweitzer's many philosophical writings and exemplified in his self-sacrificing life guided by naturalistic metaphysics and Christian ethics.

But while knowledge of Schweitzer was still confined largely to a few Bach lovers, scholars, and intellectuals, grounds for a wider public were being laid. Most of Schweitzer's writings, including his autobiography, *Out of My Life and Thought,* had been translated into English and published in the 1930s, and Schweitzer the man—and saint—had been "discovered" by Americans in the mid-forties. The first biography available in English, Otto Kraus's *Albert Schweitzer: His Work and His Philosophy*, had appeared in 1944. In 1947, following a story in *Reader's Digest* on Schweitzer as a religious thinker, *Life* magazine had made news of Schweitzer the man with a brief illustrated story under the revelatory title, cautiously placed in quotation marks: "'The Greatest Man in the World.'" "There is a small group of men today," the story opened carefully, "mostly educators, who believe the title of 'greatest man in the world' should go" to "Albert Schweitzer, jungle philosopher."[56]

These words of naive adulation had introduced Albert Schweitzer to the American public at large. Soon, a few determined followers had set about expanding the audience for the saintly man then said to be completing his magisterial *Philosophy of Civilization* with a volume on the ethics of the reverence for life. Melvin Arnold, recently appointed to his post at the Beacon Press, had vowed "to make America as familiar with the work of Albert Schweitzer as is Europe,"[57] and he had traveled to Lambaréné with Schweitzer's American translator, Charles Joy, for a firsthand look (under the sponsorship of the Unitarian publication *The Christian Register*). The visit had greatly nourished Arnold's awe over Schweitzer's extraordinary blend of moral authority and humility—dramatized by Schweitzer's striking out Arnold's entry in the Lambaréné guest book dedicated to "the greatest soul in Christendom."[58] After Arnold's return, Beacon had brought out a spate of books by or about Schweitzer: *The Africa of Albert Schweitzer* by Arnold and Joy; Schweitzer's *Psychiatric Study of Jesus* and *Two Studies of Goethe*; *Albert Schweitzer: An Anthology*; and the press had scheduled the Goethe Bicentennial volume, *Goethe: Four Studies* by Albert Schweitzer.

The immediate postwar years had also brought the publication of hagiographical biographies by Hermann Hagadorn, *Prophet in the Wilderness* (1947), and George Seaver (also author of *Albert Schweitzer, Christian Revolutionary*, 1946). Although the more scholarly of the two, Seaver's *Albert Schweitzer: The Man and His Mind* (1947) struck the typical reverential tone in the first line: "Albert Schweitzer is probably the most gifted genius of our age, as well as its most prophetic thinker."[59] Two hundred pages of pious narrative then defend this thesis.

But the growing reverence for Schweitzer had had little to do with Schweitzer's actual accomplishments in scholarship or music or thought. It had grown from an idea of the man as the embodiment of a demanding moral life, a moral life attainable only to those who reject the worldly rewards of their labors and talents. This moral life could be and was esteemed as that of the exemplary Christian, but it owed as much of its magnetism to the cultural criticism of the previous hundred years that had opposed the complacent materialism, selfishness, and hypocrisy of middle-class life to the elemental needs of human nature and truths of the spirit. Schweitzer had early demonstrated his intellectual affinity with this tradition by spurning, along with fellow Christian thinkers like Karl Barth and Paul Tillich, the ethical complacency of liberal Protestantism for a more severe interpretation of the Gospel. And he had dramatized that affinity by turning his back on the insidious comforts and satisfactions of fame and position, after a youth of precocious intellectual accomplishment, to embrace rough and unremunerative service as doctor to disease-ridden natives in central Africa. Now that history's most devastating war had thrown Western civilization into a turmoil from which it had yet to recover, Schweitzer the moral refugee from that civilization could be seen to represent a cure for the malaise that eats away the moral sinews of culture and erupts in war.

The promoters of the Goethe Festival could not have missed the opportunity to exploit Schweitzer's emergent reputation by equating the Good Doctor and Goethe as the preeminent humanistic critics of Western culture. Nor was this equation difficult to achieve since Schweitzer had stressed the affinity himself, beginning with his Goethe Prize address in 1928. Goethe's message to moderns, Schweitzer had said, is "to preserve their spiritual lives" amid spiritless circumstances and to "remain loyal" to "great humane ideals" despite the "confusion and inhumanity"[60] of the age. And not long before agreeing to come to the Goethe Festival he had written to his translator, "Goethe is the personality with which I have been most deeply concerned. . . . What attracts me in him is that he is a man of action at the same time that he is a poet, a thinker, and . . . a savant." Yet "what binds us together in the deepest depths of our beings is his philosophy of nature"[61]— by which Schweitzer meant the belief in a spiritual and organic unity underlying all living things and obligating human beings to cultivate both the powers of the spirit and feelings for nature.

But Schweitzer's professed kinship with Goethe belied profound differences between the doctor and the poet in temperament and intellectual aspirations. Charles Joy's introduction to Schweitzer's *Goethe: Four Studies*, published to coincide with the festival, pointed to sources of these differences in Goethe's irreligious spirit, personal coldness, pride, and self-conscious artistry. And Schweitzer himself had expressed to Joy his "disappointment" with parts of Goethe's character—the indecisiveness, detachment, and scattered attentions—remarking that, had he and Goethe been contemporaries, they "would have been kept apart by what in each of us was strange and incomprehensible to the other. We might even have been adversaries."[62] Schweitzer, self-sacrificing Christian humanist who fled modernity to become a jungle doctor and to issue solemn volumes on the moral decline of civilization, and Goethe, Olympian literary figure, worldly administrator, scientist, and poet of the restless and energetic modern Faustian spirit, would have made odd companions indeed.

Whatever might have divided Goethe and Schweitzer would not show up in the Goethe Festival's public relations campaign. If necessary, the affinities between the two thinkers could be drawn so close as to obscure all differences, the poet and doctor passing from loose bonds of similarity to tight bonds of identity. Soliciting the cooperation of the Associated Press for publicizing the festival, Ronald Goodman explained this strategy: "We all recognize that it is rather hard to make Goethe understandable to the so-called average guy, but working with Schweitzer who can provide us with the flesh and blood, I think the job can be done." To the ingenious Goodman, not only was Schweitzer now "more like Goethe than is any other living man," but "you could almost call Schweitzer a kind of incarnate Goethe."[63] The Goethe Festival would be promoted in fact if not in name as a Schweitzer Festival.

A major press conference was scheduled for mid-March in New York. Restating the gist of earlier press releases on the immediate purpose of the festival and the identities of its participants, Hutchins stressed the long-term goals of the festival sponsors: this celebration of the universal man, bringing together many of the greatest humanists and musicians of the postwar world, would help reunite a shattered Western culture and renew its humanistic spirit so impaired by war. When some journalists doubted the cultural value of so seemingly academic an exercise, Ronald Goodman set them straight. The questions to be discussed were not, he said, of the kind, "What pocket did Goethe carry his watch in?" but those of universal import capable of lending "meaning and direction to the lives of people today."

Goodman did not mean only philosophical direction, either. Talking up the newsworthiness of the celebration, he struck a sharply political note. No mere intellectual confab, the festival was to be an event of direct relevance to Cold War politics, then growing more tense each day. Many of the European participants would bring, he said, not just insights into Goethe and modern culture but "some very good news stories on the Berlin blockade"— which had commenced the previous summer. Even more important, the festival would itself be a political statement, countering "the Russian attempts to make" of their own forthcoming "Goethe celebration in Weimar [East Germany] a propaganda stunt" through their "silly claims" that "Goethe was an exponent of world communism." For at Aspen, without propaganda or manipulation, "free men in a free meeting will make the news to refute this Red line."[64]

Goethe the universal man had thus, to the advantage of the publicity campaign, become an object of Cold War contention: who had the right to him, West or East, capitalists or communists? At the very time that the Goethe Foundation had started publicizing its Bicentennial program in mid-

February, the East German propaganda minister had issued a rebuff to all Western designs on Goethe:

> Contrary to the infamous attempts of reactionary circles to misuse the famous name of a great poet, the militant, anti-Fascist German democratic circles decided to give a truthful and comprehensive analysis of the real importance of Goethe within the framework of the history of Germany as well as the history of all mankind. German democrats will be right to celebrate Goethe as a great protagonist of a unified, humane, industrious and productive Germany.[65]

Invited by the press to comment on such East German and Soviet assertions, Carl F. Schreiber, an originator of the Goethe Festival, said simply: "Goethe and the Communists have nothing in common," and communist spokesmen "offer no supporting evidence, not even manufactured evidence" that any affinity exists.[66] But at the same time, the conservative *Chicago Tribune*, quoting the German propaganda minister's words in an article headed "Who Owns Goethe's Soul?" had concluded that while the Russians and East Germans were exploiting Goethe for their own sinister purposes, "the Hutchins group" was not much better, obviously using Goethe "to promote its own scheme of a world state under a world constitution."[67] The *Tribune*'s antagonism toward the advocates of world government was predictable, but the newspaper's observation on the motives of "the Hutchins group" had indisputably hit the mark.

Hints of the thickening Cold War atmosphere also crept into the twenty-four-page publicity booklet prepared (in a printing of fifty thousand) by Goodman and Herbert Bayer for distribution after the March press conference. Goodman's text covered the familiar ground on Goethe's career, manifold accomplishments, and relevance to the crisis of humanism in the twentieth century. But it played upon the political theme with an emphasis on Goethe's attachment to political freedom: "Reared in an environment of freedom, the Free City of Frankfurt," Goodman wrote, Goethe had opened his career with a drama, "Goetz von Berlichingen," on "the conflict between the abuse of power and the sense of justice in the free individual" and had later poured his greatest genius into the creation of Faust, the archetypal modern hero, who "ends up before the Promised Land, in which he hopes to live with free people on a free soil." How easy it was for the East Germans to invoke the same works as evidence of Goethe's belonging to them. But Goodman also added an explanation of contemporary international tensions that drew directly upon the philosophical origins of the West's Goethe Festival: "The major problems facing the nations of the world . . . in the fourth year following Hiroshima," he wrote, "are not only political and economic, but also intellectual," and fundamentally, they are "the problems of ethics and morality."[68] The postwar Goethe might be an antiauthoritarian individualist, but he could still be cast as a moralist in the vein of the Chicago Bildungsideal.

While the voices of public relations were disseminating the political message of the postwar Goethe merging internationalism and liberal individualism, the very idea of the festival came under harsh criticism from an unexpected quarter. Father Banigan of St. Mary's Catholic Church in Aspen distributed a pamphlet attacking the festival sponsors for proposing to celebrate a man known to have criticized Christianity and to have espoused ideas printed in books "condemned by the Church." Nor did the promise of Albert Schweitzer's presence lessen the evil. "We have found a purpose in life, and a solution to life's problems in our Catholic Faith," Banigan wrote. "We don't have to seek for it in the nature philosophy of Goethe, or the 'ethical pantheism' of Albert Schweitzer." "Enjoy the music," he entreated his flock, "but stay away from the lectures on religion and philosophy."[69]

The priest's charges aroused such a storm that a public meeting was held to discuss them. Walter Paepcke rose to remind Banigan that Goethe was an honorably married man and had written a good deal of religion into *Faust*. And he pointed out that many of the festival's slated participants were deeply moral and religious men—hadn't Schweitzer himself been labeled "the greatest soul in Christendom"? Then, after reiterating his familiar line that Aspen could still lose the festival if other cities showed more cooperation, Paepcke rested his case. The meeting adjourned with all except Banigan in favor of the festival.[70] Goethe had now been saved from both the communists and the Church.

The questions of the festival's participants, politics, and newsworthiness largely resolved, the PR campaign now went into high gear. A second major news conference was held in Chicago April 18 to publicize details of the musical and academic programs. And Goodman arranged an interview for Hutchins on Douglas Edwards's CBS news program in New York on April 22, instructing the chancellor to plug the festival under the guise of an interview on world politics[71]—Hutchins having just delivered a major political-philosophical address at Marquette University on that good Chicago theme: "St. Thomas and the World State."

Next, a press release went out with a new pitch. Since preparations for the festival had themselves become news, Goodman could shape the publicity as news rather than as simple announcements. "Four thousand to attend International Goethe Convocation, Music Festival in Aspen, Colorado," read his headline. Beneath it ran the details: "Famed world scholars and leaders of international thought," headed by Schweitzer, to gather and talk about Goethe and modern culture and listen to music "inspired by the works of the poet-philosopher" performed in "an open-air band shell–auditorium now being constructed." Along with the release went a "kit of press materials" to newspapers throughout the United States with a statement signed by Hutchins on the festival's desire to balance "the alarming overemphasis on the mechanics of science and technology" by applying to "today's problems" the "basic human standards best represented in the humanities—philosophy, religion, ethics—and the social sciences."[72]

At the same time, Goodman was arranging for stories on Aspen and the festival to get onto the Associated Press wires and for printed announcements of the festival to be inserted into the concert programs of the Minneapolis Symphony Orchestra and into advertising folders of United Airlines. He saw to it that some human-interest photographs were taken in Aspen and released to the wire services recording such apposite scenes as: "a grizzled miner planking down silver dollars at the Goethe office in Aspen to pay for Convocation tickets"; "a cowboy on a horse helping in construction of open-air amphitheatre by roping a portion of the lumber to be used"; and a "miner and pretty girl in shorts erecting 'Welcome to Goethe Convocation and Music Festival' sign on outskirts of Aspen."[73] He also got the radio networks to give time to the festival. The Mutual Broadcasting System agreed to broadcast one half-hour of the festival's symphony concerts on July 1 and July 8, as well as a roundtable discussion on "Ethics and Politics" or "Goethe and the Unity of Mankind." NBC agreed to cover a lecture July 2 or July 9 and possibly some of the music. And CBS prepared to provide extensive coverage: Edward R. Murrow promised to take an advanced look at Schweitzer and the festival on his regular news program; the CBS symphony promised to devote their program of June 26 to the festival with music inspired by Goethe, and to include an interview with Thornton Wilder at intermission; and E. Power Biggs scheduled a similar program of organ music on June 26. The weekly magazines *Time, Life,* and *Newsweek* also assured Goodman they would carry stories on Schweitzer with the festival as background. The Goethe Festival might not unite Western culture, but it would not easily be ignored.

With the work of selling the festival nearly done, Goodman could claim with justification that "the event is of major news importance today."[74] He had only to arrange for the reception in New York of the principal foreign guests, prepare a statement praising Goethe for release by Herbert Hoover on the eve of the festival, and issue a "round-up story" and bulletin enticing the working press to Aspen.

Goodman and Paepcke assigned responsibility for managing press coverage in New York to the Aspen Company publicist, Delphine Carpenter. Goodman underscored for her the need to stir up as much public notice of the visitors as possible, remarking that because "the arrival of our foreign scholars is top rate news," it should be easy "to take hold of the news event itself and shape it to serve the purposes of the Goethe Bicentennial Festival." This would also mean, of course, drawing attention to the festival as the exclusive sponsor of the visits, and protecting the scholars—especially Schweitzer, who was, according to his American representatives, "very much afraid of coming to America"—from exploiters and news gatherers who could usurp and distort "our story."[75]

Goodman then prepared the final statement of "our story" for release by Herbert Hoover, emphasizing, as Hoover had requested, Goethe's pertinence to the politics of individual liberty in 1949. "A group of the most distinguished leaders of world thought," the statement read, are about to assemble in Aspen "to discuss world problems in terms of Goethe's philosophy," a philosophy holding one idea above all others: "that free men everywhere must be constantly aware of their responsibilities to preserve their own liberty and freedom." Hoover-Goodman saw this philosophy most emphatically "stated by Goethe in his great drama 'Faust' when he wrote: 'He only earns his freedom and existence who daily conquers them anew.'"[76] Although ethereal in spirit and location, the Goethe Festival continued paying its respects to Cold War politics.

After sending out a bulletin inviting the press to Aspen, Goodman drew up his final press release. And this one brought the entire prefestival PR campaign not only to a conclusion but full circle from its beginning. That campaign had begun by publicizing the celebration of Goethe and of the "Goethe spirit" as a remedy for the crisis of Western culture. Then, adding announcements of important festival participants, it had started pushing Albert Schweitzer as the contemporary exemplar of that spirit and the latter-day Goethe. Next it had put the Goethe Festival in the service of Cold War politics and begun projecting the festival as a great American cultural event newsworthy in its own right. Now, as Goodman looked back over the labors of those past seven months, he found one more publicizable topic. He labeled the release: "P.R. Program for Poet-Philosopher Goethe Sets Unusual Assignment for Chicago Counselling Firm."[77] The selling of Goethe had itself become news. The release touched on the familiar festival facts, but now the veil of PR hype and "education" was drawn aside: the story of the Goethe Bicentennial was a story of public relations as much as of cultural aspirations. Elaborating on this theme in a "case study" a short time later, Goodman described his assignment as "one of the most unusual purposes to which public relations has been applied, possibly in the history of the profession." From the planning stages onward, he said, the objectives of the festival were one with the tasks of public relations: that is, to make Goethe's humanism and "universalism" known to a wide public. And he concluded that to the extent the festival achieved its goals the credit should largely go to the publicity campaign. For "professional public relations had: (1) popularized philosophy; (2) brought the dying Goethe of 117 years before to life in the minds of a mass audience; (3) introduced a new center of world culture in the United States; and (4) shaped an intellectual centennial celebration into a potent, popular educational force."[78]

Goodman was right. Mass marketing, mass communications, and public relations, the engines of the consumer culture, made the Goethe Festival the historic public event it was, putting Aspen on the map, making a folk hero of Albert Schweitzer, and, as Hutchins bragged in the aftermath, becoming "one of the most significant programs of adult education" ever undertaken.[79] But before these triumphs could be proclaimed, the festival had to unfold. On June 20, 1949, Goodman packed his bags and set out for Aspen.

During the next few weeks the remote, formerly near-deserted mountain town was to become the cultural capital of the Western World, drawing the great and the curious to its rustic streets and novel amphitheater. Yet, as the opening day approached, doubts remained whether the public attention and visitors would add up to a sufficient audience of paying guests. "It sure seems funny," said Gary Cooper, "that such an event would be held way up there in the mountains, . . . and it may be hard to get people to go."[80] Cooper was planning to be in Aspen during the festival, but to fish, not listen to lectures—although he did play host one afternoon to Ortega y Gasset at Cooper's still uncompleted Aspen home.

The better to lure an audience, the sponsors issued a large, glossy folder containing information about transportation, accommodations, and recreation. Besides the regularly scheduled transportation, two special trains would make the round-trip from Chicago for each of the two five-day festival sessions. And besides the main events there would be plenty of diversions, planned and unplanned, including skiing twenty-five miles away, swimming in the Jerome's newly built heated pool and sunning on the hotel's recently installed sun roof, riding, hiking, even a rodeo. The pamphlet also gave suggestions on clothing for mountain novices: for riding "in the Rockies we use blue jeans, gay plaid cotton shirts" and informal apparel for most other pursuits. If the promoters got their wish, Aspen would fill with devotees of high culture ready to "rough it."

Walter Paepcke, for one, liked this combination of the dignified and the informal—he was, after all, known both for liking "the best people" and for wearing worn-out clothes. And he held to this dual inclination in charting his travel plans to Aspen with Hutchins (taking along Hutchins's gift to him for the occasion: a silver cigarette lighter signed, "Bob and Goethe"). Paepcke told Hutchins they should treat themselves to an unnecessary but assuredly rewarding stop in Colorado Springs for dinner at Gene Lilly's Cooking Club. Two years of planning and a year of travels, banquets, and press conferences promoting the festival and raising funds (about $150,000) demanded, he told Hutchins, an "appropriate climax." "I have no hesitancy," he said sportively, "in stating unequivocally that this will be it."[81] The selling of Goethe was over. The celebrating was about to begin.

6

celebrating

the postwar goethe

"The greatest cultural festival of its kind ever held in our country," Hutchins proclaimed the Goethe Bicentennial celebration at a Denver public appearance on Friday, June 24 (arranged in lieu of his attendance at the opening ceremonies in Aspen on Monday). And recalling the twin dangers of "the atomic age"—to "be blown up" or to "die of boredom"—he urged Americans to heed the festival's message of cultural unity and humanistic ideals as their deliverance.[1] The somber tone went with him to Colorado Springs the next day where at a news conference prior to the Cooking Club luncheon he lashed out at "the trivial self-adoration which is sweeping the country"[2] and which had erupted in hostility to the Goethe Foundation for being either pro-Nazi or pro-communist. Reminding the press that the festival was to be an antidote to this postwar paranoia, Hutchins sharpened the point by declaring that "Goethe's ideas are anti-Nazi, anti-Communist, anti–UnAmerican Activities Committee, in short"—Hutchins here drew upon a term then gaining currency as a catchall for undemocratic politics of the Left or Right—"they are anti-totalitarian."[3] And with this, he ended his long-running performance as, so he said, "a stuffed shirt on roller skates with records on his back"[4] spreading word of the festival across the land. After lunch, he returned to Chicago for another ten days of work before joining the festival.

Paepcke arrived in Aspen (his wife was already there) to find the town spic and span and alive with anticipation. Houses had been painted, trees planted, and new faces could be seen on every street, a few belonging to festival participants—like Thornton Wilder (who was already developing a following at the Jerome bar)—most of them those of vacationers attracted by assurances of high culture and healthful recreation. Then, as a crew from the Voice of America readied equipment to broadcast speeches, interviews, and discussions in six languages to nations around the world, Ronald Goodman, installed at the Jerome, issued Herbert Hoover's press release inviting the eyes of the country and the world to fix on Aspen and on the postwar Goethe as conceived by the West: humanist, internationalist, practical and humane individualist. The festival was ready to start.

June 27 dawned in Aspen with the usual chill that burns away under the rising run. With no events scheduled before evening, the artists, intellectuals, and vacationers diverted themselves with the pleasures of nature and informal socializing. As twilight fell, and with it the sunny temperatures, visitors and locals, numbering several hundred people in all, strolled to the tent for the formal opening ceremonies and a recital by the violinist Erica Morini (see fig. 6.1). As they seated themselves in the bowl under Saarinen's tent, they opened their handsome 160-page souvenir programs to be reminded again that this happy occasion had a deeply serious purpose.[5]

More than any previous statement of that purpose, the program expressed the aching cultural pessimism of Hutchins's pronouncements over the past decade and a half. "The difficulty of our time is a difficulty of the human spirit," the text began. For while man's material powers have increased, his sense of direction has declined. "Literacy has flourished, and taste has been debased. Things seem to be bigger; but they do not seem to be better." Goethe's life and ideas bear upon this difficulty because Goethe detected its makings in the decline of humanistic culture. And Goethe's message proved the more prophetic by originating in Germany, that "bloody battleground" that "must be planted again if the difficulty of the human spirit is to be surmounted." Hence, "we are not gathered here in an antiquarian or academic mood; still less in a sentimental one," but for the most profound and far-reaching of reasons: "to search out in ourselves the depths of the spirit that sustained the optimism of Goethe." For "if he had reason to be optimistic, we have need. We need his spirit more than he did"; it alone can help us find the "common spirit that is man." To this end, the festival would ask two questions: "What can we find in Goethe's grand plan of world literature that will serve us? What can we find in Goethe's grand conception

Fig. 6.1. Eero Saarinen's music tent and Goethe Festival visitors, Aspen, 1949. W. Eugene Smith, *Life* magazine, © 1949 Time Inc.

of *Humanität* that will save us?" The lectures would provide some direct answers and the concerts would work their effect indirectly by conveying Goethe's "lyric spirit" to the community of listeners. By the evidence of this message, the Goethe Festival was to be serious business indeed.

Governor Knous officially raised the curtain on the events with a few remarks praising the novel aims that had brought audience and notables together, and he assured everyone, as if to head off a drift into solemnity, and with a plug for all of Colorado's cultural centers, that much pleasure awaited them. Then, sitting down beside Paepcke on the dais, he listened with the small crowd, shivering now as the cold night air swept through the open sides of the tent, as Erica Morini played Mozart, Brahms, Paganini, Liszt, and a *valse caprice* by Henri Wieniawski that Felix Borowski, music editor of the *Chicago Sun-Times*, said would have caused Goethe to "shudder" from its strangeness.[6]

The music was fine, but it bore no relation to Goethe; the Goethe Festival had yet to live up to its promises. Still, neither the inauspicious debut nor the disappointing crowd, which filled less than half of the tent, nor even the uncomfortably cool evening seemed to dampen the spirit of the occasion. "Don't worry," Paepcke assured an inquisitive journalist, "things will be quite all right."[7]

Things began picking up the next day with the first of many unusual programs of music inspired by Goethe and with concerts rescheduled for late afternoon to avoid the evening's chill. Jerome Hines and Herta Glaz sang songs of Schumann, Beethoven, Hugo Wolf, Schubert, and Mendelssohn, set to lyrics taken from *Wilhelm Meister, Egmont, Faust,* and Goethe's poems of love and longing. The mood of this program was that of the lyrical, melancholy, and subjective young poet who had not yet achieved his Bildung—his completed education and character. But this could hardly have been avoided, for the Goethe who inspired music was not the Olympian observer, the scientist, the critic of life but the restless, self-conscious, and sad romantic individualist.

The festival's third day brought the first nonmusical event: a roundtable discussion, "Goethe and Art." Conceived by Alfred Frankfurter, editor of *Art News,* and Walter Paepcke after the rest of the academic schedule had been completed, it was intended to redress the neglect of Goethe's ideas of the visual arts in the rest of the program. Yet the panel, consisting of Frankfurter, Herbert Bayer, Eero Saarinen, Dorothy Adlow (art critic of the *Christian Science Monitor*), and Otto Karl Bach (director of the Denver Museum of Art), seemed ignorant of Goethe's aesthetic ideas and barely touched on them, lapsing instead into often contradictory speculations on Goethe's relation to modernism—some saying Goethe remained artistically audacious and therefore protomodernist all his life, others saying that the old Goethe was anything but audacious and if alive today would, "like Winston Churchill, be painting innocuous watercolors and sit at the head of the 'Sanity in Art League.'"[8]

But with a festive atmosphere settling over the idyllic mountain town, Alfred Frankfurter casually dismissed the morning's discussion during lunch at Pioneer Park: "Nature at Aspen is far better than talking of art."[9] And by this time nature at Aspen was giving pleasure to rapidly growing numbers of people. They came from every state except Alabama and Mississippi and they included the wealthy and leisured, the adventurous young, and many academics—like a retired professor from Illinois, whose former students had collected $780 to send him and his wife to the festival.[10] Four hundred people came from Chicago alone by train or car; and jubilant vacationers arrived in buses from Glenwood Springs bearing the sign of their destination: "Goethe."

The publicity campaign seemed to have done its job. And if the newspaper reports are to be believed, some people actually came to see Goethe in the flesh. More than one visitor asked: "Where is Mr. Goethe?"—pronounced in a delightful variety of ways: "Goth," "Goweth," or "Goity."[11]

The Aspen congregation was, as Giuseppe Borgese's wife, Elisabeth, commented, "a motley society," but its members were soon to be "welded" together by the sublime atmosphere, the music, and Goethe's ideas.[12] The first full symphony concert, on July 1, ignited the welder's flame by making not only Goethe but Faust familiar figures to Aspen music lovers. A stirring performance under Mitropoulos's baton of Wagner's *Faust Overture,* Dukas's *The Sorcerer's Apprentice,* and Liszt's *Faust Symphony* brought the near-capacity audience to its feet. More than the intimate recitals that had preceded it, this concert expressed an energetic Faustian spirit and brought closer to realization than before the high expectations of planners and visitors alike (see figs. 6.2 and 6.3). The concert proved a perfect prelude to the two-week adventure in cultural criticism that began the next day with Giuseppe Borgese's address, "The Message of Goethe."

Borgese had contributed little to planning the festival after sending the ball into Hutchins's court back in 1947. For he had left his post at the University of Chicago in 1948 to resume teaching at the University of Milan and to become almost wholly occupied in working for world government. Although Hutchins continued to honor him as the festival's "godfather," by May 1949 Borgese had begun to feel slighted in the publicity, which even omitted his name as lecturer; and he modestly pointed out to Ronald Goodman that "the project of the celebration," especially its "intellectual and political values, . . . came partly at least from an early suggestion of mine."[13]

Now his importance was reestablished by the opportunity to deliver the first lecture of the academic program. Pledging himself to the festival's objective of interpreting Goethe "if we can, in the terms of our day," and in the effusive and allusive language typical of him, Borgese located the "message of Goethe" in three "myths": the Werther myth, presented in Goethe's first novel, combining images of genius, irrationality, the impossible life, and of suicide as "surrender" to the unconditioned spirit; the Faust myth, embodied by the "suprarational" worshiper of unconditioned freedom, experienced by Faust as force, energy, and unbounded expectation leading to final self-mastery; and the myth of Goethe himself, scattered in phrases throughout his writings, more numerous late than early, portraying a man imbued with confidence in belief and action and the unity of all things, the only peer of Dante and yet, unlike Dante, a voice for *our* age. These myths, Borgese said, make Goethe fair game for exploitation by any modern ideology: "Faust could well have been a Nazi" by virtue of his appetite for energetic unreason and bold misadventures; and the author of Werther and Faust is himself an appropriate person for the Soviets to celebrate because "he is a humanist, not a democrat." But Goethe's true genius and greatest achievement, Borgese said, lie in the third myth, affirming "a treaty of peace between the individual person and cosmic order." And it is this myth that places Goethe "with those of us who are One-Worlders" and that justifies their seeing "Goethe as a One-Worlder," too.[14]

Fig. 6.2. Dimitri Mitropoulos conducting the Minneapolis Symphony Orchestra in the music tent at the Goethe Festival, Aspen, 1949. Photo by Ferenc Berko.

It was fitting that the first characterization of the postwar Goethe should have come from the inveterate exponent of world government who had enlisted the Bicentennial in this cause in the first place. Borgese's listeners applauded the speech for perfectly setting the mood of intensity and uplift that the occasion required. "His Latin enthusiasm was infectious," reported the *Aspen Times*.[15] And Anne Lindbergh, a house guest of Mrs. John P. Marquand, said to Thornton Wilder as they left the tent together: "It makes you want to start studying all over again."[16] The postwar Goethe was coming to life. And after an afternoon concert, featuring Beethoven's Overture to "Egmont" and the "Eroica" Symphony, the crowds returned to hear more about him, this time from the speaker second only to Schweitzer in reputation: José Ortega y Gasset.

No one, except possibly Hutchins, came to Aspen from a career more fully occupied with education and its cultural consequences than Ortega. And no one at the festival, besides Hutchins and Paepcke, had a more lasting effect on the course of Aspen's cultural career.

Born in 1883, Ortega had opened his intellectual career as a voice among the Spanish intellectuals known as "the Generation of '98," who, enraged by Spain's humiliation in the Spanish-American War, condemned Spanish

Fig. 6.3. Walter and Elizabeth Paepcke in music tent at the Goethe Festival, Aspen, 1949. Photo by Ferenc Berko.

culture for its bondage to a dark and mythical past, its cultural insularity, and its intellectual philistinism. Although some years younger and more theoretically inclined than the others of this group, Ortega had joined them in urging the renewal of Spanish culture through intellectual discipline and the opening of Spain to foreign influence. After a period of study in Germany, he had returned to Spain bursting with Germanic philosophical questions over ways of knowing and the relation of the ideal to the real. As a professor at the University of Madrid, he had begun working out his own philosophy, first sketched in *Meditaciones del Quijote* (1914). Steeped in the cultural experience of his generation in Spain, fired by the idea (which he had taken mainly from the writings of Friedrich Nietzsche and Wilhelm Dilthey) of life as creative energy, and determined to bridge idealism and realism, Ortega there dwelled on the relation between mind and its environment and concluded that this relation defines reality. He set forth his conclusion in a phrase that represented both his metaphysics and his psychology: "I am I and my circumstances and if I do not save my circumstances, I cannot save myself."[17]

While intensifying his criticism of Spanish circumstances in *Invertebrate Spain* (1921) and the periodical *Revista de Occidente* (1923–) in hopes of opening

Spain up to the rationality and liberalism of Western thought—"leveling the Pyrenees," as he liked to say—Ortega had taken up the condition of Western culture at large. His essay "The Dehumanization of Art" (1925), reprinted many times and in many languages, offered a path-breaking social analysis of artistic modernism, concentrating on its elitist bias, its removal from historic human experience, and its identification with the young, with sport, and with play. Ortega questioned the worth of this art, since it had turned its back on the historical world, that is, man's circumstances—and he ignored its metaphysical pretensions, but he also criticized its critics for their adherence to the past. And he generously speculated that modernism would yet achieve greatness once it overcame the tendency to dehumanization.

Ortega's international reputation had become firmly established with his powerful and sweeping critique of the mass culture gaining ascendency throughout Western Europe in the 1920s and 1930s, *The Revolt of the Masses* (1930). It was this fearless book that had commended him to the festival organizers. Here Ortega described mass culture as outwardly dominated by fashionable hedonism, the cults of youth and entertainment, and, as he put it in catch phrases of the day, the "new morality" of the "smart world."[18] And he blamed the ascendency of this culture on the wiles of psychologically persuasive advertising, seductive consumer products, and the widening standardization of life, manners, thought, and emotions. Ortega was of course describing the very culture that had brought such commercial success to his future ally in cultural reform, Walter Paepcke, and which Robert M. Hutchins and Mortimer Adler and the Goethe Bicentennial Foundation itself had hoped to reform by exploiting some of its own devices: mass adult education and the selling of ideas. But like all astute cultural critics, Ortega saw that the true evil of this culture lay not in its obvious appearances but in the personality type those appearances breed. And he named this type the Mass Man. The Mass Man is not merely a member of the mass but a man of a certain character, whether he is alone or, more likely, one among many. "Spoiled" by abundance and pleasure, brutalized by the "barbarism of 'specialization'" numbed by self-satisfaction and frivolity, the Mass Man knows nothing beyond himself and is therefore incapable of discipline, self-sacrifice, and genuine excellence.[19] Hence he exchanges a demanding culture for a cheap anti-intellectualism and for a psychologically easy political authoritarianism, like that of fascism and communism; and, from there, civilization staggers to its doom.

Ortega, like his hosts of 1949, saw some prospect for redeeming the Mass Man in international political unity. "Only the determination to construct a great nation from a group of peoples of the continent," he wrote near the end of *Revolt*, "could give new life to the pulses of Europe. She would start to believe in herself again, and automatically to make demands on, to discipline herself." Yet this redemption could not come simply from "the building-up of Europe into a great national state."[20] The Mass Man would also have to be educated. And when called upon shortly after the publication of *Revolt* on behalf of students at the University of Madrid against state interference in higher education (during the constitutional crisis that eventually saw the fledgling Spanish Republic ground under the heel of Primo de Rivera's dicta-torship), Ortega had spelled out his theory of education in a series of articles for the newspaper *El Sol,* later reprinted as *The Mission of the University.*

Because the Mass Man's most egregious fault is to hold nothing superior to himself and therefore to be incapable of self-discipline, it is the true mis-sion of the university, Ortega asserted, to shape another type of man, one possessed of keen understanding and strong will. "The great task immedi-ately before us," he wrote, is to "reassemble out of the scattered pieces" of the modern self "a complete organism, the European man. . . . What force can bring this about if it is not the university?"[21] Only the university can trans-mit a vital common culture between peoples and generations while keeping the highest standards of truth and discipline intact. Thus the university will "make the ordinary man, first of all, a cultured man,"[22] or what Ortega had labeled in *Revolt* a "noble" man, that is, a man aware of the circumstances of "shipwreck" that encompass us all and that demand struggle to survive, and also a man aware of the moral consequences of action and ideas, and capable of thinking and acting for the moral good of himself and the entire culture.[23] To create such a man, Ortega went on in words remarkably like those so often intoned by Hutchins and Adler, and by Moholy-Nagy for that matter: the university must prepare "a new integration of knowledge . . . to be taught in the 'Faculty of Culture.'"[24]

Although Ortega had not been able to put his educational ideas into practice during the 1930s, fleeing into voluntary exile when Franco drove republican Spain once again into the earth, he had returned to Spain after World War II to do just that. By this time he was becoming identified with the fashionable French existentialism of Jean-Paul Sartre and Albert Camus because he perceived man as a "shipwrecked sailor" tossed about by chaotic circumstances yet morally responsible to himself. But Ortega's true occupa-tion remained, and seemed to him more compelling than ever in the wake of world war, the reform of the Mass Man, especially through humanistic edu-cation. To accomplish this he had founded the Instituto de Humanidades in 1948. Dedicated, he said, to effecting "a profound reform in those sciences which study what is human,"[25] the institute would awaken all of Spain, Ortega hoped, intellectuals and manual laborers alike, to an understanding of hu-man life in its circumstances, existential and historical.

In January 1949, Ortega had stepped to the lectern for his first public address in Spain in a dozen years. It must have pleased him to see the hall jammed with Spaniards of many kinds—students, socialists, curiosity seekers—who, one observer reported, "clapped and shouted so long" when he entered "that they seemed almost hysterical."[26] Taking as his subject Arnold Toynbee's theory of history, he decried Toynbee's imposition of lifeless abstractions upon the panorama of historical reality and, contrary to Toynbee, he ringingly blamed the fall of civilizations not on the atrophy of religion but on the loss of respect for historical reality and for the demands that reality exacts of human beings. Toynbee's theory could only reinforce the complacent and dehumanized self-regard of the Mass Man; it would not help the Noble Man to rise. Elsewhere Ortega had said, in another of his quotable phrases, "Man, in a word, has no nature; what he has is . . . history."[27] Now, as Ortega assailed Toynbee's theories, the phrase took on a sharpened edge slashing away at bloodless categories to lay bare the historic moment of postwar man and his circumstances.

Such were Ortega's intellectual occupations when he had accepted Hutchins's invitation to lecture at the Goethe Festival. Goethe was, to be sure, no stranger to him. Seventeen years earlier Ortega had commemorated the centennial of Goethe's death with an essay playing upon that venerable Ortegan theme: "Life is, in itself and forever, shipwreck." There he urged a reappraisal of Goethe, setting aside the titan in search of "a Goethe for the shipwrecked," a Goethe for man and his circumstances in 1932. Goethe lends himself to such a reappraisal, Ortega said, because he had steeped himself in "man's struggle with his intimate and individual destiny," and had then deserted his own "destiny" by fleeing his youthful Sturm und Drang for the security and stability of court life in Weimar where he had spent his adult life. Ortega made no pretence of filling out this sketch, or of identifying with its subject, but he prodded others to look into Goethe for themselves with this advice: "There is but one way left to save a classic; . . . to bring him close to us, to make him contemporary, to set his pulse going again with an injection of blood from our own veins whose ingredients are *our* passions . . . and *our* problems."[28]

That was 1932. In 1949, after an era of fascism and world war, Ortega took up the subject where he had left it: how to make Goethe speak to "*our* passions. . . and *our* problems." He had agreed to give two lectures, presumably the same one twice. But Ortega was too full of ideas to repeat himself, and he resolved to deliver two different addresses, one composed on his journey across the Atlantic and the other in Aspen. After a difficult voyage that disrupted his concentration and delayed his writing, he nevertheless arrived in Aspen on July 1 in the buoyant spirits that marked his temperament.

That same day he gave the first interview he had ever given, remarking jovially that the high altitude must have made him forget himself. His unimposing appearance—a short stocky frame, jowly face, wide expressive mouth, large intelligent eyes, surmounted by a prominent forehead and nearly bald pate—gave him a friendly, even neighborly air, which he reinforced with a hearty smile that seldom left his lips. Asked for his impressions of America on this, his first, visit, he replied with an affection not all Europeans would share and an observation common among them. "Europe," he said, "is old and has many vices," and it "needs the faith in life and the reasons to exist which it can get from the United States." But, he added, for all its vitality and affirmation, one thing "America and her people need is training in the art of concentration."[29] Although Ortega liked America, he suspected that it might be all too hospitable to the Mass Man.

Ortega picked up the theme of concentration again as he took the podium for his first lecture. With Elio Gianturco of the Library of Congress reading from a rough translation of the speech entitled "The Bicentennial Goethe," Ortega opened with an existential question: "Why are you here?" Everyone in attendance, he said, had *chosen* to come to this mountain retreat to celebrate Goethe. And the choice had been not merely between external options but between internal potentialities. Thus it had the "grave character" of a moral and existential decision making each person "responsible before his own conscience for his presence."

Having put the audience on notice of the existential business at hand, Ortega turned to Goethe, whom he characterized as a "visceral element" in European civilization touching its every "entrail." With this civilization "going through a radical crisis," and starving for solutions, Goethe must give some clues to the crisis and a way out of it. Ortega found the first clue in Goethe's idea of personality or personhood (*Persönlichkeit*). Not a fixed psychological structure, personality for Goethe was a "task," "the being of each one of us" in process of fulfilling itself through growth and development, and as such it is our supreme act and crowning joy: "Höchster Gluck der Erdenkinder/Ist nur die Persönlichkeit" ("The highest happiness of those on Earth/Is only personality").

A second clue Ortega found in Goethe's idea of culture. Far from being an incidental ornament or an external pattern of life or, worse, an object of veneration, as it has become in modern times, culture for Goethe was a source of meaning and discipline and energy, generated and drawn upon by personalities in the act of living. The "modern Goethe," Ortega said, "the one of 1949," the "Bicentennial Goethe," is one who demands that culture be brought before the bar of humanity in a civilization that has "become a problem for itself." This was not, Ortega conceded, the Goethe of the nineteenth century, the century of progress and peace; it is the Goethe of an era of crisis, doubt, and world war, "whom neither his contemporaries nor the generations preceding our own were able to see," and one who represents for us the forces of life needed to create "a new pattern of human existence" from the ruins of the old.[30]

Then, taking a few well-directed slaps at his supposed philosophical brethren, the nihilistic existentialists of France, "who try today to push man back into nothingness and to leave him there," and at Arnold Toynbee's lugubrious and lifeless theory of history, Ortega adroitly joined his own philosophy to that of the Bicentennial Goethe to vigorously and persuasively wrest reasons for hope from mid-century despair. "European civilization has profound doubts about itself," he repeated. "Well and good! I do not recollect that any civilization ever perished from an attack of doubt. I recollect that civilizations usually die through the ossification of their traditional faith, through an arteriosclerosis of their beliefs." Hence, "instead of concealing the negative aspects of the present period, . . . we must bare them, manifest them, emphasize them, energetically define them" and put them to use.[31] For, he said, playing again on his favorite image, the "sensation of shipwreck is a great stimulant for man." Just as "the shipwrecked mariner becomes a swimmer," the civilization that knows danger will prevail.

Thus the "great Goethean task" of the postwar era, Ortega concluded, is to rebuild civilization out of "human negativities," encouraged by the "resignation" Goethe had acquired in old age, which his readers "prior to our days" could not understand. Ortega promised to say more of this resignation in his next address; now he would only hint at its meaning: the belief that "life is impossible without illusions," and that Europe was about to embrace the one illusion as yet untried: "the illusion of being disillusioned."[32]

Such was Ortega's first "Bicentennial Goethe": humanist, existentialist, prophet of renewal amid doubt and devastation, critic of dreamers and nihilists, religionists and worshipers of culture. It was a more bracing and attractive Goethe than that of Ortega's previous essay, for Ortega, following his own advice, had discovered a Goethe for "today"—understandably a Goethe hardly distinguishable from Ortega himself.

Whether or not this Goethe made any converts that night, the speaker, modestly describing himself as an "obscure, retiring man devoid of any monumentality," did.[33] For although the speech was loose and even more loosely translated, it had all the hallmarks of Ortega's strong writings: ragged in form, rambling in thought, it soared on brilliant generalization, alighted on sharp images and lapidary phrases, and took flight again only to come to rest on a riddle. If the ideas defied easy summary and ready grasp, combined as they were with Ortega's eloquent delivery, punctuated by spirited gesturing, they conveyed the sensation of powerful thought to every listener. Ortega "gave to everyone in the audience," Elisabeth Mann Borgese observed, "the illusion that he or she understood Spanish, every word of it."[34] And the young lawyer called to Aspen in 1945 to manage Walter Paepcke's real estate affairs, Sam Mitchell, became an instant convert to Ortega's belief that a wounded culture could be cured only *by exertion;* thirty years later, he was still quick to cite Ortega as the philosophical inspiration not only of the Goethe Festival but of his life.[35] The *Aspen Times* of July 7, echoing the public response, took Ortega's image of the shipwrecked mariner as the symbol of the festival itself: for two weeks, the newspaper observed, Aspen would be this mariner, struggling to save civilization from ruin.

As the convocation's first full day ended, many of Aspen's visitors might worry over the fate of Western civilization, but none could doubt that they were part of a historic event bent on shaping that fate. This impression strengthened as the days passed and as a mood of inspiriting camaraderie spread through the celebration, enhanced even by untoward incidents—like the torrential rain during the next day's concert that turned the stretched canvas tent into a kettle drum and drove audience and performers into communal clusters at protected spots between streams of water pouring through openings near the poles.

As if commenting on the unexpected conviviality of that afternoon, Stephen Spender spoke in the evening (preceded earlier in the day by Ernst R. Curtius, lecturing on the medieval bases of Western thought and saying little about Goethe) of the community underlying differences between cultures. Spender, the youngest of the speakers, just turned forty and at that time a temporary lecturer at Sarah Lawrence College, was known to Americans mainly as a member of the English literary generation of the 1930s that had put literature and criticism in the service of left-wing politics in general and antifascist politics in particular and had created a poetry of moral conscience and simple style—in opposition to the aestheticism of the older modernists, Yeats, Eliot, and Pound. Spender was also recognized, like his friends W. H. Auden and Christopher Isherwood, for having a strong association with Germany, where he had spent much of his early adulthood. Thus, when the more prominent Briton T. S. Eliot declined Hutchins's invitation, Spender was a good choice to help renew cultural ties between Germany and the West.

After an introduction by James Laughlin, Spender explored literary relations between Goethe and the English. Although Goethe was much influenced by Shakespeare, Spender said, Goethe's "uninhibited guiltless attitude" thwarted a reciprocal influence among the guilt-ridden English. Condemned for his "immorality" by Wordsworth, Goethe then fell victim to the "fruitful misunderstanding" of others like Coleridge and Carlyle, who viewed him as marmoreal, earnest, energetic, deadly serious, self-important, and objective: in short, as a Victorian patriarch. (Carlyle, Goethe's greatest friend in England, memorably expressed his ambivalence: "Goethe is the greatest genius that has lived for a century and the greatest ass that has lived for three. I could sometimes fall down and worship him; at other times I could kick him out of the room.") So thoroughly identified with the Victorian temper did Goethe become (notwithstanding G. S. Lewes's rehabilitative biography of 1855, unmentioned by Spender) that when the Victorians went wholly out of favor with the rise of modernism, Goethe went with them—as Max Beerbohm illustrated in his debunking essay, "Quia Imperfectum."

Now, Spender said, we must discover Goethe anew—and the true Goethe at that. He must be a Goethe detached from the Victorian legend and acceptable to modernists. This Goethe can be found in such places as part 2 of *Faust*, where the author wrestles with "the main problem of modern poetry: firstly to found poetry on personal experience and secondly, to enlarge personal experience until it becomes objective." Better than any writer in English, Spender added, Goethe showed how to achieve this salutary objectivity through an art that comprehends past and present, and through political responsibility. Thus Goethe at once led toward modernism and pointed a way out of the impasse of subjectivity in which the modernist languishes.[36]

Spender was right to read Goethe as a protomodernist, for no literary document better exhibits the modern pains of ambivalence and unsatisfied desire than *Faust*, and in no one was the tension between subjectivity and objectivity more sharply drawn than in Goethe himself. But, as Spender only hinted, if Goethe were to find a large literary audience in the twentieth century, the modernist tendency to subjectivity, ambivalence, and negativism would have to give way to an appetite for the kind of objectivity, will, and affirmation he admired. Spender wished such an appetite would develop but barely intimated how fundamental the change would have to be.

Aspen had now met three postwar Goethes: the one-worlder, the Ortegan existentialist, and the modernist. The next day it met a fourth (after the Indian philosopher T. M. P. Mahadevan had ignored Goethe in a lecture on the relation of Western rationalism to Eastern intuitionism) in a portrait by Italian scholar Elio Gianturco of Goethe as an Italianate philsopher of style. Other Goethes would follow. But first, the attention of everyone was drawn to the arrival of Albert Schweitzer.

Ever since his boat, the *Nieuw Amsterdam,* had docked in New York June 25—after an unsettling bump with another vessel in fog off Nantucket—Schweitzer's presence in this country had stirred public curiosity and roused the energies of publicists. The festival's publicity had at least made Schweitzer an "event" to be covered even if his importance and identity were vague: "Famed African Organist to Visit U.S." read one headline on an early Schweitzer story.[37]

But whatever Schweitzer's reputation, some sixty-five people of the press greeted the *Nieuw Amsterdam* eager for a quotable word or a historic photo. Schweitzer played to them with the public persona he wore best—humility. Bowing respectfully, he apologized in French for not speaking their language: "Ladies and gentlemen, in my youth I was a stupid young man. I learned German and French, Latin, Greek, Hebrew—but no English. In my next incarnation, English shall be my first language." Then at the request of the press he assumed an awkward, statuesque pose with the New York skyline as the backdrop. "New York et moi," he said with a chuckle. The audience was his. The press could hardly have resisted him, this physically imposing moral and intellectual giant so gentle and deferential. And he cultivated their affections by seeming to be theirs. "You are so nice to me," he said in his sweetest, almost childlike manner. "You treat me like a big banker or a prize fighter."[38]

In this humble spirit Schweitzer declined to speak on public affairs. "In view of the atomic bomb," asked one reporter, "do you have a philosophy to offer the world?"[39] And another: "How about communism? What can be done about that?" But to such queries Schweitzer would only say: "Those questions do not exist in the forest," and "One who comes out of solitude into the world can give no message to the world—just as those who come to us can give us no message in Africa." Pressed again, he added: "The best thing with which to oppose communism is noncommunism—to give all possible liberties to all possible peoples, spiritual and material." "Would you call the African native free?" came the reporter's quick response. But Schweitzer had simple wisdom on this, too. "Am I free? Are you free? The natives eat. What grows on the land belongs to them. That is an enormous thing, isn't it?"[40] The press had their story: here was a Schweitzer for Americans. Not the world-renowned scholar, philosopher, musician, and self-sacrificing moralist, but the noble innocent—wise through simplicity, and the greater man for it.

This public image was the making of the Schweitzer legend in America. Yet that legend would not have had a chance to flower had Schweitzer known exactly where the Goethe Festival was to be held. When he had first contemplated attending the festival, after receiving the invitation promising two million francs for his hospital, Schweitzer had opened a world atlas in search of Aspen. But the book was old, and he could find no listing—at that time not even an up-to-date atlas would have helped. Noticing that all the cables from Hutchins originated in Chicago, he had decided Aspen must be a new suburb of that great midwestern city. Only when he arrived in New York did Schweitzer learn that Aspen was one thousand miles west of Chicago, and worse, it lay eight thousand feet above sea level. His health might not stand it. "When I learned that Aspen was in Colorado," he said later, "and at such an altitude, I did not like that so well, when for years my heart has not been able to support the altitude."[41] Aspen was, he later confided to Paepcke with gracious ambiguity, "a little too near heaven for me."[42] But having given his word, Schweitzer kept it. At some danger and certain discomfort to himself, he entrained for the Rockies.

Pursued by reporters, Schweitzer grew in celebrity with every stage of the journey. "Albert Schweitzer has only this month hit the headlines in the American press as he made his way to a remote Colorado town,"[43] reported one midwestern newspaper. And with that celebrity grew the legend, fostered by anecdotes demonstrating the Great Man's innocence and purity of heart. At Chicago's Union Station he slipped away from his party to carry suitcases for a struggling woman. Later on the train two young women naively asked him, "Would you be good enough to autograph our books, Dr. Einstein?" He winked mischievously and wrote: "With best wishes, Albert Einstein, by his friend Albert Schweitzer."[44] He also praised the Marshall Plan as a "strong spiritual manifestation" of America's generosity; and when told of food lifts for birds stranded in the previous midwestern winter's storms, he blinked back tears and said warmly, "Ah, the poor animals. What a magnificent achievement. Vive l'Amérique!" Even the buttons in his train roomette elicited a response happily noted by journalists. "So many stops," he said; "it's like playing an organ."[45] And, clinching his host country's affections, he told reporters, "I am delighted to find that people here are almost as disorganized and leisurely as they are in Europe. I feel very much at home."[46]

It was in Aspen of course that Schweitzer found people most leisurely. But reaching that mountain destination proved even more laborious than he had imagined, adding a new and unwanted adventure to the series of surprises that had begun with the shipboard collision. Departing Denver for Glenwood Springs on the morning of the Fourth of July, the train carrying Schweitzer and his party chugged into the mountains. Two hours later it abruptly ground to a halt. Before it the tracks disappeared into a rockslide. The train lurched backward, and, returning to Denver, took another route through Colorado Springs. Instead of reaching Glenwood Springs at two in the afternoon as scheduled, the train pulled into the station at midnight.

Exhausted and already feeling the ill effects of the altitude, Schweitzer and his wife climbed into Paepcke's waiting car for the final leg of the trip. Arriving in Aspen after all was quiet and even Elizabeth Paepcke had gone to sleep, the old couple settled into the former carriage house, now the guest house at Pioneer Park—giving rise to the quip that the Paepckes had bedded a saint in their stable. Breakfast, Paepcke said, would be at 8:00 A.M. if that suited his guests.

But the misadventures were not yet past. The next morning, preparations for breakfast in the Paepcke household came to a sudden halt as desperate cries of alarm issued from the bathroom. Elizabeth Paepcke dropped everything and flew up the stairs. There in the shower stood her husband shouting helplessly, "Do something!" as water flowed up from every drain, flooding the floor and flowing over the threshold. Used to managing crises in the various Paepcke houses, Elizabeth dashed about with mop and bucket trying to hold back the deluge and ordering the bewildered maids to cut off the plumbing.

The clock chimed eight. The doorbell rang. In bathrobe and curlers, mop in hand, at once frantic and resigned, Elizabeth Paepcke opened the door. "There stood the great man himself," she remembered, "just as he had been described to me: shaggy mane of grey hair, amused brown eyes, immense drooping mustache, the black folded tie, old-fashioned long coat—and on his arm an elderly lady in grey and garnets who looked like a pale moth. I stared at the doctor."

"Oh," she cried, "our plumbing has backed up, there is water all over the floor, and I have to rescue my husband from the bathroom."

"I see," said Dr. Schweitzer slowly (in German), as he looked Elizabeth over from tousled hair to bare feet and mop. "I see," he repeated. "Mrs. Schweitzer and I are just in time to witness the second Flood."[47]

The tides at last being turned back, breakfast proceeded in good humor—and reverence for the Great Man. And now another side of Schweitzer began to appear. More than an innocent and gentle moralist, he had *the truth* and the will to live it, and this bred in him a weary impatience with lesser beings, whom he indulged only when he chose. True to his philosophy of "reverence for life," which prevented his killing any creature unnecessarily, he would eat no creatures, only vegetables and fruits. And although generous with his time, he would not allow his privacy or his chosen pursuits to be disturbed. When he wanted to play the piano in the Pioneer Park living room—as he did in the early mornings and late at night—he expected other people to accommodate him. When he wanted someone else to perform, he expected them to cooperate. He told the soprano Dorothy Maynor, also a house guest of the Paepckes, that she *would* sing Bach arias to his accompaniment before breakfast, and when she replied that she must have something to eat first, he said simply: "Have an apple; if I can play, you can sing."[48]

In later years, after the exaltation of Schweitzer's reputation had provoked a more skeptical reaction, the bon docteur's tendencies to self-righteousness and authoritarianism were often observed and reproved, and even his life of sacrifice in the African jungles was belittled as futile and self-aggrandizing. But during his American visit, coming amid the thirst for humanistic idealism and moral heroism of the postwar years (which also engendered the widespread but temporary adulation of Albert Camus), Schweitzer was almost universally revered as a hero and a saint, or more. "Sitting in his presence," one visitor at the festival said, "was like sitting in the presence of God."[49] Yet to sit beside the man or hear him speak was one thing; to play hostess to him was another: "Living with a saint," Elizabeth Paepcke remembered, "was the most uncomfortable thing imaginable."[50]

Fortunately for the Goethe Festival, Schweitzer, despite his benign authoritarianism and the physical discomfort that made him more temperamental than usual, played the role of gentle saint very well. He often said he was not of this modern world, and he looked it. His tall, imposing frame, draped in a black nineteenth-century suitcoat, rumpled trousers, and drooping string bowtie, his generally disheveled appearance—"Albert, comb your hair," his wife kept whispering[51]—and shuffling movements set him apart from the other speakers. Many of them dropped by to talk with him in the morning and evening at the Paepckes' or at the Jerome, where he sometimes sat in the afternoon (see fig. 6.4). On his first visit to the hotel an epiphany of the festival's spirit occurred. Seated for lunch, Schweitzer was seen from the far side of the room by Ortega. The Spaniard crossed over to him; Schweitzer rose, and, never having met in the flesh before, these two living monuments of Western intellectual culture—Schweitzer, the festival's spiritual symbol, and Ortega, its philosophical guide—clasped arms.[52]

Wherever Schweitzer went, people gathered to watch or listen. And many of them behaved like nothing less than fans, if a saint can be said to have fans, peering through the windows at Pioneer Park and the Jerome, perching in trees, dogging the saint's footsteps. And Schweitzer lived up to the image. When Paepcke tried to protect him from autograph-seeking hands, Schweitzer called him off, saying: "It is my duty." To spare him this duty, or to grant him benefits from it, the *Aspen Times* went so far as to recommend that people donate ten to twenty-five dollars per signature to the hospital in Lambaréné. Short of that, the newspaper said, "Give the man a break."[53]

Schweitzer's first public act in Aspen came shortly after that early ill-fated breakfast. Sitting in the yard of a neighboring house, he answered questions from some thirty members of the press (with Jean Canu translating). Apologizing for his fatigue, he revealed his displeasure on learning that the convocation was to be held in the mountains, a displeasure that had now become physical. "If you know a witch doctor who could help me," he added, "you might let me know."

Once he had decided to come to the Goethe Bicentennial, he said, "I plunged again into Goethe and into new things written about him," which brought renewed confidence "that in philosophy we were one." Goethe, he explained, "starts from material things and arrives at spiritual knowledge."

Fig. 6.4. Notables gathered in Aspen for the Goethe Festival, June 1949. Left to right: Thornton Wilder, William Ernest Hocking, José Ortega y Gasset, Jean Canu, Halvdan Koht, Giuseppe Borgese, Albert Schweitzer, Elio Gianturco, Gerardus van der Leeuw. W. Eugene Smith, *Life* magazine, © 1949 Time Inc.

Asked if the strength of American "materialism" would bar this path, Schweitzer replied: "No. Beyond the things, one goes on to the spiritual, and behind the spiritual things is often found materialism."[54] This gnomic utterance cast little philosophical light, but it strengthened Schweitzer's aura as a man of profound simplicity.

Schweitzer's remarks on politics and on the festival did the same. Praising the American good will of the Marshall Plan—assuming good will, not political self-interest, to have been its source—Schweitzer responded to a question about contemporary world politics with words attractive if puzzling to the politically attuned journalist: "The great conflict of our time is the struggle between a collective society representing the spirit of Goethe and the individualism of man representing the spirit of Goethe."[55] Although he did not say so, this was the very conflict between the Goethe festivals of Weimar and Aspen. Yet Schweitzer chose not to take sides. Instead he went on to suggest that, as the *Aspen Times* reported, Goethe had a lesson to teach the postwar Germans of both persuasions: to "lift themselves up through their own spirit, . . . face all things that come and strive to overcome them." And, he concluded, all the world would benefit from following Goethe's conviction that "the only way to further the brotherhood of man" is "to fulfill one's duty completely."

Pleading exhaustion after fifteen minutes, Schweitzer terminated the conference, posed for a few pictures, and went to rest, while his listeners returned to their typewriters or headed off to the tent for the next lecture. Schweitzer had played his part perfectly. The press and public had been repeatedly told that no living man was more like Goethe than Schweitzer; now they were learning why: Goethe, like Schweitzer, was a moralist and a sage, and something of a naif, too.

But before audiences were to learn any more of Schweitzer's Goethe, they had to meet several others. The first was Thornton Wilder's. Wilder had come to the festival from an illustrious career as an author and through a friendship with Hutchins born of similar religious backgrounds and temperaments and going back to their college days together, first at Oberlin and then at Yale. The friendship sealed in those years persisted to the end of Wilder's life in 1975, although some acquaintances believed it "less a friendship than an alliance, covered over, to be sure, by a patina of wan New England affection."[56]

While Hutchins had gone on to become dean of the Yale Law School in 1927 and then president of the University of Chicago in 1929, Wilder had become a novelist, and a famous one, with the publication first of *Cabala* (1925), a graceful and exotic tale of intellectual awakening set amid a mysterious social clique in Rome, and then of the Pulitzer Prize–winning *The Bridge of San Luis Ray* (1927), a neatly woven story of five lives united by a common death in eighteenth-century Peru. These works and the next, *The Woman of Andros* (1930), a novel of social chaos and forlorn love among ancient Greeks wistfully yearning for religious faith, had given Wilder a reputation for cosmopolitan sensibility, psychological sophistication, and Christian moralism.

At first, critics like the young Edmund Wilson had praised Wilder's "feelings for national temperaments" as well as his Proustian ways with character. But increasingly they had urged him to leave the exotic settings and, as Wilson wrote in 1928, to "study the diverse elements that go to make the United States and give us *their* national portraits."[57] Then, after a controversy surrounding a hostile essay by Michael Gold in the *New Republic* (October 22, 1930) branding Wilder "the Emily Post of culture" and condemning his limpid prose and mythological tales with their faded passions and conservative morality as symptoms of a decaying capitalist society and a sedative for an ailing America, Wilder changed direction. His next novel, *Heaven's My Destination* (1935), the comic story of a religious textbook salesman plying his trade in the American Midwest, opened Wilder's career as an observer of American life, still moralistic but now matter-of-fact rather than mythological and sentimental, a career that reached its pinnacle in the drama that won him a second Pulitzer Prize, *Our Town* (1938).

Even more important than the critics for turning Wilder to American themes was probably his stint as a teacher of creative writing and literature at the University of Chicago. Beginning in 1930, at Hutchins's invitation (as usual, over departmental opposition) and throughout the thirties, Wilder had built a keen following there among the students as a lively and attentive teacher, adding his celebrity to the intellectual ferment of the campus in those years. At the same time, Wilder had come under the fruitful guidance of another occasional lecturer, Gertrude Stein, who taught him to dramatize human emotions and actions directly, which he then did so effectively in *Our Town*.

By the time of the Goethe Festival, Wilder's reputation had shifted again. The great success of *Our Town*, followed by the comic play *The Merchant of Yonkers* (1938)—later the source of the hit Broadway musical *Hello Dolly*—and the experimental drama *The Skin of Our Teeth* (1942), had widened his popular audience. And although he had returned to a remote setting in his most recent novel, *The Ides of March* (1948), portraying Julius Caesar as something of an existentialist hero, Wilder was now regarded by most critics as merely a popular author. Thus they had largely ignored this latest novel—and so had the public. Hence Wilder, invited not only for his fame and friendship but for his lifelong preoccupation with the relation of morality to culture and politics, had arrived in Aspen a discouraged man (despite the respect of people like the publisher Kurt Wolff, also in Aspen, who said Wilder was "the American writer most near the stature of Goethe").[58] At the age of fifty-one, as a friend and biographer observed, Wilder was afflicted by "the fear of failure" and entering "fifteen years of uncertainty."[59]

But as he had done so often, Wilder masked his feelings in an urbane demeanor and emotional detachment. A student of life, not an actor in it, a man who never married and lived with his unmarried sister at the cost of guilt for consuming her life, Wilder appeared to those near him as genial but uninvolved. Yet no one in Aspen was more sociable or willing to pass the day in conversation. If Schweitzer was the festival's spiritual leader and Ortega its philosophical guide, Wilder was its social center. On the afternoon of his speech, Wilder put socializing and his own regrets aside to apply his urbane and cosmopolitan humanism to the search for a twentieth-century Goethe in an address under the auspicious title "World Literature and the Modern Mind." He took his title from Goethe himself, who conceived of "world literature" as a clue to human nature. Although Goethe prized Greek literature for having created the model of "the beautiful human being," he believed all literatures yield truths of human nature and therefore represent, in Wilder's phrase, a "planetary consciousness" needing only to become aware of itself. Sensing the dawn of this awareness late in his life, Goethe had optimistically told his friend Eckermann: "The epoch of world literature is at hand."

"Goethe spoke too soon," Wilder said, but the poet-philosopher had been prophetic. For in the second quarter of the twentieth century a literature appeared that for the first time "assumes that the world is an indivisible unit. Its subject has become planetary life," and Wilder pointed as evidence to the works of modernists, particularly Eliot, Joyce, and Pound—he could have included himself—who drew upon languages and images from all of history and culture. Goethe therefore teaches, Wilder concluded, that mankind can transcend fear and cultural provinciality by acquiring faith in the eternal creative power of life in all its forms. And he reminded his listeners that such a faith is not passive; to embrace it as Goethe did is to "feel that after these days at Aspen we must all change our lives."[60]

More homiletic than philosophical or scholarly, Wilder's address shaped a Goethe much like Wilder himself: part cosmopolitan romanticist, part modernist, part moralist, part one-worlder. And to many listeners, Wilder's Goethe was one of the most impressive of all. The *Aspen Times* reported that Wilder "brought Goethe to life, . . . made him one of us."[61] One visitor told the *Times* that Thornton Wilder's lecture was the greatest he had ever heard;[62] and Elisabeth Borgese pronounced it "one of the most celebrated highlights of the Convocation."[63] But, looked at closely, Wilder's Goethe (drawn mainly from Johann Peter Eckermann's *Conversations with Goethe in the Last Years of His Life*), although an exponent of life and the unity of culture, was, like Wilder himself, rather a man apart, not a heated lover, nor a man of affairs, but a man living for world literature and imagination and for the appreciation of life—not a man truly living life. How different in spirit from Ortega's Bicentennial Goethe, whom the Spanish philosopher had so pointedly quoted as saying: "The more I think about it, the more evident it seems to me that life exists purely in order to be lived."[64]

Wilder's Goethe represented an edifying humanistic ideal to be sure; and this was the Goethe best known to Europeans from Eckermann onward. The next day, after lectures by Halvdan Koht and Jean Canu on the image and influence of Goethe in Scandinavia and France respectively (the first emphasizing a Goethe of psychological discipline and the second an uncompromising individualist), Barker Fairley questioned the accuracy of Wilder's portrait. Taking as his theme "Goethe—The Man and the Myth," he asked whether the Goethe most revered by history, the old Goethe of universal genius and marmoreal perfection captured for posterity in Eckermann's words at Goethe's burial, "*ein vollkommener Mensch lag in grosser Schönheit vor mir*" ("a perfected human being lay in great beauty before me"), had indeed existed.

That conception of Goethe is a myth, Fairley said, and a myth unworthy of the man because it blinds its adherents to Goethe's actual nature, distorts his philosophy of life, and misrepresents his historic importance. Far from a perfectly formed being, Goethe was forever tormented by contradictory desires and incapacities of will, which caused much of his work to remain disorganized and unkempt. And far from an Olympian artist and thinker detached from the vicissitudes of emotion and the troubles of experience, Goethe possessed an unquenchable emotionality that erupted in lyric verse to the end of his days; and he was so steeped in "the problem of managing life and directing it" that his works are infused with a rare "power to change men from what they were and make them different."[65]

Here was a Goethe for Everyman, not preternatural, not perfect, but an exemplary human being, capable of mirroring human nature in strength and weakness and of improving it. At once more comprehensive and closely observed than most of the portraits of Goethe at the festival—and most like Ortega's in interpretation—Fairley's portrait deserved more attention than it got. But because it came from the hand of a cautious and modest scholar who skirted politics and demythologized the master, it had few reverberations. And besides, it had the misfortune of going on view the same day that Albert Schweitzer took the podium to present his version: "Goethe: His Personality and His Work."

People filled the tent to overflowing, anticipating the first formal appearance of the Living Goethe. Robert M. Hutchins, at last in Aspen for the occasion, introduced the one man who by now needed no introduction. As Schweitzer rose to speak, the audience rose with him. For five minutes they stood, applauding. Schweitzer, his head bowed slightly, smiled diffidently, shuffled his feet and waited. Finally the crowd quieted, and Schweitzer began, speaking in French with Wilder at his side reading a translation.

Making no mention of his hope expressed in 1932 that the Bicentennial of Goethe's birth would come at a time more hospitable to humanism than had the one-hundredth anniversary of Goethe's death, Schweitzer turned away from the contemporary world altogether to ask why the Bicentennial "is a date for the whole world," whereas a hundred years earlier the centennial of Goethe's birth "had not roused even his native town." Schweitzer's answer, framed with impressive learning and phrased with winsome grace, sketched the familiar and singular phenomenon that was Goethe: his gift for language, his "many-sidedness" as a poet, his skill as an empirical and deductive scientist, his subtlety as a thinker, his profound philosophy of nature, his "need to serve," and his powers as "a great man." But Schweitzer also noted imperfections of Goethe's character usually overlooked—his moodiness, indecisiveness, sarcasm, and "lack of naturalness" in relations with people. Of all the themes he touched upon, Schweitzer set one above the rest. "The whole philosophy of Goethe," he said, "consists in the observation of material and spiritual phenomena outside and within ourselves," that is, recognition of an organically coherent structure as well as of creative and "dark forces" in both nature and human beings. And because this philosophy attributes spiritual qualities, such as morality, religion, and love, to the natural order itself, rather than consigning them to a spiritual realm, it makes of Goethe a teacher unexcelled in "ethical and religious wisdom, so simple and so deep."

This Goethe was very much the one Schweitzer had celebrated before. But, like Schweitzer himself, this Goethe had in the intervening years become more of a sage, a man of spirit, even a saint, whose human frailties rendered his character and ideas the more inspiring. How could anyone now doubt that Schweitzer was the true heir of Goethe, this man of "ethical and religious wisdom, so simple and so deep"?[66]

"In its grand simplicity," Victor Lange said of Schweitzer's address, "it proved a deeply moving confession of faith in the Goethean way."[67] And as a confession of faith, its contents affected the audience less than the character and aura of the man who spoke. For, true to Schweitzer's growing reputation in this country, it was not Schweitzer's words and accomplishments that moved people but his image as a man of profound simplicity, inviolable conscience, and supreme self-sacrifice. "More even than his lectures," Elisabeth Mann Borgese noted, "it was the personality itself of Schweitzer, his graspable kindness and goodness, the marks on all his manners, on his language, of his all-human experience, which radiated a spirit of world community."[68] Schweitzer's aura so pervaded the atmosphere that the actual occasion for the festival could easily be forgotten. "Indeed, an uninformed onlooker—if there had been such," reported a St. Louis journalist, "would have been justified in thinking that he had wandered into a Schweitzer festival."[69]

Schweitzer's lecture brought the convocation's first week-long session to a close. After speaking, the Good Doctor sat at the back of the tent signing autographs and looking forward to a day of rest before opening the second session with a repeat performance and then beginning the long road back to Lambaréné.

The break between sessions gave everyone a chance for some idle diversion. Schweitzer walked about Aspen and relaxed at the keyboard in Pioneer Park. Others, enticed by spectacular views, rode the chairlift up Aspen Mountain—where Artur Rubinstein was among those once left swinging helplessly for half an hour while repairmen fixed a broken motor. Ortega, who struck observers as having a "childlike enjoyment of the novelty about him"[70] and who "never stopped smiling,"[71] disported himself socially, visiting people like Gary Cooper (who a few years earlier had starred in the popular movie of the Spanish Civil War, *For Whom the Bell Tolls*), strolling the streets, and attending parties. He was also given to curious behavior. Approached on the street by some ladies who asked, "Are you Señor Ortega?" he paused as if uncertain but wanting to say, as his philosophy dictated: "Madame, I am he only in a vague way. I am *à peu pres* he, because I feel so much that I am only a remote approximation of him who I should be, of him who I have to be."[72] Fortunately, he resisted the temptation and finally nodded. Other eccentricities he more openly indulged. Discovering a favorite delicacy, Westphalian ham, at a buffet dinner one evening at Pioneer Park, he asked his hostess if he might take some back with him to his room at the Jerome. "Of course, Señor Ortega," said Elizabeth Paepcke in the Spanish she had learned on business trips with her husband to South America. "I'll get you a bag." "Oh, no," he interrupted. "I have my own way." Fastidiously, the neatly attired and well-mannered Spanish philosopher gathered up some paper-thin slices of the treat and, with a grin, slapped them on his bald head, donned his hat, and said good night.[73]

Ortega may have carried informality a bit farther than his fellow celebrities, but informality typified the festival as much as did the event's serious purpose. Every evening saw gatherings at private homes, the Jerome, the Four Seasons, and numerous other venues, drawing together musicians, intellectuals, vacationers, and locals for food and casual conversation and sometimes an impromptu performance, like Stephen Spender's poetry readings. The rustic and congested living conditions also added to the cosmopolitan conviviality. Kurt Wolff found himself sleeping on the parlor sofa of a private house and washing with cold water from a pan on the back porch and loving every minute of it. The philosopher William Ernest Hocking, impressed by the extraordinary "variety of mankind" gathered in this remote place, later told Hutchins that "the incidental personal meetings were a large part of the happiness of the affair, and I mustn't forget the Jewish philosopher Ernst Simon who shared a room with me, and showed me how a practicing Jew says his prayers in the morning."[74] Elisabeth Mann Borgese hailed the same easy internationalism: "There was a Hindu sage in awesome black attire; observant Israelis would rather arrive soaking wet at the tent where the minds met than accept a car ride on a Sabbath when it rained in sheets; French was heard and Spanish; Italian and German; Hindi verses were declaimed, and passages of the Talmud were read in their original language."[75]

No one got more swept up in this polyglot congeniality than Thornton Wilder, although he experienced it rather differently than most. "The days are getting harder," he wrote to his friend the author Mabel Dodge Luhan. "The scholars are coming to me as translator-aide. Ouch! It's hard and also time consuming, but it's a privilege in such cases as Dr. Schweitzer and Don José Ortega y Gasset." Yet more than the celebrities, the nonfamous visitors moved Wilder with their curiosity and receptivity. "They stop me at every corner," he reported, "all deeply shaken and happy. . . . These unforeseen usefulnesses are the final justification."[76]

At the beginning of the second week, Schweitzer, visibly worn from physical discomfort, spoke again, repeating his previous words, this time in German, following Borgese's introduction of him as the embodiment of international-ism and a fellow "builder of the World Republic."[77] Then he left on the next train east, pausing just long enough to record his feelings in the Paepckes' guest book: "The way the red cloth affects the bull, so guest books affect me. . . . Yet not in this house, where I must entrust to this book how charmingly I have been taken into this house, how good you were to me, how well things have gone for me here, and that I would come for two months every year, if it were possible, which mournfully will probably not be the case. With all my heart, A.S."[78] He stopped briefly in Chicago to accept an honorary degree, visited Boston to see an organ, and bade America farewell.

With Schweitzer gone, the convocation continued mingling scholarly essays and general discourses on Goethe's genius and pertinence to contem-porary life. Scholars such as Ludwig Lewisohn of Brandeis, Hermann J. Weigand of Yale, Karl Reinhardt and Willy Hartner of the Goethe University in Frank-furt, Ernst Simon of Hebrew University (who had replaced Martin Buber when Buber could not come), and William Ernest Hocking of Harvard ex-plored the diversity of Goethe's pursuits in poetry and science, friendship and cosmopolitan humanism. And a symposium, "Ethics and Politics," gave Simon, Halvdan Koht, Gerardus van der Leeuw, and the anthropologist Robert Redfield an opportunity jointly to decry the amorality of modern politics and to urge a rebirth of integrity in private and public life and the creation of a "world order," in Simon's words, "in the form of a world gov-ernment."[79] The festival had its lapses into academic obscurities, but it was not to forget its political origins.

Then with Ortega's second appearance at the lectern the program took flight again. Refusing to repeat his first address because he believed "all repetition is anti-vital" and "life is essentially that which cannot be repeated," he took up his favorite theme: human life. After lauding Thornton Wilder's *Our Town* (with Wilder abashedly translating) for providing "the strongest aes-thetic emotion that I have received during these last years" because it dra-matizes "the life of one of those innumerable cities still in a state of project, of germ, of sketch,"[80] Ortega took up "Goethe's conception of human life." Goethe "meditated upon the subject of human life" more than anyone before

him, Ortega said, but his conception of life "suffers from a two-sidedness."
On the one side, Goethe's philosophy of nature leads him to interpret life as
a natural unfolding toward wholeness—an idea dear to Schweitzer but one
that Ortega criticized for denying the "constitutionally dramatic character"
of life that arises from existential uncertainty. Yet on the other side, and
despite his philosophy of nature, Goethe demonstrated in literature that
human life does *not* follow a "smooth and organic unfolding such as is enjoyed by plants" but is unpredictable and troubled and "thrown forward toward and upon the future" through its own energy, chance, necessity, and
possibilities. Thus what is valuable in Goethe's idea of life, Ortega continued, now that *human life* and the future have become "problematic to a super-
lative degree," is the dramatic side that speaks to the "human powers" of
"hazard and hope."[81]

Ortega's second address never solved the riddle left at the end of the
first about Goethe's "resignation." But it sharpened his existentialist interpretation of Goethe while adding a new note of affirmation. Although Ortega
still had reservations about Goethe's humanism, he had, it seems, found a
Goethe for 1949.

As usual, Ortega's words both confused and inspired his listeners. "I
really do not know what to think of it," Wilder remarked of the address. It
had given him the impression of "a great and fertile mind being strangely
willful and naughty—shooting out suggestive half-truths without organization or basic coherence." And yet, Wilder conceded, "there are passages in
this lecture I shall never forget or cease to be grateful for."[82]

Ortega's work was done. He could now return to his institute braced for
further battles against the Mass Man. But Wilder had one more task to
perform. And on July 15 he stood before an audience in the tent to introduce
his old friend Robert M. Hutchins, who was to crown the events of the
preceding weeks with a testimonial, "Goethe and the Unity of Mankind."

Hutchins began with words of gratitude to Goethe for having given him
"nothing less than the gift of thought." This gift had come through Goethe's
poetry, so rich in "suggestiveness" that to read it was to think, and to pursue
its suggestions was to acquire a "complete university education"—something
Hutchins said was true of only four other authors, Plato, Aristotle, Dante,
and Shakespeare. But Goethe had given Hutchins more than the stimulus to
think. He had also provided an energizing philosophy of life, which Hutchins,
earnest Calvinist and enemy of indolence, equated above all with Goethe's
"will to work." "There is no sin but indolence," he said with moralistic
gravity (paraphrasing Christopher Marlowe), and "of this sin, which is radical and original, Goethe was never guilty." Goethe's romantic "striving" meant
to Hutchins not just restless activity or endless experience; it meant productive *work*, work in the world, and above all the work of self-mastery. Unlike

those who prized Goethe's ideals of humanity and personality as representing an unlimited unfolding of self, Hutchins identified those ideals, as well as Goethe's idea of freedom, with "self-denial." Only through self-denial can the true freedom of psychic discipline, rationality, and moral community be achieved. And only in discipline, rationality, and morality, Hutchins said, is there hope of overcoming the principal evils of modern civilization: the trivialization of existence, the specialization of learning, the hegemony of fact, and nationalism in politics, all of which portend the extinction of mankind through boredom or war. Then, denouncing as a symptom of these evils the anti-Russian mood then sweeping America, he closed with a stirring appeal for what he had so long desired, a "civilization of the Dialogue" capable of bringing "about that moral, intellectual, and spiritual revolution which will unite mankind in lasting peace."[83] With Hutchins's words, the academic program ended as it had begun: in the morality, the pedagogy, and the politics of the Chicago Bildungsideal.

The postwar Goethe was now complete: one-worlder, existentialist, universal humanist, moralist, and humanistic cultural critic. It remained to be seen if this Goethe would live on and reform postwar culture. But before departing with their hopes that he could, the festival participants had one item of business remaining. Wilder returned to the dais to read a resolution signed by all of the speakers still in Aspen during those last few days. Here the postwar Goethe had his final words. The resolution called for "the formation of a world council of international relations to continue the work pioneered at these sessions."[84] Applause resounded through the tent.

The participants not only passed this resolution but some of them gathered to chart plans for renewing that spirit in Aspen. Over lunch, Wilder, Hutchins, Paepcke, and others discussed the prospects for following the Goethe Bicentennial with another cultural festival the next year. Several people had already suggested honoring the two-hundredth anniversary of the death of Johann Sebastian Bach. Wilder put forward a more ambitious alternative, and one more in line with the purposes of the Goethe Festival: bringing the world's greatest thinkers—Sartre, Einstein, Toynbee, etc.—to Aspen to contemplate the philosophical and moral imperatives of mid-century civilization.

No definite plans materialized that day, but all decided that something would be done to keep the "Goethe spirit" alive. And after the celebrants had listened to the last concert and dispersed—musicians to their concert halls, professors to their classrooms, vacationers to their everyday lives—visions of another Aspen summer dedicated to reforming modern culture began to take form.

7

the birth of

the aspen idea

"The fruitfulness of our sessions exceeded our wildest hopes," Thornton Wilder informed Herbert Hoover as the Bicentennial celebration passed into memory and summer's calm settled over Aspen once more.[1] Of course Wilder was bound to deliver a glowing report to the festival's honorary chairman. But equally laudatory accounts came from other people. Victor Lange reported that "many spoke of the Aspen days as a decisive, perhaps even the most revealing experience of their lives," and he judged the convocation "one of the great events of our time," possessing "a significance which cannot possibly be overrated."[2] Lange overrated that significance despite himself, but his enthusiasm was widely shared. "I want to congratulate you," Eero Saarinen wrote to Walter Paepcke, for "an Intellectual Mardi Gras which, if you can see your way clear to repeat it, will have far-reaching consequences on the cultural life of our country."[3] The Library of Congress agreed. Recognizing the festival as emblematic of America's cultural ascendency in the postwar world, the library requested recordings of the lectures because "such a gathering of distinguished scholars is so rare as to be an important landmark in our cultural development."[4]

Other testimonials bore a more personal tone. "Aspen doesn't leave me," wrote William Ernest Hocking to Elizabeth Paepcke; "it glows in the dark of my mind."⁵ This same distinguished philosopher had written in the Paepcke guest book: "For an old man, a new beginning." Carl Schreiber quoted Ernst R. Curtius as saying that the Aspen experience was "the crowning point of his whole life."⁶ A housewife from Boise, Idaho, sent Walter Paepcke a four-stanza poem in "appreciation of a ten-day period which gave me the deepest and finest experience of my life."⁷ And from the other end of the country Kurt Wolff sent word that "all New York talks about the Aspen success." He went on with effusions of his own—and reports of Ortega's:

> Yesterday Ortega y Gasset arrived in New York. He came to dinner, and I only wish you could have eavesdropped on our conversation. . . . Everything in Aspen united to heighten one's "Lebensgefuehl"—the beautiful setting, the atmosphere of harmony and remoteness from the stress of our normal-abnormal life in big cities, the serious dedication of all present to things of the mind, the opportunity to meet informally and to talk freely and at length with some of the most interesting and stimulating Zeitgenossen [contemporaries]. To have brought all this within our reach, and so successfully, is a near miracle.⁸

Wolff's hearty affection for the Aspen *Lebensgefühl* (the feeling of life) touched the source of the "miracle." The speeches, the music, the celebrities, the setting, the informal sociability, all combined to create an experience greater than the sum of its parts. Hutchins attempted to identify the essence of this experience. "When I try to figure out why the celebration was such a great success," he wrote to Elizabeth Paepcke, "I am finally forced to consider that it was a matter of atmosphere," for "the same people doing the same things somewhere else would have produced a quite different effect." Yet more than the remote mountain environment, he said, it was the Paepckes, and especially she, who had created the effect. "Walter's energy and imagination made the celebration possible—but you made it what it was, because you more than anybody else gave it the atmosphere."⁹

Hutchins was, to be sure, giving compliments to a friend. But he had detected something in the Aspen "atmosphere" that had affected almost everyone, transforming a cultural event into a state of mind. Even Schweitzer succumbed to this state of mind as he returned to Europe and then to Lambaréné. Although Aspen had caused him much physical discomfort because it stood "a little too near heaven," he wrote to Paepcke from Frankfurt on Goethe's birthday, August 28, that Aspen was a "lovely place" where he had enjoyed the pleasures of good conversation and of playing "das liebe Klavier" ("the dear piano," to which he asked that his "greetings" be conveyed).¹⁰ Schweitzer also wrote to Hutchins of his "joy" over having spoken "on this grand master before a public so interesting and interested" and of his belief that the "Aspen enterprise has responded to a need" and "that it has a future."[11] In later years, Schweitzer's happy memories of Aspen actually strengthened. "I am so grateful," he wrote to Paepcke in 1955, "that together with Professor Hutchins you made me come to the U.S.A. It was so wonderful for me and it had a great meaning for me." He summoned up fond images of his Aspen hosts, too: "I see you both in your house in Aspen where I spent such beautiful days beginning with piano exercises." Of "the first breakfast with you" he chose to recall not the flood but only that "your wife had such a beautiful, simple housecoat so that I was quite sad when later she changed it for a riding costume."[12] And on his ninetieth and last birthday, in 1965, thanking Elizabeth Paepcke for her birthday message, he still recalled his visit warmly and expressed his belief that Aspen had great "spiritual significance for the U.S.A."[13]

The many warm memories of the festival, coupled with all the national publicity before and after, including cover stories in *Time* magazine on both Schweitzer (July 11, 1949) and Hutchins (November 21, 1949) and a lengthy spread on Schweitzer in *Life* magazine (July 25, 1949) featuring a moving double-page photograph by Eugene Smith of the tousled doctor at the keyboard of "das liebe Klavier," could not have failed to disseminate some part of the festival's message far beyond the Aspen visitors. And soon the letters were flowing into Aspen and Chicago from all kinds of people seeking or offering information about Goethe or trying to exploit the festival's or Paepcke's success for their own purposes. "Ever since the Goethe Bicentennial," Paepcke said the next summer, bewailing the many inquiries from would-be relatives, "I have discovered there are thousands of Paepckes in the world."[14] Paepcke also heard from a wine importer in New York who had a business proposition: "Knowing of your interest in everything connected with Goethe," he wrote, wouldn't Paepcke like to stock in Aspen a nice Riesling called "Goethewein"?[15]

Some communications brought tidings of new Goethe scholarship. A Colorado historian who had attended the festival and hoped the world would "grow toward oneness through its influence" reported that he had discovered, in a small Colorado town, an old German expatriate whose father had known Goethe.[16] Amateur scholars submitted essays interpreting Goethe from every point of view. There was "Goethe and Geology," "Goethe and America," "Goethe and Pharmacy." And a professor in Gross Hessen, Germany, wrote Hutchins lamenting the lack of books "showing the main character of Goethe in his infatuation for tree and bush." He proposed to draw world attention to "Goethe as a man of trees" by creating a "Goethe World Arboretum" in Frankfurt to be planted with saplings native to every land.[17]

As tributes of all kinds continued coming in, there could be no doubt that the festival had reached many people either directly through the events and the "atmosphere" or indirectly through publicity. But exactly how it had affected them and to what ends were not yet clear.

In an unusual test of the festival's effects, the *Denver Post* published the results of a poll comparing public recognition of Goethe with that of Hollywood's comic sex idol, Mae West. Ninety-four percent of those polled recognized the buxom comedienne; 24 percent recognized the long-dead foreign poet. Still, this was not so bad a showing for Goethe in the light of Hutchins's guess that before the festival only 5 percent of Americans could have identified him. A more reliable measure of the festival's success in shaping opinion lay in individual perceptions of Goethe, like the Aspen resident who wrote in the local newspaper: "Before the lectures began Goethe registered a complete blank with me. Now he means something." Goethe meant to him a man "humble, simple, zealous, wise, religiously sincere, and dedicated to serve mankind, giving access to order in a world of utter confusion" and supplying "a motivating and sustaining force" for constructing "a World Constitution."[18]

This humanitarian and religious Goethe, this Goethe the humble soul and peacemaker, was not the Goethe of history, the often tortured and restless creator of Werther, Tasso, Wilhelm Meister, and Faust. He was not even the Goethe of subsequent tradition, the Olympian and serene observer of life and minister of a minor duchy; nor was he the Goethe of those lectures dwelling on his universal genius, vast aspirations, and human weaknesses. Rather he was the Goethe imagined by the exponents of world government and, even more, by those who identified him with the man said to be his spiritual heir, Albert Schweitzer. No wonder it was Schweitzer the humanitarian, not Goethe the humanist, who became the postwar symbol of the unity of mankind.

It was to Schweitzer, after all, not to Goethe or any of the other speakers, that magazines and newspapers devoted their lead stories, and it was Schweitzer's reputation, not Goethe's, that, as one of Schweitzer's American advocates, Norman Cousins, said, took "a quantum leap" after the festival.[19] Almost overnight, Americans began making pilgrimages to Lambaréné to witness the great man at work and to absorb his inspiration. A journalist of the *Denver Post*, Antonia Brico, was in Africa within the year, reverentially reporting to her Colorado readers on life at the jungle hospital. Norman Cousins followed to observe and write about the one man of our time "willing to make the ultimate sacrifice for a moral principle."[20] Elizabeth Paepcke later looked at the hospital and wept over the doctor's heroism and gentleness amid the adversity of his task. Others were not only moved by Schweitzer's work but became medical missionaries themselves as a result of its example— like the young American Fergus Pope, who returned from Lambaréné to take up medical studies and then joined Schweitzer's staff, and Larimer Mellon, who, after meeting Schweitzer in New York, obtained a medical degree and went on to found a hospital in Schweitzer's name in Haiti. Yet among all the tributes to Schweitzer's inspiration, one that especially pleased him came in the form of a European college student's answer to an examination question relayed to Schweitzer by the teacher. The question read: "How do you define the best hope for the culture of Europe?" The student's answer: "It is not in any part of Europe. It is in a small African village and it belongs to a man in his eighties."[21]

But whatever its successes, or shortcomings, as a representation of Goethe or, in Paepcke's words, as a "dramatization of the humanities in this all too scientific and material age,"[22] the Goethe Festival could claim one unquestioned achievement: it was a triumph of public relations. Ronald Goodman, naturally enough, wholly identified the festival with public relations and hailed the results as a coup of his profession. Agreeing with Goodman but adding a critical bite, a columnist for *Harper's* dismissed the festival as the "ultimate triumph in packaging—packaging culture and shipping it in, signed, sealed, and delivered to Aspen, Colorado, U.S.A."[23]

No one could deny that the Goethe Bicentennial was at least in part a creation, and a creature, of publicity. The celebration had even foreshadowed what would later be called a "media event," that is, an event staged for the purpose of publicity. (And it set a model of mass appeal followed by future memorials to great men like Leonardo da Vinci, Shakespeare, and Copernicus.) But this is not to say it was without substance or instruction. Rather, in the mass technological consumer culture that had made celebrities of figures like Hutchins and magnates of men like Paepcke, the lines between appearance and substance, and between publicity and education, were clouding. Thus, when Hutchins declared the festival "one of the most significant programs of adult education ever,"[24] he was both playing for space in the mass media and betraying his very modern sense that—as advertisers and publicists had been saying for half a century and more—effective publicity *is* education.

As it turned out, when memories of the festival had faded and the saintly reputation of its living symbol, the good doctor, had tarnished in the glare of public scrutiny, the most lasting effect of this *education* proved to be not public recognition of Goethe or even of Schweitzer, much less a mass following for world unity. It was rather something Ronald Goodman had noted in his appraisal of the publicity campaign, as almost an afterthought: it "introduced a new center of world culture in the United States."[25]

Talk of Aspen's cultural future began well before the Goethe Festival folded its tent. Ortega had alluded to this talk during his second address, suggesting that any future "sessions of collective meditations . . . among the heights" take up his theme, "The Experience of Life."[26] Many others thought the natural sequel to the celebration of Goethe's two-hundredth birthday would be, as noted above, to celebrate the two-hundredth anniversary of the death of Johann Sebastian Bach—passing the honors from Albert Schweitzer's philosophical to his musical mentor. Others still put in their bids for a writers' conference or a gathering of painters. One correspondent offered to supply Hutchins a list of every important birthday going back to the time of Christ, keeping Aspen in annual celebrations for the next two thousand years.[27]

But as things turned out, the next year brought no celebration of historic anniversaries, or a conference of writers or painters or world figures. Those prospects faded as deficits from the Goethe Bicentennial (close to $30,000) held discouragingly firm through the fall, and as a new proposal was advanced, mainly by Hutchins and Mortimer Adler, who had by now entered the Aspen conversations, to have done with transitory festivals and establish instead a permanent educational institution in Aspen.

By October 1949, this idea had supplanted all others: Aspen was to have a full-fledged university (or rather a small college under a bigger name). "Aspen University" would bring together the "atmosphere" of the Goethe Festival and many of the precepts, programs, and aspirations of the Chicago Bildungsideal. Paepcke explained the idea to Schweitzer in a letter of October 4: "At the present moment our minds are turning very much toward the possible establishment of a very small university at Aspen which would be without buildings, without campus, without expensive athletic fields, stadium, and even without what would usually be considered a reasonably good library." Such a "hair shirt" university, as Hutchins had labeled it, would free humanistic education from "extraneous reasons" for going to college, like social and professional advancement, athletics, and idle play. But, Paepcke went on, Aspen University would be much more than an unconventional liberal arts college. It "would have true purposes and indulge in three activities: (1) the education of young people aged seventeen or eighteen to twenty or twenty-one; (2) adult education of those grown-up people who, as during the Goethe Convocation, might like to combine a vacation with mental and spiritual stimulus; and (3) a continuing philosophical conference where some of the visiting and resident scholars could discuss, debate, and perhaps even resolve some questions of a philosophical nature."[28] Although the exact character of those "true purposes" and the intellectual content of this three-tiered organization had yet to be filled out, Aspen University would presumably provide a general education for undergraduates and adults and lead in the third phase to preparation of Adler's long-dreamed-of *Summa Dialectica,* the analytical encyclopedia of Western thought.

As an instance of American educational reform, Aspen University thus promised to unite the general education of the University of Chicago with the informal atmosphere that typified other experimental, "hair shirt" colleges like Reed, Black Mountain, and Goddard. What made the Aspen University idea unique was the combination of Hutchins's, Adler's, and Paepcke's pet projects: Hutchins's liberal education and ascetic environment, Adler's mandatory academic program and philosophical conference, and Paepcke's center of high tastes and cultural stimulation in Aspen.[29]

It seemed the natural offspring of a happy marriage, this "university for thinkers only,"[30] as the newspapers dubbed it. But despite the early enthusiasm, Aspen University—except briefly on paper—was not to be. For while the idea stayed alive over the next decade, no one came forward to head the school. The educators offered the job—like Lawrence Kimpton, Clarence H. Faust, Richard McKeon, O. Meredith Wilson, Sterling McMurrin—all had other obligations or they had doubts of a kind quite common among those invited to contribute to Aspen culture in later years: Aspen looked suspiciously like Paepcke's show, and no academician wanted to place his future so fully in the hands of an entrepreneur, however intelligent and cultivated he might be. His strong identification with culture aside, Paepcke the businessman still stood in the shadow of Babbitt and acquisitive capitalism.

While plans for Aspen University were starting on their long road to extinction, a revised scheme for reforming modern culture from Aspen was taking shape. The revision began when Paepcke opened a letter that he and Aspen would never forget. It was from Ortega, dated October 26, 1949. Paepcke had written to Ortega in early October with news of the vague plans forming for the next summer and soliciting suggestions. It was a routine inquiry, much like that sent to Schweitzer and others—although Paepcke also reminded Ortega of his pledge to contribute to Aspen's future and begged indulgence for imagining an "Aspen University," which, Paepcke said, would probably make Ortega laugh.

Ortega did not laugh—"except," he remarked with philosophic good cheer, "in the sense that all joy carries with it a smile." He followed this opening with four thousand words weaving the passions and precepts of his philosophy of culture and education around Paepcke's proposal.

"I abandoned myself entirely to Aspen during those two wonderful weeks I spent there," he began; "that is, I absorbed that atmosphere to the very marrow of my bones," and "one day there appeared to me, suddenly and altogether, along with many other subjects, the ideas I shall now succinctly expound." Aspen seemed to call for, he said, "*something like* a university" but not a university as such—rather a "*most novel* institution" embodying, like the Instituto de Humanidades, only the "nuclear meaning" of university, i.e., "advanced studies and education," without the extraneous connotations of complicated organization and formal certification. "On setting aside the term

'university,'" Ortega explained, "we have freed ourselves from the commitments—frightful for their variety and number—which the term implies, and
we can picture a 'superior school,'" or school of "advanced studies," that
"would be very limited in its instruction but highly concentrated on educational efficiency and with a clear, definite, attractive *pedagogical, thus human
style.*"

Ortega's blueprint for this school, recalling much in *The Revolt of the
Masses* and *The Mission of the University,* accorded so well with the principles
of the Chicago Bildungsideal that, but for its Ortegan rhetoric, it could almost have been written by Hutchins. (Years later, upon first reading *The
Mission of the University,* Mortimer Adler wondered if Hutchins had read it in
the thirties without telling him and framed the Chicago Plan with it in
mind.)[31] The school would, Ortega said, rectify the pernicious overemphasis
in America on "naturalistic (not humanistic), physical, biological and technical education" by providing "education in a total synthesis of human life"
through "synthetic bodies of doctrine" drawn from "all subjects." And although comprehensive, this "synthetic teaching would be made on the basis
of a *library with very few but masterly chosen volumes,*" through which students
would learn how "to *really* absorb an important book" and how to apply "the
principles of concentration or condensation and synthesis."

But more important than these pedagogical points were Ortega's notions of the spirit that should animate this "most novel institution." Like
the educational reformers from Chicago, Ortega conceived this spirit as an
antidote to cultural ills that plague modern society in general and America
in particular. The American, Ortega observed, suffers from "an excess of
comfort." And comfort is excessive when it becomes an end in itself, thereby
diminishing that "inwardness" that is man's essential nature, that is, the
ability of the "inner self to live intensely" through "thinking, imagining,
loving and feeling." Americans exhibit this loss of inwardness most bla-
tantly in their preoccupation with objects. "During my trip to the States," he
explained, "I had the impression that the American runs the risk of getting
lost in objects, of living *on* and *in* objects."

Ortega was not, of course, alone in criticizing the American attachment
to things. Most mid-century American social critics did the same, as had
generations of European observers before them. And Ortega's solution to
this and other failings of American culture took its inspiration from Ortega's
origins and experience as an antimaterialistic European. "Through the new
School," Ortega said confidently, "we shall succeed in making it fashionable
in America not to do without objects but to be capable of doing without
them gladly." This change of mind or spirit could come about by making two
educational principles preeminent: "Spartanism" and "elegance." By Spartanism Ortega meant physical discipline: "the students shall lead a highly

austere life in every sense; they shall enjoy very few conveniences as long as that discomfort cannot result in a shortage of their working capacity and joy." They would also have to do physical work: "a part of the system of school duties shall be a certain forced labor, not of an ornamental nature but useful to Aspen; opening up roads, building bridges, arranging gardens, constructing houses and community centers." These Spartan demands would breed the qualities needed to transcend American materialism (and the psychology of the Mass Man): "energy, hardness, continuity in effort, endurance, etc." And they would lead to another psychological attribute that Ortega admired, one he associated with "socially aristocratic" peoples and therefore rarely found in America, one "which is *characteristic and essential* in every truly strong people, namely elegance."

Here was the heart of Ortega's message to Aspen: *elegance*. Ortega said he would gladly give "a course of six lectures" on this theme in Aspen, adding, "if I do give such a course, you will be amazed when you realize that such obvious, evident and humanly important things as stated by me had never been mentioned upon the subject." This was not entirely correct, for Ortega's elegance was that same attribute of mind, spirit, action, and appearance recommended long before by Goethe and Nietzsche under the term *style*. Goethe had defined style as the pattern of appearances in art and life that both expresses and shapes the personality behind it. Nietzsche had gone farther toward Ortega's elitism by stressing the dependency of style on the capacity for discipline: "'Giving style' to one's character" is possible only for "the strong and domineering natures who enjoy their finest gaiety in such compulsion, in such constraint and perfection under a law of their own."[32] Like his predecessors, Ortega believed style, or elegance, has nothing to do with mere status. Elegance is a psychological discipline that "must penetrate, influence man's entire life, from his gestures and ways of walking, through his way of dressing, through his way of using language, of carrying on a conversation, of speaking in public, to the most intimate side of *moral* and intellectual actions." And true to his Spartan ideal of discipline and austerity, Ortega took as the model of elegance not aesthetics but mathematics: "Whoever takes the trouble to analyze which features make a mathematical reasoning elegant will understand, as if suddenly struck by the lightning of intellection, *everything* that I have hinted at about the *vital human* virtue called 'elegance.'" Elegance is, therefore, simplicity, the form of a thing drawn to the austere perfection of its inherent necessity—like a mathematical formula or the Doric architecture of Sparta itself.

Ortega thought this elegance could be achieved in Aspen in many ways. The school, carried on in the harsh winter climate, would be the very soul of austerity and high seriousness; and in summer the gracious pleasures of high culture and recreation would attract "'gens du monde,'" making Aspen "the most elegant summer resort." Hence students would emerge from their winter's labors to see and learn from people of "social elegance"—particularly "women of real distinction" and "high intellectual position," people like those at the Goethe Bicentennial. Reiterating his belief in the power of moral authority, Ortega said the "elegant people" would work their beneficial effects simply by allowing young people to "see them live"—as "happened in Europe fifty years ago" during "'fashion days' at the theater and at the great scientific and literary ceremonies," which, alas, had become all but impossible amid "the disorganized, vulgarized form of social life in the last years." But the "elegant people" would also be rewarded. For, "immersed in a high intellectual and moral milieu, stimulating and austere," they, too, would "promptly feel charged . . . with a new and exquisite electricity." Aspen elegance, as much a social as a moral virtue, would leave no one unchanged, and thereby create a cultural elite who "will be called upon to influence all walks of American life."

To insure this alchemy of elegance, Ortega added a final note. The school should construct a central building capable of accommodating "some one thousand *people*" for dining and conviviality, and "the grounds of the premises must be terraced so that everyone can see each other within the enormous space. This humble physical detail is *vital*," he emphasized, because "spirit" (a word he detested) "cannot exist without the so-called matter" and without the "humility to count on matter."[33] Although Ortega did not say so, these last proposals gave practical expression to his philosophical credo: Aspen's education in elegance would stand materially and spiritually as a monument to his conviction: "I am I and my circumstances."

Walter Paepcke reacted to Ortega's message with the ardor of a disciple. He had the letter translated, reproduced, and mailed out to everyone associated with or curious about the future of Aspen. He also began adopting some of Ortega's phrases in talking about that future. References to a "hair shirt" university now yielded to the idea of an "Institute for Humanistic Studies" to be "done in a very simple manner as far as physical comfort is concerned,"[34] and with the purposes of opposing vulgar materialism and exemplifying cultural elegance. Some of Paepcke's correspondents responded to Ortega's letter with keen assent. James Laughlin wrote: "That letter from Ortega is simply a classic. His way of putting things makes it at first sound quite mad, but when you dig down into it there are some wonderful ideas."[35] The political scientist Harold Lasswell, sharing Ortega's doubts about the idea of a "university," agreed that "the mind and the creative talent of America need to be liberated from the steam-roller impact of the academic paraphernalia involved in the granting of degrees," and in place of a university he suggested establishing a "world center for intellectual and artistic creation."[36]

Paepcke welcomed such agreeable thoughts. But he also encountered some dissent, as when he later passed the letter on to Jacques Barzun, professor of history at Columbia and one of America's subtlest cultural critics. Barzun applauded Ortega's admiration of elegance and of the humanistic curriculum, but, he said, "I disagree entirely with his interpretation of American comfort and his desire for Spartan discipline." Where Ortega had gone wrong, Barzun remarked, was in believing "American gadgetry is a form of self-indulgence," whereas it is just "a substitute for domestic service." Prefiguring an idea elaborated in his book *God's Country and Mine* (1954), Barzun reproached Ortega and "the Europeans who accuse us of seeking the easy life" as self-deceiving since they blithely exploit "a couple of poor slaveys who live in an attic and work from six in the morning to ten at night, and who are given less consideration than actual slaves because they do not represent property." The important cultural question was not whether one used gadgets or not but whether their use enhanced or diminished life. Ortega had compounded this error, Barzun went on, by advising unnecessary and detrimental austerity for students. Restating his own conviction that education depends on intellectual discipline, not on practical tasks, Barzun chided Paepcke for confusing earthy innovations with genuine learning. "I can't see that Yale students will be intellectually better off for having to make their own beds, or that Black Mountain College gives a better education because the whole community builds its own equipment." And with a friendly dig at both Ortega and Paepcke he concluded: "Of course, if Señor Ortega wants to draw his own water from the well or wash his face at the pump, I am sure that your generous management at Aspen will provide these bracers for him!"[37]

Not to be deterred from his adherence to Ortega's Spartan ideals, Paepcke replied to Barzun's good-natured barbs with some cultural criticism of his own. Betraying his strong aversion to the Mass Man and his identification with High Culture, Paepcke complained that "most people nowadays have become enslaved to gadgets without ever having had slaveys"; and worse, whether through a dependence on gadgets or not, most young people have become intellectually and morally lazy and "could do with a little more self-discipline, be that making their own beds and cleaning up their rooms, . . . or in restraining themselves from putting their feet on the seats beside them in a train, sticking their chewing gum under the chairs in restaurants, movies or church pews, or refraining from the excessive use of the jargon of the day."[38]

Like Ortega, Paepcke conceived of elegance in Aspen as the unity of Spartan austerity and cultural refinement. But since both Paepcke and Ortega had themselves acquired elegance more through economic and cultural privilege than through Spartan difficulty—Paepcke had always depended on servants or his resourceful wife for every material convenience—it is nicely ironic that they should have felt the need to impose, by severe means, the elegance they enjoyed on their social opposites: the unprivileged, indisciplined, unrefined Mass Man.

Whatever else Aspen might become, then, if Paepcke and Ortega had their way it would be the home of an institution dedicated to saving American culture from the Mass Man and to shaping that culture in the image of elegance. Still uncertain was exactly how those ends were to be accomplished. But seized by the Ortegan vision, Paepcke cast uncertainties aside and brought the institution to life. On December 30, 1949, Aspen University, incorporated December 8, formally became the Aspen Institute for Humanistic Studies.

The vision of cultural reform loosely shared by Ortega, Paepcke, Hutchins, and Adler at last embodied in the Aspen Institute, the actual work of organization remained. Paepcke quickly put together a distinguished board of trustees drawn largely from participants in the Goethe Festival or supporters of the Great Books, including Schweitzer (who accepted in an honorary capacity), Ortega, Hutchins, Wilder, and John Erskine, the father of the Great Books idea itself. Then, while hopes of expanding to a year-round schedule of classes hung in the air, Paepcke and Hutchins decided to concentrate that year on a summer program of adult education patterned on the Goethe Festival.

Reckoning the need for paying customers and still wincing from the previous summer's deficit, Paepcke planned to have a roster of famous lecturers as "drawing cards."[39] And he and his colleagues soon came up with several suitably prominent figures, such as T. S. Eliot (whose recent book *Notes Toward the Definition of Culture*, 1948, had so roundly blasted the prevailing anarchy, indiscipline, and vulgarity of culture that Hutchins had already arranged for him to speak at the University of Chicago in the fall of 1950 on "the aim of education"), Herbert Read, Archibald MacLeish, Arnold Toynbee, and Dwight D. Eisenhower (invited less for reasons of philosophy than of public relations). Then the planning took a decisive turn after Ortega advised Paepcke to determine "the themes with which this conference will deal" before scheduling the speakers.[40] Paepcke fired off a memo to his associates: "Have you any suggestions about the 'theme'?"[41] Of the several responses, the most influential in shaping the institute's future came from Mortimer Adler.

Adler's reply had been quick and predictable: the "Unity of Western Culture" as expressed in the Great Ideas that Adler had been indexing for nearly seven years.[42] Now that he had nearly finished the index, Adler saw in the Aspen Institute a chance to expand upon his accomplishment and perhaps fulfill his "youthful vision" of preparing a dialectical encyclopedia of Western thought. As he enthusiastically informed a friend: "The kind of discussions which we can set up at Aspen might further the work on the *Summa Dialectica*."[43] The *Syntopicon* had laid the groundwork, now the Aspen Institute, representing Adler's favorite part of the Aspen University idea, could demonstrate the dialectical unity of Western thought to all comers in lectures and seminars year after year.

As it happened, Adler was not the only one to have a personal interest in associating the Great Ideas with the Aspen Institute. Paepcke had acquired such an interest, too. For not long after Adler had made his recommendation, Paepcke had received a kindred proposal pertaining not to the institute but to the advertising of the Container Corporation. Pointing out that the ideas of great thinkers could be effective in corporate advertising, Egbert Jacobson wrote to his boss in early January 1950: "With your indulgence I should like to make one more suggestion for the Company advertising." Referring to an attached copy of the "Preliminary Draft of a World Constitution" published by the Borgese-Hutchins-Adler Committee to Frame a World Constitution in 1948, Jacobson recommended taking "some of the ideas of its authors" and some of the historic statements quoted in it and publishing them as advertisements "strikingly illustrated by Picasso, Le Corbusier, Portinari, Chagall, and others." The object, he said, would be "to join these minds in giving publicity" to their ideas and in providing the company a new "means of maintaining our acceptance with the public."[44] By becoming identified with the "Great Ideas of Western Man," as the advertising campaign was later labeled, Container's corporate image would thus acquire fresh sophistication as well as greater distance from the emblems of vulgar capitalist acquisitiveness—and critics would cringe to see consumer capitalism now openly enlist in its cause not only the once subversive modern artists but the entire Western intellectual tradition.[45]

Perfectly adapted to Container's reputation as a stylish innovator in advertising, Jacobson's suggestion also caught the wind of perfect timing. Coming alongside Adler's proposal for Aspen, it opened Paepcke's eyes to the opportunity of making his two pet enterprises, the Container Corporation and the Aspen Institute, allied agents of publicity and cultural reform through the Great Ideas. Paepcke later characterized the inception of the "Great Ideas" advertising campaign in words echoing the ideology adopted by the institute: "Here, indeed, we thought, was an opportunity to stimulate thinking and discussion about the ideas at the roots of what the philosophers call 'the good life'; ideas that are infinitely more important to the preservation of our society and our liberties than the pursuit of material gain."[46]

Swept along by his idealism, Paepcke failed to notice the irony in this latest piece of corporate ingenuity. For the ideas he deemed "more important . . . than the pursuit of material gain" were to be put, under his guidance, into the service of material gain, just as modern art and good design had been—notwithstanding the benefits of these tactics to public taste and enlightenment. And who better to consummate this supreme alliance of commerce and culture, advertising and education, than the doyen of mass adult education and cataloguer of ideas, Mortimer Adler himself.

Placed on retainer to the Container Corporation, Adler flipped through his *Syntopicon* index cards and came up with, as Paepcke reported, "an ample supply of statements . . . of the ideas that are the very foundation of the Western tradition."[47] Each month Adler would send a new batch of statements to a committee at Container, which, assisted by the N. W. Ayer & Son advertising agency, would choose one and select an artist to illustrate it as the artist saw fit. The Great Ideas of Western Man, in the form of an advertising campaign destined to run for a generation and more, bringing Container numerous awards and peerless national recognition, had found a use that not even Adler had previously imagined.

Persuaded by the corporate and cultural uses of the Great Ideas, Paepcke threw in his lot with Mortimer Adler at both Container and the institute in the spring of 1950. Adler's duties for the Container Corporation were simple enough, but the demands made upon him by the institute proved rather greater than he had anticipated. He encountered the unexpected on his first visit to Aspen that April. In the company of Elizabeth Paepcke, Adler reached the mud-sodden unpaved streets to experience what residents knew and visitors quickly learned: falling between winter's gleaming snow and summer's sun and green hills, April in Aspen is the cruelest month—gray, messy, and depressing. "I cannot remember what I expected it to look like," Adler recalled, "but I do remember how appalled I was by the sea of mud that, in the spring thaw, filled all of Aspen's unpaved streets and almost prevented me from appreciating the beauty of the mountains and the clarity of the atmosphere."[48]

But casting the displeasure of the moment aside, Adler recognized the potential of Aspen as a summer haven for intellectuals with a yen for thought and talk. He started at once to lay out a full eleven-week summer program. It should open, he decided, with a week of lectures and Great Books seminars under the rubric "The Essence of Humanism," followed by several weeks on the nature of society and politics, science and philosophy, morality and religion, and winding up with "The Individual and the Species."

To carry out this program, Adler, Paepcke, and their colleagues selected a notable group of willing lecturers and moderators—although not quite the luminaries they had hoped for. Besides Adler, who scheduled himself for several lectures, there would be Ortega, Hutchins, Clarence Faust, Adler's old friend Clifton Fadiman, the theologian Reinhold Niebuhr, the philosophers Alexander Meiklejohn, Erich Kahler, and Charles Malik, the literary scholar A. F. B. Clark, the psychoanalyst Karl Menninger, the music scholars and critics Carleton Sprague Smith and Olin Downes, and others. To capture the earnest spirit of this program, Adler and Paepcke chose as the publicity label for the summer: "Great Books, Great Men, Great Music."

Ever since the Goethe Festival, Paepcke had been putting together a music program for the summer of 1950, originally inspired by the idea of holding a Bach festival. But Paepcke didn't want to bring just a few stars to Aspen for a brief stint that, like the Goethe Festival, might lose "the balance between the cultural and the recreational." He wanted instead to hold a music festival extending over the entire summer. And he believed most artists would agree to long-term summer fees lower than their winter concert rates, especially if they could be guaranteed income from teaching as well. He was right. The internationally respected Aspen summer music school and festival were here in the making.

The first publicity releases for the Aspen Institute went out in mid-March announcing the music program and lectures to be given by Olin Downes, the music critic of the *New York Times,* and Carleton Sprague Smith, chief of the music division of the New York Public Library. Although these said nothing of the far-reaching cultural aspirations of the institute, the publicity statements for the academic program, as written by Adler, left no doubt that the Aspen Institute did not exist for entertainment. "At the mid-point of the twentieth century," Adler wrote in the first of these publications and in words familiar to his pen, human beings "are dominated more than ever before by science." Indeed, they live "in a world which almost worships science and technology" to the detriment of those "moral and spiritual truths" that could "enable men to control science and all its machinery." As he had done so many times before, Adler supported this claim with an excursion into the philosophical division between truths of fact and truths of value. Because science belongs to the first, it must forever inhabit its value-free, nonhuman home: "Science does not and cannot appoint the goals men should seek; science does not and cannot direct us in the good life or to a good society; science does not and cannot determine which among competing values are true and which false." Only the humanities, he said, as embodied "in the arts and in philosophy, in morals and religion," can point the way to "the fundamental truths which can give human life direction and which can create a society to be served by science rather than ruled by it." For only the humanities inhabit the realm of values.

Then deploring the moral aimlessness of a world dominated by science, and with a gesture toward contemporary politics and the recent detonation of the Soviets' first atom bomb, he described the mission of the Aspen Institute as that of saving Western civilization from itself and from its destruction "by instruments which should serve to enrich it." Only "the vision of greatness in the human tradition," he said, can provide civilization with "spiritual bulwarks stronger than the blast of atoms"[49] and give hope, as a second publicity release put it, for "Humanism in a World of Science."[50]

Thus the Aspen Institute for Humanistic Studies, born of the Goethe Festival's universalism and Ortega's cultural elitism, went forward waving above all others the banner of the Chicago Bildungsideal: humanism versus science, value versus fact, idealism versus pragmatism.

Whether or not Adler could make his ideals prevail this time, he early made it known to Paepcke that he did not live on ideals alone. Not for nothing would his publishers later tout him as "the world's highest-paid philosopher."[51] And although this could not have been said of him in 1950, he was learning his worth in dollars and acquiring a sybarite's tastes. When the time came to fix a price for his contribution to the institute, he pronounced Paepcke's offer of $1,000 "definitely too little." After all, Adler said, he was both planning the summer program and preparing to give five or six lectures and conduct nine seminars. At $1,000 he would be getting a lower rate than other participants. And besides the time and energy, he reminded Paepcke, the Adler name was itself an attraction: "Recent publicity about the Great Books and the Syntopicon, and the fact that I am nationally known as 'the great bookie,' makes my name as good a drawing card for Aspen—hell, better than Niebuhr's," although, he conceded with a note of becoming modesty, "I admit it's not quite as bright a neon light as Churchill's would be, if we could get him."[52] In sum, he said, the appropriate fee would be $1,750 or $2,000. Paepcke, true to his pragmatic and frugal ways, agreed to the lower figure two days before the institute's opening.

In a happy prelude to that debut the first "Great Ideas of Western Man" advertisement hit the news stands in the June 19 issue of *Time* magazine (see fig. 7.1). Illustrated by Arthur Williams, it showed a scales of justice, a medallion portrait of Alexander Hamilton, and a book lying open to Hamilton's words on the twin imperatives of government: "to control the governed" and "to control itself." The Container Corporation's selling of the Great Ideas had begun. Next, the curtain went up on the Aspen Institute's celebration of these same ideas.

Paepcke rose before a handful of people gathered under Saarinen's tent on June 26 to speak the first words of the Aspen Institute's public career. Briefly commending the moral authority of the humanities in a world of science and alluding to the Ortegan social criticism that flowed through the institute's veins (Ortega had been forced by illness to cancel his visit at the last minute; he died in 1955, never having returned to Aspen), Paepcke committed the institute's resources to the instruction of people's lives, energies, and leisure in an increasingly egalitarian and technological society. Defender of the

Fig. 7.1. Arthur Williams, Container Corporation magazine advertisement, Great Ideas of Western Man series, no. 1, 1950. Courtesy of CCA (Smithsonian American Art Museum).

Fig. 7.2. Herbert Bayer, Container Corporation magazine advertisement, Great Ideas of Western Man series, no. 11, 1951. Courtesy of CCA (Smithsonian American Art Museum).

humanities against science, the Aspen Institute would also be a champion of high culture against low, of the Noble Man's elegance against the Mass Man's sloth.

Robert Hutchins expanded upon Paepcke's theme in the formal address that followed, "On Education." He blamed the failures of education on the reigning assumption that education in a democracy means adapting schools to the wants of students. Since Americans seem inclined "to make it as easy as possible for the child," he said, the young lose all energy and discipline of mind, with the result that they are helpless before the predatory popular culture that provides easy escape and seductive stupefaction. And among the chief enemies of education, Hutchins went on, restating conclusions from his study of the freedom of the press, is the radio, which induces intellectual lethargy and offers nothing but "a good time filled with bad things." As for television, he snapped, of that the less said the better, for it is "the complete degradation of culture."[53]

Although the small audience was not altogether persuaded by Hutchins's indictment of mass culture (and some critics, like David Riesman, whose book The Lonely Crowd had just appeared, would have dissented from Hutchins's dismissal of entertainment as mere escapism), the chancellor had set the tone of humanistic cultural criticism and Ortegan elegance that would guide the Aspen Institute for the next decade. That tone, although resonant with political implications, reflected, at least for the moment, nothing of contemporary political events. This is odd, because just two days before Paepcke and Hutchins took the podium to summon Americans to a more demanding cultural life, North Korean armies had flowed across the 38th parallel into South Korea in the first act of open military aggression since World War II. Even as Hutchins spoke on June 27, President Truman was committing U.S. forces to battle. Yet Hutchins and Paepcke could well have justified the omission on principle. For the educational philosophy behind the institute held that the problems of the modern world, be they moral, social, or political, can be solved only by exploring the perennial questions of value—what ought to be, not what is—that underlie them. And during its first decade or so, the institute attempted fairly consistently to do just this: contemporary events provided only the backdrop for discussions of the Great Ideas of Western Civilization.

Hutchins emphasized this principle when he opened the first Great Books seminar the next day on the stage of the slightly repaired Opera House. "It is not the object of the Great Books seminars to reach general and clear conclusions," he told the small audience. The object "is to raise the important questions and begin the discussion of them" in hopes that "these discussions will go on throughout your lives and ours."[54] The seminar itself, devoted to Aristotle's Poetics, seemed to have the desired effect, at least temporarily, arousing bursts of applause, numerous questions from the floor, and thoughtful criticism of Hutchins's "Thomistic smugness" in asserting absolute standards of good and bad even while disclaiming any intent of leading the participants toward definite answers.[55]

A similarly spirited response greeted Adler's first address a few days later. Repeating his battle cry from the academic wars at the University of Chicago, "Questions Science Cannot Answer," he declared that the truths of reason and faith simply cannot be judged by science, whose realm is fact. Science could never prove the moral worth of democracy over dictatorship; but a good humanist could do so, and could go on to prove that world peace necessarily depends on world government.

As always, Adler's facile presentation convinced some and vexed others. The *Aspen Times*, in an unwitting confirmation of Adler's charges against the hegemony of science, reported that Adler had claimed he could "prove with scientific methods" every assertion he made.[56] Adler's very thesis, stated endless times over the years, that there *are* answers to "the questions science cannot answer," and that these are to be found in a type of knowledge *outside* of science, had been wholly lost on the local journalist, as it had been lost before on so many people who also implicitly equated knowledge with science—quite apart from those who deemed the thesis false.

Although Hutchins's and Adler's contributions to the general theme, "The Essence of Humanism," covered well-trodden philosophical ground and made no reference to contemporary politics, Clifton Fadiman openly linked the contemporary crisis of humanism with political conditions in his address, "A Post-Hiroshima Planet." The atomic bomb, he said, had divided people into three groups: those of a pre-Hiroshima cast of mind, who regard the bombing as merely a military act; those of an authoritarian temper, who believe that peace and world order are possible only through a totalitarian regime of Left or Right; and those of humanistic vision, who believe universal peace, order, and human freedom can be achieved only through world government. The ideals of this third group justified the "Police Action" just then getting underway in Korea. "We are not employing force," he explained, "except insofar as we are simply obeying and executing the law." And "this law is not our national law but is the law laid down in the charter of the United Nations." The U.N. may not be the global government desired, Fadiman concluded, but it is "the nearest we have so far come to a conception of world law operating in the interests of world freedom."[57]

The political note having been struck, it was held, although in a philosophical key, through the week of the Fourth of July in seminars and lectures about "The American Republic." On Independence Day, Fadiman gave a public reading of the Declaration of Independence, later broadcast nationally, and a panel led by Adler and Lawrence Kimpton scrutinized this document for its moral, political, and intellectual implications. Subsequent weeks brought public seminars on the ideas of freedom, authority, and human nature as set forth by thinkers from Plato to Mill and lectures on kindred themes, such as Alexander Meiklejohn on "The Philosophy of Self-Government," Erich Kahler on "The Problem of Values," and Adler on a variety of topics, including "The Unity of Civilization" and "The Intellectual Community: The Great Ideas."

Spirited intellectual conflicts also erupted. Clare Boothe Luce and Elizabeth Paepcke captivated an audience with a brilliant display of philosophical and feminine rivalry in a panel discussion of Machiavelli. And Adler attacked Niebuhr's interpretation of human nature. Niebuhr, a severe, neo-orthodox Augustinian—another of those twentieth-century theologians, like Albert Schweitzer, to revolt against the liberal Protestantism of previous generations—chose to dwell on the evils of pride. "Pride of spirit or mind," he said, is the essence of sin and a sympton of human fallibility. Man does not gain but loses by exalting his own powers of body or mind, for only by submitting himself to "grace" can man be redeemed from his weaknesses, only in grace is there "a new strength which enters the will."[58] Adler might have shared Niebuhr's estimation of faith as higher than secular intelligence, but as a thoroughgoing humanist Adler had no use for people lacking confidence in human nature. And he stated this confidence unequivocally—as he had done so many times before—in his lecture "The Nature of Man," later elaborated in his book, *The Difference of Man and the Difference It Makes* (1967). Following the Aristotelian line that man possesses an inherent nature comprised of the natural *needs* of intellect and appetite (by contrast to man's many "wants"), Adler argued that man has an obligation to satisfy those needs. And since the only needs unique to man are those of the intellect, the chief imperative of human beings is to cultivate the mind—even at the risk of pride.

Niebuhr's Augustinian fatalism was unlikely to win many converts in Aspen in that summer of 1950. The hopes of humanism had staked their claims there too solidly. And the people who took part in mining these claims saw their hopes visibly strengthened by the effort. The Chicago journalist Sydney Harris, brought in as a moderator, enthusiastically reported the experience to his readers. "Instead of making unpleasant noises at the Russians," he wrote, "we were engaged in probing into the fundamentals of government—all government—to disclose how society can be organized on a peaceful basis." These were not just conversations among academicians, either, he noted. "A housewife, a college student, a businessman, a local judge, a musician, an Olympic skier, and a Czechoslovakian refugee" all searched together for "the very basis of our political beliefs" and "some kind of agreement as to the kind of world we would like to live in."[59] Another journalist took these conversations so to heart that he vowed to change the direction of his professional life and to begin philosophizing about fundamental questions—Right, Ends, "The Common Good," etc.—in his newspaper column.[60]

The very atmosphere was alive with intellectual curiosity and humanistic idealism and with what Paepcke called a "mystic something" that seemed to affect everyone who came under Aspen's spell[61]—what Hutchins had previously called "atmosphere." Walter and Ise Gropius, who stopped for a few days after a stay at the Paepcke ranch, found themselves enchanted by the "intellectual heights," as well as by the signs of an architectural renaissance that, despite the absence of a master plan, seemed to "begin a new chapter in Aspen history."[62] William Gorman saw a living incarnation of the True, the Good, and the Beautiful in the philosophical discussions and the physical beauty of the environment as well as of women like Elizabeth Paepcke and Clare Boothe Luce (one of Ortega's wishes come true).[63] Mortimer Adler, who fell so in love with Aspen that he was to return virtually every summer for over thirty years, added a variation on Gorman's theme. The "Aspen experience," he later wrote, uniquely demonstrated "that, in the scale of values the Platonic triad of the true, the good, and the beautiful takes precedence over the Machiavellian triad of money, fame, and power."[64]

The Jerome was again the social center of the "Aspen experience," drawing together at its bar, dining room, and sparkling swimming pool famous intellectuals and musicians, vacationers and curious locals to lounge about and discuss philosophy and the Good Life. If the institute lacked the Great Hall Ortega had envisioned, it could at least thank the Jerome for performing much the same function. And to one of the college students hired as a busboy, the Jerome and its environs achieved even more: the atmosphere of lofty meditation, serene sociability, and sublime leisure fostered there made Aspen resemble nothing so much as the fabled Alpine outpost of high civilization and exquisite sensibility portrayed in Thomas Mann's famous novel *The Magic Mountain*.[65]

The Wagner concerts by opera stars Lauritz Melchior and Helen Traubel played in perfect harmony with the serious yet convivial mood. The last of these concerts even played in harmony with nature. As the Denver Symphony's conductor, Saul Caston, called up the first bars of the overture to the *Flying Dutchman*, thunder roared overhead and rain began pelting the roof. Then, with the rousing *Ride of the Walküre*, the storm gathered force with the music, only to subside as if in preparation for Traubel's performance of the heartrending Vorspiel and Liebestod from *Tristan and Isolde*. The dramatic accompaniment of nature continued through "Siegfried's Rhine Journey" and "Funeral March" and then faded in the quiet semidarkness of evening after "Brunnhilde's Immolation." When the music stopped, the audience rose as one, applauding the unexpectedly dramatic concert of nature and culture.

After the Wagner concerts, the music was mainly by Bach or his contemporaries, in honor of the Bach bicentennial. But the height of the music program came with the appearance of Igor Stravinsky. In shirtsleeves because his luggage had not yet arrived, he brought the full house (the only capacity audience all summer) to its feet in ovation by conducting the Denver Symphony Orchestra in a performance of his own *Firebird* suite and *Divertimento*.

Music critics hailed the concert series and with it the advent of Aspen as a unique cultural center. Writing in the *New York Times*, Olin Downes praised the music program for "an eclecticism and richness of perspective simply not in the customary concert hall offering."[66] And Virgil Thomson, critic for the *New York Herald Tribune*, observing that "the tone of the whole place is intellectual, civilized, agreeable," declared the "musical entertainment unmatched, to my knowledge, in the United States and, I am sure, in Europe as well."[67]

At the summer's end, several of the performers traveled to the home of pianists Victor Babin and Vitya Vronsky in Santa Fe, where they savored their experience and contemplated their return the next summer. Aspen is unique among summer festivals, the tenor Mack Harrell told a local journalist, because of Paepcke's "vision" that "the world today needs more and more spiritual activity and impetus" and because Paepcke had brought together a "staff of world-famed, brilliant lecturers, writers, musicians, all devoted to the same ideal."[68] Harrell and the others acclaimed Aspen as a magnificent departure in American musical and cultural life, and they all hoped to be part of it—as some of them, including Harrell, Vronsky and Babin, and Robert Mann of the Juilliard String Quartet, were to be for years to come.

The "mystic something" had worked its charm. Everyone seemed to agree: the Aspen Institute was a singular invention—not Tanglewood or Salzburg, Sun Valley or Garmisch, but a little bit of all of them, and more. And nearly everyone wanted it to thrive.

One who did not was John P. Marquand, whose wife owned a vacation home in Aspen. Unable to tolerate the "rarified intellectual atmosphere of Aspen," he eventually refused even to pronounce the name of the town, dubbing the place his "Ass-pain."[69] Another dizzied if not repelled by Aspen's new cultural climate was Harold Ross. Ross was, according to his colleague at *The New Yorker* James Thurber, affected by a "profound uneasiness in the presence of anything smacking of scholarship or specialized knowledge."[70] Paepcke discovered this for himself when trying to coax Ross into joining the seminars and discussions. The editor of the nation's most sophisticated literary magazine would have no part of it. Ross came to Aspen to fish, he said, not to contemplate the True, the Good, and the Beautiful. Paepcke finally gave up, chiding Ross for not only resisting "culture at Aspen" but for being "allergic to it, which, as you know, means breaking out all over, losing one's health, or turning one's stomach."[71] Aspen's most famous son could never be at home in the Aspen of high culture. (But Ross proved his attachment to the home town the next year when, shortly before he died in December, he requested that his cremated remains be strewn over the mountains around Aspen, if his daughter would consent after her twenty-first birthday. Five years later, in December 1956, the consent came, and mortician Tom Sardy took to the skies scattering the ashes of Harold W. Ross into the mountain winds.)[72]

Paepcke and his colleagues at the institute did not, of course, expect to convert every visitor or transform American culture overnight. The institute's goals would be accomplished in time if only enough people could be brought under Aspen's spell. But as the summer progressed, it became all too evident that the people were all too few. None of the events, except the concerts by Melchior and Traubel and by Stravinsky, drew anything like capacity crowds. And most events played to less than half-filled halls—even in the six-hundred-seat Opera House. It was bad enough for Robert M. Hutchins to address an opening-day audience of three hundred in an auditorium built for two thousand. But the diplomat and philosopher Charles Malik spoke to a mere sixty-five people, and Isaac Stern played once to a house yielding $131, and a second time, in a concert with the Juilliard String Quartet, to box office receipts of $164.

The entire revenue from attendance at all events during the summer came to $14,917 (during the same time the ski lift took in $20,000). Total expenses ran to $121,937. After contributions of $48,756 (of which $15,000 came from Paepcke and the Aspen Company) and all other revenues had been tallied, Paepcke's anticipated surplus had collapsed into a loss of $53,133, almost double that of the Goethe Festival.

There was no shortage of explanations. International tensions and a threatened railroad strike possibly kept distant travelers away, but Aspen residents stayed away as well, prompting the *Aspen Times* to conduct a survey. Some locals said the institute was too highbrow, others that its program lasted too long, others still that the daytime schedule of events was inconvenient or that the participants were unprepared or insensitive to the interests of the audience.[73]

Participants and people close to the institute also had advice to give. Thornton Wilder, who had not attended because of other obligations, chastised Paepcke for not understanding "the laws of show business," from which "cultural matters" are not exempted—namely, the institute must attract an audience.[74] Mrs. Sam Mitchell said more people might have come, at least to the seminars, had the Hutchins-Adler Aristotelian bias been less dominant, and had the program employed fewer speakers and moderators. The exclusive attention to Western culture also roused dissent from those who thought the institute would have to take world literature and ideas as its province if it hoped to live up to its name.

Mortimer Adler recognized that Great Books seminars can only work among people who have read the book under discussion. Although an occasional demonstration seminar in front of an audience could dramatize the procedure, a regular schedule of such demonstrations before audiences ignorant of the books must soon lose effect for all but the participants. And since most of the Aspen seminars followed this public format, they had to fall short as "drawing cards." "For the most part," Adler admitted, "these panel discussions failed to be genuinely intelligible," and "it would be an understatement to say that they did not serve the educational objectives we had in mind."[75]

Signaling the institute's failure to reach enough people, Hutchins cancelled his scheduled return appearance at the summer's end for an address on "the essence of education." In its place Adler conducted a panel, "What Aspen Can Mean to America." Aspen could mean cultural reform, as the panel reiterated. But in the wake of that disappointing summer, the more important question was, how could the ill-attended institute bring it off?

Much of the advice offered by outsiders brought little cause for confidence. A man locked in a Mexico City jail promised—after reading newspaper accounts of the institute and its economic needs—to split a cache of $385,000 with Paepcke in exchange for assistance in getting hold of it. Paepcke's sense of adventure might have been tempted, but he let the deal pass. And to suggestions that he deck out the institute's program with popular entertainments, like jazz and theater, Paepcke retorted: "I, for one, would frankly rather lose something on a Goethe Bicentennial or an Aspen Institute for Humanistic Studies than be protected against the loss, assured of probably greater income, but filled with a feeling of great dissatisfaction in every other way."[76] Again, with a note of cheerful affirmation, he told a journalist: "It is against my principles to lose money, but it is almost a pleasure to watch it go down the drain on something as much fun as the Institute."[77]

But Paepcke's good cheer could flag. After gauging the extent of the losses, he occasionally allowed discouragement to break through—at least to people who might be moved to lend assistance. "It just isn't worth all the time, energy, and expense," he complained to one correspondent, "to have all these programs unless more people attend."[78] But how could the institute live by "the laws of show business" without abandoning its cultural aspirations?

One plausible answer came from none other than the mogul of the mass news magazine, Henry Luce. Luce and his wife, Clare, had arrived in Aspen on August 17, 1950, after Clare had been induced by Mortimer Adler, following a radio broadcast together in Chicago dealing with the *Syntopicon*, to participate in some of the institute's Great Books seminars. Henry Luce, an acquaintance of Paepcke's since their days at Yale, had come only to look and listen, willing on such occasions (in part from inhibition over a stutter in his speech) to bask in the glow of Clare's beauty and intelligence.

Yet if Clare Luce added luster to the institute's program, Henry changed its history. Sitting among the small clusters of people attending the sessions, he noticed something curious. Not only were the listeners few in number; they all had the bookish air of teachers, librarians, and scholars. These people, he thought, had nothing to gain from the Aspen Institute that they couldn't get at home among their own books and colleagues. Why should the institute direct itself to such an audience when it could serve culture so much better by addressing people who have little humanistic education and who need it desperately? And whom did Luce have in mind but the same ones he had been trying to elevate culturally through the pages of *Fortune* for twenty years. As he told Paepcke: Don't worry about the academicians, they will always be with you, however few in numbers; turn the institute instead toward "the great intellectually unwashed of America: *the businessman*."[79] For if businessmen could be drawn to the institute, its work would have reverberations throughout American life. "His suggestion," Paepcke explained a few days later to a friend, Clarence Randall, head of Inland Steel, "was that we literally take the scholar and the business man into the mountains and let them converse on subjects of basic interest to both of them on a high philosophical plane and not because either one of them then and there has an axe to grind."[80] And best of all, the institute would then surely become solvent, since business executives could attend at company expense under the guise of a working vacation. The strategy couldn't fail.

With the promise of helping to recruit these executives, Luce returned to New York, and Paepcke, himself a Reconstructed Businessman, hastened to spread the news. It should not be difficult, Paepcke told Gene Lilly, "to get various business tycoons . . . to send out at company expense five or ten of their top coming young men because a little philosophizing for the industrial leaders of tomorrow would be good." And besides, he added, striking a chord much played in the 1950s amid a growing tension between intellectuals and anti-intellectuals, "top educators and top business leaders should get to know each other better."[81] "The advantage" of the plan, he went on to a former administrator of the Rockefeller Foundation, "is to get the business man and the educator to understand each other better and to have a simple and unforced method of communication develop between them."[82] Both businessmen and educators, he explained, would benefit from the exchange: the practical and tough-minded men of business would learn to trust the intellectuals who educate their children; and the intellectuals, analytical and tentative as they are, would gain respect for the businessmen who supply their goods and give financial support to their institutions. Thus the institute would bring to an end, in the words of historian Richard Hofstadter, the "estrangement between businessmen and . . . men of critical intellect" that had been "profound and continuous" in America since the dawn of industrialization.[83] Businessmen and intellectuals could then join together to supplant the vulgarity, scientism, and aimlessness of American life with cultural refinement and humanistic idealism.

Thanks to Henry Luce, the Aspen Institute for Humanistic Studies had found yet another vocation. To its original ideals of postwar internationalism, Ortega's elegance, and the Chicago Bildungsideal, the institute would now add a more distant paternity: the cultural discontents and aspirations of the businessman. And Walter Paepcke, who had long felt those discontents and pursued those aspirations both within business and outside it, would now round out his varied career by translating them into the reform of business culture itself.

aspen and
america in
the fifties —and after

8

consensus,
criticism,

and the new
american elite

Reforming business culture would require more than the idealistic puffery of "great bookies" or Chautauquan exercises in moral and cultural uplift. The aim was, after all, no less than to convert to humanism, by persuasion or promised advantage, what Richard Hofstadter has called "the most powerful and pervasive interest in American life"—business.[1] And not only was this "interest" powerful and pervasive. From the mid-nineteenth century onward it had also seemed to many to be the very antithesis of humanistic culture. As a British observer had complained of American businessmen in 1859: "They are incapable of acquiring general knowledge on a broad or a liberal scale. All are confined to trade, finance, law, and small, local provincial information. Art, science, literature, are nearly dead to them."[2] Over a hundred years later this complaint still echoed in the sneering remark of the Latin American author Jorge Luis Borges: "Who respects businessmen? No one. People look at America and all they see are traveling salesmen. So they laugh."[3]

But by the middle of the twentieth century, changes in business and American culture were beginning to dim the stereotype. The crude "business culture," so distasteful to social critics in the twenties, was fading in the convergence of commerce and culture and of their old polarities—practice and theory, trade and intellect, promotion and taste, profits and public responsibility. Not that these polarities were dissolving into blissful union. The old tensions between material progress, secularity, and egalitarianism on the one side and spiritual ideals, social stability, and cultural elitism on the other remained. And quarrels between intellectuals and businessmen, or eggheads and fatheads, as they labeled each other, were a common motif of the fifties. As earlier chapters have shown, however, alliances were being formed—or at least, in Hofstadter's words again, "an uneasy symbiosis."[4] Thus an author in *Saturday Review* could confidently assert in 1957: "No sensible businessman would be prepared to do without the critical and analytical activity of the academic men; no sensible academician would be prepared to sacrifice the agreeable economic corollaries—scholarships, foundations, subsidies—of a sound prosperity."[5]

Reasons for the alliance of business with culture and intellect are not hard to find. For one, the consumer economy had turned many corporations, like CCA, into promoters of benign and appealing "images" of themselves, and some had also become exponents, not to say exploiters, of art and good taste. At the same time, the cultural philanthropies of businessmen like Carnegie, Guggenheim, Vanderbilt, and Rockefeller (followed by those of foundations and, later, corporations) had, in the absence of government support for cultural institutions, given the businessman not only an identification with high culture but a dominant place in it. On what if not capitalist profits did America's major museums, concert halls, and private universities depend for their origins and sustenance? Whether prompted by capitalist guilt or gain, such philanthropies proved the interdependence, not the antipathy, of wealth and high culture in America.

But more than the philanthropic largesse of businessmen, the economic and political ascendency of America in the twentieth century elevated the stature of business by boosting the traditional American confidence in the businessman's creed of practicality. Hadn't American practicality won a world war and made this country the richest and most powerful in the world? Who could gainsay success? Charles E. Wilson, the president of General Motors who became secretary of defense in 1952, caught the essence of this mood in a proposition that entered American folklore as "what's good for General Motors is good for the country and vice versa." The remark (a reversal of Wilson's actual words) gained infamy for Wilson, but it also spoke a truth that the atmosphere of Cold War competition strengthened: capitalism is the bulwark of American democracy and of America's position in the world. Little wonder that Eisenhower appointed to his cabinet not contemplative men but people like Wilson, or, as TRB in *The New Republic* quipped, "eight millionaires and a plumber," whose actions were often, as a journalist noted of Wilson, "neither 'conservative' nor 'liberal.' They were, however, practical."[6]

This praise of practicality sometimes masked an anti-intellectual distrust of mind and education. Charles E. Wilson, for one, frequently dismissed intellectuals as mere temporizers. But by mid-century, "practicality" was loosening its ties to anti-intellectualism and joining forces with intellect to produce, among other things, a new type of businessman. No more the roughshod or even genteel entrepreneur who founded and ran his own company. The very size and diversity, as well as the public ownership of the modern corporation, had all but driven him from the scene and set in his place the wage-earning executive trained in administration and economic planning.

This "managerial revolution" was, to be sure, latent in capitalism itself. The nineteenth-century British critic Walter Bagehot had noted its makings in the "matter-of-factness" and prosaic "'stock-taking' habit" created by "perpetual commerce."[7] And the German social theorist Max Weber had translated such observations into a comprehensive theory of capitalism as the supremely rationalized, bureaucratic system. By the 1950s, consumer commerce, public ownership, and government regulations had made the latent manifest. Rational matter-of-factness was spreading throughout economic life in the form of professional business administration. "The Tycoon Is Dead," declared the editors of Fortune in 1951.[8] As Max Lerner observed in his mid-century summing-up, America as a Civilization (1957), "in place of the heroic adventurism of the Titans came a group of 'managerial skills' that required talent and judgement in the art of management but seemed earth-creeping by comparison."[9]

Acquiring these "managerial skills" demanded one thing above all: education. But this education would not come simply from the "school of experience" that had once served as the only training deemed necessary for a business career. "The day has quite gone by," the Commercial and Financial Chronicle had announced as early as 1916, "when it is sufficient for a young man to begin at the bottom and without more training than he can gather in the daily routine, . . . to acquire that breadth of knowledge and completeness of training which are necessary" for competence in modern business.[10] The businessman's education would increasingly come in college and professional school. In 1900, 39.4 percent of top business executives had some college education; in 1925 the figure had risen to 51.4 percent, and in 1950, 76 percent. At mid-century, about 20 percent of the top executives had also attended graduate school in law, engineering, or at one of the several business schools founded in the late decades of the nineteenth century and the early decades of the twentieth expressly to provide training in "business administration."[11] In the 1960s, Fortune magazine reported that 85 percent of top executives in a survey had college degrees and 40 percent of them had also done graduate work.[12] And the most important managerial skills that these new businessmen needed to acquire were those for handling policy and people in the large organizations of the new American economy. "The mid-century businessman has had to go to school—in labor, in politics, in social welfare," said *Fortune* magazine.[13] "We don't care if you're a Phi Beta Kappa or a Tau Beta Phi," one company president cautioned prospective executives. "We want a well-rounded person who can handle well-rounded people."[14]

The result was a businessman most unlike Sinclair Lewis's Babbitt or Theodore Dreiser's dynamic Titans. He was instead a cautious organization man like the central figure of Sloan Wilson's *Man in the Grey Flannel Suit* (1955) or a corporate manipulator like the title character of Cameron Hawley's *Cash McCall* (1955). These were men of calculating mind and studied social performance—the kind meticulously, and critically, examined by sociologist C. Wright Mills in *White Collar* (1951) and by social critic William H. Whyte, Jr., in *The Organization Man* (1956). And as Mills, Wright, and other observers implied, the new businessmen were becoming interchangeable with their counterparts in labor, government, and other large organizations. They were men, in Frederick Lewis Allen's words of those years, "to whom government service and public service of other sorts came naturally" in consequence of "the wide range of techniques and public responsibilities which present-day business confronts."[15] Such facts were to induce historian Eric Goldman to say of the businessmen in Eisenhower's cabinet that they were "decidedly not businessmen of the 1920s type. They were part of the new, more adaptable managerial class."[16] Who can blame Charles E. Wilson for readily equating the interests of the United States with those of General Motors and for seeing no difference between running GM and the Defense Department—they were all becoming one.

The rise of the professional manager, and the new-found friendship between business and intellect, alongside the political and economic triumphs of American practicality, thus gave business a social and cultural status it had not known before—at least not since the passing of the traditional mercantile class. "When I was growing up," the journalist Ralph Coghlan told a conference of businessmen in 1951, "the word 'soulless' corporation was a very common term. . . . Well, in my lifetime I have seen a remarkable change in this. I don't know whether it could be said that corporations have obtained souls, but at least they have obtained intelligence."[17] And with this change in the stature of business came a reappraisal of American culture itself.

The postwar political eminence of America made such a reappraisal inevitable. American freedom and know-how were certain to come in for some kudos. But the newly forming relation between practicality and intellect was also bound to prompt scrutiny of the place of mind in America and of the

health of American cultural life in general. And so it did, yielding the discovery that American culture had at last come of age and was gaining ascendancy over the Western world.

The new estimation of American culture owed much to America's good fortune as a haven for Europeans fleeing their homelands during the dark years
of fascist domination. The notables who sought refuge on these shores, many
of them permanently, in this wave of migration brought a new cosmopoli-
tanism and excellence to virtually every field of American artistic and intellectual life in the middle third of the century.[18] But this fresh identity did
not come from emigrés alone. Native energies were also fueling the cultural
fires. Alongside immigrant painters, Americans like Jackson Pollack and
Barnett Newman helped move the Western capital of the arts from Paris to
New York. Designers, like Walter Dorwin Teague, Norman Bel Geddes, and
Henry Dreyfuss, and architects, like Philip Johnson and Edward Durrell Stone
(to say nothing of Frank Lloyd Wright), insured the Americanization of
modernist design. Social scientists, physical scientists, and scholars of all
kinds were joining immigrant colleagues in making American universities
unexcelled in the world. And American writers, led by Sinclair Lewis, Eugene
O'Neill, Faulkner and Hemingway, were winning international reputations
and prizes, while those who had sought escape from American commerce
and vulgarity in the twenties were returning home.

No wonder critics and historians started revising America's place in the
scheme of Western culture. Many of these revisions dwelled on America's
surging affluence—for example, David M. Potter's *People of Plenty: Economic
Abundance and the American Character* (1954), Max Lerner's *America as a
Civilization* (1957), and John Kenneth Galbraith's *The Affluent Society* (1957).
But others took the measure of the cultural life itself. And none did so more
suggestively than the proceedings of a symposium sponsored by *Partisan Review* and published in 1952 under the title "Our Country and Our Culture."

"Until little more than a decade ago," the editors began, "America was
commonly thought to be hostile to art and culture. Since then, however, the
tide has begun to turn, and many writers and intellectuals now feel closer to
their country and its culture. . . . Europe is no longer regarded as a sanctuary;
it no longer assures that rich experience of culture which inspired and justified a criticism of American life. The wheel has come full circle, and now
America has become the protector of Western civilization."

The editors tempered this effusion by cautioning against complacent
pride and above all against the evils of mass culture (no longer, like the
critics of the twenties, against the evils of business culture). But optimism
dominated the discussion of the "reaffirmation and rediscovery of America."
David Riesman, Reinhold Niebuhr, James Burnham, Leslie Fiedler, Mark

Schorer, Lionel Trilling, and others agreed that artists and intellectuals were unquestionably abandoning their traditional hostility to American life. Trilling voiced the common view (kept short of unanimity by Norman Mailer and one or two others) when he observed: "For the first time in the history of the modern American intellectual America is not to be conceived of as *a priori* the vulgarest and stupidest nation in the world." And he attributed this improvement to none other than the cultural fact stressed earlier: a "change in the relation of wealth to intellect." Wealth, he went on, nowadays "shows a tendency to submit itself to the rule of mind and imagination, to refine itself, and to apologize for its existence by a show of taste and sensitivity," with the result that "art and thought" are "more generally and happily received and recognized . . . than they have ever been before in America."[19] (Trilling and some of the other participants displayed rather more optimism about American culture at this symposium than they would in later years after the mood of cultural pride that typified the early fifties had taken on the appearance of a self-deceiving approbation. Trilling's Jefferson Lecture at the Library of Congress in 1972, for example, expressed a disappointment bordering on despair that mind in America had lost ground again.)[20]

Trilling, in his more optimistic mood, was describing an America educated by both modernism and advanced capitalism and strengthened by both victory in war and a Europe in eclipse. But within the cultural awakening that so pleased him and his colleagues, Trilling also discerned a social fact of mounting importance—and one that formed a direct link between American society at large and the Aspen Institute. The ascendancy of mind in America, he said, not only prefigured an era of intellectual vitality, it was also creating "a new intellectual class"[21] to administer the ever more demanding political, economic, and cultural life.

The sociologist C. Wright Mills, writing a few years later, called this class (although he slighted the academicians) the "power elite."[22] He defined it as a segment of society marked by common economic and educational origins, power, wealth, celebrity, and high social status, and supported by bonds of reciprocal privileges and advantages among its members. Trilling and Mills detected a truth. Since the fifties, this "new intellectual class" or "power elite" has become a pervasive presence in American life, exercising influence through the intellectual expertise and common interests of its members, who move comfortably from academe to government to foundations to corporations and back again. They are the new American elite (see also Chapter 10).

It is not surprising that this class supplied the clientele of the Aspen Institute, and that the institute became its agent. For the institute's ambitions to reform business culture at mid-century meant inducing members of this class to contemplate their status and responsibilities as leaders of a country that had become the military and economic might of the world and that aspired to cultural preeminence as well. These occupations were not laid out when the institute embarked on its new course in 1951. But they soon came to dominate institute affairs, just as they had gained prominence in American intellectual life.

Most of these consequences lay far ahead when Paepcke began beckoning businessmen and intellectuals to Aspen. His chief worry at the time was that the practical minds would prevail and lead discussion away from universals toward particulars, from eternal verities toward everyday minutiae, thus thwarting the institute's aspiration to rejuvenate humanistic culture. "We want to keep away from the current and contemporary and stay with more basic ideas," Paepcke explained to an inquiring industrial relations expert who assumed the Aspen Institute shared his company's preoccupation with management principles and the tactics of commerce. "The contemporary phase of American Government, present day economics, and the like is some-thing which we would probably leave for someone else to do."

In disclaiming such pursuits for Aspen, Paepcke referred his correspon-dent to the forthcoming "discussions and seminars . . . of exactly this type"[23] at Dwight D. Eisenhower's recently established conference center near New York City, the American Assembly. For unlike the American Assembly, which took the immediate affairs of the country and of the world as its province, the Aspen Institute would, if Paepcke had his way, serve civiliza-tion by being a bastion of culture transcending those affairs. As Clifton Fadiman somberly put it in late 1950: "Aspen could be very important in the increasingly bleak two or three centuries ahead of us, just as the monasteries were during the centuries from the fall of Rome to the 12th century."[24] But despite his yen to make the institute an ivory tower, Paepcke did take some cues from the American Assembly. He consulted with Eisenhower in No-vember 1950, and shortly thereafter seemed willing to inch the institute a bit closer to the assembly's format. "I had a very nice hour's chat with Gen-eral Eisenhower at Columbia" (of which Eisenhower was president), Paepcke informed his brother-in-law, Paul Nitze. "He is very excited about the 'Ameri-can Assembly'" where he "expects to invite businessmen, educators, labor leaders and some political people to discuss important problems of the day. . . . While we do not expect, for the coming year," Paepcke added, to make the Aspen sessions "absolutely topical or contemporary in nature, I think we should try to strike a happy middle ground between the entirely abstract and the completely current."[25]

This gesture toward contemporaneity had reverberations in a proposal drawn up to solicit foundation support. The institute, it said, existed not only to help remedy "the plight of our culture" (that is, the inability of a science-saturated society to "make progress in human relations"), but to resolve the "urgent practical problems of our society." These "practical problems," in those disquieted Cold War days, centered on how "the democratic way of life can survive the dangers, external and internal, with which it is confronted." The institute proposed to help by "clarifying the questions of ends and values" underlying the dangers and by promoting "a fuller understanding of the ideas on which [the American way of life] is based."[26]

Paepcke then took another step to expand the institute's appeal and its potential influence. Perhaps the institute should not rely on the "great ideas" alone to reform culture by way of the businessman. Falling in line with what a contemporary historian perceived as a "widespread and contagious . . . desire for synthesis and reconciliation" of "supposedly contrasting interests in American society,"[27] Paepcke suggested that the institute bring together leaders of all sectors of American life, not just businessmen and intellectuals, to dispel misunderstandings and forge ties among them, thus enabling them the better to serve America, and America to serve the world. Paepcke set forth the revised plan in an address to his fellow trustees of the University of Chicago in January 1951. "We now in the United States have the leadership of the world in our laps," he said, and yet we "are without any appealing ideology around which other peoples of the world may rally." This failure clings to us, he went on, because "the four major groups running our country: Government, Labor, Business, and Education [he included the arts under Education] . . . do not really know each other and they definitely distrust each other. . . . When so little understanding and confidence exist between these various groups, is it to be wondered at that as a nation we" fail to provide "ideological and cultural leadership?" Hence, he concluded, "should not and must not some of the wiser representatives of these various groups sit down together and attempt to arrive at some basic understanding?"[28] Although Paepcke did not tell his audience, he had a place for such a gathering picked out.

By shaping itself in the image of these aspirations, the Aspen Institute added still another ingredient to its recipe for cultural reform. The Chicago Bildungsideal, postwar internationalism, Ortega's criticism of the Mass Man, and Henry Luce's humanizing of business were now joined by the mid-century desire to forge a consensus among America's economic, political, and cultural leaders capable of lending ideological guidance and thereby insuring America's global eminence.

The trustees of the institute formally adopted these goals in late January 1951: "To bring together thoughtful leaders from the fields of government, education, business and labor in an attempt to find a meeting ground which all of these groups will recognize as a common foundation for citizenship."[29] To help find that "meeting ground," the trustees decided the seminars and lectures should dwell on "the broad principles which underlie our Western ideology"[30] as found in four categories of "the American heritage": political philosophy, literature, economic theory and reforms, and theology and philosophy.

This program set the pattern loosely followed by the institute for a decade or more, delicately balancing the universal and the particular, the immemorial and the immediate. And to administer that balance, and facilitate formation of the network of people to be drawn to the institute, the trustees appointed a full-time resident manager. For three years—until fired amid an administrative upheaval that saw the music festival and music school break off from the institute—Richard Leach, an agent for the National Concerts and Artists Corporation with whom Paepcke had first negotiated contracts for the musicians, relieved Paepcke of the increasingly complicated task of overseeing the "Aspen Summer Festival" (including the academic and music programs, the Design Conference, begun in 1951, and America's first national Photo Conference, also held in 1951). Leach's appointment also enabled Paepcke to fill a void on the board of trustees left by the resignation and withdrawal from Aspen affairs of one of the institute's founders: Robert M. Hutchins.

Hutchins had several reasons for resigning. Chief among them was his decision in late 1950 to leave the University of Chicago and join his friend Paul G. Hoffman in spending the billions held by the newly reorganized and endowed Ford Foundation. "It was a tremendous opportunity," he said, to do just the kind of thing he had always wanted to do; in other words: "the proclamation of the Ford Foundation in 1950 could be summarized by saying it was going to save the world."[31] How could Hutchins have resisted? Taking as his part of the enterprise his own brainchild, the subsidiary Fund for the Advancement of Education, he hoped the fund would "ultimately result in the reorganization of the educational system."[32] Hutchins's hopes proved unavailing, in part because his and Hoffman's liberal leanings made the foundation a target of McCarthyite witch-hunting, which charged the foundation with dispensing the profits of capitalism to leftist causes. By 1953, both Hoffman and Hutchins had been purged, although they won the small victory of a $915 million grant to set up the Fund for the Republic, dedicated to the study and protection of civil liberties. Hutchins headed the Fund for the Republic, issuing studies of black history and the like, until 1959, when, the Ford money gone, he obtained new support and set up the Center for the Study of Democratic Institutions to continue and expand the fund's work.

The Ford Foundation job gave Hutchins a far more promising opportunity to alter the course of American education than anything he could have done for the Aspen Institute. The job also made Paepcke rub his hands and joke that now "the all-year-round dream university, sometimes known as the Aspen Institute for Humanistic Studies, will be financed by Robert Maynard Ford."[33] But the Ford post was not Hutchins's only reason for disengaging from Aspen. For one, his second wife could not travel into the mountains for reasons of health. And for another, he wasn't all that keen on spending time there himself after the discouraging showing of the previous summer. Hutchins's last communication as a trustee to Paepcke hinted, with customary brevity and aplomb, at his readiness to let others make Aspen their arena. Upon reading Paepcke's announcement of a trustees' meeting set for January 28—at which his resignation was to be tendered—Hutchins's eye had fixed on its concluding statements: "As summer plans are somewhat more definitized, further information will be sent to all the trustees. Meanwhile, if you have any suggestions, please let us have them." In a few swift strokes he had jotted his reply at the bottom and returned the announcement to Paepcke: "My suggestion is that you stop using such words as definitized."[34] In the future, Hutchins was to deliver a few lectures at the institute and offer occasional advice, and he received an award in 1965, but his days as a shaper of Aspen's crusade for cultural reform were over.

Hutchins's departure did not directly affect the intellectual direction or character of the institute, since these were already in the hands of Paepcke, Adler (who also left the University of Chicago in 1951 to join Hutchins in spending Ford money by establishing his own Institute for Philosophical Research to complete the *Summa Dialectica*), Clarence Faust, and others. It is possible that had Hutchins stayed on, he might have restrained the eventual movement of the institute away from its original humanistic idealism toward more worldly pursuits. But this is unlikely. For the institute had cast its lot with the leaders of American society; and the course followed thereafter was bound to mirror the interests of those leaders and their times, not just the ideals of mid-century humanism.

The institute set off on that course in the summer of 1951 with an eleven-week series of lectures and seminars labeled "Our American Heritage." Promising a bracing experience of cultural self-scrutiny amid war abroad and anticommunist witch-hunting at home, the institute managed to attract an impressive variety of intellectuals and executives. The executives included such Paepcke loyalists as Meyer Kestnbaum and Clarence Randall, as well as many having little or no connection to the Aspen entrepreneur—like the head of a small sulphur company; the head of a printing company; young Charles Percy, president of Bell and Howell, later senator from Illinois; and union officials from the International Ladies Garment Workers, the Oil Workers, the Steel Workers, the Printing Pressmen, and the Building Service Employees. The intellectuals also included friends and strangers: Hutchins and Adler, of course, and several of their colleagues and acquaintances from past and present—Mark Van Doren and Jacques Barzun of Columbia; Theodore Hesburgh, president of Notre Dame; O. Meredith Wilson, president of the University of Oregon; Norman Cousins, editor of *Saturday Review;* Edward Weeks, editor of *Atlantic Monthly;* Raymond Moley, columnist for *Newsweek;* and prize-winning physicist Leo Szilard; as well as lesser lights recommended by academic friends. This assembly, although not altogether C. Wright Mills's "power elite," was a representative part of it and unmistakably signaled a new mandarin class.

Gathering together for forums, lectures, and seminars in the Opera House (finally renovated to Herbert Bayer's modern but respectful design) and on the lawn at Pioneer Park, these disparate spokesmen of American culture explored their common heritage through a few dominant ideas, chief among them (predictably in that chill Cold War year): individualism, liberty, and practicality. Lest anyone miss the pertinence of these ideas to contemporary life, some of the lecturers took pains to drive the message home. A professor of biochemistry from the University of Texas, in an address entitled "Natural Science in the Service of American Ideals," attempted to reveal the physics (or metaphysics) of individualism. Chemistry, he explained, demonstrates that nature consists of discrete, individual entities rather than collective "averages," and can therefore "help undermine communism, which is designed to deal with people as they are not"[35] (a theory that had its Soviet counterpart in Lysenkoism, which presumed that organisms interact so thoroughly with their environments that atomistic individuality is impossible).

Others, like Norman Cousins, spoke more modestly of "America's assets in the present crisis," which Cousins discerned in America's military might, tradition of liberty, and willingness to work for the future. Striking a similar note in a lecture on "the conditions of peace," Hutchins reiterated his unwavering faith in "the civilization of the dialogue" as the hope of democracy and world peace, and he affirmed the responsibility of America as global leader to keep that dialogue alive and make it universal.

But probably the most learned and thought-provoking of the many appraisals of the American heritage that summer was Jacques Barzun's graceful portrait of "America's romance with practicality." Barzun's words, later published in *Harper's* magazine, were singularly apposite because they questioned some of the assumptions behind the institute's program and at the same time exemplified the affirmation in Aspen and beyond of American culture and "practicality" during the early fifties.

Like Adler, Barzun had been an early beneficiary of John Erskine's seminal great books course at Columbia, and had also joined Adler in teaching great books at the People's Institute in New York. But unlike his colleague,

Barzun had made his career expounding the particulars of history rather than the universals of philosophy. And the particulars that had most occupied him were those of romanticism, whose variousness, vitality, and humanity he commended to the troubled, anti-romantic twentieth century. In his many writings on this subject (especially his magisterial *Berlioz and the Romantic Century*) and others, Barzun had exhibited extraordinary abilities to comprehend variousness and complexity, to write with lucidity and grace, and to unmask misuses of intellect. These abilities also marked Barzun's meditations on American practicality—and his later contributions to the institute's fare.

Spurning the widely accepted notion that America invented practicality and that practicality is a vice, Barzun defended some of the ideas that Adler and Hutchins had been attacking for years. Modernity should not, he said, be denigrated for its acceptance of relativism and for its praise of practicality in favor of a more confident and spiritual past. For relativism, meaning provisional truths derived from experience, and practicality, meaning the *pragmatic* weighing of means and ends, have given civilization most of its material and moral advantages, advantages not even the idealists propose to live without.

Echoing John Dewey in the battle over the Chicago Bildungsideal, Barzun asserted an inherent bond between pragmatism, democracy, and diversity: "Pragmatic relativism is both a safeguard *against* absolutes which when ambitious invariably turn tyrannical; and a safeguard *for* those absolutes when their claims to universality remain within the bounds of decent social behavior." Addressing those who would defend democracy by propounding certainties, he warned: "In ideological conflicts, the forces of wisdom, experience, and emotional maturity must resist the urge to meet absolutes with absolutes. The repeated demand that democracy must have 'an ideology' stiffnecked and verbose like the Communists' is as foolish as it would be fatal."[36] Far from desirable for democracy, abstract ideology is inimical to it and "precisely the trouble with the modern world," for democracy depends on "unverbalized convictions" that insure variety and vitality.[37] In short, democracy depends on practicality.

Barzun's celebration of diversity and practicality plainly contradicted Adler's reverence for theory and truth as set forth, for instance, in Adler's own Aspen lecture near the same time, "The Theoretical and the Practical," and in Paepcke's appeals for a democratic ideology. Nor did the contradictions go unnoticed. When participants gathered on the lawn at Pioneer Park to discuss Barzun's remarks and William James's *Pragmatism*, Barzun and Adler fell into such an energetic debate on the character and merits of pragmatism that, as Father Theodore Hesburgh (who was present) recalled nearly thirty years later, "no one could get a word in edgewise."[38]

Nor was this the only fissure of disagreement that opened during the sessions. Barzun and Adler joined forces to argue against business executive Clarence Randall that profits are a means not an end; Randall quarreled with union leader William Gomberg over the respective roles of labor and management in the American economy; and sometimes everybody seemed to be at odds with everybody—one listener remarked after a forum that the only thing the participants "had in common was that they all needed a haircut."[39]

However diverse in opinion, the participants seemed to enjoy the experience of expressing those opinions and hearing others express theirs. One businessman stuck in Barzun's memory by greeting every intellectual revelation with an astonished "Gee whiz!" then sitting back, wide-eyed, to absorb the shock.[40] A union vice-president said the experience of encountering "many new and sometimes disturbing thoughts is . . . something that I will remember and cherish all the rest of my life."[41] William Gomberg echoed the sentiment: "I did massacre a few mild prejudices I held, but I suppose that is all to the good."[42] On the side of business, Clarence Randall was more than taken aback by the vigorous debates. "It has done a great deal for me," he confessed. "The discipline involved in facing up to that many keen minds, both to say what you believe and to think out why you believe it is a very salutary experience. It ought to be required for every man holding substantial responsibility in the business world."[43] So taken was Randall by the Aspen experience that he refused payment for his services and expenses and soon joined the institute's board of trustees.

The institute's prescription for reforming American culture with a dose of what Paepcke now liked to call "the cross-fertilization of ideas" seemed to be working. At least it had proved its curative potential. But an old sore rankled: costs far exceeded receipts. For all its high-powered program, the institute was still not drawing enough paying guests. And when the season closed with a deficit of more than $60,000, Paepcke acidly joked that the institute was not only "not for profit"; it was a "first-class loser."[44]

To keep his hopes for Aspen alive, Paepcke sought to strengthen the institute in any way he could. He formed a permanent administration, with himself as president, supported by a vice-president, a director of the music school, and a director of the music festival, and he began turning over his Aspen Company stock—1,500 shares, nearly three-quarters of the total, appraised at $178 each—to the institute in hopes of convincing potential donors that he had no financial stake in the institute's success. This last move was not, to be sure, entirely selfless, since it yielded tax advantages, and the Aspen Company had never turned a profit or paid dividends anyway. But it earned Paepcke new respect among Aspenites, who signed a petition registering their admiration and gratitude that Paepcke was truly in Aspen for culture not profit—notwithstanding the appreciating value of his land hold-ings unaffected by the stock divestment. He also vowed to enliven future summer programs with some light entertainment "for the larger prospective audience we must have."[45] And he told Adler to spice up the academic offer-ings by using more familiar American authors in the seminars and employ-ing catchy names for the lectures. Don't "change the contents," he advised jocularly, "but make the titles lurid."[46]

Alongside these cosmetic alterations, Paepcke made the first of several new public concessions to the interests of the mid-century businessmen whom, together with representatives of government, he wanted to entice to Aspen. From this time onward, the lofty philosophical pronouncements of the institute's early publicity, exalting the humanities over the sciences, value over fact, and urging the humanistic unity of Western civilization and an ideological consensus among America's leaders, gave way to more pragmatic statements of the advantages, especially to business executives, of the Aspen experience. The publicity folder of 1952 was the last one to repeat the old slogans. And even as it was being mailed, the institute issued a special an-nouncement over Paepcke's name advertising "The Aspen Program for Busi-ness Leadership." Playing heavily upon the changed character of corporate capitalism at mid-century—namely the importance of the "human prob-lems" born of social relations, management, and government regulation—this document summoned executives to prepare for their widened responsi-bilities by attending the Aspen Institute. "What will these businessmen get out of it?" Paepcke was quoted as asking and answering in words he would have shunned two years earlier: "First I think they will be better businessmen."[47]

After 1952, this pitch to the interests of Aspen's executive clientele dominated institute publicity (no longer written by Mortimer Adler but by others, like the articulate banker Gaylord Freeman). Formally promoted from 1953 onward as "The Aspen Executives' Program," and taking as their pe-rennial theme in 1956 "The Responsibilities of Leadership," the seminars were closed to the public and explicitly promised benefits to the modern business culture. They would explore the "modern executive's position as a business leader" and, above all, the executive's "obligation to champion the principles upon which personal freedom and the free economy are founded."[48] And by doing this, as Paepcke wrote in the last publicity pamphlet prepared during the fifties—and the last in Paepcke's lifetime—they would make the executive "a more effective business leader and can be expected to make his enterprise a more profitable one. This is the purpose of the Aspen program."[49]

These words barely recalled the institute's early aspirations for cultural reform. But, printed to sell businesses on the institute as a good investment in education for their employees, those words were dictated by economic necessity—a concession that became more pronounced and took on more philosophical conviction after Paepcke's death in 1960, when the entire institute program went forth under the heading "Management Development for American Leadership," with the seminars labeled "Liberal Arts Management Development Seminars."[50]

Such words paid off, at least modestly. For the institute gradually hosted increasing numbers of executives (more than 400 enrolled during the first decade). And this growth brought the creation of a permanent campus of specially designed seminar rooms (see fig. 8.1), offices, lodges, and dining and recreational facilities, as well as a fully equipped and staffed health center that won national attention in 1957 as Paepcke's crowning ingenuity in educating "the Whole Man"[51]—although, as an idea ahead of its time, the center failed to pay its way and eventually became merely a casual recreational facility.

To help finance the physical expansion, the institute also began opening its doors to conventions having nothing to do with humanistic studies or the "cross-fertilization of ideas." Half a dozen such gatherings took place for the first time in 1958, followed by a dozen more the next year, drawing to Aspen such disparate organizations as the National Restaurant Association and the Rocky Mountain Society of Orthodontists.

Thus under the pressures of financial constraints, and guided by Paepcke's determination and inventiveness, the institute altered its public identity several times in the 1950s. In doing so it sacrificed some of its early idealism. But by the decade's end Paepcke could at least take pride in having ensured Aspen's place on the cultural map, and having set in motion a chain of events that showed every prospect of making Aspen internationally renowned for hosting the best and the brightest, the powerful and the celebrated of America and the Western world in the second half of the twentieth century.

But the institute's ascending reputation came from more than facile promotion, courageous expansion, Paepcke's money, and good will. As the fifties moved along, the Aspen intellectual experience openly reflected and addressed several preoccupations of American culture and the new American elite.

These historical resonances were most conspicuous in the public lectures and discussions. Some lecture topics were perennial favorites, notably the idea of freedom and the character of American culture. Freedom was explored in dozens of lectures and from every angle—in its relation to truth, law, license, security, equality, authority, technology, and so on. Understandably, discussions of the subject often revolved around the twin threats of communism and anticommunism. On the one side stood intellectuals like Adler, Hutchins, Clarence Faust, and others who advocated studying Marx

Fig. 8.1. Jacques Barzun (far left center) moderating executive seminar in Aspen, 1959. Supreme Court Justice Hugo Black sits two to Barzun's left. Photo by Ferenc Berko.

and who castigated rabid anticommunism as a peril to freedom and truth. On the other stood executives who assailed intellectuals displaying the least sympathy for Marx as "tools of communism."[52] One opponent, asked by Adler to explain "what's wrong with the Russian system," amused and silenced her redoubtable interrogator with the retort: "It's un-American."[53]

Although McCarthyite hysteria had few strong reverberations in Aspen (it did cost the institute a return visit by Senator J. William Fulbright in 1954 when the Army-McCarthy hearings forced him to cancel, pleading the pressing threat of McCarthy to both domestic politics and foreign policy),[54] the institute was unmistakably a defender of individual liberty and capitalist economics. Adler demonstrated this loyalty in a brief for capitalism presented in 1958 (prepared with Louis O. Kelso and published as *The Capitalist Manifesto*). Jettisoning the socialist morality that he had clung to since youth, Adler pointed to a logical connection between political and economic freedom: only by diffusing political and economic power throughout society in the forms of democratic political liberty and capitalist economic self-sufficiency can true human freedom be preserved. Democracy and capitalism must be treated as means, not ends: they must promote self-perfection, not self-indulgence.

While the discussions of freedom fairly consistently mirrored the American concern at mid-century with the defense of political and economic liberties against the dangers of communism or false ideology, the meditations on American culture traced a wider and less predictable course. Beginning in a spirit of consensus, by the decade's end they had grown less confident and more critical, reflecting the shifting perspectives of social criticism in the fifties. Following their affirming explorations of the American heritage in 1951, the institute's participants dwelled on the shared interests and affluence and new-found cultural pride of Americans at mid-century. Leaders of the labor movement, for instance, spoke of the mounting contentment of the American working class. No more the aggrieved discontents, socialist militancy, and revolutionary ambitions of yesteryear. Walter Reuther, head of the United Auto Workers, could speak confidently of labor's new desire to function within the established political and economic system, because working men, he said, want neither political power for themselves nor the socialist economy dreamed of by their early champions, like Reuther himself; they want instead politicians responsive to their needs. Thus he brushed aside the idea that labor should have its own political party, conceding that "there can be no successful party on such a narrow base." In place of his old socialist formulas, Reuther laid down a strictly humanistic prescription for improving the lot of labor and society. Decrying the American "emphasis on practical things," he said, our laggard "moral and spiritual development" has created a compelling "need for humanistic thought."[55] The battles, ideological and organizational, of the labor movement behind him, Reuther had become one of the new mandarins, and a middle-class sage.

Reuther's colleague, William Gomberg, agreed with Reuther's prescription but offered his own version of what had made it necessary. By the mid-century, he told an Aspen audience, affluence had robbed the trade union movement of any need for militancy, with the result that old labor fighters like himself and Reuther had abandoned their socialist ambitions and lost enthusiasm for the movement itself. "Labor leaders are victims of their own success," he said. For "the most creative tasks" of the trade union movement "are behind it rather than ahead." This may be good for the rank and file, he went on, but executives like Reuther and himself who had "set out to be arbiters and controllers of our industrial destiny . . . are now serving out their middle years and old age as cops, desperately attempting to conceal the true nature of their roles from themselves and from the public." The result is "frustration and ennui," expressed in corruption or "a fight for status," or, as Gomberg's own actions later proved, departure from the labor movement for academe altogether.[56]

Gomberg's words had a different ring from Reuther's but they described the same historical reality. And this was the reality mirrored in the aspirations, the clientele, and the discussions of the Aspen Institute itself: the relative affluence and ideological unity and cultural conscience of America at the mid-century.

A finely drawn variation on this theme came with a discourse by Jacques Barzun on the American appetite for "culture." Barzun thought this topic tailor-made for the institute. But when he proposed as the title "Our Country's Devotion to Culture," Paepcke, a living illustration of Barzun's point, questioned "whether 'devotion' is right" and how "a pragmatist" like Barzun could be so "very optimistic." Paepcke maintained that "our country has no particular devotion to culture" and offered alternatives such as "Our Country's Attitude to Culture" or "Approach to Culture."[57] Not to be swayed in principle but "ever willing to oblige" in practice, and with a friendly dismissal of Paepcke's alternatives—"I do *not* like 'attitude' and I loathe 'approach' (I like to get near things and not always be approaching them)"—Barzun agreed to replace "devotion" with "concern." Weaker words would not do, he said, because he intended to address "the concern that many people now feel for culture—yourself a shining example of same. That is the ground of fact that led me to speak of devotion: it wasn't optimism or hopefulness, but a very real cult [that] has developed in this country in the last thirty years."[58]

Paepcke the pessimist was not to be persuaded. He gave in on the decisive word but not on the idea behind it, insisting that most of the businessmen and "average citizens" he knew "have no 'concern' whatsoever for culture"[59]—as evidenced by the paltry audiences for chamber music at Aspen compared to those for popular entertainment. Barzun hit back quickly and at a vulnerable spot, one often exposed in arguments over universal education. That spot was "an assumption," Barzun said, "which you make and I don't, namely: that everybody ought to be interested in culture."[60] Paepcke could hardly have denied the charge. He had dedicated much of his adult life to disseminating culture in hopes of redeeming a vulgar technological and philistine civilization. As a cultural pessimist he had become exactly what Barzun proposed to talk about: an American devoted to culture.

Barzun likely had Paepcke in mind when he opened his lecture: "Whatever department of life one thinks of today, one must admit that the *idea* of culture is in the ascendant." On all sides one could see art and learning organized, distributed, promoted, patronized, esteemed. But Barzun wondered what justification can be given for urging culture upon people when, by its nature, culture must deprive them of some pleasures and exact from them some pains. Culture or, rather, cultivation of the arts, Barzun observed, neither notably strengthens a people nor makes them wiser or better, and can even dull sensibilities if pushed to excess. Nevertheless, America's concern for culture signaled for him "our coming of age." It "betokens self-confidence," and "it proves—if any proof were needed—that we are not money maniacs, and that our powers of design and organization are transferable to other things than consumer goods. We have even made a happy blend of industrial production and artistic form, so that more and more of the things we handle every day have art mixed with them—surely a sign of general culture."[61]

Barzun's cautions against the excesses of culture might not have won Paepcke's assent; but the honor Barzun paid to the marriage of art and industry must have brought Paepcke a flush of pride. For here Paepcke's own style of commerce was credited not only with improving the quality of commerce but elevating the "general culture."

Barzun's lecture on culture in American life, delivered in 1953, like his address on practicality two years earlier, and like so many other Aspen discourses of those years, expressed more confidence in America's new-found status than doubts about the future. But by the time Barzun spoke in Aspen again in 1959, his tone was different, more critical, less sanguine—a contrast reflected also in his two books of those years, *God's Country and Mine* (1954) and *The House of Intellect* (1959). And it wasn't just Barzun who had changed. Something had happened to American intellectual culture. Patriotic pride was yielding to criticism, confidence to doubt.

The changing mood was boldly voiced by Adlai Stevenson in an Aspen lecture not long after his return from a trip to the Soviet Union in 1958. Remarking the emergence in the Soviet Union of an able and aggressive "managerial class" composed (like its counterpart in the United States) of "career administrators, career engineers and scientists and industrial executives" dedicated to the advancement of Soviet interests, he denounced the flaccidity of American will and energy in advancing the cause of freedom. "In our fat, dumb, happy fashion," he said (repeating and embellishing some of his earlier reports of the Russian journey), "we assume that we can't lose, that if we persevere, if we damn the communists every morning and noon and night right will surely prevail in the end." But, he asserted, "we are not taking the measures necessary" to prevail. As Stevenson described those measures, they would amount to shaking off the cultural mood that was coming to typify the fifties in the eyes of many social critics: comfortable consensus and complacent acceptance of America's affluence and dominant position in the world. "I believe we have had enough of adjustment, of conformity, of easy option, and of the lowest common denominator in our social system," Stevenson went on. Americans must learn that they have misunderstood the "true nature of happiness and of the conditions of its pursuit" and that this misunderstanding "is simply an aspect of something else—our misunderstanding of the real nature of freedom." For Stevenson (no less than for Mortimer Alder), true freedom consisted not in willfulness or pleasure but in self-discipline and the pursuit of self-perfection. "We shall not have a free society," Stevenson concluded, "unless we have free men."[62]

This solemn mood descended upon Aspen with shadows that fell across American cultural life between the early and late fifties. One shadow was cast by social critics, like Lionel Trilling, John Kenneth Galbraith, William H. Whyte, Jr., and Herbert Marcuse, who discerned evil effects of America's burgeoning affluence and political preeminence. An even darker shadow than this was cast on an October day in 1957, when the Soviet Union sent the world's first man-made satellite into orbit, putting a sudden end to the implicit confidence of Americans in their postwar global technological and military supremacy. The Soviets had already achieved nuclear parity with the United States three years before with their detonation of a hydrogen bomb. But Sputnik I, followed a month later by the much larger Sputnik II, represented a triumph of concerted national energies extending from the highest government officials and the new "managerial class" on down to the elementary schools. "The launching," complained Senator Henry M. Jackson, expressing a common emotion, was "a devastating blow to the prestige of the United States as the leader in the scientific and technical world."[63]

The blow struck, doubts about American culture became the order of the day. John Kenneth Galbraith had the good fortune of having his *Affluent Society* ready for publication. He had not originally expected a large public for the book, but Sputnik turned the trick. "No action was ever so admirably timed," he joked. "I knew my book was home." For "Sputnik meant we were in for one of those orgies of anguished soul-searching" prompted by the truth that "a vastly less productive society" than ours "had brought off a breathtaking and also, who could tell, very alarming achievement."[64]

Much of the soul-searching centered on education. Not that American education had gone uncriticized before. In 1950, *Life* magazine had brought out an issue devoted to the theme: "U.S. Schools: They Face a Crisis."[65] And in 1953 several books had appeared assailing the abuses and misdirection of the educational system, among them Robert Hutchins's *The Conflict in Education*, Albert Lynd's *Quackery in Public Schools*, and Arthur Bestor's *Educational Wastelands*. (Walter Paepcke, the same year, had published an article in *Saturday Review* pressing the case for corporate giving to education.) These critics had offered mainly traditional complaints about insufficient support for the schools, the low salaries of teachers, the perils of lax "progressive" methods, and the absence of truly demanding academic goals. Hutchins had, of course, belabored such deficiencies for years.

Sputnik threw the scrutiny of American education into high gear and fired it with a sense of urgency. "The real challenge we face," Senator J. William Fulbright cried, "involves the very roots of our society. It involves our educational system, the source of our knowledge and cultural values."[66] *Life* magazine took up the challenge in a series of lengthy articles headed "Crisis in Education." "What has long been an ignored national problem," the editors wrote, "Sputnik has made a recognized crisis." And they went on to draw uncomplimentary comparisons between American and Russian educational practices, decrying American schools for their preoccupation with "adjustment," for discouraging gifted students, and for their appallingly low standards of intellectual achievement.[67] Admiral Hyman G. Rickover, scientist and sage, called in his *Education and Freedom* for "nothing short of a complete reorganization of American education, preceded by a revolutionary reversal of educational aims."[68]

Within a year of Sputnik, Congress responded to the wave of criticism by enacting the National Defense Education Act providing $900 million in scholarships and loans for students of the sciences and foreign languages— later expanded to cover other subjects. This was a token response, perhaps, but it registered the new-born fears of national weakness and the dawning certainty that this weakness could be remedied only by strengthening the intellectual culture, which meant fostering the educated class responsible for administering a technocratic society.

It is not surprising that the post-Sputnik tide of national soul-searching reached Aspen, for the institute existed to rectify the wrongs of American culture. The Aspen air did not, of course, fill completely with the crisis of the hour. But the solemn criticism of American culture in post-Sputnik days got a wide hearing. Beside William Gomberg's critical words on the growing complacency of labor and Adlai Stevenson's on the enervation of the American will, Yale historian John Blum attributed the decline in America's image to a long-standing tolerance of materialistic interests, self-righteousness, and social injustice. To redeem itself, Blum said, America would have to revive the all-but-forgotten ideas of frugality, nationalism, economic strength, and true democracy. Norman Corwin, the radio and screen writer, picked up where Blum left off with a diatribe against the mediocrity of radio and television and against the insidious power of advertising to mold a self-satisfied, conformist public. (Presumably unknown to Corwin, not long before his appearance, Walter Paepcke had been named Advertising Man of the Year by *Industrial Marketing*.)

The institute further fell in with the national mood by staging a forum in 1959 on "the problem of America's image of itself." The panel broke no new ground, but its title alone signaled the national uncertainty and the mounting occupation with public image as the measure of reality. One of the panelists, Barry Bingham, editor of the Louisville *Courier-Journal*, blamed America's poor image on the image-making industry itself—the mass media, especially films—which represent the "seamy" and unappealing or melodramatic sides of American life rather than the healthy actuality. But another panelist, Jacques Barzun, criticized the very assumption that efforts should be made to improve America's image abroad—he pointed to a proposal then in the news for a "white fleet" to carry American food, medicine, and good will across the world. These efforts betray, he said, nothing so much as America's "desire to be loved," and, although well-intentioned, they could only be received elsewhere as arrogant and paternalistic. The desire to be loved is itself "a very American thing," he concluded, as much a part of our self-image as of our image in others' eyes. But it should be held in check.[69]

Barzun came close here to unmasking not only America's self-image but the bewitching powers of *image* itself, then extending its magical sway over American life. The consumer economy, advertising, publicity, and the mass media had made of *image* both the secret and the measure of success in commerce, culture, and politics—as Paepcke had discovered through the successful promotion of corporate image at the Container Corporation. As Daniel J. Boorstin remarked in *The Image, or What Happened to the American Dream*, a book completed as the fifties ended, "We are haunted, not by reality, but by those images we have put in place of reality."[70]

It was in part to help jostle America out of its illusions, false worries, and futile hopes that Jacques Barzun returned to the stage a few days after the panel to speak on the contemporary degradation of language and intellect. Taking a page from a book he published the same year, *The House of Intellect*, he indicted those "at the top," the educators and intellectuals themselves, for damaging the authority of intellect in America by spreading noxious habits in language. Vagueness, jargon, misuse, and pseudoscientific quantification are all practices that induce intellectual imprecision, laxity, and self-deception. How, he asked, can a culture hope to thrive when the very sinews of intellect are allowed to go flaccid through the abuse of language? A "loose language first makes analysis difficult, then absence of thought is hidden by technical discourse, as if the words were doing the analyzing," and finally cogent thought becomes all but impossible.[71] No wonder, as Barzun noted, America has faltered in scientific accomplishment and educational excellence: we can no longer distinguish the genuine requirements and fruits of thought from their imitators, the appearance or the image of intellect from the real article.

Barzun's chastening words, so different from those of his Aspen addresses early in the decade, put a sharp edge on the post-Sputnik criticism of American culture at Aspen. A subsequent lecture by Alvin Eurich, vice-president of the Fund for the Advancement of Education, under the title "American and Russian Education since Sputnik," added the finishing touches to the theme. While the Russians had grown ever more disciplined and vocational, Eurich said, American education had failed to keep abreast of American needs and foreign competition because Americans shamefully undervalued education and hopelessly understaffed their schools. Eurich saw little prospect for improvement; too much needed changing too soon.

With these somber reflections on American culture, the Aspen Institute came to the end of its first decade.

The mood of national self-doubt that surfaced in those last years not only marked a departure from the early fifties; it also pointed to the anguished idealism and cultural criticism of the sixties and beyond. John F. Kennedy made good use of this mood in paving his way to the White House in 1960 with America's tarnished image and promises of renewed national discipline and purpose. It was a symptom of both the character of the Aspen Institute and of its role as a gathering place for members of the new American elite that the Kennedy administration numbered among its members several Aspen alumni—so many in fact that journalists could say: "If you are not a graduate of Harvard, membership in the Aspen Institute will qualify you for a place on President Kennedy's 'New Frontier' team."[72] This was overstatement, but the New Frontiersmen who had passed through Aspen make an impressive list: Adlai Stevenson, ambassador to the United Nations; Byron R. White, assistant attorney general and later Supreme Court justice; Robert McNamara, secretary of defense; Paul H. Nitze, assistant secretary of defense; Charles E. Bohlen, ambassador to France; Llewellyn Thompson, ambassador to the Soviet Union; George C. McGhee, undersecretary of state; Sterling McMurrin, U.S. commissioner of education; Najeeb E. Halaby, chairman of the Federal Aviation Administration; and others.

The recruitment of Aspen alumni by the Kennedy administration and the visit to Aspen by scores of other notables demonstrate the importance of Aspen as a crossroads of the American establishment as early as 1960. And the intellectual life of the institute clearly mirrored the shifting American moods of the fifties. But could the Aspen Institute claim any other accomplishments at the end of its first decade? Did it achieve what its founders wanted? Did it actually breathe the ideals of humanism into those who passed through the doors, listened to the lectures, conversed in seminars, and pored over great ideas?

By the testimony of participants, the Aspen experience left ineffaceable marks and memories. "The intellectuals have made quite an impression on me," admitted a vice-president of National City Bank of New York. "Ten days ago, I would have complained that the discussions starting with principles failed to proceed to an application to contemporary problems." But "the best thing the Aspen Executives Program did for me was to re-emphasize the value of principle." A partner of the investment house of Kidder, Peabody, and Company had a similar response. "The very fact that 'Liberalism in Business' or 'Human Freedom' etc. seemed far removed from my business life, and even trite," he said, "is proof of how completely provincial I and thousands of my contemporaries have become. . . . After four or five Executive Sessions, my entire perspective on many points came into focus," and he added, "I can say without any equivocation whatsoever that the two weeks in Aspen this summer" were "the most stimulating that I have ever enjoyed."[73]

This closing compliment became the refrain of most testimonials. An Episcopal clergyman: "I have never had as exhilarating and interesting an experience as the Aspen Institute provided." An executive of the Studebaker Corporation: "For myself, it was one of the most stimulating experiences in my adult life."[74] John M. Harlan, justice of the Supreme Court: "[My wife and I] both consider the two weeks there quite one of the most pleasant and stimulating we have ever had."[75] Congressman Gerald R. Ford, the future president of the United States: "I can say without hesitation or qualification that this experience was one of the most rewarding in my lifetime. . . . It filled a void in the past and will give me greater understanding in the future. I have benefitted immeasurably."[76]

Dozens of tributes like these poured in throughout the decade. And Paepcke made the most of them by reprinting passages as advertising for prospective participants. But for all their effusions of pleasure and intellectual stimulation, few of those who sampled the Aspen experience saw fit to specify its lasting influence, possibly because that influence was more often transitory than permanent. One journalist, for instance, reported turning to the man sitting next to him at the close of a rousing lecture and asking: "What did that mean to you?" "Not a damned thing," the man replied, "but a get-together like this has a way of lifting us out of our usual selves."[77]

To be "lifted out of our usual selves" or, in the words of another participant, to be released from "the routine details of our jobs" was perhaps the most one could expect from a two-week stint of "philosophizing on the wherefores of life," as one executive put it.[78] But that was not nothing. And some participants took away with them more than the sweet memory of a fleeting philosophic flight. They bore at least a residue of intellectual curiosity. One labor union executive reported a year after his visit: "I got a good deal out of it and still carry a copy of those Federalist papers which I had never even heard about prior to Aspen."[79] Another told Alvin Eurich that before Aspen, "I used to think of business when I rode the bus to work, but now I think of ideas."[80] And the chairman of Standard Oil of California, Western Division, confessed that after exposure to the intellectual ferment, he could not "help but think in a little different vein than that practiced in the regular business routine."[81]

A few alumni were more deeply affected. The Aspen experience helped convince William Gomberg to put his union career behind him and take up professorial robes—first at Washington University and then at the Wharton School of Economics at the University of Pennsylvania. Gaylord Freeman, vice-president of the First National Bank of Chicago, said Aspen had so awakened him to issues of principle that he made the institute a part of his career and undertook to guide the First National Bank on a course of cultural and moral leadership, becoming himself a spokesman for the moral responsibilities of corporations. (Freeman later expanded upon this calling by installing at the institute an annual series of seminars on the corporation and society.) A colleague of Gomberg and Freeman at Aspen from 1954 onward, Robert O. Anderson, later chairman of Atlantic Richfield Oil Company, was so moved by the executive seminars' innovative attention to the social responsibilities of corporations that he willingly succeeded Paepcke as president and, after Paepcke's death in 1960, built up the institute largely out of his own resources into a globe-encircling agency publicly dedicated to the discussion and intellectual resolution of major issues of the day.

The encounters with thoughtful executives also altered the perceptions of intellectuals. Norman Cousins, for one, had his very conception of the businessman overturned. Expecting a "body of stumblers" mindful only of economics and "the bottom line," he had discovered instead a group of educated and intellectually alert men who marked for him, as for history, an end to the "Babbitt period of American culture" and thus the momentous "shift to brain power from money power" in the leadership of American society near the mid-century.[82]

The many affirmations of the Aspen experience, be they testimonials to temporary elation, aroused curiosity, or a change in the perception or even the conduct of life, raise a question invariably answered by Aspen partisans with a resounding *no*: Was there an "Aspen line"? There was not, they say, because the very nature of the institute prevented it. As Gaylord Freeman said publicly: "There was no Aspen school of thought, no 'party line,' no prepared conclusions to be accepted and carried home." There was nothing more than "a carefully selected series of readings, a trio of brilliant moderators, a panel of challenging guests and an interested group of 'students' brought together in an atmosphere conducive to thought."[83]

True, the institute had no hard doctrine to force upon its participants and audiences. And the participants were themselves diverse enough to represent a variety of opinions rather than uniformity—just as the organizers had desired. But despite this diversity—and partly because of it—the institute was not without its "line," its hints of ideology, its preferred perception of the world.

The Aspen Institute was, after all, more than a place to meet for idle conversation and a romp in the hills. From the beginning, it had stood for some very definite judgments of modern and particularly of American culture. Though they grew less idealistic and more pragmatic, these judgments consistently revolved around the idea of humanism.

This humanism was no systematic doctrine, but, in both the Hutchins-Adler and Ortegan versions, it stressed the stringent application of reason to questions of principle and value—by contrast to the scientific dismissal of those questions as irresolvable. Thus "humanistic studies" meant an analytical way of thinking sharpened by repudiation of the moral relativism associated with empirical science. This way of thinking is what the New York banker had in mind when he said that the Aspen Executives' Program had reemphasized for him the value of principles.

But the Aspen idea had ideological implications reaching well beyond this humanistic creed. These implications derived from both the lectures and the executive seminars. In the first place, despite its origins in the criticism of modern culture, the Aspen Institute did not beckon America's leaders into the mountains for the purpose of finding fault with American traditions and institutions. Quite the contrary, the institute aimed to stiffen moral and intellectual energies in defense of those traditions and institutions. And the participants got the message. "Aspen represents . . . an outstandingly worthwhile project for the betterment of America," wrote the chairman of Montgomery Ward: "Men who experience . . . this program cannot help but be both better businessmen and better citizens." An executive of General Electric agreed: "I am sure we will all return to work with more understanding and improved zeal for appropriate and significant contributions which American businessmen can make to their country."[84]

No one linked the institute with the defense of the American way more emphatically than Walter Reuther. "It is a frightening fact," he wrote to Paepcke in July 1957, "that many of the most important people of America" take "no time to think about ideas and values which relate fundamentally to the whole future of freedom and the values which we cherish." For this reason, he went on, "the Aspen Institute is the beginning of an idea that I think needs the fullest possible development."[85] A few months later, Reuther had cause to strengthen his affirmation. "With the launching of the Soviet earth satellite," he wrote to Paepcke, "there is even greater urgency" to keep the institute going. For Sputnik was "a dramatic warning signal for the free world of the kind of competition we face in the struggle for survival." And that survival, as well as "our capacity to provide moral leadership in the free world in the struggle against communist tyranny," he concluded, "depend upon the priority that we are prepared to give our educational effort."[86] Reuther thus saw the Aspen Institute as a beacon of educational and moral guidance in a nation he said had become more concerned with its plumbing than its schools.

No wonder the deputy director of the CIA hailed the institute for exposing people to "the current philosophy . . . of American business leaders,"[87] and that Justice Hugo L. Black said he wished there were a hundred Aspens where the principles of democracy could be discussed. For despite the critical tone that surfaced in the late fifties, the institute consistently stood for a natural affinity between humanism and the democratic liberties and economic individualism of the American tradition. The "leaders" of American society who constituted the institute's clientele could hardly have interpreted humanism differently during these Cold War years.

The ideological line running through the Aspen Institute left still sharper traces than this veiled nationalism. For the institute came to embody a specific set of beliefs about how best to defend the American way. These beliefs held that the keenest threat to America's strength lay in misunderstandings and disunity among the country's "leading groups"; hence, if members of those groups could be brought together to discuss the American tradition, dangerous misunderstandings would dissolve into a healthy consensus.

This was not a bad idea, at least assuming the grounds for such a consensus existed. And the sponsors of the Aspen Institute were not alone in pressing that assumption. Most of the social thinkers of the early fifties did so, too. Echoing the critics who proclaimed America's cultural coming of age, historians, sociologists, and psychologists alike discovered a community of interests or shared values or common strategies of adjustment beneath all surface disharmonies. David M. Potter, Edmund S. Morgan, and Richard Hofstadter, for example, rewrote American history to bring to light common political and economic interests long obscured by more visible conflicts of classes, regions, and ideologies. "An unsuspected degree of uniformity and agreement appeared in the welter of America's historical experience," remarked a historian of the historians; "instead of a polarized culture . . . young scholars glimpsed an essentially homogeneous culture full of small impermanent variations."[88]

Social theorists said the same kind of thing not only about American society but about society itself—and several published influential, exemplary works in the same year. David Riesman cleverly charted the growth of conformity as a social fact and fashion in *The Lonely Crowd* (1950); and others, like the young Erving Goffman and the eminent Talcott Parsons, went farther to explain how *all* social life entails elemental agreement. Goffman's seminal study *The Presentation of Self in Everyday Life* (1950) described how society functions as a network of reciprocally reinforcing expectations and performances amounting to a "celebration" of unity. Parsons devoted abundant

writings, most comprehensive among them *The Social System* (1950), to elaborating in theory how society depends for its existence on the common values
that mitigate conflict and maintain a benign equilibrium among all members
of society.

Psychological theorists produced their variation on the same theme under
the label of "ego psychology." Following Anna Freud, ego psychologists like
Heinz Hartmann and, most prominently, Erik Erikson—whose book *Childhood
and Society* (also published in 1950) systematized and popularized the theory—
turned from the irreconcilable conflicts between the psyche and society emphasized by Freud to dwell on the patterns of adaptation employed by the
ego. Not for them—and especially for such men of good cheer as A. H.
Maslow and Carl Rogers—the constitutionally troubled, ill-adjusted personality. Happiness and self-fulfillment were available to all through the resolution
of Erikson's famed "identity crises" and reasoned adjustment to the world.

The list could go on, each item bearing the same message: conflict in
society is a marginal fact signifying superficial differences over means, not elemental differences over ends, incidental battles of ideas, not inevitable wars of
interests. Such was the ideology of consensus that stands as a hallmark of the
fifties. And the Aspen Institute exemplified this ideology with earnest hopes
and innocent pride. No elemental and intractable conflicts of interest exist
among the "leading groups" of American society, so the Aspen assumption
ran; there is only misunderstanding of what the common interests are.

The consensus theory was, to be sure, a little naive; and it received
considerable criticism from social thinkers and would-be revolutionaries in
the 1960s. But it was more right than wrong, particularly as represented by
the clientele of Aspen Institute. For the differences of interest among America's
"leading groups" were diminishing with the ascendancy of a society marked
by mass markets, advanced technology, professional management, and inter-
dependent public and private institutions. This was a society witnessing, in
Daniel Bell's memorable phrase, penned as the decade ended, "the end of
ideology," that is, the end of passionate ideological differences over the organization of society, government, and the economy.[89] Such differences were
dissipating under the pressures of technical necessities and analytical knowledge. The leaders of American society (intellectuals, executives, politicians,
lawyers, bureaucrats), possessing similar abilities, education, and responsibilities and attuned to the rationality of their tasks, were likely to discover
many affinities with each other and to seek the benefits of fraternization. A
certain consensus among them was waiting to be formed, if not around their
common heritage, then around their similar professional experience. And
Aspen helped them form it.

After two weeks of fraternizing and philosophizing in Aspen, the institute's
participants usually returned to their professional lives with new confidence

that America's leading institutions and their personnel do indeed share attributes, responsibilities, interests, and values, and have less cause for conflict than previously thought. Numerous businessmen came away with a new appreciation of ideas, and many intellectuals, like Norman Cousins, Jacques Barzun, and Mortimer Adler, acquired a new respect for the intellectual sophistication of businessmen. (Adler picked up a few tough business practices from them, too, prompting Paepcke to dub him a "philosopher turned businessman.")[90] Representatives of labor and management also saw each other with new eyes. William Gomberg praised the informal philosophical meetings of labor and corporate executives for shaking prejudices on both sides. And one union man from Chicago was so awakened to the interdependence of business and labor that he later asked Paepcke to mediate a dispute between his striking union and Montgomery Ward. (Paepcke declined, pleading the impossibility of pleasing both the union, which would distrust him as a corporation head, and Montgomery Ward, which was one of his own customers.)

This last incident betrays another of Aspen's contributions to the culture of consensus: the institute proved a boon to "making contacts." Few alumni failed to remark this as one of the high rewards of their Aspen days. "I gained a lot," wrote one board chairman, "particularly through the acquaintances." Dozens of others sang the same refrain of gratitude for "the associations made" and the "many friendships which we are sure we will value in the years to come."[91] Many such associations lasted, too, bringing opportunities for employment, investment, and influence, quite apart from enlightenment.

In the end, therefore, probably more than Ortegan "elegance" or the humanism of the Chicago Bildungsideal, more even than the celebration of American liberty and individualism, the ideology of consensus proved to be the Aspen line. And it worked, lending unity to American culture and thereby in an unexpected way at least partially fulfilling that emblematic modern desire for cultural integration shared by Ortega, the Chicago humanists, and the Bauhäusler. For the institute participants embraced that line not because it reflected the unity of American society as a whole but because it mirrored the interests of the participants themselves and aided their emergence as part of the new American elite. National magazines (like *Newsweek*, in a story headlined "Plato, Aristotle, and the Businessman")[92] said as much by publicizing the institute as an innovative educator of the rising managerial class. The Kennedy administration confirmed the fact by endowing Aspen alumni with prominent posts. And this was barely the beginning. Long after the mid-century search for consensus had passed, and the mandarin class was well established, the institute was to be one of the chief instruments of this class, playing host to leaders of governments, corporations, and culture from around the world, and endeavoring to influence public policy on subjects from corporate responsibility and ecology to arms control and the arts. By then, Aspen's mid-century ideals of humanism would seem obsolete. And in many ways they would be. For the responsibilities and rewards of leadership had consumed them. But it could not be denied that Aspen had significantly furthered the cause so dear to Walter Paepcke: unifying the worlds of commerce and culture.

Paepcke did not live to see the ends to which the "cross-fertilization of ideas" among the Aspen visitors would lead. But even as the institute started moving along this path by attracting ever more executives and notables and opening its doors to conventions unrelated to its original aims, Paepcke began turning some of his energies away from the institute to other pursuits. This redirection began after the Music Festival declared its independence of him in 1954 when he embarked on development of the European branch of the Container Corporation. It took on institutional form in 1957 when he became chairman of the institute's board of trustees and turned the presidency over to Robert O. Anderson.

The transition came, Anderson recalled, at a time of discouragement for Paepcke. The economic recession of 1956–1957 had hurt him badly, and the institute, which had just opened its expensive Health Center to virtually no business, was costing him more and more. Paepcke needed someone like Anderson (at that time a moderately wealthy oilman and a friend since his first visits to Aspen and the purchase of a home there in 1953) to help manage and win new financial support for the institute if it were to survive. At the same time, Paepcke was finding satisfaction far from Aspen in the European expansion of the Container Corporation, an enterprise that provided the gambler's thrills he could not resist.

But Anderson accepted Paepcke's invitation only as a temporary measure. "I was called in just to hold the phone," he later said, until Paepcke could devote his energies once again to running the institute's affairs.[93] After all, Anderson thought, Paepcke had a long-standing involvement in virtually every aspect of Aspen, an involvement not likely to be abandoned, and one not to be matched or desired by any newcomer like himself. Anderson agreed to help the institute survive and grow, but he would not take on Paepcke's role as what many people named the Baron of Aspen.

With Paepcke's cooperation and the assistance of the institute's personable full-time manager, Robert Craig (who replaced Richard Leach in 1954 after Leach was fired), Anderson took over the routine responsibilities of organization, fund-raising, preparing additions to the facilities, including plans for an auditorium, as well as developing a new clientele of conventioneers. From that time on, Anderson recalled, "Walter's visits to Aspen became more infrequent," while the Container Corporation moved "rapidly ahead in its European operations and Walter and Pussy traveled extensively."[94]

Still, Paepcke was far from losing touch with Aspen. And in early 1959 he started working on an amibitious new scheme for enlarging the institute's place on the cultural map. This scheme (treated fully in Chapter 9) was to build an architectual village adjacent to the institute, consisting of a dozen houses designed by the world's leading architects. The idea had all the earmarks of Paepcke's promotional attachment to good design, his appreciation of good designers, and his determination to identify Aspen with first-class attractions. But no sooner had he begun exploring the idea than his life took a fateful turn: his health weakened.

Nagging bursitis unresponsive to medical care and a worried wife finally forced the stubborn Paepcke to have X-rays taken in the fall of 1959. The X-rays revealed something much worse than bursitis: lung and bone cancer. The doctors told Elizabeth Paepcke her husband had six months to live.

Elizabeth kept the grim news from her sixty-three-year-old husband, knowing his disdain for the medical profession and the hopelessness of his condition. Confidently ignorant, he carried on as usual. Visiting Aspen in December, full of ideas and equipped with some designs for his architectual village, he seemed very much himself and felt certain the ailment would pass. But in January he had to cancel engagements, pleading "a few aches and pains." And in February those near him could see the end approaching. Learning the worst, Robert Anderson traveled to Chicago. "Pussy met me at the door," he remembered, "and Walter called out a word of welcome from the bedroom. In two months he was a changed man. . . . He was unable to raise his head from his bed, but his [wife] propped him up so we could talk over a number of Aspen matters. He showed me his current letters and many favorable responses on his contemporary architecture program. . . . In parting we shook hands, he asked me to come again when possible. I replied, 'Take care of yourself, Walter. I'll keep an eye on things until you are up and about.' As I passed through the door we both knew that we would never see each other again."[95]

A few weeks later, on April 13, 1960, Walter Paepcke died. The groundbreaking for the architectural village had been set for the same month. Instead, that same ground opened to receive Paepcke's remains.

With Paepcke gone, the architectural village would never materialize, and under Anderson's guidance the Aspen Institute would move on to new purposes and achievements. But it was fitting that Paepcke's last amibition should have been to build a monument in Aspen to the movement that had first brought him prominence as an innovator in commerce: modern design. In Paepcke's mind, the Aspen idea of humanism had always included the arts, traditional and modern.

9

the aspen muses

and the twilight of modernism

Aspen became a haven of the new American elite not only by providing a place to fraternize and contemplate American culture and the responsibilities of leadership. It also beckoned with recreation and the pleasures of art.

Almost from the beginning of his Aspen adventures, Paepcke had hoped to draw people to the former Crystal City with good music. Aspen could well become a summer music capital, he thought, perhaps the American Salzburg. The triumph of the Goethe Festival, followed by creation of the Aspen Institute and the continuing deficits, strengthened this ambition. By playing host to name musicians, so Paepcke believed, the institute could fill its own coffers while enriching Aspen's cultural life and contributing to the "cross-fertilization of ideas."

So it was that Aspen opened its arms to the arts. Through Paepcke's encouragement and benefactions in the early fifties, musicians established there a permanent home for the Aspen Music Festival and Music School; photographers gathered for a unique conference on their fledgling art; industrial designers and graphic artists founded the annual International Design Conference; and only death kept Paepcke from building there a museum of modern architecture. These were the Aspen muses: music, photography, design. Each had its part in shaping Aspen's character and enabling Aspen to mirror currents in mid-century culture at large. Their stories, especially that of design, continue the history begun in Chapter 1, pointing to the cultural legacy of the alliance of modern art and commerce, and to the career of modernism beyond the mid-century.

The story of music in Aspen originated in Paepcke's life-long affection for classical music and his extensive knowledge of musical repertoire. When the Goethe Festival proved Aspen could be the stage for a first-rate music festival, Paepcke resolved to make such a festival part of the annual fare.

But the depressing scarcity of paying customers in the summer of 1950, combined with the high cost of stellar talent, forced Paepcke to rethink the music festival, just as he did the academic program. This rethinking led to the founding—largely through the efforts of Mack Harrell and Henri Temianka (a member of the Paganini String Quartet, which had performed in Aspen in 1950)—of the Aspen Music School.

By the time the school opened in June 1951, its first director, Grace Denton, former director of the Music Academy of the West at Santa Barbara, had resigned in protest of Paepcke's tight-fisted policy. But the promotional work of Temianka and others had paid off. From thirty-five states, 183 students came to enroll—a healthy increase over the 34 informally instructed the previous summer. However shaky its start, the Aspen Music School was on its way to being the preeminent summer institution of its kind in the country.

The list of superior artists who taught and performed at the school, many becoming identified with Aspen over the years, would eventually read like a Who's Who of mid-twentieth-century musical culture. The summer of 1951 alone brought not only the return of alumni like Harrell, Temianka, and Robert Mann, but the addition of such other artists destined to become Aspen regulars as violinist Albert Tipton, pianists Brooks Smith and Rudolf Firkusny, clarinetist Reginald Kell, composer Charles Jones, and, most illustrious of all, composer Darius Milhaud.

One of the many Europeans who had sought refuge in America during the Nazi years, Milhaud had joined the faculty of Mills College in California in 1940. There Grace Denton had met him, and it was she who first invited him to Aspen—although she had long since departed when he arrived. Milhaud had won early fame in France as one of the young avant-garde composers known as "Les Six," who were united mainly by a staunch rejection of the lush chromatism of Wagner, Debussy, and Richard Strauss in favor of the light musical eccentricities of Erik Satie, as well as by their own experiments with dry sonorities and jazz rhythms. Milhaud's own works bore the marks of his particular taste for polytonality, dissonance, and dramatic effects spiced with lyricism (as in the ballets *L'Homme et son desir* and *Le Boeuf sur le toit*, and in *Sodades do Brasil*). Milhaud also earned a lasting, if uncelebrated, place in the annals of modern music by creating, together with Erik Satie, one of the twentieth century's distinctive musical forms: *musique d'ameublement*, "furniture music." First performed in 1920 during an intermission of a concert featuring works by "Les Six" and a play by Max Jacob, furniture music was intended to filter through the air without quite catching the ear. "Talk, keep on talking," Satie had urged the bemused audience. "Whatever you do, don't listen." "Furniture music creates a vibration," he explained, "it has no other goal; it fills the same role as light and heat—as *comfort* in every form." And it should be played—everywhere: "Furniture music for law offices, banks, etc."[1]

By the time Milhaud arrived in Aspen in June 1951, such youthful musical experiments lay far behind—although he still paid whimsical respect to "furniture music" by telling companions as they exited elevators: "Wait. I want to hear how the music ends."[2] He had just completed his eighteenth string quartet—thereby surpassing Beethoven, a goal he had set himself forty years earlier—which was given its world première in Aspen that August in a performance by the Paganini Quartet. And for the next generation, Milhaud and his music were to be a constant part of Aspen, despite the arthritis that slowly crippled him. In later years, Milhaud immortalized his affections for Aspen by composing an "Aspen Suite" in five movements, one for each letter of the name. It was a *beau geste*. But some listeners at the première thought the *geste* better than the music; one was heard to say: "I'm glad as hell this place isn't Garmisch-Partenkirchen."[3]

Milhaud was the most eminent but not the only composer to have works premiered in the early years under the Aspen tent. Others came from the hands of Aspen regular Charles Jones, who had come to Aspen as Milhaud's assistant, and visitors like Virgil Thomson and Alexander Tcherepnin, whose one-act opera *The Farmer and the Fairy* Paepcke commissioned. Although none of these works had great musical distinction, they strengthened the camaraderie of the Aspen musicians and added spice to Aspen's musical life.

That life also benefited from the unexpected, as when jazz clarinetist Benny Goodman wandered into Aspen in search of good fishing. He hooked no fish but discovered his classical clarinet teacher, the world-renowned Reginald Kell, in residence. Struck by the idea of performing together, the two ascended the stage a couple of nights later, along with a young bassoonist, to play Mozart's *Divertimento* no. 4. The audience loved it and demanded more. Then, amid rounds of applause, Goodman was handed a bouquet of flowers—along with a string of trout. He gamely hung the trout from the bell of his clarinet and, smiling, took his remaining bows. Goodman later returned the favor with a donation to the institute, making him perhaps the only world-class performer to pay for the privilege of playing Aspen.

But while the Music School and Music Festival were building their reputations, they were also moving toward a permanent rupture with Paepcke and the institute.

By late summer 1954, tensions between Paepcke and Richard Leach, vice-president of the institute and manager of the overall summer program since 1952, had been smoldering for months. Leach, a former managing agent for many of the musicians, was chafing under the obligation to carry out and often anticipate Paepcke's wishes, particularly when those wishes seemed to conflict with those of his former clients. Paepcke suspected that Leach's divided loyalties were working to the detriment of the institute. There seemed to be only one solution: get rid of Leach. Paepcke justified the action in a lengthy letter listing Leach's failures—such as making misleading statements; underestimating costs; lavishing unnecessary attentions and money on the musicians; and altering contracts to allow musicians to perform elsewhere in Colorado while scheduled at Aspen.[4]

But Paepcke hadn't reckoned Leach's powerful support among the musicians, especially on the subject of Paepcke's influence over their affairs. They rallied to Leach's side. "Mr. Leach has been more than an administrator—he has been a friend," read a petition (stating what Paepcke feared) requesting Paepcke to allow Leach "to continue his important role in the Aspen Festival."[5] Several individual artists, including Reginald Kell and Mack Harrell, allied themselves with Leach, believing Paepcke wished for more control than he deserved.

Paepcke responded by taking his familiar stand: if the musicians didn't like the way he handled things, they could do without his financial backing. This had worked before with Aspenites, but it didn't work with the artists. Buoyed by their own confidence and Leach's encouragement, the musicians said they would go it alone. And what Leach now described as "a unique experiment having no precedent anywhere" began.[6]

The musicians still needed Paepcke's cooperation, however, since the institute owned the music tent and most of the public space in town. After a series of negotiations, Paepcke agreed to provide temporary use of the institute's facilities, and the musicians agreed not to compete with the institute's program and fund-raising. The musicians also won a pledge from Aspenites to raise half of the next summer's budget; and upon Leach's diplomatic departure, they established their own organization, the Music Associates of Aspen (MAA). Filing articles of incorporation in December 1954, they created a board of trustees and named Norman Singer, an administrator at the Juilliard School of Music, dean of the Music School.

As tempers cooled and as the MAA freed itself from dependence on Paepcke's largesse and influence, a good working relationship grew up between the musicians and their former patron. Paepcke even saw his personal relations with many of the musicians improve; and he continued donating funds to their cause, never ceasing to prize the contribution of music to Aspen's cultivation of the Whole Human Being—mind, soul, and body.

But things had changed. The Music Associates of Aspen belonged to Aspen, not to Paepcke or the institute—the citizens themselves raised enough money to fully finance the first independent festival (more than double what they had promised). Losing control of the music festival as he had—despite his public statements of amicable parting—shook Paepcke deeply. Aspen culture was not quite his any more. The effects on him were even physical: breathing became difficult and energy flagged. When dragged to a doctor by his wife, Paepcke was told that he should get away from Aspen and all worldly pressures for a while lest the nervous disorders produce serious ill effects.

Acting on the doctor's advice, Paepcke fled the pressures of Aspen and business in the fall of 1954 by taking his first trip to Europe in twenty-five years. Driving through the Bavarian Alps, he caught a whiff of pulp processing fumes in the air. He stopped the car and then detoured to a nearby plant. His eyes lit up. The idea of Europa Carton, a European branch of the Container Corporation, was born. Paepcke was healthy again.

While the Music Festival and Music School were putting down their own roots in Aspen—enabling them to become permanent and internationally renowned Aspen institutions, eventually acquiring a year-round concert hall at the Aspen Meadows in 1993 and a lasting music tent structure in 2000—certain visual arts were finding homes there too, temporary or permanent. One of these was photography. In the late summer of 1950, when Paepcke was casting about for ways of ensuring the Aspen Institute's future, he invited two of his artistic friends and colleagues, Ferenc Berko, a freelance photographer who had worked for CCA and had settled in Aspen in 1948, and Egbert Jacobson, to meet him at the Jerome pool. As the three men tossed ideas about, Paepcke turned to Berko with an ingenious proposal: why not gather the country's leading photographers for a conference in Aspen at the end of the next summer when the magnificent fall colors begin to show? It's never been done, Berko replied, but it's a nice prospect and could be great fun.[7] So Berko started laying the groundwork for a photography conference while Paepcke informed interested Aspen alumni that "a conference of color film and Kodachrome photography people is apt to take place from the 25th of September on for a week or two."[8]

Sluggish responses from the photographers first queried, who questioned the benefits of such a gathering, prompted Jacobson to step in. Long familiar with the stubborn independence of freelance artists, Jacobson proposed forming a steering committee of prominent photographers to lay out the objectives of the conference and generate professional interest in it. The committee met in New York in July and included such notables as Edward Steichen, the pioneer American photographer and exponent of artistic modernism and at that time head of the photography department at the Museum of Modern Art, and a historian of photography, Beaumont Newhall. "In general," Jacobson reported, "the group liked the idea of having a meeting on photography at Aspen." But, he went on, "after three hours of discussion, it was still not quite clear what the overall subject should be, how the program might be organized, and what eventual purpose it should serve."[9] So the committee decided the conference should be put off for another year to allow adequate preparations.

Paepcke balked. Since the conference had already been publicized in hopes of attracting amateurs and professionals from all over the country, they must, he said, go ahead with it, if only as a prelude to a full-scale meeting the next year. The risk of proceeding with only partial representation from the fledgling profession would have to be taken.

It paid off. More important photographers and amateurs assembled in Aspen that September than had gathered in one place to talk photography before. There was Ansel Adams, the lyric poet of natural imagery, and his disciple Minor White, the symbolist poet of that imagery; Dorothea Lange, master portraitist of human hardship and the rural life; Berenice Abbott, supreme perceiver of the urban landscape and its spirit; and others from journalism and freelance careers, like Laura Gilpin, Eliot Porter, Will Connell, Paul Berg, Fritz Henle, Wayne Miller, Fritz Kaeser, Robert C. Bishop, and Berko, as well as some two dozen other professionals and amateurs (see fig. 9.1). Beaumont Newhall was there, too, as was the consultant in iconography at the Library of Congress, Paul Vanderbilt. And they all took to the experience like a thirsty man to water. "We talked photography from breakfast until after midnight," Newhall reported. "Every meal in the Hotel Jerome was a symposium. No table was large enough to accommodate all who wanted to sit together. . . . Around the swimming pool, in the bar, on the street corner, little groups continued discussions. . . . As one of the conferees said, 'I had to expand or explode.'" What electrified everyone was the discovery, taken for granted thirty years later, that photography was no longer just a technically ingenious medium of communication; it had become a full-fledged art form. As "art" it demanded definition and comprehension. "We did not ask if photography is an art," Newhall said. "Instead we tried to determine what kind of art it is," and "we talked of the place of photography, and particularly the photographer, in the world today."

Fig. 9.1. Participants at Aspen photography conference, September 1951, in lobby of the Hotel Jerome. Left to right, standing: Herbert Bayer, Eliot Porter, Joella Bayer, Mrs. Paul Vanderbilt, Connie Steele, John Morris, Ferenc Berko, Laura Gilpin, Fritz Kaeser, Paul Vanderbilt. Left to right, seated: Millie Kaeser, Ansel Adams, Mrs. Eliot Porter, Dorothea Lange (front), Minor White, Walter Paepcke, Berenice Abbott, Frederick Sommer, Nancy and Beaumont Newhall. On floor: Will Connell, Wayne Miller. Photo by R. C. Bishop.

Here was an aesthetics of photography in the making—and the breath-less naiveté and philosophical excitement of those treading uncharted terri-tory. And although they represented diverse schools and styles within their art, the photographers agreed on one thing at least: photography must assert its artistic autonomy against the twin threats of being either an artless mir-ror of fact or a pretentious imitator of painting. Minor White, a careful student of visual patterns in nature whose work was tending toward ever greater abstractness, distinguished photography from painting by the "total-ity" of the photographic image, its "tether to reality, its immediacy, and its lack of the mark of the hand." Berenice Abbott, a resolute realist, warned against abstract photography as "the final fling of pictorialism." At its best, she said, photography lies closer to literature than to painting since it "does not record alone," but "probes and explores the subject" and "proclaims the dignity of man." Agreeing with Abbott, fellow realist Dorothea Lange dismissed the term "documentary," insisting that the photographer portrays reality only through an artful selection of images signifying time and change. Asked to demonstrate the point with a hypothetical assignment, she told the story of Aspen and the photo conference in pictures: the first picture, she said, would give an aerial view of the town and the autumn foliage to establish place and time of year; the second, a picture of battered jeeps near an old building to convey a sense of the postwar period; the third, a photograph of the beautiful brass clock in the lobby of the Hotel Jerome to indicate the charm of the place. She did not complete this "shooting script" but left all convinced, if they needed convincing, according to Newhall, "that the documentary photographer does not merely record."

Appealing to the photographers' practical instincts, Ansel Adams cautioned against overintellectualizing photography in both theory and practice lest the new art lose the "sympathy" that makes all art human; and he urged his colleagues to concentrate on establishing a profession for themselves equipped with publications, organizations, and standards of quality. Sounding a similar theme, several of the commercial photographers spoke of the demanding constraints they must work under: the requirements of editors and advertisers and, behind these, public taste. These complaints prompted Walter Paepcke to ask one of his favorite questions: why "the public could not be given what it should have rather than what it wants"; and they led Jacobson to sing one of his favorite tunes: artists must convert businessmen to the merits of good art and not just submit to the lead of commerce. Herbert Bayer (who was at that time preparing a unique and magnificent new geographical atlas for CCA) followed by reiterating his belief that the limitations of a commission often help rather than hinder creativity, favorably citing Le Corbusier's dictum that architecture is easier than painting because the client does so much of the thinking.

The photographers also found time to put some of their aesthetic ideas into practice. They wandered around snapping pictures of the natural beauties, the potpourri of Victorian architecture, and the plush Victorian atmosphere of the Hotel Jerome (much photographed by Berenice Abbott). And with them went crowds of amateurs hoping for clues to the art of photography—and sometimes getting them, as when Ansel Adams pronounced his credo to listeners in front of an old Aspen house: "Exposure is not the thing of first importance; it is the picture in your mind."[10]

"The picture in your mind," more than anything else, characterized the conception of photography formulated in Aspen. Photographers neither merely record nor invent. They arrange a pattern of images in the mind's eye, then capture it on film. Thirty years later, in the first full-scale appraisal of photography's influence on culture, the critic Susan Sontag assailed photography on exactly this count: that it renders reality through distorted images and thus trains the eye to equate those images with fact. Sontag could have been reproaching the Aspen photographers for discovering the secret of their art. For the chief accomplishment of the Aspen conference was just this, that despite a certain bias against abstract photography, the photographers demonstrated the automony of photography as art and, as Newhall concluded, proved that photography in America had come of age as a "medium . . . so powerful and so beautiful, so potentially informative and persuasive that it demands responsibility and commands dignity."[11]

The photographers departed Aspen dizzied from the intellectual rather than the geographic heights. And they wanted more: "The Aspen conference was simply terrific," Ansel Adams and Nancy Newhall wrote to Paepcke. "We keep meeting happily dazed participants all over the West. It was easily one of the most important events in contemporary photography. We are still in the state of superlatives."[12] Seven months later Adams was still awed: "The Aspen venture was about the best thing that ever happened to photography." And, like everyone else associated with the conference, Adams vowed "to do everything I possibly can to help" with next year's conference.[13]

But a second Aspen photography conference was not to be, despite an earnest and lively planning session held the next June under Steichen's direction at the Museum of Modem Art—"What we need," he declared at that time, is "to learn what photography is all about."[14] For when several photographers hesitated to attend without compensation, and when time to properly arrange and publicize the event fell short, Paepcke decided he had too many other struggling Aspen enterprises to warrant further investment in photography's search for its identity. He let the idea drop, and no one picked it up.

Although it produced no successor, the photography conference and the discussions it prompted helped put Aspen in the mainstream of American culture at the mid-century, while also exhibiting the rising stature and self-consciousness of that culture. The same claim can be made for another Aspen venture in the arts that soon took precedence over photography and left an enduring legacy in Aspen: the International Design Conference.

A conference of designers was a natural for Aspen, because it would exemplify and strengthen the alliance of art and commerce that Walter Paepcke's career, both in business and out, had thrived on. And like much in that career, the Design Conference owed a lot to Egbert Jacobson.

No sooner had the Aspen Institute come into being at the end of 1949 than Egbert Jacobson had suggested (about the same time that he proposed the Great Ideas advertising campaign) holding a meeting for designers in Aspen. But Paepcke had been at that time full of ambitions to reform Western culture through great books, great men, and great music, so he had let Jacobson's idea pass. Then, after paltry audiences that first summer forced a reappraisal of the institute's program and promotions, Jacobson repeated his proposal at the meeting with Paepcke and Berko by the Jerome pool, recommending that a design seminar be made a permanent part of the summer fare. "I am sure you will agree," he wrote to Paepcke, drawing on years of shared proselytizing for good design, "that questions of design are as vital to humanism as music, literature, and philosophy." Quoting Walter Gropius on how "design embraces the whole orbit of man-made, visible surroundings, from simple, everyday goods to the complex patterns of a whole town," he suggested that Gropius be appointed seminar director and that noted architects, graphic artists, painters, and museum directors be invited as guests and speakers. It would be a conference without precedence in this country, a modernist assembly demonstrating the importance of design "in the life of American communities."[15]

This time Paepcke snapped the notion up and set Jacobson to work organizing the first of what was to become the annual International Design Conference in Aspen, whose life goes on over fifty years later.

Paepcke had put the right man on the job; for Jacobson brought the conference into being almost single-handedly, hoping it would bring a "better understanding of the value of first-class design to industry and incidentally improve public taste." This meant that the conference would have to attract not only those active in the arts but businessmen "who already have demonstrated publicly their appreciation of good design" and who could thus entice "others who need influencing."[16]

At the beginning of 1951, Jacobson was hard at work drumming up support in New York. In February he held a planning session with some of his converts—including Frank Stanton, president of CBS; Philip Johnson, architect and director of the department of architecture and design at the Museum of Modern Art; Leo Lionni, art director of *Fortune* magazine; and the artist Ben Shawn. Agreeing first of all that "without the attendance of important businessmen there would be no point to the conference," the group decided the program should establish "once and for all the relation of design to business." It must examine "every aspect of design in business from the graphic arts through industrial design, furniture, interiors, and architecture"[17]—thereby furthering the integration of the consumer economy, if not culture itself as envisioned at the Bauhaus. And to insure the attendance of businessmen the title was slanted toward them: "Design—A Function of

Management." The most ambitious conference on industrial design ever held in this country was off the ground.

The time was ripe for it, too. The "second machine age"—characterized by electric power, synthetic materials, and consumer products rather than heavy industry—was making the designer indispensable to ever more manufacturers (although not all manufacturers recognized the fact). Industrial design had itself come of age as a profession in America only in the previous two decades through the work of designers like Teague, Loewy, Bel Geddes, Dreyfuss, and Moholy-Nagy—as the Museum of Modern Art confirmed in 1946 by holding a conference on "Industrial Design as a New Profession," which Paepcke and Moholy-Nagy had attended. And since World War II, industrial design had flowered anew, experiencing some of the same kind of international competition as had followed World War I: Britain created the Council of Industrial Design (1944) and France the Institut d'Esthétique Industrielle (1951) to advance good design in domestic industries; Scandinavian designers, like Alvar Aalto and Hans Wegner, fashioned a style of furniture that swept America in the fifties as "Danish modern"; and Italy surpassed all competitors aesthetically thanks to young talents like Gio Ponti and Enrico Peressutti, who designed sleek and ingenious forms in the new synthetic materials.

The Museum of Modern Art paid homage to the aesthetic, economic, and professional prestige of industrial design at mid-century by inaugurating in 1950 an annual "Good Design" exhibition devoted to exemplary contemporary products and graphics. This same year the Corning Glass Company was able to boast that fully half of its sales were in products that had not existed a decade earlier; and the following year the company would host a widely publicized conference of businessmen, scholars, public officials, and designers to explore the place of design in industry, and industry in society, under the heading "Living in Industrial Civilization."[18] The year 1951 also brought a twentieth-century version of the Great Exhibition of 1851 in Britain with a festival of industrial design that, according to a designer who later reported on the event in Aspen, achieved for the first time, at least in Britain, a completely "coordinated policy" in design encompassing everything from admission tickets to public buildings.[19]

But "good design" was not in itself responsible for the growth of the design profession. The public had been besieged for more than a generation by advertisers, packagers, and manufacturers bent on making design a commodity that consumers would pay for, and would pay for as often as the design changed. Partly because of this campaign, "good taste" was becoming an emblem of status among Americans who increasingly valued social acceptance and were attuned to the subtle signs of social prestige—as remarked by observers like David Riesman in The Lonely Crowd (1950), Russell Lynes in his *Harper's* articles published as *The Tastemakers* (1954), and Jacques Barzun in his Aspen lecture "America's Concern with Culture." (The popular novelist Cameron Hawley even saw a compelling subject for fiction in the saga of a furniture company and its chief designer, which he told in *Executive Suite,* 1952.) Thus at the mid-century a popular cult of taste, art, and culture was rising and spreading modernist design, in authentic and bastardized versions, across the landscape of American life.

Coming when it did, the Design Conference had a ready-made and eager clientele. Some 250 designers and their spouses assembled in the amphitheater on June 28 to hear the first Aspen words on "design as a function of management" from the godfather of the conference, Walter Paepcke. Reciting his regrets about the modern division of art, craft, and commerce, and about the cultural backwardness of American business, Paepcke went on to urge businessmen not only to employ an occasional designer but to "believe in the philosophy of design." Good design pays off only when it "extends through the whole organization"—as it did at the Container Corporation and at Olivetti, which had an exhibit at the conference—from the stationery and office furniture to the marketable goods. To stop short of this is to present an inconsistent design image and risk losing potential customers. Executives must therefore learn to grant their designer the same importance as the production manager. It was to foster such an alliance between designers and management, Paepcke concluded, that the Design Conference was being held. And he invited the conferees to return to Aspen for more meetings the next year.[20]

Paepcke's apologia introduced four days of pronouncements on the theory and practice of industrial design that were a harbinger of the conference's future. Stanley Marcus, head of the department store Neiman-Marcus, followed Paepcke to the podium to describe his own use of good design as a merchandizing policy aimed at selling first "the mood of the store, then the merchandise." With a nod to cultural conscience, he claimed this policy had not only helped profits but had made Neiman-Marcus as important in elevating public taste as any museum—an understandable overstatement, in light of the commercial origins and purpose of modern design. Playing on the same theme, William Connally of Johnson's Wax noted the benefits to his company in publicity and corporate image of its striking modern headquarters building designed by Frank Lloyd Wright (which also marked a turning point in Wright's reputation). Charles Zadok of Gimbel's department store in Milwaukee stated flatly that "good design" had "resulted in more sales" in his store of "articles from hardware to high fashion." Flushed with enthusiasm and whistling a familiar mid-century tune, Zadok went on to recommend holding an annual "World Series" among designers to help make America "as strong culturally as it is militarily" by achieving leadership of "the world in design." Not to let business take all the credit for encouraging good design, Edgar Kaufmann, Jr., of the Museum of Modern Art, reviewed the accomplishments of the museum over the previous seventeen years in advancing modern design through exhibitions, publications, and advice to manufacturers and retailers.

But for all the compliments to design by businessmen and publicists, many designers seemed to think that full cooperation between business and their profession was still a long way off. George Nelson, noted furniture designer and architect, for one, chastised businessmen and designers for talking different languages, the one "military," the other "moral," and failing to "realize they are all in the same boat" and must pull together. Herbert Bayer took the same tack, albeit in softer words, repeating his belief that "the artist needs business, and business needs useful art," and that together the two partners could "greatly enrich the visual experience of society." Charles T. Coiner, pioneering art director and then vice-president of the advertising firm of N. W. Ayer & Sons, complained that advertising design had made no advances in twenty years and that many advertisers are irresponsible, violating good taste and truth by making "fantastic claims" for their products (the same complaint that had governed his advice to the Container Corporation in the 1930s and after). And Charles Eames, designer of the famous chair that bears his name, underscored the importance of practical "objectives" in all types of design—such as those for a chair: maximum service, minimum space, low upkeep, and low cost. The architect Louis I. Kahn also cautioned against the doctrinaire modernist hostility to tradition and advised uniting what is best in the "architecture of the past" with the advantages of modern engineering. Don Wallance, an industrial designer and consultant, agreed, reminding his listeners that the practical must dominate the ideal.[21]

These and other addresses and exchanges did not produce agreement over the relation of managers and designers. But they did lay out anew some common ground and set the Design Conference on its course as a forum for the theory, practice, and criticism of modern design and its nascent profession.

A few of the businessmen were even converted to the *philosophy* of good design. An executive of du Pont de Nemours wrote to Paepcke soon after the conference for further word on "how 'Design as a Function of Management' has been successfully employed by your company."[22] The president of a Denver cosmetics company contracted Bayer to redesign "every single thing we have that is printed, from the forms we use routinely inter-office, up to and including our packages and our national advertising."[23] The good will and intellectual pleasures of the conference infected even businessmen and designers who had not attended, and a group of them in Chicago prevailed upon Paepcke and Jacobson to present a review of the proceedings at the Art Institute that fall. By then, of course, the Aspen conferees had already decided the work begun should not be allowed to lapse. Before leaving Aspen they had agreed to return to Aspen for another round the next year. Good design, a driving force of the consumer economy as well as of the Container Corporation's corporate image campaign, had found a place in the rarefied atmosphere of Aspen alongside great ideas, great music, and the ideology of consensus.

The Design Conference was not without its critics. Some participants thought too many of the speakers were artistic types who "talked themselves starry-eyed" and seemed "completely incapable of intercourse with management."[24] The president of the Society of Industrial Designers advised Paepcke that the only hope of enabling businessmen and designers to work together lay in giving precedence to stolid practitioners rather than those inclined toward the "aesthetic and theoretical."[25] Paepcke agreed, at least in part, informing Bayer that the businessmen "*must* be our target."[26]

But this concession to the practical did not throw the Design Conference into the arms of pragmatists. After all, the conference had come into existence (like the Aspen Institute) not to boost the profits of business but ostensibly to awaken businessmen to their cultural responsibilities and bring wholeness—aesthetic and economic—to American culture. In achieving this, as Paepcke pointed out at the beginning of the next year's session, it would also help to satisfy that other pressing mid-century American need: to gain a primacy for America in culture equal to that held in military might—and some participants believed the conference was doing just that. One designer said the conference signified progress toward a "cultural level never before attainable. Comes the American Renaissance!"[27] No one envisioned the contributions of the conference more grandiloquently than R. Buckminster Fuller, a participant for the first time in 1952: "So vividly persistent in my awareness are . . . the Aspen potentials, thoughts, questions, challenges that I realize I have been admitted to a newly, but certainly and logically forming regenerative source of historical verities, inspirations, and transcendental initiatives"[28] (see fig. 9.2).

Paepcke and the conference planners tried to resolve the tensions between the imperatives of practicality and the ideals of cultural reform in setting up future sessions. They did not wholly succeed, but the Design Conference went on its way all the same, forming its own character and adding distinctive and very lively colors to Aspen's cultural landscape. And it became so quickly established as a forum for designers and those interested in design—if not for the businessmen Paepcke had hoped to win over—that four years after it began the conference set down permanent institutional

Fig. 9.2. Richard Neutra (left), R. Buckminster Fuller, and Herbert Bayer (right) on the porch of Bayer's house during the Aspen Design Conference in the mid-1950s. A construction by Bayer stands in the foreground. Photo by Ferenc Berko.

roots in Aspen. Virtually self-sufficient (no longer dependent, as at the beginning, on the Container Corporation), enjoying a regular and growing clientele, the Design Conference was incorporated, with Paepcke's blessing, on October 22, 1954, as the International Design Conference in Aspen (IDCA). Thereafter, the history of the conference through the fifties was, at its most significant and despite an array of topics ranging from city planning to film, a history of ideas on the character, uses, abuses, and future of design and the designer in modern life.

It is not surprising, given the cultural history of industrial design from Sir Robert Peel and William Morris down through the Bauhaus and its kindred organizations, that the IDCA heard paeans aplenty to design as the salvation of modern industry and modern civilization. Will Burtin, in opening the first independent conference in 1955, called for designers, artists of all kinds, as well as scientists, intellectuals, and businessmen to join together "to control mechanization, to control power, to control our environment" by "understanding the historic challenge that is ours" and promoting "a fuller appreciation of the arts in our lives."[29] Taking up the challenge, Lancelot Law Whyte, scientist and philosopher, spoke twice during the fifties on design as the ordering principle in nature and imagination; the mathematician and humanist Jacob Bronowski pronounced design the dynamic unity in nature that admits change and provides human beings the freedom to better their world. And the computer scientist and author Bruce MacKenzie hailed the dawn of a new type of designer who could serve as a "bridge" between art and science "whether he designs film or textbooks, computers or can openers, buildings or boats."[30] Two former members of the New Bauhaus faculty in Chicago, Hin Bredendieck and Gyorgy Kepes, restated the Bauhaus ideal of cultural integration through the unity of intellect and intuition, art and science, human beings and their environment, all to be made possible by an inclusive conception of design or, in Kepes's words (which recall Moholy-Nagy) a "new vision" of the "'whole'. . . dynamic continuity" of existence.[31] Openly invoking Moholy's "new vision," the British designer William M. de Majo extolled the Festival of Britain exhibition of 1951 for achieving, if only fleetingly, "the ideal toward which industrial design . . . should move": that is, a completely coordinated policy of good design affecting everything, ash cans and doorknobs no less than the urban landscape.[32] Architects and city planners like E. A. Gutkind and Max Frisch (later famous as a novelist) sounded the same exalted notes, criticizing the disorder and disintegration of modern society and advocating comprehensive design of the urban environment to create, in Frisch's words, a "New City" for "social and sovereign democracy,"[33] or, as Gutkind put it, "a new pattern of life."[34]

But alongside this high and well-trod road of idealism, which promised to lead to the familiar modern utopia of an architectonic civilization, there ran a path of pragmatic caution, doubt, and criticism. For throughout the fifties, and far more then than later, no topic more frequently occupied the Aspen designers than that raised in the first year: what is the relation *in fact* of design to business and to the culture business serves? Understandably, most designers believed their importance to business was only just gaining notice, and that too slowly. Such was the criticism of William de Majo when he lamented that the achievements in design of the 1951 Festival of Britain were "not much more than a brilliant meteor in a rather dull sky" because British industry was dragging its heels.[35] Gordon Lippincott, designer and author, followed, noting that although "each year *design* is playing a more powerful role in influencing buyer decisions," executives still fail to give designers the central place in management they must have to be able to affect policy. Instead of "management-oriented designs," he said, we should have "design-oriented management."[36]

But behind such plainspoken and traditional cries of designers for more recognition, there could be heard another complaint, which came forward only in the second half of the decade. This grievance was less specific and yet more strident than the first because it arose from an emerging ambiguity in the designer's economic and cultural identity. And the revelation and exploration of this ambiguity by both designers and their critics constituted the major contribution of the Aspen conferences to the intellectual history of modern design.

Hints of this ambiguity appeared in remarks (by British designer Lancelot Hogben, CBS advertising art director William Golden, and architects Ernesto N. Rogers and Paul Rudolph) criticizing modern designers and architects for complaining and theorizing too much, for being slaves to doctrinaire "functionalism," and for disregarding the practical imperatives of their craft. But it was met head-on by those who detected an insidious decline of integrity in the design profession itself resulting from the designer's enslavement to commercialism. British designer Abram Games, noting the profound influence of graphic design on public attitudes (which he had seen during the war from his position as War Office poster designer), cautioned designers against letting their power be put to questionable ends. They must be most wary of serving political authority—like the designers of Nazi Germany—but neither should they submit to the wiles of "motivational research," which had come forward since the war as the supreme technique for selling through psychological manipulation. (A spokesman for motivational research at the same conference, William Capitman, commended the technique on exactly the same grounds: design only sells products when it speaks to human desires.) For if the designer does submit, "he will in fact have become a peddlar in commodities—much less, the peddlar's dog, led by a fancy lead."[37]

Several speakers saw the chief threat to the integrity of modern design in the very success of the designer's commercial credo: "eye-value" sells products. Richard S. Latham, former director of design for Raymond Loewy Associates and then head of his own firm, attacked the cult of "good taste" that had grown up alongside the artificiality of industrial production and the modernist dogma of "newness." Implying a debt to Marx's notion of "the fetishism of commodities," Latham said that manufactured objects, mysterious of origin and unnecessary in purpose, had come to possess a value much greater than practical worth. They have psychological power as symbols of status and character. For they betray our "taste," which is in truth a measure of *our* worth as judges of quality. Perhaps, Latham added, this would not be so bad a thing if "good taste" and good design went together. But taste is a slave to fashion, and fashion seeks novelty. Hence designers as the purveyors rather than the arbiter's of taste wind up catering to the desire for novelty rather than producing good design. Eventually they too lose the ability to see the difference. And when this is lost, nothing remains but vulgarity.[38]

Observations on the hegemony of "taste" were not unique to Aspen in the fifties. Social critics had been making them since the decade began. But it was an observation new to designers and disturbing to many of them. And they probed it endlessly. Lippincott, Will Burtin, and Jacques Vienot (founder of the French Institut d'Esthétique Industrielle), among others, warned their fellow designers of the trouble they had all let themselves in for. Having convinced business that "eye-value" sells products, the designer had become trapped by the perverse economic logic of his position: "eye-value" not only sells products, it *is* a product. Hence designs must be kept fresh to keep sales alive, and the designer thus becomes a hack harnessed, in Lippincott's words, to "style obsolescence" or "new look by gimmick."[39] Even Herbert Bayer, a pathbreaking graphic and typographic artist whose images excelled in arresting attention and rapidly conveying messages, had by the mid-fifties come to see advertising as an ingeniously manipulative and often pernicious device. Turning the clock of advertising history back a hundred years, he said he "would replace this super-technique, which interferes unnecessarily with our thought energies, generally speaking, with the simple idea of *information*. All that is required is a straightforward message . . . : what kind of product, its utility, its price, where to find it."[40]

These remarks brought the intellectual history of advertising and design full circle—back to the pre-twentieth-century assumption that products exist to satisfy needs, so advertising has only to supply literal descriptions of the products. But Bayer and his fellow designers neglected to observe that advertising and product design in a highly competitive consumer economy exist not to help satisfy actual needs but to generate artificial needs in the form of strong psychological desires. Those desires belong less to the consumers who feel and act on them than to the producers and advertisers who arouse them for the purpose of profit.

A firmer grasp of the designer's troubles and complicity in them had to await two more critical speakers—one at the academic edge of design, James Real, a designer and consultant to Robert M. Hutchins's Fund for the Republic and director of the fund's Education Project, and another speaker far beyond that edge, C. Wright Mills, professor of sociology at Columbia. James Real attacked if not the theory at least the practice of design as a tool of management for fabricating a corporate image. Image, he said, does not stand as an emblem of reality, it is a "facade" that conceals reality. Corporations project themselves not as they are, huge and powerful organizations bent on profit, but as friendly, accessible clubs devoted to service. By mobilizing design in the service of image, corporations create the impression that all economic realities, however upsetting, can be controlled by simply altering appearances—"clean typography, neighborly-neighbor advertisements, Bauhaus factories or lemon yellow box-cars." In sum, Real asked, is the modern designer improving the world, "or is he building masks, behind which the verities and strengths of the free society are slowly eroding away?"[41]

C. Wright Mills, a sociologist with strongly Marxist leanings, was a fierce and penetrating critic of American society, particularly of its unstated ideologies and hidden systems of authority—political, economic, intellectual. He had recently set forth many of his observations and criticisms in *The Power Elite* (1956), a book that had come close to describing the Aspen Institute's clientele. When he stood before the designers in 1958, he did not hesitate to identify the painful ambiguities and bitter ironies of their profession.

Design became important in business, he said, not because design was seen to improve products but because capitalist production so outruns demand that demand must be created. The designer was invented to create this demand by adding to products "the magical gloss and dazzle of prestige" that brings status to the owner. The designer is therefore part victim, part villain of the modern economy, because "his art is a business, but his business is art," and since his purpose is "to make people ashamed of last year's model," thereby causing "a panic for status" and keeping the machinery of selling purring along on the treadmill of "status obsolescence."

But this is not all. By throwing his talents into the service of selling, the designer turns all society into "a great sales room" where "beauty itself becomes identified with the designer's speed-up and debasement of imagination, taste and sensibility," and where the entire "cultural apparatus" becomes the tool of advertising and the servant of rapacious consumer capitalism.[42]

Although Mills held out a faint promise of redemption for designers in a return to craft, his words stand as the most severe and probing indictment of modern design in the fifties, condemning as they do virtually every achievement of the designer's art over the previous half-century. Here we see modern design as no longer an idealistic youth asserting itself against tradition; it had become the dominant tradition thrown on the defensive by those who saw in its alliance with commerce an insidious victory of commerce.

The criticism of modern design in the late fifties closed a chapter in the history of modernism and in the history of the International Design Conference in Aspen. After the fifties, a critical social conscience and aesthetic discontent would put the Aspen designers on the defensive. Reyner Banham, a historian of modern design and an Aspen regular, wrote of the IDCA that "the brashly elitist self-confidence of the early Fifties, when designers apparently held it as a self-evident truth that it was a manifest cultural duty of the world to owe them a living, dissolved before the social introspection and cultural awareness of the Sixties"; at the same time the "mystique" of the "progressive corporation" faded into "the old principle of guilt by association" that made "the design profession culpable of complicity with big business in the corruption of society and the pollution of the environment." By the end of the 1960s, this critical spirit had grown so intense that it erupted, alongside the widespread radicalism of those years, in an upheaval "that buried the old style Aspen" in a call by the young for political activism—workshops, be-ins, etc.—in place of buoyant discourses on the contributions of modern design to commerce. After this, Banham noted, "we got ourselves together again, but an epoch had ended."[43] The Design Conference as a novel forum for a young design profession to advance itself through modernist ideals of art and commerce was finished—and soon the cultural tide in the country at large would turn against modernism itself, beginning with architecture, as urged on by "post-modernist" theorists like Robert Venturi in his seminal book, *Complexity and Contradiction in Architecture* (1966).

The ideas of the Design Conference did not expire with this changing cultural mood, but they could never carry the same force of originality and possibility. Walter Paepcke did not live to see this decline, and he did not anticipate it. For his last adventure in the arts in Aspen was nothing less than a celebration of modern architecture itself with the construction of a modern architectural village.

Conceived by Paepcke early in the 1950s as a means of inducing important architects to settle in Aspen, the idea of constructing a collection of houses exemplifying the distinctive styles of such architects seemed timely.[44] The fifties saw the architect become something of a folk hero in America. Uniting intrepid individualism, cultural refinement, utopian idealism, and practicality, the architect easily symbolized the soaring American spirit at the mid-century—just as he had symbolized the humanist ideal of the Renaissance, the *uomo universale*. And national news magazines, especially Henry Luce's *Time,* gave frequent publicity to The New Architecture and its creators. A *Time* cover story in 1949, featuring Richard Neutra, announced, "modern houses are here to stay." And they should stay because they are practical and honest: "instead of concealing the purposes and technique of the construction," the architects accentuate them so "one can tell at a glance what the house is made of and how it was put together."[45] These statements appeared just after Philip Johnson had completed his famed "glass house" in Connecticut and just as Mies van der Rohe's influential apartment houses were rising on Chicago's Lake Shore Drive, all monuments to the style *Time* celebrated. A few years later, in a cover story on Eero Saarinen, *Time* could observe that "the greatest progress" in modern architecture "has come in a land not otherwise noted for its leadership in the world of art: the U.S."[46]

So taken were *Time*'s editors with the flowering of American architecture that they organized a traveling exhibition of models and photographs of sixty-six modern buildings representing the work of thirteen architects under the heading "Form-Givers at Mid-Century." And they proclaimed these architects peerless, visionary shapers of the future.[47]

While *Time* was helping awaken a public for modern achitecture and arousing reverence for modern architects, Paepcke was preparing lists of architects to design his architectural museum. He also hit upon what seemed to be the perfect source of financing: Henry Luce and Time Inc. He reported to Thornton Wilder in January 1959 that he had got Luce "somewhat interested in doing the original financing until the houses are sold."[48] A month later Time Inc. received a proposal to sponsor the project jointly with the Aspen Institute, Time supplying approximately one million dollars and the institute spending it. Nor was the project to be just an experiment in practical aesthetics. Like most of Paepcke's undertakings, it aimed at cultural uplift. "It is our genuine belief," the proposal read, that the village "might have a very radical and positive impact upon the standards of new housing in this country and might very well open a new era in terms of upgrading these standards."[49]

With prospects for financing looking bright, Paepcke invited seventeen noted architects to Aspen in early 1959 to lay out, as he told Le Corbusier, who was one of them, a "museum of living architecture."[50] Most accepted and some did so with relish. Philip Johnson was delighted to accept because "such a group of houses is most important for the cause of modern architecture."[51] Walter Gropius, however, said that he and his associates at the Architects' Collaborative were "most interested" but wanted assurances about overall planning. "As you may know," he explained to Paepcke, "the emphasis of all my architectural doings is on how to reach 'unity in diversity' which seems to me the most necessary aim for the building of our future communities." But he required that "an organic layout . . . and certain basic directives be worked out . . . in order to create a common denominator of design to be abided by by all. Without such a safeguard, a heterogeneous group of houses may result in spite of the high quality of the individual designs."[52]

Others, like I. M. Pei and Harry Weese, voiced similar concerns at the Aspen meeting. But Paepcke silenced them with appeals to their idealism, pledges to support their interests, and consent that they have control over interior design as well as the architecture. An agreement was struck. Twelve to fifteen houses costing $40,000 to $50,000 each would rise from the Aspen Meadows over the next three years.

In the fall of 1959, Paepcke informed the institute's board of trustees that he had firm commitments from Gropius, Marcel Breuer, Pei, Edward Durrell Stone, Weese, John Warnecke, John Lyon Reid, José Luis Sert, and Minoru Yamasaki. Asked if the institute would have to pick up the tab, because the Time Inc. deal had not come through, he conceded: "Probably. If not I might take a crack at it myself."[53] In any case, he added, financing for the first three houses, to be designed by Breuer, Weese, and Reid, was already in hand from outside the institute (mainly from his own pockets). Accepting these assurances, the trustees voted to back the plan. The ground-breaking was set for the spring thaw.

Paepcke was poring over the first sketches when Robert O. Anderson visited him in his sickbed in February. A few weeks later, as if to honor his work in progress, and explicitly in honor of his long service to modern design, the Architectural League of Chicago awarded Paepcke a medal of distinction. (At the same time, the league gave another medal to Mies van der Rohe, placing "the prosaic boxmaker" in the most distinguished architectural company.) But Paepcke could not receive the honor in person. He was dying. And before shovels could break the Aspen ground to bring his last grand design to life, he was dead.

A week after Paepcke died, a letter went out from the Aspen Institute to all the architects who had agreed to submit plans: "In view of the death of Walter Paepcke, the Board of the Aspen Institute for Humanistic Studies has decided to suspend for now all activities on the architectural project. We will contact you further at the earliest appropriate time."[54] Paepcke's dream died with him, for no one at the institute thought the architectural museum worth taking on.

And why should they have? Aspen was Paepcke's creation, not theirs. It was he who had envisioned Aspen as the American Athens and who had set himself to make it so—or as Marquis W. Childs put it in a laudatory article of 1958, "here was to be another Renaissance, with Paepcke as Medici in chief."[55] With his death, Aspen and its cultural institutions would be shaped by other hands, some belonging to people with ambitions of their own, others to those of a culture leaving behind the innocent hopes and earnest idealism of the early 1950s and moving off toward the postindustrial complexities, postmodernist aesthetics, and narcissistic appetites of the late twentieth century and after.

10

epilogue:

the romance of commerce and culture, 2002

The death of Walter Paepcke marked a passage in American culture as the 1960s dawned. For Paepcke had been an intermediary, a catalyst, and a shaping presence in American commercial and cultural life for a generation. His friends sensed the historical significance of his passing. They suffered not only a personal loss—Paepcke was actually not a very "personal" man—but the loss of an exemplary figure who had stood for a peculiarly energetic and resourceful brand of cultural idealism.

The president of the American Society of Industrial Designers said Paepcke was irreplaceable in the world of design because he "was and will always remain the noble human spirit in our profession."[1] Herbert Bayer memorialized his friend and patron in a long poem, published in an issue of the graphic magazine *Print* dedicated to Paepcke and to the first decade of the Design Conference, honoring Paepcke's impatience with "weakness," "softness," waste, and indolence, and eulogizing him for being "relentlessly driven by his imagination" to lead "the community of man . . . towards a more complete life."[2] The musician Victor Babin echoed this sentiment in a reminiscence of Paepcke's capacious appetite for "practically every kind of human achievement" and thanking him in memoriam for supplying "a new dimension to our lives."[3] Norman Cousins confessed he could "think of few men of our time who have more effectively and constructively served the cause of the thinking mind than [Paepcke] did."[4] And photographer Ansel Adams let brevity speak his feelings: "Walter," he wrote, "was a truly great man."[5] Perhaps the most affecting tribute, summing up many, and one that would have brought Paepcke special pride, came from the historian and critic Jacques Barzun. Paepcke "did more for learning in this country," Barzun wrote, "than ten colleges and universities, and this simply by caring and *doing*. With twenty men of his caliber in the land, the cultural complexion of the United States would be unrecognizable. But there aren't twenty, there aren't two, and now we are without one."[6]

These eulogies and others like them were, of course, the generous, pardonably exaggerated words of friendly voices in mourning. Yet events confirmed one of their salient messages: without the resolute, if occasionally the reckless, idealism and restless, even compulsive, energies of Paepcke behind them, the causes he served and the institutions he built would never be the same. They would come under new leaders and travel off through new historical terrain, all but leaving behind the world that Walter Paepcke knew and had helped to shape.

The Container Corporation wound its way along a course of domestic and Latin American expansion (and divestiture in Europe) until it fell into the maw of late-twentieth-century conglomerate ownership. This started in its partnership with Montgomery Ward as Marcor, which became a subsidiary of gigantic Mobil Oil Corporation in the late 1970s. Mobil then sold a half interest in CCA to the Scottish box maker Jefferson Smurfit in 1986 and the rest in 1989. With this last transaction, the Container Corporation of America ceased to exist, its name lingering only as a historical note in the records of what became Smurfit-Stone Container Corporation, known as the world's largest box maker—but not known for any interest in what had made CCA important: good commercial design.

Before CCA's definitive extinction, the advertisements that had brought the company its highest renown, "The Great Ideas of Western Man," continued to appear occasionally in national magazines, and a collection of them had traveled back and forth across the country in a museum exhibition. In 1976, on the eve of CCA's full acquisition by Mobil, the company had published a handsome hard-bound volume of those advertisements to commemorate the historic twenty-five-year advertising campaign, along with a slick, 100-page history in pictures of CCA's first fifty years. But in 1984, as Jefferson Smurfit was preparing to take over, this collection and the rest of CCA's advertising art were given to the National Museum of American Art at the

Smithsonian Institution in Washington, D.C. A year later, the Smithsonian held an exhibition devoted to this collection entitled "Art, Design, and the Modern Corporation: The Collection of Container Corporation of America," complete with a catalogue featuring CCA's advertising art and a lengthy scholarly essay by the historian Neil Harris elaborating on the historical context of CCA's contribution to advertising and corporate design.[7] The exhibit and its catalogue were an appropriate swan song for the Container Corporation of America.

But the gift of CCA's advertising art to the Smithsonian Museum, followed by the demise of CCA itself, bespoke more than the end of a pioneering and emblematic corporation in twentieth-century America. It also betrayed a sea change in the consumer culture and in industrial and commercial design. While the consumer economy was swelling to proportions hardly imagined before World War II, many of the old institutions that had once driven this economy—such as numerous traditional urban department stores—were succumbing to new mass marketing techniques and technologies propelled by television advertising, abetted by automobiles and suburban malls, and eventually attaining virtually boundless reach through the Internet. With this marketing boom, what had once been a pioneering crusade to transform modern commerce through "good design" in products, packaging, advertising, and corporate images became a commonplace practice. Modernist design and stylish corporate images had come to pervade the consumer economy.

If this signaled a victory for modernism and commercial design, it also stirred deepening doubts in some designers that serious design really mattered anymore. The commerce of their profession seemed to consume the culture of design. One graphic designer who started his career at CCA, Bill Bonnell (who also prepared the fiftieth anniversary history of the company, then left in 1978 for New York where he would head his own design firm), regretted that while corporations now commonly assumed they needed to have a design image, they would often meet this need by arbitrarily creating flashy logos overnight and generally treating "design as nothing more than a marketing tool." Not that this was entirely novel, he acknowledged, but it had become the norm, as it had not been when CCA and other companies had given design "deep roots in corporate values." To keep up with the galloping demand for quick design images, he added, designers multiplied, many with marginal training and uncertain purposes, transforming the profession into a mass marketplace of mediocrity.[8]

Echoing Bonnell's sentiments, the head of another New York graphic design firm observed that the advent of the personal computer in the 1980s sealed the fate of the commercial design profession as a leading force in the consumer culture. With their sophisticated graphics software, computers enabled virtually anyone to become a designer, sparing companies the need to hire highly talented professionals.[9] Submitting to these trends, another graphic designer, renowned in the 1970s and 1980s for his artful logos and other corporate design images, left the profession altogether in the late 1990s because, he said, "clients don't really care about distinctive design any more. They use design as a mere window dressing. Anybody can create that."[10]

This journey of commercial design from its pioneering spirit of the early and mid-twentieth century to its more routine status at the end of that century also surfaced in the institution created by Paepcke and Egbert Jacobson to help foster good design (while bringing paying guests to Aspen)—the grandly named International Design Conference in Aspen. When the IDCA celebrated its fiftieth anniversary in the summer of 2001, its members were not blind to the changing conditions of their profession. Taking as its theme "The More Things Change," the conference rather ambiguously addressed "design that matters today . . . in the light of what mattered, or seemed to matter, in the past" and "that produced the professions of design as we now know them." Turning from that exuberant past to the uncertain future, the conference promised to identify continuing roles for designers amidst the "ticking technology," "global marketing," "biospheres and ecosystems," and "affairs of state" of the early twenty-first century.[11] Some of the lofty rhetoric of the early IDCA was still here, but not the presence of the mid-twentieth-century America that the IDCA had been organized to serve when commercial design was relatively young and seemingly boundless. Making waves in the vast sea of twenty-first-century commercial design would not be so easy.

Walter Paepcke's prize cultural creation (besides the Aspen Music Festival, which had broken with Paepcke in 1954), the Aspen Institute for Humanistic Studies, also followed a path after 1960 that led it into territory unforeseen by its founders. As early as 1962, some visitors detected movement "away from the broad humanistic" spirit of the institute's early days and toward "more specific economic, social and political problems of American society."[12] In the same year, William Benton, a long-time devotee of the Chicago-Aspen humanism, complained to Adler (absent from the roster of moderators for the first time in 1961, although he would return and be a mainstay of the executive seminars into the 1990s): "Do you know what happened here? Is it felt that Aristotle will scare the businessmen away while Teddy Roosevelt's 1910 speech in Kansas will attract them?"[13]

The institute had, to be sure, been moving in this direction ever since the executive seminars had become routine in the mid-fifties. But the pace accelerated after Paepcke's death. The 1960s brought a variety of programs and conferences dealing with such current subjects as economics, ecology, demography, and the social responsibilities of science and technology. The Aspen Center for Theoretical Physics was also established in 1961, and a (short-lived) Aspen Film Conference was launched in 1963 with a keynote address by the critic Lionel Trilling on the artistic significance of movies. But these were minor additions compared to those of the 1970s and 1980s when the original Aspen idea of humanistic cultural reform was unmistakably overshadowed by new ambitions.

These new ambitions mushroomed with the appointment of Joseph E. Slater as president in 1969 (under Robert O. Anderson as chairman—a role Anderson had played since 1963, after serving as president since 1957). For the next seventeen years, Slater, coming from a background in cultural and philanthropic organizations, would persistently widen the institute's horizons far beyond its executive seminars and place it firmly on the world stage as an international center for public policy discussions. As he said in 1975, the institute should focus its "unique characteristics on the central problems of today" and provide "an annual *Overview* of the human condition."[14]

To these ends, Slater swiftly installed half a dozen on-going programs under the rubric "Thought Leading to Action," dealing with communications, education, justice, science, technology, the environment, and international affairs, each program headed by a notable authority in its field. These "Action Programs," as they became known, gave rise to all kinds of new conferences, seminars, workshops, projects, and publications on such topical themes as "The Future of Commercial Entertainment Television," "Mankind and Freedom—Planning for 1984," "Arms Control," "Europe and the United States: The Future of the Relationship," "The Environment, Energy, and Institutional Structures," "Women and Men: Changing Roles, Relationships, and Perceptions." At the same time, the institute formed ties and sponsored conferences with numerous international organizations, and it established outposts or partnerships around the world—in France, Italy, Germany, Israel, Iran (although the latter two proved temporary, and the institute's relations with Iran aroused controversy in the light of the Islamic revolution there),[15] and later Japan.

But this expansion did not unfold without difficulties. The most acute of these came from the city of Aspen itself. Robert O. Anderson might bankroll operations with his oil money (which he did for many years and beyond anything Paepcke could ever have afforded), but relations between the institute and its home town became very rocky for a while. Those relations had been somewhat strained ever since the early 1950s, owing to the institute's perceived elitist airs and to conflicts between town and gown over the scheduling of summer events. But when the ski boom of the 1960s and 1970s caused local officials to start clamping down on the city's growth for fear of being overwhelmed by development and newcomers (following in the footsteps of Paepcke in the late 1940s), the institute found its own needs thwarted.

By the late 1970s, the tensions erupted into open battle over the city's refusal to allow the institute to build new accommodations for its multiplying participants. Complaining that "a fun-oriented, anything-goes town may not be consistent with an organization which is trying to deal with major problems in a serious manner," Anderson threatened to pull the institute out of Aspen and advised his colleagues that "we must assess our future role in Aspen and whether or not it will be a desirable base for the major portion of our activities."[16] This was not an idle threat, as Paepcke's testy words to Aspenites had usually been. Unlike Paepcke, Anderson had sought no role for himself in shaping Aspen's society and economy. He had underscored this disinclination the year Paepcke died by abruptly selling off the Hotel Jerome, which the institute had controlled since Paepcke's donation of the Aspen Company stock, and letting it drift where the market would take it (after periods of insolvency and closed doors, it was renovated in 1985 and earned a listing on the National Register of Historic Places as well as membership in The Leading Hotels of the World). But city officials still balked at the pressure. Further negotiations foundered. Elizabeth Paepcke, whose personal relationship with Anderson had soured since her husband's death as she saw the institute's ambitions widening and Anderson eclipsing Walter's legacy by, for instance, letting the institute's campus be named for himself), nonetheless feared that the city government was needlessly chasing the institute away. "The city seems totally ignorant of the role the Aspen Institute has had in the history of Aspen," she told the Aspen Times in 1979. "They're doing a terrible thing."[17]

The gift to the institute in 1978 by Arthur A. Houghton of his Wye River estate on the eastern shore of Maryland, and the gift the next year by trustee Maurice Strong of his Baca Grande ranch in southeast Colorado—equipped with an inn, golf course, tennis court, swimming pool, and several houses—made the institute's departure from Aspen not only possible but probable. And in 1980 preparations began to transfer the institute's activities to those two properties. To emblazon this fact, Anderson and the trustees sold the institute's campus and all of its buildings to developer Hans Cantrup. Although the institute subsequently took out a ninety-nine-year lease on the campus, the message was clear: the Aspen Institute did not need Aspen anymore.

The Wye River estate near Washington, D.C., became the institute's chief conference center (President Clinton would hold Middle East peace talks there in 1998). And a headquarters was set up in New York, then later moved to Washington, D.C., the seat of political power toward which the institute had been gravitating in function and goals. But as it turned out, the Aspen Institute did not leave Aspen after all, or not completely.

In the late 1980s, after city officials lessened their resistance to develop-ment, the institute got much of its Aspen campus back. This occurred when a new developer, Mohammed Hadid, who was lobbying to build a luxury hotel at the base of Aspen Mountain—which would become the St. Regis—took over the property. Recognizing the value of the institute and its related cultural organizations to Aspen, Hadid donated forty acres of the property back to the institute; he gave the music tent to the Music Associates and the physics building to the Physics Center; then he sold a sizeable piece to the city for a park and the rest to individuals for private uses. The donation secured the Aspen Institute's presence in Aspen, and encouraged the reno-vation and expansion in 1995 of the original accommodations in the Aspen Meadows, keeping the Aspen campus very much alive.[18] In 2001, a spokes-man for the institute would proudly say that while half of the institute's staff works in the Washington office, and another high-level contingent works in the Chicago office where the current president is based, the Aspen Institute actually has no formal headquarters—although its true home is Aspen, at least in spirit.[19]

Today, with good relations between the institute and Aspen carefully cultivated, the Aspen campus anchors the most traditional of the institute's programs, the executive seminars, held there through most of the year (and at the Wye River campus periodically). Those seminars have also continued to affect many participants much as they had done in the early years (while representing a wider range of constituencies in American life than they had then). As one recent participant put it, the seminar experience stimulated him to "rethink . . . my own values, our society, and my role as a citizen."[20] The journalist Bill Moyers, a frequent participant and moderator, remarked in 2000 that the seminars had taught him "just how potent ideas were when people were confronted by them and wrestled with them," leading him to conclude that "people could never be the same again after they had been there."[21] In such reactions as these, the formative Aspen idea of cultural reform lived on.

But that idea lived on in very different circumstances. By the year 2000 (thanks especially to Slater and Anderson, followed by David McGlaughlin, who served as either president or chairman for the decade from 1986 to 1997, and then to Elmer W. Johnson, who assumed the presidency in 1999), there were more than half a dozen new "Seminar Programs" in addition to the traditional executive seminars, and others in the works, as well as fifteen "Policy Programs" (formerly the "Action Programs") ranging across the political, economic, and social landscape. In all, the institute was then organizing, running, or sponsoring in excess of a hundred events each year involving thousands of people, and issuing well over a hundred publications.

Clearly this was no longer the Aspen Institute for Humanistic Studies of Ortega, Paepcke, Hutchins, and Adler, aspiring to reform American culture through Ortegan elegance and Great Books. Confirming this historic fact, the board of trustees of the institute voted in October 1988 to drop the words "Humanistic Studies" from the institute's name. The next year the "Aspen Institute for Humanistic Studies" officially became simply the "Aspen Institute." Another end to another era.

There can be no denying that its move in the direction of public policy and global reach won for the institute an international reputation as a forum for high-level confabulations among movers and shakers on pressing public policy issues. A participant at the Aspen Institute in Berlin noted, for instance, that "some long telegrams are sent after the meetings and some meaty reports return to presidents and prime ministers."[22] But old-time institute hands like Mortimer Adler rued the decline of the original humanistic ethos into amorphous political conferences—Adler also fought the "corruption," as he labeled it, of the executive seminars through the introduction of insufficiently "great" writings—and some conference attendees found some of the proceedings themselves rather thin. "It's like the Powder River," cracked former Urban League president and now Washington insider Vernon Jordan, "about a mile wide and an inch deep." Another said the "thought leading to action programs" are "mostly thought leading to more thought—and thence to slumber." And in 1980 the journalist Joseph Kraft rather dismissively dubbed the institute itself "The Great American Salon."[23]

No conferences held on the plane of the latter-day Aspen Institute's could satisfy everyone, of course. But besides their contents, these conferences have served the institute's long-standing purpose of promoting "networking" and Paepcke's "cross-fertilization of ideas" among the "leaders of American life." And the institute has also tried to retain a semblance of the original Aspen idea of humanism even in its public policy discussions. Reaffirming that idea in 2000, the president, Elmer W. Johnson, declared that the discussion of policy issues at the institute should be "informed by the same humanistic perspective" as "the seminar programs, a perspective that is often under-emphasized in policy discourse and decision making." Conceding, however, that "the more you get involved in policy, the easier it is to lose sight" of larger humanistic concerns,[24] Johnson then put a contemporary spin on the institute's humanism: "Leveraging the power of leaders to improve the human condition—that is our global mission."[25]

Johnson renewed both the institute's humanistic heritage and its worldly twenty-first-century aspirations in commemorating the institute's fiftieth anniversary with several events around the country in 2000, capped by a four-day summer convocation in Aspen. Taking a cue from the Goethe Bicentennial Festival of 1949, Johnson and his colleagues chose to honor the occasion by exploring a contemporary version of the Goethe Bicentennial's theme of universal humanism. But whereas the Goethe Festival had aimed to heal wounds of World War II and to ameliorate the intensifying Cold War by unifying humankind through humanistic ideas, the institute's fiftieth anniversary celebration in Aspen took up the less idealistic task of grappling with the social, political, and economic consequences of what had come to be known at the turn of the twenty-first century as "globalization."

Under the heading "Globalization and the Human Condition," this celebration brought together a host of notables from politics, economics, academia, and journalism—albeit no one of the stature of Albert Schweitzer or Ortega y Gasset, for no such preeminent philosophical figures remained in a world that no longer exalted philosophers as guides to life for their worldly wisdom. Among the luminati who assembled in Aspen this time, the top names came from politics and economics, including former United States president Jimmy Carter, president of the World Bank, James D. Wolfenson, Secretary of the Interior Bruce Babbitt, and Librarian of Congress James H. Billington. In workshops, panels, and lectures, they and their many colleagues spoke soberly of how globalization is a fact of modern technology and economics that must be guided toward humane purposes, lest it do more harm to more people than the good it does for a few.

Elmer Johnson set the tone by asking, "Do our public and private institutions have the capacity, and do those who lead them have the wisdom, to harness and humanize the forces of globalization in the interests of a more just and mutually supportive world?"[26] Again and again the implicit answer came that for globalization to create a "just" and "supportive" world, it must conquer the poverty and inequalities that rule the lives of most people on earth. A few participants saw gains already being made through global capitalism itself. But most voiced concern over the widening gulf throughout the world between rich and poor, and over its portentous consequences. Oscar Arias Sanchez, former president of Costa Rica and Nobel Laureate, struck the dominant theme: "The enemy of world peace is injustice, hunger, poverty, and inequality," so "we must speak out for a new ethic of globalization—one that respects human dignity and holds governments and corporations accountable for their actions in the international community, one that promotes respect for all peoples and nations."[27]

When the curtain came down on the four-day celebration, and the speakers and their listeners departed, the idea of globalization in the twenty-first century had clearly received a humanistic stamp—just as prospects for the postwar world of the mid-twentieth century had received a humanistic stamp from the Goethe Bicentennial festival. But times had changed, for both the better and the worse. The Goethe Festival had been held against a background of postwar American ascendancy and Cold War tensions. The

Aspen Institute's fiftieth anniversary celebration came with America fully ascendant in a post–Cold War world that was nonetheless unsure how to secure peace, rectify inequities, and establish universal justice in an age of inevitable globalization.

This celebration addressing the problems globalization poses, rather than merely idealizing the unity it might bring, made a fitting climax to the Aspen Institute's first half century. For while honoring the legacy of the Goethe Bicentennial's humanistic idealism, the institute's fiftieth anniversary convocation reflected a deepening sense at the turn of the twenty-first century that despite the social, economic, and political gains of the previous fifty years, globalization was creating more complicated international challenges and potential dangers than ever.

As it happened, just over a year after this anniversary celebration, Arab terrorist attacks on New York and Washington, D.C., exposed a very dark side of globalization indeed, justifying the worries voiced in Aspen that globalization threatened to divide the world more than to unite it, and to thwart world peace in ways unforseen fifty years earlier. Within weeks of those attacks, the institute had launched its own response with "an agenda of long-term actions for working toward a much more stable and just world." That agenda, as Elmer Johnson put it in a memorandum to the trustees, called for policy discussions and seminars appropriate to the institute's "mission," focusing on such topics as: "the values and perspectives of other cultures," including "the revivalism that has swept across the Islamic world over the last 30 years"; the "legitimate grievances of those who feel they have no stake in the benefits of globalization"; and how to build "stronger bridges of understanding" between "Islam and the West" and improve "the wealth-creating power of the poor around the globe."[28] If the Aspen Institute could help meet the new economic and political challenges of globalization and create "a more stable and just world," it would live up to the humanistic legacy of the Goethe Bicentennial festival.

While the Aspen Institute was traveling its historic path after Walter Paepcke's death from being a small idealistic educational institution in the Rocky Mountains toward becoming a globe-encircling organization hosting policy discussions with a humanistic slant on the most urgent matters of the day, the institute's home town was going through kindred changes. Some of these matched the institute's widening ambitions as a center for the movers and shakers of American life, but others clashed with the institute's intellectual seriousness, as Robert O. Anderson had complained in the 1970s.

This disharmony actually had origins in the Janus-like character of Aspen as shaped by Walter Paepcke from the beginning. Aspen's marriage of culture and recreation had never been entirely stable: people who came to town for the one seldom came for the other. The split followed the seasons: summer the season of culture, winter the season of play—as the *Aspen Times* had unwittingly foreshadowed on the November day in 1948 when its front page had carried lead stories on both the forthcoming Goethe Bicentennial festival and the FIS ski competition.

Yet the gulf between culture and recreation opened up only after Paepcke's death. Harbingers of things to come appeared with the 1960s. The year 1960 saw the United States host the Winter Olympics for the first time since 1932, this time in Squaw Valley and on national television. If the Lake Placid games of 1932 had created an American public for skiing as a rather primitive thrill, Squaw Valley created a mass public for skiing as fashion. Not only had ski equipment become more manageable and versatile in the intervening years, sparking greater speed and more downhill dramatics, ski clothing had acquired style. No more bulky, formless woolens making skiers resemble bundled snowmen. Now flashy nylon parkas clung to slender torsos, and stretch pants by Bogdner snaked from hip to heel. The skier's "look" became as prized as the skier's thrills. The inauguration of John F. Kennedy in January 1961, and the landing of the first jet in Aspen (a prop-jet) in the same month, further spurred the cult of stylish recreation. The era of youth and the glittery jet-set had arrived—and soon the extended Kennedy family (almost all of them except the president himself) were frequent visitors to the Aspen slopes.

To accommodate the influx of pleasure seekers, Aspen's first modern public lodgings opened—the Aspen Inn (1962) and the Aspen Alps (1963)—followed by dozens of lodges and, later, condominiums. By the late sixties the city and its environs could house some 10,000 guests; ten years later the number had nearly tripled; and when the century ended the Aspen/Snowmass region was bedding many thousands more, at the most exorbitant rates. The Aspen Skiing Corporation (and some early short-lived competitors) fed the demand by financing new runs and lifts until Aspen became one of the largest ski areas in the country and the corporation ripe for acquisition. In 1978, nearly $50 million changed hands, and the Aspen Skiing Corporation became a subsidiary of Twentieth Century Fox. Another tie with Aspen's past was broken, and the floodgates of Hollywood opened wide. The skiing corporation, continuing to expand beyond Aspen Mountain to include the Aspen Highlands, Buttermilk, and Snowmass, later returned to private hands. And it would even publicize itself in 2001 with "Guiding Principles" pledged to "sustain the 'Aspen Idea'" of "the complete life where mind, body, and spirit are enriched."[29] But Aspen's skiing culture now blended better with show business than it did with Walter Paepcke's original humanistic ideals.

Paepcke's desire to make Aspen a home for a "high type of person" had become an invitation to the famous and affluent and their acolytes to come for fashionable recreation and social cachet. In the 1970s, the town was often caught up in carnival revelry, the whiff of drugs, and a fad for ecstatic self-discovery through Werner Erhard's zealous therapeutic regimen of *est*— and Erhard himself became a lionized local presence. A trashy novel came out taking its name from the town and exposing the worldly and sometimes dissolute delights of the new Aspen. This new ethos also found both dramatic and poignant expression in the career of an actress named Claudine Longet. Acquitted, in a sensational nationally publicized trial at Aspen's courthouse, of murdering her lover, a professional skier, in their Aspen residence, she then purchased the Red Mountain home of Herbert Bayer. Bayer, aging and increasingly uncomfortable in the mountain altitudes, left Aspen in 1978 for Montecito, California, where he died in 1985, closing another chapter in Aspen's history.

From the 1970s onward, Aspen developed an ever livelier sense of itself as the quintessence of late-twentieth-century celebrity, wealth, and style. By the opening of the new century, the local airport, named for Tom Sardy, was often clogged with private jets bringing movie stars and corporate magnates, socialites and financiers—the "über-hip," as *Aspen Magazine* crowed[30]—to vacation or to fraternize with each other, and scores of these people purchased or built fabulous residences in Aspen or nearby. Real estate values told the story. Modest frame houses, some bought for taxes in the late forties, became nearly half-million dollar properties in the 1970s (Herbert Bayer's Red Mountain house went for the then grand sum $350,000) and kept rising in value from there. In the first half of 2000, the *average* price of all houses sold in Aspen, as well as in neighboring Snowmass, surpassed $3.5 million, and condominiums in Aspen averaged over $1 million.[31] Those prices might have reflected the widespread real estate boom of the late 1990s, but they made it indisputable that Aspen was not a place for anyone of modest means. "How do you define success? Money? Power? Invites to Aspen's top soirées?" asked an article in *Aspen Magazine* in 2001.[32] The question and these answers ran together in the Aspen of the 1990s and later.

By then, Aspen had shed much of its seventies' eccentricities and provided most of the sophisticated cosmopolitan pleasures and diversions of great cities—not only cultural institutions but dozens of posh restaurants, boutique shops, galleries, and a glittery social scene to match—all freed from the urban maelstrom and nestled in a spectacular mountain recreational setting. New organizations and events were also multiplying to burnish the local luster. The nearby Anderson Ranch Arts Center, for example, became an international establishment for the discussion and teaching of the visual arts—and some said that winning one of its "prestigious awards" for service to the arts was a sure sign that "you've truly arrived."[33] "Jazz Aspen at Snowmass" brought in the leading lights of jazz and other show business

Fig, 10.1. Aspen, Colorado, in the 1970s. The Aspen Institute campus lies in the center foreground; Aspen Mountain (left center) and the Aspen Highlands dominate the background. Photo by Robert C. Bishop.

luminaries. A chic Aspen film festival paid local homage to Hollywood. And the annual *Food and Wine Magazine* culinary festival, featuring "seminars, tastings, demonstrations," with "the shining stars of the epicurean universe,"[34] made foodies happy and played a "major role in Aspen's becoming a magnet for adventurous chefs and committed restaurateurs."[35] *Aspen Magazine* mirrored the new style while chronicling it. Founded in the 1970s, the magazine came to burst with lavish advertisements pitched to the rich, and fervently boosted Aspen's unique blend of culture and recreation, celebrity and society, art and nature. Other cities and regions produced similarly slick magazines in these years, but *Aspen Magazine* was unsurpassed. As its capable, long-time editor, Janet O'Grady—a transplanted Easterner—enthused in 2001, "I'm still in awe of how Aspen truly has it all."[36]

"Aspen is not only a celebrity watering hole," quipped an author who handled the social beat for the *Aspen Times* in the late eighties, "it is a celebrity itself"—and something of a "circus."[37] Another journalist, who lived in Aspen for twenty-five years, remarked after departing that "the people of Aspen have always believed the town was special, unique," and although she criticized this as "hubris," she concluded that Aspen is "more than the sum of its parts": it is "a way of life," "an idea."[38] It has been these things

ever since the Paepckes first arrived in May 1945, or, rather, ever since Elizabeth Paepcke, seeing Aspen in 1939 under a blanket of snow, thought of it as
a "Sleeping Beauty." But it has become an idea that Walter Paepcke would
not readily recognize—as one native Aspenite born before Paepcke arrived
says, nowadays "there is more stress on Gucci than on culture."[39]

For her part, Elizabeth Paepcke looked on with a questioning eye and
wry amusement at the changes in the town she had once seen sleeping and
had come to love and to become identified with as its matron—or, in the
words of Aspen Magazine, "the soul and conscience of Aspen."[40] She would
recall with longing affection her early years in Aspen, and she would never
become part of the Hollywood and international celebrity scene there. "Aspen is going off in a different direction from everything we cared about," she
would say in her last years. "My heart is broken."[41] But she nevertheless
worked hard to keep the Aspen Institute there, and she continued to play
her role as inimitable hostess to cultural leaders at her spacious Aspen home
with its expansive secluded gardens overlooking Hallam Lake, where she
established the Aspen Institute for Environmental Studies. While tending
those precious gardens one morning in June of 1994, she fell, hit her head,
and lost consciousness, never to reawaken. She would have been ninety-two
that same summer. She might have chosen this ending in this setting. But
Aspen mourned. Aspenites who knew her felt that Aspen had lost a bit of its
soul and would never be the same without her. Even people who did not know
her personally sensed her presence as she traveled about the town on errands
in her signature jeep, with a smile for anyone, and often with unexpected
gifts. When she was gone, no one in Aspen could fail to feel her absence—
and the New York Times Magazine featured her photograph on the cover of its
memorial issue the next January devoted to "Lives Well Lived," honoring
her as "Eve in the Garden of Aspen."[42]

Aspen's idea of itself in the early twenty-first century might be far from what it
once was. But different as it may be, it had its origins in Walter Paepcke's
ambition to build a cultural, social, and recreational center in Aspen for "a
high type of person" to cultivate mind, soul, and body. That both the town
of Aspen and the Aspen Institute should have drifted away from the original
dreams that Paepcke had for them owed something to his premature death.
But much more than this, Aspen and the institute—along with the other
enterprises of Paepcke and his allies in cultural reform—were swept up in
historical currents that took them and America from the culture of the mid-
twentieth-century to the culture of the early twenty-first century.

Some signs of those currents have already been noted here in the latter-
day careers of the Container Corporation, the Aspen Institute, and Aspen

itself. But more widely, those currents brought such changes as the emergence of what has been called a postindustrial, technocratic, and postmodern society, the passing of artistic modernism, and the decline of a traditional, self-denying personality type. All of these changes affected the Chicago-Aspen crusade for cultural reform and its leaders in illuminating ways. The history of Aspen from the mid-twentieth century to the twenty-first century is therefore the history of an epochal era in American culture—and beyond.

The transition to postindustrial, technocratic, postmodern society made America increasingly dependent on services rather than manufacturing, on intellect, technical knowledge, and information rather than on practical experience, and on a professional class educated to execute its cognitive tasks and to administer its "organized complexity."[43] This kind of society—by whatever name—had supplied the Aspen Institute much of its clientele from the outset as the "power elite," in C. Wright Mills's term, that Paepkce had wanted to nurture through "the cross-fertilization of ideas." But Mills had also pointed out that historical conditions were calling forth "a power elite that is of a new caliber" from any of its predecessors, because increasingly "the sweep of matters" involved in "the making of decisions is vast and interrelated" and "the information needed for judgments" has become "complex"[44] to an unprecedented degree. This new elite would therefore be characterized as much by intellectual skills as by the possession of power itself. In 1994, a book entitled *The Bell Curve: Intelligence and Class Structure in American Life* supported Mills's prediction by arguing with abundant statistics that the modern economy and its related educational institutions were indeed producing nothing less than a "cognitive elite" of those mentally best able to conduct the affairs of professional life.[45] The contention of this book had many unattractive and controversial social implications, but the historical fact at its heart remained: leadership in late-twentieth-century America demanded intellectual skills and education on a scale previously unknown—by the late twentieth century virtually all top executives in America had gone to college, and close to a majority had attended graduate school as well (on this theme, see Chapter 8).

These developments, which brought to maturity what one historian has labeled "the culture of professionalism,"[46] inevitably placed the original intellectual aspirations of the Chicago Bildungsideal and the Aspen Institute in a new light. For to meet the mounting educational demands of American life, the best colleges and professional schools were advancing analytical skills and intellectual sophistication in their graduates akin to some of what Hutchins and Adler had promoted through the study of Great Books. Those institutions did not typically consider the Great Books necessary to do this (Columbia remained a stalwart exception, while even the University of Chicago moved substantially away from its Great Books curriculum after Adler and Hutchins left), but some used analogous techniques. The Harvard Business School, for instance, refined the case method of teaching after World War II along conceptual and pedagogical lines loosely analogous to the study of Great Books.[47] However far removed from the humanism of Hutchins and Adler, the success of such educational innovations could not help but make the Chicago Bildungsideal seem more parochial.

The Aspen Institute had first acknowledged the expanding role of intellect and education in American professional life by trying to educate the new "power elite" through the "humanistic studies" of Great Books in the executive seminars. Later the institute expanded its mission to serve and influence that elite more widely—if not more deeply—by becoming less of an educational institution and more of a forum for the discussion of public policy among leaders of the already well-educated "cognitive elite" at large. But in both its beginnings and its evolution, the institute reflected American educational, professional, and political culture.

Meanwhile, many humanists complained that, amidst the pressures to "train" people for professional life, general humanistic education was getting slighted more than ever. And in the sixties and seventies, influential humanists (some in meetings at the Aspen Institute) successfully lobbied to create the National Endowment for the Humanities, and then the National Association for the Advancement of the Humanities and the National Center for the Humanities. But in 1980 a national Commission on the Humanities could still report that there was cause for "profound disquiet about the state of the humanities in our culture."[48] Shortly thereafter, a new wave of educational reforms swelled to remedy the neglect not only of the humanities but of all "basic" learning in the primary and secondary schools. The "cultural literacy" campaign of E. D. Hirsch, bent on eradicating American students' ignorance of general humanistic matters, was one of these.[49] The "Paideia Proposal" of Mortimer Adler was another. And this brings us back to the Chicago Bildungsideal and the fate of its two chief crusaders in cultural reform.

Mortimer Adler's turn to primary and secondary school reform came as he and his old comrade-in-arms, Hutchins, found themselves and their educational ideas largely shunted to the sidelines of higher education as American culture made its way through the second half of the century. But confronting most disappointments with resilience, they kept up a good fight.

Hutchins carried on his defense of their humanistic cause through his Center for the Study of Democratic Institutions in Santa Barbara. Holding philosophical gatherings among fellows and guests, and gaining a large circulation for its thought-provoking publications, *The Center Magazine* and *The Center Report*, Hutchins's center won considerable attention and respect in the 1960s. But the next decade saw its stature wane and financial troubles engulf it as Hutchins began withdrawing. When he died in 1977, Hutchins was, according to many of those close to him, a disillusioned man. And, lacking his leadership to sustain it, the center was taken over two years later by the University of California at Santa Barbara, which moved it to Los Angeles, where in 1988 it was faintly reconstituted as the publisher of *New Perspectives Quarterly*. Tallying Hutchins's career, a biographer concluded that Hutchins's most lasting legacies probably amounted only to his "stand on academic freedom" and his campaign to "reexamine the ends of educational institutions."[50] But it should not be forgotten that through the Chicago Bildungsideal and the institutions it shaped, Hutchins gave humanism a vital presence in American life for a generation and more that it had not had before and has not had since.

Adler, always brimming with intellectual energies and philosophy, and having a keen eye for promoting himself and his ideas, kept trying with diverse strategies to advance the principles of the Chicago Bildungsideal. Criticism failed to daunt him. Dismissed by many academicians and critics as a philosophical showman who hadn't had a new idea since the 1920s—"the Lawrence Welk of the philosophy trade," the writer Nelson Algren once quipped—he would characteristically retort with aplomb, "I thumbed my nose at them, so why should they pay any attention to me?"[51] Even occasional bouts of discouragement didn't thwart him. "My hopes for the reform of the American college and university have dwindled to the verge of despair," he confessed in a *Newsweek* essay of 1978. "The evil that confronts us" now, he concluded, is "the demise of culture itself."[52] But then he threw himself into the Paideia Project, aiming to bring an "enlarged understanding of ideas and values"[53] to the lower schools. He also continued to conduct traditional executive seminars in Aspen, uncompromisingly combating the "corruption" of the seminars introduced by works he disapproved—although he was viewed by some participants as a relic of the past. And he continued pouring forth popular philosophical books and articles, while pushing on with the *Summa Dialectica* at his Institute for Philosophical Research, making frequent television appearances as philosopher, revamping the entire structure of the Encyclopedia Britannica, and preparing a new edition of the *Great Books of the Western World* and its *Syntopicon*, which came out in 1990 featuring fifty new authors in six additional volumes. The man was indefatigable.

Adler was also able to take pride that some of his oldest educational offspring (or those that would not have come into existence without him) persisted. St. John's College, for one, where he often lectured, held fast to its Great Books curriculum and even added a second campus in Santa Fe, New Mexico, in 1964. The Great Books Foundation, for another, could still boast some 900 adult groups around the country in 2001, as well as many new programs and publications, including a selection of global classics distributed to a million schoolchildren each year (albeit Adler characteristically derided these ecumenical efforts as "phony tolerance," because no "Great Conversation" on common topics exists globally and no *Syntopicon* is possible).[54] At the same time, Adler's youngest educational offspring, the Paideia Project, thrived as a national organization for shaping school curriculums, advising educators, and training teachers. In 1988, he gave it a permanent home at the University of North Carolina at Durham, where he held a faculty position for three years.

Recognizing his many contributions to the humanities, the National Endowment for the Humanities awarded Adler its Charles Frankel Prize in 1990. In that same year, with his disciple and colleague Max Weismann, Adler founded the Center for the Study of Great Ideas in Chicago. A successor to his Institute for Philosophical Research, this organization crowned Adler's career. In fact, it was very much a monument to Adler himself. Dedicated to teaching "why philosophy is everybody's business," the center promised "tireless efforts" to disseminate "the insights and ideals in Dr. Adler's lifelong intellectual work in the fields of Philosophy, Liberal Education, Ethics and Politics." To this end, the center publicized all of Adler's writings— scores of books and articles—and provided Internet links to the organizations he had helped create, along with access to related Adlerian educational activities.[55] A uniquely industrious and influential intellectual figure in twentieth-century America, Mortimer Adler certainly deserved a monument when he died in 2001 approaching his ninety-ninth birthday. And what monument could have been more appropriate than the one he erected himself enshrining his life's work?

With Adler's death as the new century was aborning, the original Chicago-Aspen crusade for cultural reform lost its last surviving creator. And the world Adler left behind would not likely see anyone with his philosophical energies and ideals again. For by then, notwithstanding its notable achievements, the crusade for cultural reform inspired by the "Great Conversation" among Western thinkers that Adler and Hutchins had championed in so many ways for so long had become, along with other modes of mid-twentieth-century American idealism, something of an artifact of an earlier age. That was neither a loss nor a gain in itself. It was history.

We might also say that Adler's passing symbolized the departure from American life of a certain kind of person shaped by a certain time. Most of the leading figures in this story (including Adler and Hutchins, Walter and Elizabeth Paepcke, László Moholy-Nagy, Herbert Bayer, as well as Egbert Jacobson, Henry Luce, Thornton Wilder, Jacques Barzun, and others) were of the same generation (all born between about 1896 and 1907) or of the previous one, like Walter Gropius, Ortega y Gasset (both born in 1883), and

Albert Schweitzer (born in 1875). And they shared some distinctive attributes. They all possessed rigorous moral discipline, respect for psychic restraint, a dedication to work, and a deep sense of social responsibility. Schweitzer and Ortega made self-discipline the hallmark of their lives and thought. Adler was a compulsive worker and uncompromising rationalist who had unwavering confidence in himself, distrusted emotion, disdained psychological motivation, and, by his own admission, never experienced love until he was well past middle age. Hutchins, the pastor's son, insistently equated leisure with sin and resolutely shunned it, while exhibiting "little tolerance for uncertainty" and "discomfort with the emotional and nonrational elements" in other people.[56] Moholy-Nagy, the man closest to Walter Paepcke, openly eschewed all emotion, allowing no trace of it to enter his art or recognizably to alter his life before his last years. And Paepcke put himself under such severe restraints that his hands trembled with tension, and he could never permit himself emotional intimacy. The list could go on and on.

These people and so many others whose names dot these pages were, as noted at the outset, the kind that Sigmund Freud had in mind when he concluded that the work of high civilization can be done only at the cost of some psychological sacrifice—although that need not entail unhappiness. They were also the kind that David Riesman described at the mid-century in *The Lonely Crowd* as "inner-directed" characters—fired by an internal flame to accomplish important worldly work whatever the loss in emotional ease. Riesman also knew that their days as the reigning character type were numbered, for the era of the boldly ambitious, morally righteous, emotionally self-denying individualist was fading. That age would be succeeded, Riesman predicted, by that of the "other-directed" personality, one driven not so much by self-confidence, self-restraint, moral rectitude, and the will to excel as by a placid desire to be "well liked" and contented.[57]

Social critics of the 1970s saw the American character and its culture going even beyond this socially insecure and emotionally self-conscious "other-directed" personality to create what the emblematic book of that decade dubbed the character and "culture of narcissism."[58] Striving less for social acceptance than for intense psychological satisfactions, the narcissistic personality was said to live for itself and within itself more than any character type before it, tolerating no psychic sacrifices of any kind. As one partisan of this new type proclaimed, extolling the qualities that the critics derided, "those who have awakened to the summons of self-discovery, who have found their way to the point of saying, 'I *matter*, I am *special*, there is something more in me waiting to be discovered, named, liberated,'" will at last throw off the burdens of "history" and "society," along with "the tyranny of excellence," and "the culture of guilt."[59] Werner Erhard's therapeutic *est* promised the same selfish exaltations.

The Freudian-Marxist Herbert Marcuse had detected a variety of this character type during the 1960s in a spreading cult of "the happy consciousness."[60] And long before that, from a more conservative angle, Ortega y Gasset had foreseen something like it in the ascendancy of the selfishly myopic "Mass Man." In the late twentieth century, observers would offer a multitude of variations on the theme. Critics of the 1980s and 1990s found Americans losing their very capacity for self-discipline and seriousness amid rampant consumerism and an insatiable appetite for diversion. A pair of prominent books in these decades belabored Americans for "amusing ourselves to death" and for turning life itself into an "entertainment."[61] In the late nineties, an ambitious historical work blamed America's commercial "mass culture" for purveying homogenized pleasures that induce passivity and enervate cultural life, and a biting critical study foresaw the impending demise of all culture itself through the democratic cancer of "mass individualism."[62] In a similar *fin-de-siécle* mood, the one-time Aspen hand Jacques Barzun (at the age of ninety-two) published in 2000 a monumental history of Western civilization over the previous 500 years, pronouncing this entire civilization sinking into terminal "decadence" owing to the spread of a "demotic" character type that spurns authority, despises discipline, debunks standards, forsakes morals, and so on. Barzun had voiced some of these criticisms earlier in lectures at the Aspen Institute. And his fellow early Aspenites would have applauded his high-minded values, just as they would have approved his conclusion that the deepening cultural decadence of the West would end only with the rise of a new culture inspired to fresh creativity by renewed respect for great works of the past.[63]

Whether or not these late-twentieth-century diagnoses of the decline of the American character and culture would prove accurate or not—thinkers have, after all, lamented the decline of character and culture ever since Confucius and the ancient Greeks—there could be little doubt that the strenuous, moralistic, self-denying character type of Walter Paepcke's generation belonged more to the past than to the dawning twenty-first century. This was true not just because that generation had all but passed from the scene. It was true because American culture had become marked by consumerism, affluence, self-indulgence, and diversion to a degree that Paepcke's generation had not known and could not have readily endorsed—as Barzun's *From Dawn to Decadence* demonstrated. In a telling irony, the town of Aspen, shaped by that generation, had become a capital of this culture.

The changing social, economic, and cultural landscape of the late twentieth century that largely brought to a close the Chicago-Aspen crusade for cultural reform can also be said to have closed a chapter in the modern romance of commerce and culture overall. That romance had flourished in the twen-

tieth century as conflicts between modern commercial and cultural interests—intensified by modernism's adversarial spirit—had diminished through
budding alliances among those interests. These alliances started to form when
artists and intellectuals who criticized modern industrialism, commercialism, and specialization for disintegrating culture and impairing humanity
acted to reverse the tide by creating a culture of humanistic wholeness.

Artist/designers like the Bauhäusler Walter Gropius, Lázsló Moholy-Nagy,
and Herbert Bayer proposed to achieve this end by producing artworks, architecture, and useful objects embodying the singular spirit of modernity,
and by educating other artists, architects, and designers to comprehend that
spirit and contribute to its style—in Moholy-Nagy's words, only by seeing
the modern world through the "new vision" of abstraction could the Whole
Human Being come to life. Intellectuals like Ortega y Gasset, Robert M.
Hutchins, and Mortimer J. Adler proposed to reach the same end by promoting the disciplined exercise of intellect and the pursuit of humanistic values,
in part through study of the great ideas of Western culture since antiquity.
These were rather odd alliances, often divided by different inclinations toward modernity (and in Chicago by conflicting views of John Dewey's pragmatism), but they were revealing. For different as they were, those modern
artists and those more traditionalist intellectuals acted to integrate and humanize culture through not only education but the techniques of modern
commercial culture—e.g., product and graphic design, advertising, public relations, book publishing, nationwide organizations, conferences, and seminars. Both Walter Gropius and Robert M. Hutchins might, for instance,
extol the unity of medieval culture, but they also deftly used the commercial
devices of the twentieth century to renew it.

The ambitions on both sides were grand, and so were many of the accomplishments. Modernist art and design transformed the visual environment of our lives from consumer products to cityscapes (although, to be sure,
this transformation came from many more artist/designers than those treated
here, and some of them with other purposes). And in America the "Great
Books" became a household term, a commercial enterprise, and a familiar
formula for a traditional humanistic curriculum (stirring another round of
"culture wars" in the 1980s and 1990s over the preeminence of the classics
by "Dead White European Males" that Adler steadfastly defended, as did
that other Chicago traditionalist Allan Bloom in his widely read *The Closing
of the American Mind* [1987]). But such accomplishments did not in themselves mean that the purposes behind them had been achieved.

If the modernist style in art and design surrounds us, has culture attained the humanistic wholeness desired by Gropius and Moholy-Nagy, or
has modernism simply been tamed and absorbed into the consumer culture?
If bold modernist images accompanied by Great Ideas attract wide notice in

advertisements, have those images and ideas provoked thought, or have they merely become catchy emblems of a corporate image? If the *Great Books of the Western World* sit in a million homes and many thousands of Americans participate in Great Books discussion groups, has the Chicago Bildungsideal prevailed, or has it just provided middle-class Americans with a high-brow, unread library and occasions for book-chat socializing? If the Aspen Institute summons thousands of executives and other leaders of American life to its chambers to discuss the classics or pressing issues of the day, have humanistic ideas taken hold among those leaders, or have these ideas only become a pretext for members of the "power elite" to "network" and strengthen their hand in American society?

These were the kinds of questions that critics on the political left had been asking about capitalist culture since the 1920s, with the likes of Antonio Gramsci and the thinkers of the Frankfurt Institute for Social Research. In the late sixties, such questions became the battle cries of anticapitalist radicals fired by the writings of the former Frankfurt Institute theorist Herbert Marcuse. By the 1980s and 1990s, legions of "postmodern" critics considered the answers obvious, if ironic (irony having become the hallmark of postmodern historical understanding). Namely, the deepening relations between commerce and culture over the course of the twentieth century had brought the wholesale, if ironically deceptive, domination of culture by commercial interests that ingeniously use culture to mask that domination. For when artists and intellectuals allied their cultural aspirations with commercial interests, they helped unify modern culture all right, but they did so in the service of commerce and at the cost of diminishing the power of art and ideas to stir thought, to criticize the world as it is, and to provide guidance for change. To the postmodern temper, that was the irony of postmodern times, proving the insidiously malleable and relentless power of advanced, postindustrial consumer capitalism.[64] Or, as a prominent postmodern theorist puts it, drawing on the title of this book, the postmodern historical condition is a child of "the romance of commerce and culture."[65] Even if this postmodern, capitalist, consumer culture could be said to have helped bring about the decline and fall of the oppressive Soviet communist empire, critics would see it threatening to devour all cultures in the name of globalization.[66] This prospect was not lost on the fiftieth anniversary celebration of the Aspen Institute, which carried on its sobering explorations of the theme while protesters against the domination of global capitalism marched in the streets of Aspen (and as Arab terrorists were plotting strategies to bring America's global power to its knees).

But such anticapitalist "postmodern critiques" aside, when the arts and ideas have become the allies, and sometimes the servants, of commerce, we know that at least times have changed from the heady ambitions for cultural reform during the high tide of modernism. The reaction against modernism in the arts that arose in the 1960s, spread in the 1970s and 1980s, and became the creed of artistic "postmodernism" by the 1990s, confirmed the fact. Books and articles flowed from the presses proclaiming the cultural watershed of postmodernism, from architecture, design, and painting, to literature, dance, and photography.[67] Under this onslaught, the modernist idea of the arts, which had regarded modern artistic creation as a revelation of elemental human and metaphysical realities, and as a means of lending aesthetic form to the modern spirit and of bringing spiritual and humanistic unity to modern culture, gave way to a "postmodern" rationale for whimsical experiment, eclectic forms, and a pop-consumer style (amounting to a mirror image of the "postmodern critique" of some of the same practices).

Postmodern artists and their advocates therefore debunked the earnest ideology of early modernists like the Bauhaus artist/designers for their "prissily puristic aesthetic,"[68] and promoted instead the witty virtues of, say, Las Vegas casino signs[69] and "business art."[70] Many critics deemed modern architecture a particular "failure," even a "fiasco," and blamed Gropius for it.[71] Undoubtedly, this postmodern artistic temper marked a departure from the ideals of modernism, for good or ill.

At the beginning of the twenty-first century, it was therefore evident for manifold reasons that the era of early consumer capitalism, modernism, and the dominance of a moralistic, self-denying character type, along with that of the Chicago-Aspen crusade for cultural reform, had run its course. With this collective passing, the romance of commerce and culture did not altogether come to an end. But it surely shed its youthfully ardent passions and idealistic hopes and settled into a comfortable, if uncertain, marriage of convenience.

notes

Unless otherwise credited, all unpublished documents and printed institutional materials come from the Walter Paul Paepcke Archives by permission of the late Elizabeth H. Paepcke. Those archives now constitute the Walter P. Paepcke Papers, 1912–1961, in the Special Collections of the University of Chicago Library. All interviews were conducted by the author.

Abbreviations

MJA	Mortimer J. Adler
RG	Ronald Goodman
RMH	Robert Maynard Hutchins
LM-N	László Moholy-Nagy
SM-N	Sibyl Moholy-Nagy
EHP	Elizabeth H. Paepcke (Mrs. Walter Paul Paepcke)
WPP	Walter Paul Paepcke

Introduction

1. For perceptive, frequently persuasive, criticisms of the kinds of historical develop ments recorded herein, see, e.g., Daniel J. Boorstin, *The Image: A Guide to*

Pseudo-Events in America, originally published as *The Image, or What Happened to the American Dream* (New York: Atheneum, 1961); Dwight MacDonald, *Against the American Grain* (New York: Random House, 1962); *Power Politics and People: The Collected Essays of C. Wright Mills*, ed. Irving Louis Horowitz (New York: Oxford University Press Paperback, 1967); Herbert Marcuse, *One-Dimensional Man: Studies in the Ideology of Advanced Industrial Society* (Boston: Beacon Press, 1964); Stuart Ewen, *Captains of Consciousness: Advertising and the Social Roots of the Consumer Culture* (New York: McGraw-Hill, 1976), and *All-Consuming Images: The Politics of Style in Contemporary Culture* (New York: Basic Books, 1988); Jeffrey L. Meikle, *Twentieth Century Limited: Industrial Design in America, 1925–1939* (Philadelphia: Temple University Press, 1979); Fredric Jameson, *Postmodernism: The Cultural Logic of Late Capitalism* (Durham: Duke University Press, 1991); Jean Baudrillard, *The Consumer Society: Myths and Structures* (London: Sage, 1998).

Chapter I

1. Alexander Dorner, *The Way Beyond "Art": The Work of Herbert Bayer*, Problems of Contemporary Art, no. 3 (New York: Wittenborn, Schultz, 1947).
2. Andy Warhol, *The Philosophy of Andy Warhol (From A to B and Back Again)* (New York: Harcourt Brace Jovanovich, 1975; Harbrace Paperbound Library, 1977), 92.
3. Quoted in Daniel J. Boorstin, *The Americans: The Democratic Experience* (New York: Random House, 1973), 107.
4. On the consumer revolution, see, e.g., ibid., pt. 2; Alfred D. Chandler, Jr., *The Visible Hand: The Managerial Revolution in American Business* (Cambridge: Harvard University Press, 1977), pts. 3, 4; Peter Mathias, *Retailing Revolution: A History of Multiple Retailing in the Food Trades Based on the Allied Suppliers Group of Companies* (London: Longmans, 1967); William Leach, *Land of Desire: Merchants, Power, and the Rise of a New American Culture* (New York: Pantheon, 1993).
5. Boorstin, *The Americans*, 106; on the "agate rule," ibid., 106, 138–142.
6. Ibid., 149–150.
7. Quoted in Gilman M. Ostrander, *American Civilization in the First Machine Age, 1890–1940* (New York: Harper Torchbooks, 1972), 223.
8. Boorstin, *The Americans*, 146; Otto Pease, *The Responsibilities of American Advertising: Private Control and Public Influence, 1920–1940* (New Haven: Yale University Press, 1958), 12, 13. For recent figures, see, e.g., "Advertising," *New York Times Almanac 2001* (New York: Penguin Group, 2000). On the history of advertising, see also Daniel Pope, *The Making of Modern Advertising* (New York: Basic Books, 1983); Roland Marchand, *Advertising the American Dream: Making Way for Modernity, 1920–1940* (Berkeley: University of California Press, 1985); L. Jackson Lears, *Fables of Abundance: A Cultural History of American Advertising* (New York: Basic Books, 1994).
9. Kasimir Malevich, *The Non-Objective World (1918)*, trans. Howard Dearstyne (Chicago: Theobald, 1959). On Impressionism and abstraction, see Meyer

Schapiro's early essays "Matisse and Impressionism," A Review of the Retrospective Exhibition of Matisse at the Museum of Modern Art, New York, November 1931 (New York: Meyer Schapiro, 1931); and "The Nature of Abstract Art" (1937), in Meyer Schapiro, *Modern Art: 19th and 20th Centuries. Selected Papers* (New York: George Braziller, 1978), 185–211.

10. See E. H. Gombrich, *The Sense of Order: A Study in the Psychology of Decorative Art* (Ithaca, N.Y.: Cornell University Press, 1979), chaps. 2, 4.

11. Quoted in ibid., 58.

12. Charles W. Mears, "Advertising That Appeals to the Senses—the Coming Type," *Printers' Ink* 90 (21 January 1915); Fred W. Hunter, "Suggestion in Advertising," *Printers' Ink* 50 (15 March 1905); Frank H. Holman, "Applying 'New Thought' or Psychotherapy to the Dealer," *Printers' Ink* 72 (25 August 1910). All cited in Merle Curti, "The Changing Concept of 'Human Nature' in the Literature of American Advertising," *Business History Review* 41, no. 4 (Winter 1967), 347, 348.

13. Ernest Elmo Calkins, *Modern Advertising* (New York: Appleton, 1905), 3; Ernest Elmo Calkins, *"And Hearing Not—" Annals of an Adman* (New York: Scribner, 1946), 239. Both quoted in Meikle, *Twentieth Century Limited* (see intro., n. 1), 10.

14. Perry Duis, *Chicago: Creating New Traditions* (Chicago: Chicago Historical Society, 1976), 112; Curti, "Changing Concept," 342–343.

15. "Taking Art to the People through Outdoor Advertising," interview by G. A. Nichols with Lorado Taft, *Printers' Ink Monthly* 8, no. 6 (June 1924), 21, 22.

16. John B. Watson, *Psychological Care of Infant and Child* (New York, 1928), 187, excerpted in Robert Sklar, ed., *The Plastic Age (1917–1930)* (New York: Braziller, 1970), 315.

17. Quoted in Edward T. Hill, "Do Most People Really Think?" *Printers' Ink* 135 (17 June 1926), 150.

18. E. P. Corbett, "The Sales Letter and the Personal Appeal," *Printers' Ink* 110 (12 February 1920), 161–169.

19. Frederick Parker Anderson, "'Conscious' Advertising Copy," *Printers' Ink* 136, no. 8 (19 August 1926), 130. Quoted in Stuart Ewen, *Captains* (see intro., n. 1), 39.

20. Robert Atwan, Donald McQuade, and John W. Wright, *Edsels, Luckies and Frigidaires: Advertising the American Way* (New York: Dell, 1979), 268.

21. Frank Presbrey, *The History and Development of Advertising* (Garden City, N.Y.: Doubleday, 1929), "Advertising Appendix." Quoted in Ewen, *Captains*, 102.

22. Atwan, McQuade, and Wright, *Edsels,* 270.

23. Quoted in Ostrander, *American Civilization,* 223.

24. László Moholy-Nagy, "Modern Typography: Aims, Practice, Criticism," *Offset, Buch und Werbekunst,* no. 7 (1926), in Hans M. Wingler, *The Bauhaus: Weimar, Dessau, Berlin, Chicago,* trans. Wolfgang Jabs and Basil Gilbert, ed. Joseph Stein (Cambridge: MIT Press, 1969), 80.

25. "The Impressionistic Poster as the Sign of the Product," *Westvaco Inspirations for Printers,* no. 5 (1925).

26. *Westvaco Inspirations,* no. 33 (1928), cover.

27. Ibid., no. 53.

28. Ibid., no. 53, 1047.
29. Ibid., no. 53, 1056.
30. Roy Dickenson, "Freshen Up Your Product," *Printers' Ink* 150, no. 6 (6 February 1930), 163. Quoted in Ewen, *Captains*, 39.
31. See Boorstin, *The Americans*, chap. 49.
32. Richard B. Franken and Carroll B. Larrabee, *Packages That Sell* (New York: Harper, 1928), 87ff.
33. Frank H. Young, "Modern Layouts Must Sell Rather Than Startle," *Advertising and Selling* 14, no. 6, sec. 2, "Advertising Arts" (8 January 1930), 25–27; Ernest Elmo Calkins, "Art as a Means to an End," ibid., 17–23.
34. Henry Eckhard, "The Demise of Quality," *Advertising and Selling* 15, no. 8 (20 August 1930), 17.
35. Richard Hofstadter, *Anti-Intellectualism in American Life* (New York: Knopf, 1963), 234.
36. Fritz Stern, "Capitalism and the Cultural Historian," in *From Parnassus: Essays in Honor of Jacques Barzun*, ed. Dora B. Weiner and William Keylor (New York: Harper and Row, 1976), 217; Fritz Stern, *Gold and Iron: Bismarck, Bleichröder, and the Building of the German Empire* (New York: Knopf, 1977), 228.
37. Edith Wharton, *A Backward Glance* (1934). Quoted in Joseph Epstein, *Ambition: The Secret Passion* (New York: Dutton, 1981), 170.
38. Quoted in Stern, *Gold and Iron*, 228 n.
39. Quoted in John G. Cawelti, *Apostles of the Self-Made Man* (Chicago: University of Chicago Press, 1965), 159.
40. Quoted in Hofstadter, *Anti-Intellectualism*, 245.
41. Charles L. Hutchinson, "Art: Its Influence and Excellence in Modern Times." Quoted in Helen Lefkowitz Horowitz, *Culture and the City: Cultural Philanthropy in Chicago from the 1880s to 1917* (Lexington: University of Kentucky Press, 1976), 75.
42. Quoted in Hofstadter, *Anti-Intellectualism*, 259.
43. Quoted in Horowitz, *Culture and the City*, 88.
44. Quoted in Ostrander, *American Civilization*, 225.
45. Sinclair Lewis, *Babbitt* (New York: Grosset & Dunlap, 1922), 18, 13.
46. Roger Babson, *What Is Success?* (1923), quoted in Cawelti, *Apostles*, 185.
47. Quoted in Robert T. Elson, *The World of Time Inc.: The Intimate History of a Publishing Enterprise*, vol 2: *1941–1960* (New York: Atheneum, 1973), 199.
48. Quoted in Frederick J. Hoffman, *The Twenties: American Writing in the Postwar Decade* (New York: Viking, 1955), 326.
49. Quoted in Ewen, *Captains*, 100.
50. Quoted in ibid., 101.
51. Alice Paepcke Guenzel, interview, Chicago, 29 June 1977.
52. EHP, interview, Aspen, 26 July 1977.
53. Letter to Herbert Bayer, 28 October 1953 (courtesy Herbert and Joella Bayer).
54. Quoted in Arthur Van Vlissingen, "He Knows How to Kill Price Wars," *Forbes*, 15 September 1937, 15.

55. "War in Container," *Time*, 23 March 1931, 52.

56. Sydney Harris, interview, Chicago, 17 April 1979.

57. WPP, interoffice memo to Wesley Dixon, 5 April 1932.

58. Van Vlissingen, "He Knows How," 38.

59. "Biggest Unit in the Paperboard Industry," *Barron's*, 11 October 1937, 13.

60. "Container Kraft," *Time*, 1 June 1936, 58.

61. "Biggest Unit," 13.

62. Quoted in Russell Lynes, *The Tastemakers* (New York: Grosset & Dunlap, 1954), 291.

63. WPP's words quoted in letter to him, 27 December 1938; WPP to M. J. Lacey, 28 December 1938.

64. Ralph M. Hower, *The History of an Advertising Agency: N.W. Ayer & Son at Work, 1869–1949* (Cambridge: Harvard University Press, 1949), 212.

65. "Container Kraft," *Time*, 1 June 1936, 58.

66. WPP to Mary Farrell, 23 April 1932.

67. EHP, interview, Chicago, 17 January 1978.

68. Russell Lynes, *Good Old Modern* (New York: Atheneum, 1973), 104.

69. EHP, interview, Chicago, 17 January 1978.

70. WPP, address delivered at the meeting of the Art Directors' Club of Chicago, 19 May 1936, 1–25 passim.

71. Noel Coward to WPP, n.d. [1936].

72. WPP, address, 19 May 1936, 18.

73. WPP, "'Great Ideas' Recall Our Heritage, Help Build Container," *Industrial Marketing,* January 1955.

74. Charles T. Coiner, telephone interview, 14 February 1978.

75. WPP to Egbert Jacobson, 5 August 1937.

76. Quoted in "Prepackaged War," *Fortune*, December 1941, 170.

77. Letter to Container Corporation of America, 1 June 1945.

78. Letter to President, Container Corporation of America, 27 May 1945.

79. WPP, "'Great Ideas,'" *Industrial Marketing*, January 1955.

80. John E. Mertes, "Corporate Response to the Artist," *MSU Business Topics* 22 no. 4 (Autumn 1974), 45–46.

81. "Container Corporation of America," *Gebrauchsgraphik* 15, no. 7 (July 1938), 19, 28.

82. Quoted in "The Art Department: A Review of Five Years' Work," *Concora News* (Container Corporation of America), 1940.

83. Lynes, *Tastemakers,* 295.

84. "Charles Coiner, Art Director," *Portfolio* 1, no. 2 (Summer 1950).

85. Franklin Baker and Gladys Hinnus, "Does Fine Art Pay?" *Printers' Ink* 122, no.1 (January 1948), 30–31.

86. Lynes, *Tastemakers,* 295; Mertes, "Corporate Response," 46–51.

87. Hal Burnett, "Container Corporation's Design for Business," *Industrial Marketing,* April 1948, 35.

88. Copy Chasers, "Board Chairman Surprise Choice as Advertising Man of Year," *Industrial Marketing,* January 1955.

89. WPP, address, 19 May 1936, 12.

90. Egbert Jacobson, "The Science of Color," *More Business* 2, no. 11 (November 1937), 2.

91. Burnett, "Container Corporation's Design," 38.

92. "Prepackaged War," 87.

93. WPP to Tirey L. Ford, 25 January 1943.

94. Letter to WPP, 26 May 1950.

95. Letter to WPP, 25 February 1952.

96. Letter to Egbert Jacobson, 12 December 1951.

97. Norman DeHaan, interview, Chicago, 6 May 1977.

98. See *Art, Design and the Modern Corporation: The Collection of Container Corporation of America.* Catalogue by Martina Roudabush Norelli; essay, "Designs on Demand: Art and the Modern Corporation," by Neil Harris (Washington, D.C.: Smithsonian Institution Press, 1985).

Chapter 2

1. LM-N to SM-N, 4 July 1937, quoted in SM-N, *Moholy-Nagy: Experiment in Totality*, 2d ed. (Cambridge: MIT Press, 1969), 141. This biography is reverent and not wholly reliable but a moving and largely persuasive portrait of its subject.

2. LM-N to SM-N, 5 July 1937, quoted in ibid.

3. LM-N to SM-N, 8 July 1937, quoted in ibid., 142–143.

4. LM-N to SM-N, 16 July 1937, quoted in ibid., 143.

5. LM-N to SM-N, 27 July 1937, quoted in ibid., 144–145.

6. Norma K. Stahle to LM-N, 29 May 1937, quoted in ibid., 140.

7. A detailed history of the association and the circumstances leading to the settling of the Bauhaus in Chicago is given in Lloyd C. Engelbrecht, "The Association of Arts and Industries: Background and Origins of the Bauhaus Movement in Chicago," Ph.D. diss., University of Chicago, 1973.

8. Quoted in Sidney C. Hutchinson, *The History of the Royal Academy, 1768–1968* (New York: Taplinger, 1968), 43.

9. Quoted in Herbert Read, *Art and Industry: The Principles of Industrial Design* (1934; reprint, Bloomington: Indiana University Press, 1961), 6.

10. Quoted in ibid., 7.

11. Nicholas Pevsner, *Pioneers of Modern Design: From William Morris to Walter Gropius*, rev ed. (Harmondsworth, England: Penguin, 1960), 29.

12. Quoted in H. Montgomery Hyde, *Oscar Wilde: A Biography* (New York: Farrar, Straus & Giroux, 1975), 65, 66.

13. See Gwendolyn Wright, *Moralism and the Modern Home: Domestic Architecture and Cultural Conflict in Chicago, 1873–1913* (Chicago: University of Chicago Press, 1980). For an earlier moralistic impetus to artistic design in everyday objects, see Neil Harris, *Humbug: The Art of P. T. Barnum* (Boston: Little, Brown, 1973; Chicago: University of Chicago Press, Phoenix Books, 1981), 80–82.

14. William Morris, "The Aims of Art," in Eugen Weber, ed., *Paths to the Present: Aspects of European Thought from Romanticism to Existentialism* (New York: Dodd, Mead, 1973), 319.

15. Frank Lloyd Wright, "The Art and Craft of the Machine," in *Frank Lloyd Wright: Writings and Buildings*, selected by Edgar Kaufmann and Ben Raeburn (New York: Horizon Press, 1960), 55.

16. Hermann Muthesius, *The English House*, excerpted in Tim and Charlotte Benton, eds., *Architecture and Design, 1890–1939: An International Anthology of Original Articles* (New York: Whitney Library of Design, 1975), 35.

17. Quoted in Reyner Banham, *Theory and Design in the First Machine Age*, 2d ed. (New York: Praeger, 1967), 70.

18. Quoted in Pevsner, *Pioneers*, 35.

19. Quoted in ibid., 36.

20. Ibid.

21. H. H. Peach, "Museums and the Design and Industries Association," *American Magazine of Art* 7, no. 5 (March 1916), 198.

22. Quoted in Peter Gay, *Art and Act: On Causes in History—Manet, Gropius, Mondrian* (New York: Harper & Row, 1976), 121.

23. Quoted in ibid., 169. On the developments described here and especially Gropius's relation to them, see ibid., chap. 3. On Behrens in particular, see Alan Windsor, *Peter Behrens: Architect and Designer, 1869–1940* (New York: Whitney Library of Design, 1981).

24. Quoted in *Chicago Daily News*, 23 May 1922, 16; Engelbrecht, "The Association," 126, 127.

25. Louis H. Sullivan, *The Autobiography of an Idea* (1924; reprint, New York: Dover [1956]), 325.

26. See Stanley Tigerman, comp., *Late Entries to the Tribune Tower Competition*, introduction by Stuart E. Cohen and critical essays by George Baird and others (New York: Rizzoli, 1980).

27. Charles Norman, *Ezra Pound* (New York: Macmillan, 1960), 199.

28. Katharine Kuh, interview, New York, 12 May 1977.

29. *Chicago Evening Post Magazine of the Art World*, 27 January 1931, 6, quoted in Engelbrecht, "The Association," 135.

30. *Chicago Evening Post Magazine of the Art World*, 31 March 1931, 3, quoted in ibid.

31. *Report of Commission Appointed by the Secretary of Commerce to Visit and Report upon the International Exposition of Modern Decorative and Industrial Art in Paris, 1925*, 13.

32. Unsigned editorial, *American Magazine of Art*, 15, no. 10 (October 1924), 540.

33. *Report of Commission*, 17, 18.

34. Joseph Breck, assistant director of the Metropolitan Museum of Art, New York, quoted in unsigned article, "Modern Decorative Arts from Paris at the Metropolitan Museum of Art," *American Magazine of Art*, 17, no. 4 (April 1926), 170.

35. *Report of Commission*, 16.

36. Ibid., 21.

37. Emily Genauer, *Modern Interiors Today and Tomorrow: A Critical Analysis of Trends in Contemporary Decoration as Seen at the Paris Exposition of Arts and Techniques and Reflected at the New York World's Fair* (New York: Illustrated Editions, 1939), 14.

38. "Current Topics of Trade Interest," *Good Furniture Magazine* 31, no. 3 (September 1928), 116.

39. Douglas C. McMurtrie, *Modern Typography and Layout* (Chicago: Eyncourt Press, 1929), 16.

40. Ibid., 143.

41. Quoted in Olga Gueft, "A Salute to the American Society of Interior Designers," *Interiors*, January 1975, 79.

42. Sullivan, *Autobiography*, 324.

43. *Architecture of Skidmore, Owings & Merrill, 1950–1962*, text by Ernest Danz, introduction by Henry-Russell Hitchcock (New York: Praeger, 1963), 9.

44. On the best of these American designers, see Meikle, *Twentieth Century Limited* (see intro., n. 1).

45. C. J. Bulliet, *Apples and Madonnas: Emotional Expression in Modern Art* (Chicago: Pascal Covici, 1927), 182.

46. E. N. Benson, "Wanted: An American Bauhaus," *American Magazine of Art* 27, no. 6 (June 1934), 307–311.

47. George Fred Keck, "A History of the Institute of Design," unpublished lecture at the Institute of Design, 18 August 1955.

48. Quoted in Banham, *Theory and Design*, 76–77.

49. See Peter Gay, *Weimar Culture: The Outsider as Insider* (New York: Harper & Row, 1968), chap. 4, "The Hunger for Wholeness: Trials of Modernity."

50. Walter Gropius, *Program of the Staatliche Bauhaus in Weimar*, April 1919; "Address to the Students of the Staatliche Bauhaus," July 1919, both in Wingler, *The Bauhaus* (see chap. 1, n. 24), 31, 36.

51. Walter Gropius, *The Theory and Organization of the Bauhaus* (1923), in Herbert Bayer, Walter Gropius, and Ise Gropius eds., *Bauhaus, 1919–1928* (1938; paperbound edition, New York: Museum of Modern Art, 1975), 20.

52. Gropius, "Address to the Students"; Walter Gropius, "The Work of the Bauhaus Stage," October 1922, both in Wingler, *The Bauhaus*, 36, 58.

53. Walter Gropius, *The New Architecture and the Bauhaus*, trans. P. Morton Shand (1935; Cambridge: MIT Press, paperbound, 1965), 75.

54. Ibid., 65.

55. Gropius, *Program of the Staatliche Bauhaus*, in Wingler, *The Bauhaus*, 132.

56. Gropius, *The New Architecture*, 71.

57. Walter Gropius, "The Viability of the Bauhaus Idea," in Wingler, *The Bauhaus*, 52.

58. Lyonel Feininger to Julia Feininger, 12 March 1925, in Wingler, *The Bauhaus*, 97.

59. Walter Gropius, Preface to LM-N, *The New Vision*, 3d ed., trans. Daphne M. Hoffman, published with *Abstract of an Artist*, The Documents of Modern Art, Robert Motherwell, director (New York: Wittenborn, 1946), 5.

60. Gillian Naylor, *The Bauhaus* (London: Studio Vista/Dutton Pictureback, 1968), 109.

61. LM-N, *Malerei—Photography—Film*, 28. Quoted in SM-N, *Moholy-Nagy*, 37, 38.

62. LM-N, "From Pigment to Light," *Telehor* (1936), in *Moholy-Nagy*, ed. Richard Kostelanetz, Documentary Monographs in Modern Art (New York: Praeger, 1970), 33.

63. See LM-N, *Painting, Photography, Film*, 2d ed. of *Malerei—Photography—Film* (1927), trans. Janet Seligman with a note by Hans M. Wingler and postscript by Otto Stelzer (Cambridge: MIT Press, 1969; paperbound ed., 1973); Andreas Haus, *Moholy-Nagy: Photographs and Photograms*, trans. Frederic Samson (New York: Pantheon Books, 1980); Richard Kostelanetz, "Moholy-Nagy: Risk and Necessity of Artistic Adventurism," *Salmagundi*, 10–11 (Fall 1969–Winter 1970), in *Moholy-Nagy*, ed. Kostelanetz, 3–16.

64. Quoted in SM-N, *Moholy-Nagy*, 12.

65. LM-N, *New Vision*, 15, 32.

66. LM-N, "Subject without Art," *The Studio* 12, no. 259 (November 4, 1936), in *Moholy-Nagy*, ed. Kostelanetz, 43.

67. See Gyorgy Kepes, *Language of Vision* (Chicago: Theobald, 1944); Alexander Dorner, *The Way Beyond "Art"* (see chap. 1, n. 1); Sigfried Giedion, *Space, Time, and Architecture*, 5th ed. (Cambridge: Harvard University Press, 1967); Giedion, *Mechanization Takes Command* (New York: Oxford University Press, 1948).

68. Quoted in SM-N, *Moholy-Nagy*, 46.

69. Walter Gropius to Norma K. Stahle, 18 May 1937, in Wingler, *The Bauhaus*, 192.

70. Quoted in SM-N, *Moholy-Nagy*, 137.

71. Norma K. Stahle to LM-N, 7 June 1937, quoted in ibid., 139.

72. SM-N to LM-N, 8 June 1937, quoted in ibid., 139.

73. Norma K. Stahle to LM-N, 13 June 1937, quoted in ibid., 139.

74. Norma K. Stahle to LM-N, 29 May 1937, quoted in ibid., 140.

75. LM-N to SM-N, 8 August 1937, quoted in ibid., 145.

76. See A. Conger Goodyear, *The Museum of Modern Art: The First Ten Years* (Goodyear, 1943), 70.

77. Quoted in Katharine Kuh, *Saturday Review*, 23 January 1965, 61.

78. Katharine Kuh, interview, New York, 26 January 1977.

79. Norman DeHaan, interview, Chicago, 16 May 1977.

80. Quoted by Robert Jay Wolff, interview, New Preston, Conn., 30 March 1977.

81. SM-N, *Moholy-Nagy*, 191.

82. LM-N, "The Contribution of the Arts to Social Reconstruction," lecture, 1943, in *Moholy-Nagy*, ed. Kostelanetz, 19, 21.

83. LM-N, *New Vision*, 17.

84. Norma K. Stahle, quoted in *Chicago Daily News*, 23 August 1937, 11, quoted in Engelbrecht, "The Association," 231.

85. SM-N, *Moholy-Nagy*, 148.

86. Quoted in ibid., 149–150.

87. Quoted in ibid., 150.

88. Quoted in ibid., 150–151.

89. Herbert Feigl, "The Wiener Kreis in America," in Donald Fleming and Bernard Bailyn, eds., *The Intellectual Migration: Europe and America, 1930–1960* (Cambridge: Harvard University Press, 1969), 637.

90. Charles Morris, "The Contribution of Science to the Designer's Task," prospectus, *The New Bauhaus, Chicago, 1937–1938*, in Wingler, *The Bauhaus*, 195.

91. LM-N to Executive Committee, 30 October 1937, quoted in SM-N, *Moholy-Nagy*, 155.

92. Quoted in ibid., 154–155.

93. See Joseph Mileck, *Hermann Hesse: Life and Art* (Berkeley and Los Angeles: University of California Press, 1977), 255–264.

94. Norma K. Stahle to Walter Gropius, 30 August 1938, quoted in SM-N, *Moholy-Nagy*, 162.

95. LM-N to WPP, 25 January 1939.

96. Quoted by EHP, interview, Chicago, 16 April 1979.

97. *School of Design*, prospectus (1939–1940), 1.

98. *The School of Design in Chicago*, prospectus, n.d. [1940–], 1–24 passim.

99. Quoted in SM-N, *Moholy-Nagy*, 172.

100. Robert Jay Wolff, interview, New Preston, Conn., 30 March 1977.

101. SM-N, "Moholy-Nagy: The Chicago Years," in *Moholy-Nagy*, ed. Kostelanetz, 23.

102. SM-N to WPP, 6 March 1939.

103. LM-N to WPP, 20 April 1939.

104. Quoted in SM-N, *Moholy-Nagy*, 213.

105. Quoted by Katharine Kuh, interview, New York, 12 May 1977.

106. Letter to WPP, 12 June 1945.

107. Letter to WPP, 25 July 1945.

108. Quoted in John Chancellor, "The Rocky Road from the Bauhaus," *Chicago Magazine*, July 1955.

109. Robert Yoder, "Are You a Contemporary?" *Saturday Evening Post*, July 1943.

110. LM-N, "Better Than Before?" *Technology Review* 46, no. 1 (November 1943).

111. Letter to WPP, 19 August 1942.

112. LM-N to WPP, 5 August 1942.

113. Quoted in letter of Rockefeller Foundation official to WPP, 12 June 1945.

114. Quoted in SM-N, *Moholy-Nagy*, 216.

115. WPP to LM-N, 14 April 1944.

116. WPP to George Fred Keck, 8 February 1944.

117. WPP to Walter Gropius, 7 February 1944.

118. WPP memorandum to Donald Fairchild, n.d. [1944].

119. Letter to Mr. [Jesse A.] Jacobs, 12 December 1944.

120. WPP to Arnold Epstein, 9 January 1945.

121. "A Presentation of the Institute of Design," April 1944.

122. Catalogue, *Institute of Design, 1945–1946*, 14.

123. Letter to W. A. Patterson, 16 July 1945.

124. Walter Gropius to WPP, 28 February 1945.

125. Letter of 11 May 1945, quoted in SM-N, *Moholy-Nagy*, 218.

126. Quoted in ibid., 224.

127. Minutes of meeting of the Board of Directors, Institute of Design, 1 May 1945.

128. Walter Gropius to WPP, 28 February 1945.

129. *Exhibition of the Advance Guard of Advertising Artists*, exhibition catalogue, Katharine Kuh Gallery, Chicago, December 1941.

130. Walter Gropius to WPP, 12 March 1945.

131. *Modern Art in Advertising: An Exhibition of Designs for Container Corporation of America*, exhibition catalogue, Art Institute of Chicago (27 April–23 June 1945), 25.

132. Sigfried Giedion to WPP, 29 June 1945.

133. Rosamund Frost, "This Business Ties Art into a Neat Package," *Art News*, 15–31 May 1945, 13.

134. Hal Burnett, "Container Corporation's Design for Business," *Industrial Marketing*, April 1948, 39.

135. WPP to Houston McBain, 10 April 1945.

136. WPP to Houston McBain, 21 March 1946.

137. Letter to WPP, 22 September 1945.

138. LM-N to WPP, 31 July 1946.

139. LM-N to WPP, 21 November 1946.

140. Ibid.

141. Quoted in SM-N, *Moholy-Nagy*, 243.

142. Quoted in ibid., 243.

143. Robert Jay Wolff to SM-N, 2 May 1949, quoted in ibid., 251.

144. Quoted in ibid., 148.

145. Quoted in ibid., 236.

146. LM-N, *Vision in Motion* (Chicago: Theobald, 1947; reprint, 1969), 114.

147. Ibid., *153*.

148. Ibid., 360-61.

149. EHP, interview, Chicago, 16 May 1977.

150. Walter Gropius to WPP, 3 December 1946.

151. Quoted in SM-N, *Moholy-Nagy*, 241.

152. Some critics have viewed Moholy's career in Chicago as a betrayal of his previous experimental spirit for the rewards of commercialism. See Andreas Haus, *Moholy-Nagy* (n. 63 above), and Hilton Kramer, "Moholy-Nagy," in Kramer's *The Age of the Avant Garde: An Art Chronicle of 1956–1972* (New York: Farrar, Straus & Giroux, 1973), 144–147.

153. Gropius and Mies to John T. Rattalieta, president, IIT, 6 November 1954.

154. Harry Weese, interview, Chicago, 21 January 1978.

155. Quoted in William H. Jordy, "The Aftermath of the Bauhaus in America," in Fleming and Bailyn, eds., *Intellectual Migration* (see n. 89), 506.

Chapter 3

1. Quoted in obituary, *New York Times*, 16 May 1977. See Mary Ann Dzuback, *Robert M. Hutchins: Portrait of an Educator* (Chicago: University of Chicago Press, 1991).
2. Daniel J. Boorstin, *The Image* (see intro., n. 1), 188.
3. Ibid., 188–189.
4. *Time*, 21 November 1949, cover.
5. Quoted in obituary, *New York Times*, 16 May 1977.
6. RMH, Convocation address, University of Chicago, 1930; published as "Education and Research, II," in RMH, *No Friendly Voice* (Chicago: University of Chicago Press, 1936), 184.
7. Quoted in MJA, *Philosopher at Large: An Intellectual Autobiography* (New York: Macmillan, 1977), 129.
8. Ibid., 42.
9. Ibid., 25.
10. Justus Buchler, "Reconstruction in the Liberal Arts," in *A History of Columbia College on Morningside* (New York: Columbia University Press, 1954).
11. Quoted in MJA, *Philosopher at Large*, 31.
12. Ibid., 31.
13. MJA to RMH, December 1929, quoted in ibid., 131.
14. Ibid., 132.
15. RMH to MJA, June 1930, quoted in ibid., 132.
16. The account of the curricular reforms is largely derived from: RMH, "The Chicago Plan," in *No Friendly Voice*, 188–196; MJA, *Philosopher at Large*, chaps. 7–9; Daniel Bell, *The Reforming of General Education: The Columbia College Experience in Its National Setting* (New York: Columbia University Press, 1966), 26–38. See also Dzuback, *Robert M. Hutchins*.
17. John Chamberlain, quoted in MJA, *Philosopher at Large*, 149.
18. RMH, "The Chicago Plan," 191.
19. Quoted in obituary, *New York Times*, 16 May 1977.
20. Matthew Arnold, *Culture and Anarchy* (1869; New York: Macmillan, 1925), 67.
21. RMH, "The Higher Learning, I," in *No Friendly Voice*, 25, 30.
22. MJA, *Philosopher at Large*, 171.
23. Quoted in MJA, "The Chicago School," *Harper's Magazine*, September 1941, in MJA, *Reforming Education: The Schooling of a People and Their Education Beyond Schooling* (Boulder, Colo.: Westview Press, 1977), 38.
24. Ibid., 39.
25. MJA, "Liberalism and Liberal Education," *Educational Record*, July 1939, in MJA, *Reforming Education*, 48.
26. MJA, "Are There Absolute and Universal Principles on Which Education Should Be Founded?" *Educational Trends*, July–August 1941, in MJA, *Reforming Education*, 61–73.
27. MJA, "An Analysis of the Kinds of Knowledge," unpublished manuscript dated May 1935, RMH Papers, University of Chicago Library.

28. RMH, *The Higher Learning in America* (New Haven: Yale University Press, 1936), 94.

29. MJA to RMH, 26 March 1937, RMH Papers, University of Chicago Library.

30. RMH, *Higher Learning*, 99, 100.

31. Ibid., 105.

32. Ibid., 87.

33. Ibid.

34. Ibid., 105.

35. John Erskine, *Memory of Certain Persons* (Philadelphia, New York: Lippincott, 1947), 343.

36. John Dewey, review of RMH, *The Higher Learning, Social Frontier*, January 1937. Quoted in MJA, *Philosopher at Large*, 183.

37. John Dewey, "Challenge to Liberal Thought," *Fortune* 30 (August 1944), 155, 156.

38. Quoted in *Time*, 21 November 1949, 62.

39. Quoted in MJA, *Philosopher at Large*, 184.

40. Quoted in *Chicago Tribune*, 13 April 1935, front page.

41. *Chicago Tribune*, 12 April 1935.

42. Quoted in obituary, *New York Times*, 16 May 1977.

43. MJA, *Philosopher at Large*, 184–185.

44. Ibid., 188–189.

45. MJA, "This Pre-War Generation," *Harper's Magazine*, October 1940, in MJA, *Reforming Education*, 13.

46. Quoted in ibid., 24–25.

47. Dewey, "Challenge to Liberal Thought," 190.

48. Giuseppe Antonio Borgese, *Goliath: The March of Fascism* (New York: Viking, 1937), 218, 289.

49. Lewis Mumford, *My Works and Days: A Personal Chronicle* (New York: Harcourt Brace Jovanovich, 1979), 389–390.

50. Ibid., 391.

51. Ibid., 394.

52. Quoted in obituary, *New York Times*, 16 May 1977.

53. Quoted in "How Great Books Course Had Its Beginning Here," *Chicago Sun-Times*, 1 June 1958.

54. Quoted in *Great Books Foundation*, booklet, Spring 1947, 4.

55. WPP to RMH, 15 October 1943.

56. RMH to WPP, 1 December 1943.

57. "How Great Books Course."

58. Quoted in ibid.

59. William Benton to RMH, 3 June 1943, Presidents' Papers, c1925–1945, University of Chicago Library.

60. MJA, *Philosopher at Large*, 238.

61. MJA, interview, Chicago, 18 May 1977.

62. William Benton to E. H. Powell, 25 October 1943, Presidents' Papers, c1925–1945, University of Chicago Library.

63. RMH to John Erskine, 13 October 1943, Presidents' Papers, c1925–1945, University of Chicago Library.

64. MJA, *Philosopher at Large*, chap. 12.

65. Letter to RMH, 11 December 1945, RMH Papers, University of Chicago Library.

66. Dwight MacDonald, "The Book of the Millennium Club," *New Yorker,* 29 November 1952, in Dwight MacDonald, *Against the American Grain* (New York: Random House, 1962), 256.

67. Quoted in ibid., 257–258.

68. MJA, "Adult Education," lecture published by the Great Books Foundation (Chicago, 1952), 3.

69. Memorandum, Great Books publicity release, June 1947, 6.

70. WPP to John H. Jameson, 18 July 1947.

71. MJA, *Philosopher at Large*, 229.

72. The Commission on Freedom of the Press, *A Free and Responsible Press. A General Report on Mass Communication: Newspapers, Radio, Motion Pictures, Magazines, and Books* (Chicago: University of Chicago Press, 1947).

73. RMH, "The New Realism," mimeographed address, Convocation, 15 June 1945.

74. "A Manifesto," Committee on Social Thought, John U. Nef to WPP, 16 April 1946, enclosure.

75. RMH, "Science and Wisdom in the Atomic Age: The Uses of Knowledge," mimeographed lecture, University of Chicago, December 1945, 11, 15.

76. WPP to James Laughlin, 22 February 1947.

Chapter 4

1. WPP to Mr. and Mrs. William A. Nitze, 1945, n.d.

2. Tom Sardy, interview, Aspen, 21 August 1978.

3. EHP, interview, Chicago, 19 May 1977.

4. Ibid.

5. Oscar Wilde to Mrs. Bernard Beere, 17 April 1882, in *The Letters of Oscar Wilde,* ed. Rupert Hart-Davis (New York: Harcourt Brace & World, 1962), 111–112.

6. Frank Hall, "The Valley of the Roaring Fork." In Frank L. Wentworth, comp., *Aspen on the Roaring Fork: An Illustrated History of Colorado's "Greatest Silver Camp,"* 3d ed. (Denver: Sundance Publications, 1976), 26.

7. Warner A. Root, "The New Mining Camp and the Men Who Led the Way Over the Divide," *Aspen Weekly Times,* 18 April 1881. In Wentworth, *Aspen,* 65.

8. *Rocky Mountain News,* 16 February 1881. Quoted in Wentworth, *Aspen,* 70.

9. Root, "The New Mining Camp," in Wentworth, *Aspen,* 72.

10. Quoted in *Aspen Times,* 22 March 1951.

11. Ralph M. Hower, *History of Macy's of New York, 1858–1919: Chapters in the Evolution of the Department Store.* Harvard Studies in Business History, 7 (Cambridge: Harvard University Press, 1943), 172.

12. Malcolm J. Rohrbough, *Aspen: The History of a Silver Mining Town, 1879–1893* (Boulder: University Press of Colorado, 2000); Wentworth, *Aspen,* chaps. 8–10;

Caroline Bancroft, *Famous Aspen: Its Fabulous Past—Its Lively Present,* 8th ed. (Boulder, Colo.: Johnson Publishing Co., 1975), chap. 1.

13. *Daily Chronicle,* 28 November 1889, quoted in *Aspen Times,* 26 February 1960.
14. Bancroft, *Famous Aspen,* 27.
15. Ibid., 25–26; Wentworth, *Aspen,* chap. 9; Heather Hopton and Lilo Shuldner, *Aspen's Early Days: A Walking Tour.* Aspen Historical Society Heritage Series, 1. (Boulder, Colo.: Johnson Publishing Co., 1975), passim.
16. EHP interview, Aspen, 25 July 1977.
17. Quoted in Doug Oppenheimer and Jim Poore, *Sun Valley: A Biography* (Boise, Idaho: Beatty Books, 1976), 13–14.
18. The story of Sun Valley comes from Oppenheimer and Poore, *Sun Valley,* passim.
19. Bancroft, *Famous Aspen,* 24–25.
20. *Aspen Times,* 19 November 1936.
21. *Aspen Times,* 24 December 1936.
22. *Aspen Times,* 19 November 1936.
23. Lowell Thomas, "Introduction," John and Frankie O'Rear, *The Aspen Story. Including Skiing the Aspen Way* (New York: A. S. Barnes & Co., 1966), 9.
24. Quoted in Bancroft, *Famous Aspen,* 41.
25. WPP to Eugene Lilly, 18 May 1945.
26. Memorandum to WPP, n.d.
27. Letter to *Rocky Mountain Winter Sports News,* 30 April 1945.
28. Letter to Editor, *Aspen Times,* 30 April 1945.
29. Letter to Aspen Bank, "Attention President," 30 April 1945.
30. Letter to WPP, 1 May 1945.
31. WPP to realtor, 3 May 1945.
32. WPP to Albin Dearing, 3 May 1945.
33. Secretary to W. Lucas Woodall, 15 May 1945.
34. Floyd N. Gibbs to WPP, 24 May 1945.
35. WPP to Floyd N. Gibbs, 25 May 1945.
36. Joella Bayer to WPP and EHP, 10 June 1945.
37. Walter Gropius to WPP, 28 February 1945.
38. *Boston Post,* 11 March 1946.
39. WPP to Herber Bayer, 22 May 1945.
40. Quoted in Eugene Lilly to EHP, April 1960.
41. Unsigned note in handwriting of WPP.
42. Lloyd Gould to Floyd N. Gibbs, 31 May 1945.
43. E. E. Jackson to secretary, 1 June 1945.
44. WPP to Judge William Shaw, 8 June 1945.
45. WPP to Tom Sardy, 14 June 1945.
46. EHP, interview, Aspen, 24 July 1977.
47. *Aspen Times,* 14 June 1945.
48. WPP to Judge William Shaw, 8 June 1945.
49. Judge William Shaw to WPP, 6 June 1945.
50. WPP to Floyd N. Gibbs, 6 June 1945.

51. WPP to Eugene Lilly, 13 June 1945.
52. WPP to Herbert Bayer, 14 June 1945.
53. WPP to Eugene Lilly, 13 June 1945.
54. Floyd N. Gibbs to WPP, 17 June 1945.
55. WPP to Floyd N. Gibbs, 20 June 1945.
56. WPP to Floyd N. Gibbs, 23 June 1945.
57. WPP to Mountain States Telephone and Telegraph Co., 27 June 1945.
58. WPP to Albin Dearing, 23 June 1945.
59. "Aspen Quakings," *Aspen Times*, 5 July 1945.
60. Mrs. William Shaw to WPP, 6 July 1945.
61. *Aspen Times*, 12 June 1945.
62. Ibid., front page.
63. WPP to Floyd N. Gibbs, 12 July 1945.
64. WPP to Tom Sardy, 14 July 1945.
65. WPP to E. E. Jackson, 19 July 1945.
66. Judge William Shaw to WPP, 17 July 1945.
67. WPP to Judge William Shaw, 17 July 1945.
68. Sam Mitchell, interview, Aspen, 23 July 1977.
69. WPP to Sam Mitchell, 1 August 1945.
70. WPP to Charles Wiley, 26 September 1945.
71. Walter Gropius, *New Architecture* (see chap. 2, n. 53), 19.
72. WPP to Charles Wiley, 26 September 1945.
73. Walter Gropius to WPP, 6 September 1945.
74. Ibid.
75. WPP to Charles Wiley, 25 September 1945.
76. WPP to Laurence Elisha and others, 12 September 1945.
77. Walter Gropius to WPP, 6 September 1945, 20 September 1945.
78. *Business Week*, 17 November 1945, 17.
79. WPP to Frank Rising, 28 November 1945.
80. Albin Dearing to WPP, 20 November 1945.
81. SM-N to WPP, n.d. (probably 21 November 1945).
82. WPP to Joella and Herbert Bayer, 1 February 1946.
83. WPP to Joella and Herbert Bayer, 29 January 1946.
84. WPP to Joella and Herbert Bayer, 14 February 1946.
85. WPP to Joella and Herbert Bayer, 29 January 1946.
86. Paul Nitze, interview, New York City, 22 February 1977.
87. WPP to Paul Nitze, 30 January 1946.
88. WPP to Harold W. Ross, 22 April 1946.
89. Harold W. Ross to WPP, 8 May 1946.
90. Harold W. Ross to WPP, 14 May 1946.
91. WPP to V. E. Ringle, 11 June 1946.
92. Henry L. Stein, interview, Aspen, 18 August 1978.
93. WPP to Paul Nitze, 26 September 1946.
94. *Time*, 20 January 1947, 83–84.

95. WPP, memorandum, 16 December 1947.
96. WPP to Noel Coward, 27 October 1947.
97. Noel Coward to WPP, 1 November 1947.
98. EHP, interview, Aspen, 24 July 1977.
99. WPP to James Laughlin, 17 December 1946.
100. WPP to Gene Lilly, 21 July 1947.
101. WPP to Charles Bayley, 25 September 1947.
102. WPP to Lowell Thomas, 4 June 1947.

Chapter 5

1. WPP to James Laughlin, 22 February 1947.
2. WPP to James Laughlin, 13 March 1947.
3. Carl Schreiber to WPP, 8 February 1948.
4. WPP to James Laughlin, 13 March 1947.
5. MJA, interview, Chicago, 6 May 1978.
6. E.g., Johannes Hoffmeister, *Die Heimkehr des Geistes: Studien zur Dichtung und Philosophie der Goethezeit* (Hameln: F. Seifert, 1946).
7. WPP to William Benton, 14 April 1947.
8. William Benton to WPP, 22 April 1947.
9. RMH to WPP, 24 April 1947.
10. Quoted in memorandum to RMH, 9 January 1948.
11. Arnold Bergstraesser, memorandum to Board of Directors, Goethe Bicentennial Foundation, 28 January 1948.
12. WPP to Carl Schreiber, 10 March 1948.
13. Quoted in memorandum to RMH, 17 June 1948.
14. Mitchell McKeown to Sims Carter, 21 June 1948.
15. Memo to Siegmund Jeremias, 13 July 1948.
16. WPP to Gene Lilly, 20 May 1948.
17. EHP, interview, Chicago, 18 January 1978.
18. Albert Schweitzer, "The One Hundredth Anniversary Memorial Address Delivered at the Centennial Celebration of Goethe's Death in His Native City, Frankfort on the Main, March 22, 1932," in *Goethe: Four Studies by Albert Schweitzer,* Goethe Bicentennial edition, trans. with introduction by Charles R. Joy (Boston: Beacon, 1949), 59–60.
19. WPP to RMH, 11 October 1948.
20. RMH to WPP, 12 October 1948.
21. WPP to D. S. Gottesman, 27 October 1948.
22. Quoted in letter to Mitchell McKeown, 14 October 1948.
23. Sims Carter to Mitchell McKeown, 14 October 1948.
24. The Mitchell McKeown Organization, "Program of Public Relations for the Goethe Bicentennial Foundation," October 1948, 1–10 passim.
25. David Riesman, with Nathan Glazer and Reuel Denney, *The Lonely Crowd: A Study of the Changing American Character* (New Haven: Yale University Press,

1950; abridged, paperbound ed., 1961), chaps. 4, 5.

26. McKeown Organization, "Fact Sheet on Goethe Bicentennial Foundation," 8 November 1948.

27. RMH, "Press Conference by the Board of Directors of the Goethe Bicentennial Foundation at the University Club, Chicago, Illinois, Tuesday, November 9, 1948," 1–10 passim.

28. McKeown Organization, "Public Relations Schedule for Goethe Bicentennial Foundation," n.d. [late 1948].

29. *The Goethe Bicentennial,* pamphlet (Chicago: Goethe Bicentennial Foundation, n.d.), 1.

30. RG to Morris Siegel, 12 January 1949.

31. WPP to Gary Cooper, 13 November 1948.

32. WPP to Howard Hohl, 15 September 1948.

33. WPP to Gaylen Broyles, 30 October 1948.

34. *Aspen Times,* 11 November 1948, front page.

35. WPP, "A Statement," prospectus of the Institute of Design, 1948, in Wingler, *The Bauhaus* (see chap. 1, n. 24), 204.

36. Serge Chermayeff to WPP, 2 November 1948.

37. Ibid.

38. Quoted in Martin Duberman, *Black Mountain: An Exploration in Community* (New York: Dutton, 1972), 40.

39. WPP to Herbert Bayer, 9 November 1948; WPP to Herbert Bayer, 17 November 1948.

40. Letter to Sims Carter, 30 December 1948.

41. WPP to J. Quigg Newton, 19 March 1949.

42. RMH to Albert Schweitzer, 19 January 1949.

43. RMH to José Ortega y Gasset, 19 January 1949.

44. RMH to Ernst R. Curtius, 19 January 1949.

45. RMH to Thornton Wilder, 19 January 1949.

46 Albert Schweitzer to RMH, 2 February 1949.

47. Sims Carter to WPP, 2 February 1949.

48. Melvin Arnold to Sims Carter, 4 February 1949.

49 WPP to Alfred C. Newton, 18 June 1949.

50. WPP to J. Quigg Newton, 19 March 1949.

51. Quoted in RG to Edward Darling, 4 February 1949.

52. "Distinguished Artists to Appear at Goethe Music Festival," press release, Goethe Bicentennial Foundation, 16 February 1949.

53. "Announce First Group of World Scholars and Authors to Participate in U.S. Goethe Convocation," press release, Goethe Bicentennial Foundation, 16 February 1949.

54. RG to Edward Darling, 15 February 1949; Edward Darling to RG, 18 February 1949.

55. "Dr. Albert Schweitzer, Famed Philosopher-Doctor, to Participate in World Goethe Convocation in U.S.," press release, Goethe Bicentennial Foundation, 22 February 1949.

56. "'The Greatest Man in the World,'" *Life*, 6 October 1947, 95.

57. Quoted in James Brabazon, *Albert Schweitzer* (New York: Putnam, 1975), 373.

58. Ibid., 374.

59. George Seaver, *Albert Schweitzer: The Man and His Mind* (New York: Harper, 1947), 3.

60. Albert Schweitzer, "The Goethe Prize Address," 28 August 1928, in *Goethe: Four Studies*, 112–113.

61. Quoted in Charles R. Joy, Introduction to *Goethe: Four Studies*, 14–15.

62. Quoted in ibid., 18.

63. RG to Lewis Hankins, 23 March 1949.

64. Ibid.

65. "Soviet Enrolls Goethe (Who Died in 1832) as Apostle in Germany of World Communism," *New York Times*, 17 February 1949.

66. Quoted in "Refutes Reds' Recent Claim to J. Goethe," *Journal-Courier* (New Haven, Conn.), 21 March 1949.

67. "Who Owns Goethe's Soul?" *Chicago Tribune*, 21 February 1949.

68. *Goethe Bicentennial Convocation and Music Festival, 1949: Aspen, Colorado, U.S.A., June 27–July 16*, publicity booklet, 5–10 passim.

69. *Second Sunday after Easter, May 1, 1949*, pamphlet for mass, Saint Mary's Church, Aspen, Colorado.

70. Minutes of meeting of Citizens Interested in the Goethe Bicentennial Foundation, 28 March 1949.

71. RG to RMH, 15 March 1949.

72. "Four Thousand to Attend International Goethe Convocation, Music Festival in Aspen, Colorado," press release, Goethe Bicentennial Foundation, 26 May 1949.

73. RG, "Report of New York City Press-Radio Arrangements, May 24–27," 5 May 1949.

74. RG to Ludwig Lewisohn, 14 June 1949.

75. RG to Delphine Carpenter, 15 June 1949.

76. "Goethe Bicentennial Convocation and Music Festival at Aspen, Colorado," draft of press release for 26 June 1949, in RG to RMH, 15 June 1949.

77. "P.R. Program for Poet Philosopher Goethe Sets Unusual Assignment for Chicago Counselling Firm," press release, Mitchell McKeown Organization, 11 June 1949.

78. RG, "Case Study on the AMERICAN OBSERVANCE OF THE GOETHE BICENTENNIAL," unpublished typed copy, n.d., 5 pp.

79. Quoted in ibid., 5.

80. Quoted in letter from McKeown Organization to WPP, 17 June 1949.

81. WPP to RMH, 21 June 1949, RMH Papers, Addenda #1, University of Chicago Library.

Chapter 6

1. Quoted in *Denver Post*, 24 June 1949.

2. Quoted in *Denver Colorado News*, 26 June 1949.

3. Quoted in *Colorado Springs Gazette Telegram*, 26 June 1949.

4. Quoted in ibid.

5. *Goethe Bicentennial Convocation and Music Festival, Souvenir Program, Aspen, Colorado, U.S.A. June 27–July 16 1949* (n.p., n.d., 160 pp.). The account that follows is based on pp. 5–8.

6. Felix Borowski, *Chicago Sun-Times*, 29 June 1949.

7. Quoted in Richard J. Davis, *Milwaukee Journal*, 27 June 1949.

8. Quoted in *New York Herald Tribune*, 30 June 1949.

9. Alfred Frankfurter, guest book, Pioneer Park, 29 June 1949.

10. Jacksonville, Illinois, *Journal*, 20 April 1949.

11. Quoted in Lucy Key Miller, "Front Views and Profiles," *Chicago Sun-Times*, 27 July 1949.

12. Elisabeth Mann Borgese, "Goethe and the Unity of Mankind: A Report on the Goethe Bicentennial Convocation in Aspen, Colorado," *Common Cause* 3, no. 3 (October 1949), 113.

13. Giuseppe Borgese to RG, 23 May 1949.

14. Giuseppe Borgese, "The Message of Goethe," in Arnold Bergstraesser, ed., *Goethe and the Modern Age: The International Convocation at Aspen, Colorado, 1949* (Chicago: Regnery, 1950), 3–32 passim.

15. Wolfgang Koessler, "Lecture Reports as of July 5, 1949," *Aspen Times*, 7 July 1949.

16. Quoted in *Christian Science Monitor*, 18 July 1949.

17. José Ortega y Gasset, *Meditaciones del Quijote* (1914), in *Obras completas*, 11 vols. (Madrid: Revista de Occidente, 1946–1969), 1:322. Quoted in Robert McClintock, *Man and His Circumstances: Ortega as Educator* (New York: Teachers College Press, 1971), 5.

18. José Ortega y Gasset, *The Revolt of the Masses* (New York: Norton, 1932), 201, 23.

19. Ibid., 63, 108, 119.

20. Ibid., 197–198, 200.

21. José Ortega y Gasset, *Mission of the University* (1930), trans. and ed. Howard Lee Nostrand (1944; New York: Norton, Norton Library, 1966), 43.

22. Ibid., 59.

23. Ortega, *Revolt*, 67–74 passim, 170.

24. Ortega, *Mission*, 79, 80.

25. José Ortega y Gasset, *An Interpretation of Universal History*, trans. Mildred Adams (1973; New York: Norton Library, 1975), 150–151.

26. *Time*, 17 January 1949.

27. José Ortega y Gasset, "History as a System," in *History as a System and Other Essays Toward a Philosophy of History*, trans. Helene Wyle (New York: Norton, 1941; Norton Library, 1962), 217.

28. José Ortega y Gasset, "In Search of Goethe from Within," *Die Neue Rundschau*, 1932, trans. Willard Trask, *Partisan Review* (1949), in *The Dehumanization of Art and Other Essays on Art, Culture, and Literature* (Princeton: Princeton University Press, 1968), 136, 146, 174.

29. Quoted in *Tulsa Oklahoma World*, 2 July 1949.

30. José Ortega y Gasset, untitled lecture (announced as "The Bicentennial Goethe"), unpublished typescript (18 pp.; missing pp. 14, 16, 18), 1–13 passim.

31. Missing pages of ibid. published as "The Bicentennial Goethe" in Elisabeth Mann Borgese, "Goethe and the Unity of Mankind" (see n. 12), 118–119.

32. José Ortega y Gasset, untitled lecture (announced as "The Bicentennial Goethe"), 15, 17.

33. Ibid., 1.

34. Elisabeth Mann Borgese, "Goethe and the Unity of Mankind," 118.

35. Samuel Mitchell, interview, Aspen, 19 July 1977.

36. Stephen Spender, "Goethe and the Modern Mind," in Bergstraesser, ed., *Goethe and the Modern Mind*, 113–134 passim.

37. Austin, Texas, *American*, 13 May 1949.

38. Quoted in *Time*, 11 July 1949, 68.

39. Quoted in *New York Herald Tribune*, 29 June 1949.

40. Quoted in *Chicago Tribune*, 30 June 1949.

41. Quoted in *Aspen Times*, 7 July 1949.

42. Quoted in WPP to Albert Schweitzer, 4 October 1949.

43. Minneapolis *Sunday Tribune*, 17 July 1949.

44. Quoted in Emory Ross, "Schweitzer in America," *Saturday Review*, 25 September 1965, 25.

45. Quoted in *Life*, 25 July 1949, 76–77.

46. Quoted in *Time*, 11 July 1949.

47. EHP, Address at the Schweitzer Convocation in Aspen, Colorado, 1966, n.p.

48. Quoted by Antonia Paepcke Dubrul, interview, New York, 16 March 1978.

49. Quoted in Spokane *Chronicle*, 16 July 1949.

50. EHP, interview, Aspen, 22 August 1978.

51. Quoted by Antonia Paepcke Dubrul, interview, New York, 16 March 1978.

52. *Christian Science Monitor*, 18 July 1949.

53. "Why Autographs?" *Aspen Times*, 7 July 1949.

54. Quoted in *Aspen Times*, 7 July 1949.

55. Quoted in Albuquerque *Journal*, 6 July 1949.

56. Richard H. Goldstone, *Thornton Wilder: An Intimate Portrait* (New York: Saturday Review Press/Dutton, 1975), 32.

57. Edmund Wilson, "Thornton Wilder," in *Shores of Light: A Literary Chronicle of the Twenties and Thirties* (New York: Random House, Vintage Books, 1952), 391.

58. Quoted in *Chicago Sun-Times*, 10 July 1949.

59. Goldstone, *Thornton Wilder*, 223.

60. Thornton Wilder, "World Literature and the Modern Mind," in Bergstraesser, ed., *Goethe and the Modern Age*, 213–224 passim.

61. *Aspen Times*, 7 July 1949.

62. Quoted in ibid.

63. Elisabeth Mann Borgese, "Goethe and the Unity of Mankind," 129.

64. Quoted in Ortega, untitled lecture (announced as "The Bicentennial Goethe"), 15.

65. Barker Fairley, "Goethe—The Man and the Myth," in Bergstraesser, ed., *Goethe and the Modern Age*, 23–37 passim.
66. Albert Schweitzer, "Goethe: His Personality and His Work," in ibid., 95–110 passim.
67. Victor Lange, "The Goethe Convocation at Aspen," *American-German Review* 15, no. 6 (August 1949), 34.
68. Elisabeth Mann Borgese, "Goethe and the Unity of Mankind," 223.
69. Thomas Sherman, *St. Louis Post-Dispatch*, 13 July 1949.
70. Thornton Wilder to EHP, 6 August 1949.
71. EHP, interview, Aspen, 22 August 1978.
72. José Ortega y Gasset, "Concerning a Bicentennial Goethe," in Bergstraesser, ed., *Goethe and the Modern Age*, 357.
73. EHP, interview, Aspen, 22 August 1978.
74. William Ernest Hocking to RMH, n.d., RMH Papers, Addenda #1, University of Chicago Library.
75. Elisabeth Mann Borgese, "Goethe and the Unity of Mankind," 114.
76. Thornton Wilder to Mabel Dodge Luhan. Quoted in Taos, N.M., *El Crepusculo*, 14 September 1949.
77. Quoted in Elisabeth Mann Borgese, "Goethe and the Unity of Mankind," 124.
78. Albert Schweitzer, guest book, Pioneer Park, n.d.
79. "Symposium of Ethics and Politics," in Bergstraesser, ed., *Goethe and the Modern Age*, 365–381 passim.
80. José Ortega y Gasset, "Goethe, 1749–1949" (typescript of lecture published in Bergstraesser, ed., *Goethe and the Modern World* as "Concerning a Bicentennial Goethe" with pp. 1–2 omitted), 1–2.
81. Ortega, "Concerning a Bicentennial Goethe," 349–362 passim.
82. Thornton Wilder to EHP, 6 August 1949.
83. RMH, "Goethe and the Unity of Mankind," in Bergstraesser, ed., *Goethe and the Modern Age*, 385–402 passim.
84. Quoted in *San Francisco Chronicle*, 14 July 1949.

Chapter 7

1. Thornton Wilder to Herbert Hoover, n.d.
2. Lange, "The Goethe Convocation" (see chap. 6, n. 67), 33–34.
3. Eero Saarinen to WPP, 4 July 1949.
4. Letter to WPP, 28 December 1949.
5. William Ernest Hocking to EHP, 15 July 1949.
6. Carl Schreiber to WPP, 22 July 1949.
7. Quoted in WPP to RMH, 6 December 1949.
8. Kurt Wolff to EHP, 18 July 1949.
9. RMH to EHP, 22 July 1949.
10. Albert Schweitzer to WPP, 28 August 1949.
11. Albert Schweitzer to RMH, 21 August 1949, RMH Papers, Addenda # 1, University of Chicago Library.

12. Albert Schweitzer to WPP, 7 July 1955.
13. Albert Scheitzer to EHP, 17 February 1965.
14. WPP to Paul Nitze, 25 June 1950.
15. Letter to WPP, 16 October 1950.
16. Letter to WPP, 8 July 1949.
17. Letter to RMH, 21 October 1949, RMH Papers, Addenda #1, University of Chicago Library.
18. William Longmaid in *Aspen Times,* 17 July 1949.
19. Norman Cousins, interview, New York, 22 June 1978.
20. Norman Cousins, "What Matters about Schweitzer," *Saturday Review,* 25 September 1965, 31.
21. Quoted in ibid., 32.
22. WPP to James T. Babb, 5 November 1949.
23. "After Hours," *Harper's,* July 1949, 100.
24. Quoted in RG, "Case Study" (see chap. 5, n. 78), 5.
25. Ibid.
26. José Ortega y Gasset, "Concerning a Bicentennial Goethe," in Bergstraesser, ed., *Goethe and the Modern Age* (see chap. 6, n. 14), 351.
27. Joshua L. Baily, Jr., to RMH, 9 February 1950, RMH Papers, Addenda #1, University of Chicago Library.
28. WPP to Albert Schweitzer, 4 October 1949.
29. See C. Faust and F. Champion Ward, "Aspen College," *Journal of General Education* 30, no. 2 (Summer 1978), 67–72—an essay by two proponents of Aspen University originally written as a memorial to Paepcke.
30. Quoted in *Aspen Times,* 17 November 1949.
31. MJA, interview, Chicago, 23 April 1979.
32. Friedrich Nietzsche, *The Gay Science,* section 290, in *The Portable Nietzsche,* trans. and ed. Walter Kaufmann (New York: Viking, 1954), 98–99.
33. José Ortega y Gasset to WPP, 26 October 1949; published in Spanish and English under the title *Aspen Institute for Humanistic Studies, 1974, 25th Anniversary Year* (Revista de Occidente and Aspen Institute for Humanistic Studies, 1974), 35–48 passim.
34. WPP to Mrs. E. M. Holden, 6 December 1949.
35. James Laughlin to WPP, 3 January 1950.
36. Harold Lasswell to WPP, 21 November 1949.
37. Jacques Barzun to WPP, 27 September 1951.
38. WPP to Jacques Barzun, 9 October 1951.
39. WPP to RMH, 4 February 1950.
40. José Ortega y Gasset to WPP, 7 December 1949, RMH Papers, Addenda #1, University of Chicago Library.
41. WPP to RMH, 15 December 1949, RMH Papers, Addenda #1, University of Chicago Library.
42. Quoted in WPP to RMH, 15 December, 1949 (see n. 41).
43. MJA to Axel Wenner-Gren, 28 July 1950 (courtesy MJA).

44. Egbert Jacobson to WPP, CCA memorandum, 5 January 1950.

45. For a deft criticism of Mortimer Adler and the Container Corporation Great Ideas advertising campaign, see Hugh Kenner, "Please Welcome My Next Idea," *Harper's*, December 1982, 60.

46. WPP, "The 'Great Ideas' Campaign," *Advertising Review*, Autumn 1954, 26.

47. Ibid., 28.

48. MJA, *Philosopher at Large* (see chap. 3, n. 7), 263.

49. *Aspen Institute for Humanistic Studies Presents Summer Program, 1950: Great Books, Great Men, Great Music*, publicity pamphlet and program.

50. *Humanism in a World of Science: Aspen Institute for Humanistic Studies Presents Great Books, Great Men, Great Music. June 26 through September 10 in Aspen, Colorado*, publicity folder.

51. Clare Boothe Luce, quoted on dust jacket of MJA, *Philosopher at Large*.

52. MJA to WPP, 21 May 1950.

53. Quoted in *Aspen Times*, 29 June 1950.

54. Quoted in *Aspen Times*, 29 June 1950.

55. Quoted in Joseph Przudzik, "Peace—Or Else," *America*, 19 August 1950, 512.

56. *Aspen Times*, 6 July 1950.

57. Quoted in *Grand Junction Daily Sentinel*, 30 June 1950.

58. Quoted in *Aspen Times*, 20 July 1950.

59. Sydney Harris, "Strictly Personal," *Chicago Daily News*, 7 August 1950.

60. Harry C. Schnibbe, "The Common Good," *Cervi's Journal*, 10 August 1950.

61. Quoted in Mildred Shaw, *Grand Junction Daily Sentinel*, 29 June 1950.

62. Ise and Walter Gropius to EHP and WPP, 6 September 1950.

63. William Gorman, interview, Santa Barbara, 9 August 1977.

64. MJA, *Philosopher at Large*, 265.

65. Friedel Ungeheuer, interview, New York, 24 March 1977.

66. Olin Downes, *New York Times*, 23 July 1950.

67. Virgil Thompson, *New York Herald Tribune Music Review*, 10 September 1950.

68. Quoted in *Santa Fe New Mexican*, 13 September 1950.

69. John P. Marquand to King Vidor, 1952. Quoted in Millicent Bell, *Marquand: An American Life* (Boston: Little, Brown and Co., 1979), 383.

70. James Thurber, *The Years with Ross* (Boston: Little, Brown, 1959), 96.

71. WPP to Harold W. Ross, 24 August 1950.

72. *Aspen Times*, 27 December 1956.

73. *Aspen Times*, 14 September 1950.

74. Thornton Wilder to EHP, n.d.

75. MJA, *Philosopher at Large*, 264.

76. WPP to Miriam Ingebretson, 25 April 1950.

77. Quoted in Marshall Sprague, "Aspen Appraised," *Denver Times*, 6 August 1950.

78. WPP to Harry Forwood, 19 October 1950.

79. MJA, interview, Chicago, 18 May 1977.

80. WPP to Clarence Randall, 15 August 1950.

81. WPP to Gene Lilly, 25 August 1950.

82. WPP to David H. Stevens, 24 August 1950.
83. Hofstadter, *Anti-Intellectualism* (see chap. 1, n. 35), 234.

Chapter 8

1. Richard Hofstadter, *Anti-Intellectualism* (see chap. 1, n. 35), 237.
2. Thomas Colley Grattan, *Civilized America* (London, 1859), quoted in ibid., 250.
3. Quoted in Paul Theroux, *New York Times Book Review*, 21 July 1979, 18.
4. Hofstadter, *Anti-Intellectualism*, 236.
5. Crawford H. Greenwalt, "The Culture of the Businessman," *Saturday Review*, 19 January 1957. Quoted in Douglas T. Miller and Marion Nowak, *The Fifties: The Way We Really Were* (Garden City, N.Y.: Doubleday, 1977), 241.
6. Charles E. Wilson, TRB, and the journalist Ralph Coghlan are quoted in Eric F. Goldman, *The Crucial Decade—and After: America, 1945–1960* (New York: Vintage Books, 1960), 239, 269.
7. Walter Bagehot, *The English Constitution* (1867). Excerpted in Roland Stromberg, ed., *Realism, Naturalism, and Symbolism: Modes of Thought and Expression in Europe, 1848–1914* (New York: Harper Torchbooks, 1968), 31.
8. Advertisement for the *Fortune* editors' book *U.S.A., the Permanent Revolution* (1951). Quoted in Frederick Lewis Allen, *The Big Change, 1900–1950* (1952; paperbound ed., New York: Bantam Books, 1965), 215.
9. Max Lerner, *America as a Civilization* (New York: Simon & Schuster, 1957), 281. See also Thomas C. Cochran, *Business in American Life: A History* (New York: McGraw-Hill, 1972), chap. 26; Chandler, *The Visible Hand* (see chap.1, n. 4), pt. 4 and concl.
10. Quoted in Hofstadter, *Anti-Intellectualism*, 261.
11. Ibid.
12. Cochran, *Business in American Life*, 256.
13. Quoted in Allen, *The Big Change*, 215.
14. Quoted in Hofstadter, *Anti-Intellectualism*, 264.
15. Allen, *The Big Change*, 217.
16. Goldman, *Crucial Decade*, 269.
17. Quoted in Allen, *The Big Change*, 221.
18. See Fleming and Bailyn, eds., *Intellectual Migration* (see chap. 2, n. 89).
19. "Our Country and Our Culture: A Symposium," *Partisan Review* 19 (September–October 1952), 283, 284, 319, 321.
20. Lionel Trilling, *Mind in the Modern World* (New York: Viking, 1972).
21. Trilling, "Our Country . . . Symposium," 320.
22. C. Wright Mills, *The Power Elite* (New York: Oxford University Press, 1956).
23. WPP to George L. Treadwell, 25 October 1950.
24. Clifton Fadiman to Clarence Faust, 2 November 1950.
25. WPP to Paul Nitze, 29 November 1950.
26. Statement on the purposes of the Aspen Insitute for Humanistic Studies with solicitation for funds, enclosed in WPP to Clarence Faust, 12 October 1950.

27. Allen, *The Big Change,* 219.
28. WPP, address at annual trustees' dinner, University of Chicago, 10 January 1951, typescript.
29. Notes of trustees' meeting, 28 January 1951, quoted in J. S. Doughty to WPP, 29 January 1951.
30. Quoted in J. S. Doughty to WPP, 29 January 1951.
31. Quoted in obituary, *New York Times,* 16 May 1977.
32. Quoted in Leonard Silk and Mark Silk, *The American Establishment* (New York: Basic Books, 1980), 127.
33. WPP to RMH, 18 December 1950, RMH Papers, Addenda #1, University of Chicago Library.
34. WPP to RMH, 26 January 1951.
35. Letter to WPP, 29 March 1951.
36. Jacques Barzun, "America's Romance with Practicality," *Harper's,* February 1952, 76, 77.
37. Jacques Barzun to WPP, 27 September 1951.
38. Theodore Hesburgh, lecture, Aspen, 22 July 1977.
39. Quoted in letter to WPP, 27 August 1951.
40. Quoted by Jacques Barzun, interview, New York, 10 November 1977.
41. Letter to WPP, 16 July 1951, quoted in letter to WPP, 23 July 1951.
42. William Gomberg to WPP, 21 August 1951.
43. Clarence Randall to WPP, 27 August 1951.
44. WPP to James Laughlin, n.d. [October 1951].
45. WPP to Richard P. Leach, 26 February 1952.
46. Quoted in ibid.
47. *Aspen Institute for Humanistic Studies: The Aspen Program for Business Leadership,* 1952, pamphlet.
48. *The Aspen Executives Progam, Summer of 1955,* pamphlet, 1.
49. WPP in *Aspen Institute for Humanistic Studies, 1959–60,* pamphlet, 1.
50. *Aspen Institute for Humanistic Studies, Founded by Walter Paepcke. The Aspen Executive Program. Management Development for America's Leadership, 1961–62,* pamphlet, 1.
51. *Time,* 27 August 1957.
52. Quoted in letter to WPP, 30 August 1953.
53. Quoted in MJA to WPP, 9 July 1956.
54. J. William Fulbright to WPP, 4 May 1954.
55. Quoted in *Aspen Times,* 19 July 1956.
56. Quoted in *Aspen Times,* 14 August 1958.
57. WPP to Jacques Barzun, 18 May 1953.
58. Jacques Barzun to WPP, 21 May 1953.
59. WPP to Jacques Barzun, May 1953.
60. Jacques Barzun to WPP, 25 May 1953.
61. Jacques Barzun, "America's Passion for Culture," *Harper's,* March 1954, 40–47 passim.

62. Quoted in *Aspen Times*, 19 Feburary 1959.
63. Quoted in Goldman, *Crucial Decade*, 308.
64. John Kenneth Galbraith, "Introduction to the Second Edition," *The Affluent Society*, 2d ed. (Boston: Houghton Mifflin, 1959), xxiii–xxiv.
65. "U.S. Schools: They Face a Crisis," *Life*, 16 October 1950.
66. Quoted in William Manchester, *The Glory and the Dream: A Narrative History of America, 1932–1972* (Boston: Little, Brown, 1974), 965.
67. *Life*, 24 March 1958, 25.
68. Quoted in Miller and Nowak, *The Fifties*, 262. On the criticism of education in general, see *The Fifties*, ch. 9.
69. All from *Aspen Times*, 30 July 1959.
70. Boorstin, *The Image* (see intro., n. 1).
71. Jacques Barzun, *The House of Intellect* (New York: Harper, 1959), 239–240.
72. *Chicago Sun-Times*, 15 February 1961, sec. 2.
73. These statements all come from "Comments on Aspen Institute Conferences," publicity sheets, n.d., 2.
74. Quoted in ibid., 3, 4.
75. Quoted in "Comments on the Aspen Executives' Program," publicity sheets, n.d., 2.
76. Gerald R. Ford to WPP, 17 February 1960.
77. William Harlan Hale, "Culture with a Sun Tan in the Rockies," *The Reporter*, 8 August 1957, 27.
78. Quoted in "Comments on Aspen Institute Conferences," 1.
79. Letter to WPP, 25 September 1952.
80. Quoted by Alvin Eurich, interview, New York, 4 December 1978.
81. Quoted in "Comments on Aspen Institute Conferences," 3.
82. Norman Cousins, interview, New York, 22 June 1978.
83. Quoted in "Comments on Aspen Institute Conferences," 2.
84. All quoted in ibid., 4.
85. Walter P. Reuther to WPP, 17 July 1957.
86. Walter P. Reuther to WPP, 19 December 1957.
87. Letter to WPP, 17 February 1959.
88. John Higham, *History: The Development of Historical Studies in the United States* (Englewood Cliffs, N.J.: Prentice-Hall, Spectrum Books, 1965), 214.
89. Daniel Bell, *The End of Ideology* (Glencoe, Ill.: Free Press, 1960).
90. WPP to MJA, 24 June 1955.
91. All quotations from "Comments on Aspen Institute Conferences," 1–4.
92. "Plato, Aristotle, and the Businessman," *Newsweek*, 20 July 1958, 79–80.
93. Robert O. Anderson, interview, New York, 8 November 1978.
94. Robert O. Anderson, "Aspen—The Once and Future City," unpublished essay, photocopy, 14 (courtesy Robert O. Anderson).
95. Ibid.

Chapter 9

1. Quoted in Roger Shattuck, *The Banquet Years: The Origins of the Avant Garde in France, 1885 to World War I*, rev. ed. (New York: Vintage Books, 1968), 168, 169.
2. Quoted by Charles Jones, interview, New York, 18 March 1980.
3. Quoted by Mrs. Robert Gonner, interview, Aspen, 22 August 1978.
4. WPP to Richard P. Leach, 11 December 1954.
5. Petition of the Aspen Festival Orchestra, 29 August 1954.
6. Quoted in *Aspen Times Extra*, 3 September 1954.
7. Ferenc Berko, interview, Aspen, 17 July 1977.
8. WPP to Mack Harrell, 17 October 1950.
9. Egbert Jacobson, report of luncheon meeting, Regis Hotel, New York, 20 July 1951.
10. This account of the photography conference is based on Beaumont Newhall, "The Aspen Photo Conference," typescript dated 30 October 1951, 1–12 passim. The last quotation from Ansel Adams comes from *Aspen Times*, 4 October 1951.
11. Newhall, "Aspen Photo Conference," 12.
12. Nancy Newhall and Ansel Adams to WPP, 12 October 1951.
13. Ansel Adams to WPP, 12 May 1952.
14. Quoted in Egbert Jacobson, "Notes on a Meeting Held on July 26, 1952, at the Museum of Modern Art," typescript.
15. Egbert Jacobson to WPP, CCA intercompany correspondence, 23 August 1950.
16. Ibid.
17. Egbert Jacobson, report of meeting, CBS board room, 19 February 1951.
18. Allen, *The Big Change* (see chap. 8, n. 8), 173, 221.
19. William M. de Majo, "Live Wires or Dead Ends," *Conference Papers*, International Design Conference in Aspen, 1955. (All *Conference Papers* courtesy of Herbert Pinzke.)
20. WPP, untitled address, typescript, dated 28 June 1951.
21. All references to the proceedings of the Design Conference of 1951 come from R. Hunter Middleton and Alexander Ebin, *Impressions from the Design Conference held at Aspen, Colorado, June 28 through July 1, 1951*, booklet.
22. Letter to WPP, 27 July 1951.
23. Letter to WPP, 28 November 1951.
24. Letter to Russel Wright, 7 May 1952, copy to WPP.
25. Letter to WPP, 19 May 1952.
26. WPP to Herbert Bayer, 27 February 1952.
27. Letter to Leo Leonni, 12 December 1952.
28. R. Buckminster Fuller to WPP, 13 July 1952.
29. Will Burtin, "Opening Remarks," in *Conference Papers*, 1955.
30. Bruce MacKenzie, "Design, Science and the Future," in *Communication: The Image Speaks*, Conference Papers, Ninth International Design Conference in Aspen, June 21–27, 1959.
31. Gyorgy Kepes, untitled paper in ibid.

32. De Majo, "Live Wires."

33. Max Frisch, "Why Don't We Have the Cities We Need?" in *Conference Papers*, Sixth International Design Conference in Aspen, 1956.

34. E. A. Gutkind, "How Does Our World Look Today?" in *Design and Human Problems*, Conference Papers, Eighth International Design Conference in Aspen, June 22–29, 1958.

35. De Majo, "Live Wires."

36. Gordon Lippincott, "Management and Design," in *Conference Papers*, Sixth International Design Conference in Aspen, 1956.

37. Abram Games, "Pattern and Purpose," in *Communication: The Image Speaks*.

38. Richard S. Latham, "Communications of Values through Design," in *Conference Papers*, Seventh International Design Conference in Aspen, 1957.

39. Lippincott, "Management and Design."

40. Herbert Bayer, "On Communication," in *Conference Papers*, 1955.

41. James Real, "Image or Facade," in *Communication: The Image Speaks*.

42. C. Wright Mills, "Man in the Middle: The Designer," in *Design and Human Problems*, reprinted in *Power, Politics, and People: The Collected Essays of C. Wright Mills*, ed. Irving Horowitz (1963; New York: Oxford University Press paperback, 1967), 374–386 passim.

43. Reyner Banham, "Aspen into the Seventies," in *The Aspen Papers: Twenty Years of Design Theory from the International Design Conference in Aspen*, ed. Reyner Banham (London: Pall Mall Press, 1974), 223–224.

44. WPP to R. Buckminster Fuller, Charles Eames, George Nelson, 7 August 1952.

45. *Time*, 15 August 1949, 60.

46. *Time*, 7 July 1956, 50.

47. *Time*, 27 April 1959, 67.

48. WPP to Thornton Wilder, 23 January 1959.

49. Letter from Aspen Institute to C. D. Jackson of *Time*, 25 February 1959.

50. WPP to Le Corbusier, 18 August 1959.

51. Philip Johnson to WPP, 2 March 1959.

52. Walter Gropius to WPP, 28 April 1959.

53. Minutes of board meeting, 28 November 1959.

54. Letter to Marcel Breuer et al., 19 April 1959.

55. Marquis W. Childs, "The World of Walter Paepcke," *Horizon*, September 1958, 99.

Chapter 10

1. Letter to EHP, 14 April 1960.

2. Herbert Bayer, "Walter Paepcke," *Print* 14, no. 5 (September–October 1960), 37, 38.

3. Victor Babin, unpublished essay, photocopy.

4. Norman Cousins to EHP, 18 April 1960.

5. Ansel Adams to EHP, 23 April 1960.

6. Jacques Barzun to EHP, 14 April 1960.

7. *Art, Design and the Modern Corporation. The Collection of Container Corporation of America* (see chap. 1, n. 98).

8. Bill Bonnell, interview, New York, 10 October 2001.

9. Jessica Weber, interview, New York, 18 September 2001.

10. Alan Peckolick, interview, New York, 18 September 2001.

11. *The More Things Change*, Fifty-first International Design Conference in Aspen (June 6–9, 2001), web site, www.idca.org., 1–3.

12. Letter to MJA, 29 August 1962.

13. William Benton to MJA, 21 August 1962.

14. Joseph E. Slater, "President's Letter" (1975). Quoted in Sidney Hyman, *The Aspen Idea* (Norman: University of Oklahoma Press, 1975), 377–378.

15. Allyn Harvey, "Global Reach: How One Group Claims the Aspen Institute Launched a Fundamentalist Revolution," *Aspen Times Weekly*, 19–20 August 2000, 14A. Harvey quotes extensively from Robert Dreyfuss, with Thierry LeMarc, *Hostage to Khomeini* (New York: Franklin House, c1980).

16. Anderson, "Aspen" (see chap. 8, n. 94), 26.

17. Quoted in Allyn Harvey, "The Aspen Institute: The First Fifty Years," *Aspen Times Weekly*, 19–20 August 2000, 17A.

18. See ibid., 14A–17A.

19. James M. Spiegelman, telephone interview, 27 November 2001.

20. Harry Saal, quoted in Larry Borowsky, "The Executive Seminars: The Institute's Mark on Corporate America," *Aspen Magazine*, Special Issue, 2000, 47.

21. Quoted in Larry Borowsky, "I Saw Lives Change," *Aspen Magazine*, Special Issue, 2000, 48, 49.

22. Quoted in "The Great American Salon," *Newsweek*, 14 July 1980, 66.

23. All quotations from ibid., 66, 67.

24. Quoted in Janet O'Grady, "An Interview with the President," *Aspen Magazine*, Special Issue, 2000, 71.

25. Quoted in Allyn Harvey, "The Aspen Institute: The First Fifty Years," 17A.

26. *The Great Conversation. On the Occasion of the Fiftieth Anniversary of the Aspen Institute* (Aspen Institute, 2000), 29.

27. Ibid., 62, 33.

28. Memorandum, Elmer Johnson to Board of Trustees of the Aspen Institute, 23 October 2001, pp. 1–6 passim (courtesy of Mr. Johnson and the Aspen Institute).

29. Aspen Skiing Company (the name since 1981), web site, www.aspensnowmass.com, 2001.

30. "Insider Town," *Aspen Magazine*, Late Summer/Fall, 2001, 20.

31. "Real Estate," *Aspen Times Weekly*, 19–20 August 2000, 21A.

32. Jamie Miller, "And the Winners Are . . . ," *Aspen Magazine*, Summer 2001, 52.

33. Ibid.

34. "Picked Fresh," *Aspen Magazine*, Summer 2001, 46.

35. Janet O'Grady, "Editor's Letter," ibid., 20.

36. Ibid.

37. Ted Conover, *Whiteout: Lost in Aspen* (New York: Random House, 1991), 58, 117.

38. Peggy Clifford, *To Aspen and Back: An American Journey* (New York: St. Martins Press, 1980), 164, 215.

39. Ann Crockett, e-mail to author, 11 October 2001.

40. Loren Jenkins, "Elizabeth Paepcke: The Conscience of Aspen," *Aspen Magazine*, Mid-Summer 1990, 60.

41. Quoted from the *Aspen Times* in Conover, *Whiteout*; quoted in Ted Conover, "Eve in the Garden of Aspen," *New York Times Magazine*, 1 January 1995, 21.

42. *New York Times Magazine*, 1 January 1995, 20.

43. See, e.g., Daniel Bell, *The Coming of Post-Industrial Society: A Venture in Social Forecasting* (New York: Basic Books, 1973); William Weaver, "Science and Complexity," in *The Scientists Speak*, ed. Warren Weaver (1947), quoted in ibid., 29; Neil Postman, *Technopoly: The Surrender of Culture to Technology* (New York: Random House, 1992); Jean-Francois Lyotard, *The Post-Modern Condition: A Report on Knowledge*, trans. Geoff Bennington and Brian Massumi (Minneapolis: University of Minnesota Press, 1984); Fredric Jameson, *Postmodernism: The Cultural Logic of Late Capitalism* (see intro., n. 1); Alfred D. Chandler, Jr., and James W. Cortada, eds., *A Nation Transformed by Information* (New York: Oxford University Press, 2000).

44. Mills, *The Power Elite* (see chap. 8, n. 22), 295–296.

45. Richard J. Hernstein and Charles Murray, *The Bell Curve: Intelligence and Class Structure in American Life* (New York: The Free Press, 1994), 25–27.

46. Burton J. Bledstein, *The Culture of Professionalism: The Middle Class and the Development of Higher Education in America* (New York: W. W. Norton & Co., 1976).

47. See C. Roland Christensen, with Abbey J. Hansen, "Teaching with Cases at the Harvard Business School," and James Sloan Allen, "The Use and Abuse of Humanistic Education," both in C. Roland Christensen, with Abbey J. Hansen, *Teaching and the Case Method* (Boston: Harvard Business School, 1987).

48. *The Humanities in American Life*, Report of the Commission on the Humanities (Berkeley and Los Angeles: University of California Press, 1980), xi.

49. E. D. Hirsch, Jr., *Cultural Literacy: What Every American Needs to Know* (Boston: Houghton Mifflin Company, 1987).

50. Mary Ann Dzuback, *Robert M. Hutchins: Portrait of an Educator* (see chap. 3, n.1), 254.

51. Algren and Adler quoted in Adler obituary, *New York Times*, 29 June 2001, B8.

52. MJA, "The Disappearance of Culture," *Newsweek*, 21 August 1978.

53. MJA, on behalf of the members of the Paideia Group, *The Paideia Proposal: An Educational Manifesto* (New York: Macmillan, 1982), 23.

54. Quoted in Peter Temes, "Death of a Great Reader—and Philosopher," *Chicago Sun-Times*, 3 July 2001. Also MJA, *A Second Look in the Rear-View Mirror: Further Reflections of a Philosopher at Large* (New York: Macmillan, 1992), 137.

55. Center for the Study of Great Ideas, web site, www.thegreatideas.org.

56. Dzuback, *Hutchins*, 254, 271.

57. Riesman, *The Lonely Crowd* (see chap. 5, n. 25), pt. I.

58. Christopher Lasch, *The Culture of Narcissism: American Life in an Age of Diminishing Expectations* (New York: W.W. Norton & Co., 1978).

59. Theodore Roszak, *Person/Planet: The Creative Disintegration of Industrial Society* (New York: Anchor Press/Doubleday, 1978), 27, 4, 86.

60. Herbert Marcuse, *One Dimensional Man* (see intro., n. 1), chap. 3.

61. Neil Postman, *Amusing Ourselves to Death: Public Discourse in the Age of Show Business* (New York: Penguin Books, 1985); Neal Gabler, *Life the Movie: How Entertainment Conquered Reality* (New York: Random House, 1998).

62. Michael Kammen, *American Culture, American Tastes: Social Change and the Twentieth Century* (New York: Knopf, 1999); Christopher Clausen, *Faded Mosaic: The Emergence of Post-Cultural America* (Chicago: Ivan R. Dee, 2000).

63. Jacques Barzun, *From Dawn to Decadence: 500 Years of Western Cultural Life, from 1500 to the Present* (New York: Harper/Collins, 2000), pt. IV.

64. See, e.g., Francois Lyotard, *The Post-Modern Condition* (see n. 43); Pierre Bourdieu, *The Field of Cultural Production: Essays on Art and Literature*, ed. Randal Johnson (Cambridge: Polity, 1993); Jean Baudrillard, *The Consumer Society* (see intro., n. 1); Mike Featherstone, *Consumer Culture and Postmodernism* (London: Sage, 1991); Fredric Jameson, *Postmodernism* (see intro., n. 1); Martin P. Davidson, *The Consumerist Manifesto: Advertising in Postmodern Times* (London: Routledge, 1992); Stephen Brown, *Postmodern Marketing* (London: Routledge, 1995).

65. Featherstone, *Consumer Culture and Postmodernism*, 116.

66. See, e.g., Mike Featherstone, *Undoing Culture: Globalization, Postmodernism, and Identity* (London: Sage, 1995); Walter La Feber, *Michael Jordan and the New Global Capitalism* (New York: W.W. Norton & Co.,1999).

67. See, e.g., Nigel Wheale, ed., *The Postmodern Arts: An Introductory Reader* (London: Routledge, 1995); Steven Connor, *Postmodernist Culture: An Introduction to Theories of the Contemporary*, 2d ed. (Oxford; Cambridge, Mass.: Blackwell, 1997); Johannes Hans Willem Bertens, *The Idea of the Postmodern: A History* (London: Routledge, 1995).

68. Vincent Scully, "Introduction," in Robert Venturi, *Complexity and Contradiction in Architecture*, 2d ed. (New York: Museum of Modern Art, 1977), 11. Venturi's text, originally published in 1966, was a seminal work of postmodern architectural criticism.

69. Robert Venturi, Denise Scott Brown, Steven Izenour, *Learning from Las Vegas* (Cambridge: MIT Press, 1972, rev. ed. 1977).

70. Warhol, *Philosophy* (see chap. 1, n. 2), 92.

71. Brent C. Brolin, *The Failure of Modern Architecture* (New York: Van Nostrand, Reinhold, 1976); Peter Blake, *Form Follows Fiasco: Why Modern Architecture Hasn't Worked* (Boston: Little, Brown, 1977); Tom Wolfe, *From Bauhaus to Our House* (New York: Farrar Straus Giroux, 1981).

index

postmodern criticism of, 312; and
School of Design, 65, 70, 71
Gutkind, E. A., 283

Halaby, Najeeb E., 259
Harlan, John M., 260
Harrell, Mack, 165, 230, 269, 271
Harriman, Averell: and Sun Valley, 129,
130
Harris, Sydney: on Aspen Institute, 228
Hartmann, Heinz, 264
Hartner, Willy, 205
Harvard University: Business School of,
6, 306; and W. Gropius, 57, 58; Red
Book of, 112
Hawley, Cameron: *Cash McCall*, 240;
Executive Suite, 279
Hayden, F. V.: geological survey of
Aspen region by, 122
Hélion, Jean, 33, 62, 64
Hemingway, Ernest, 241; *The Sun Also
Rises*, 16
Henle, Fritz: and Aspen photography
conference, 273
Hesburgh, Theodore, 98; and Aspen
Institute, 248
Hesse, Hermann: *Demian*, 53–54; *The
Glass Bead Game*, 64; *Steppenwolf*,
xiv, 16, 26
Hines, Jerome, 165, 183
Hirsch, E. D., 306
Hitchcock, H.-R.: and "International
Style," 50, 51
Hocking, William Ernest, *198*, 204, 205,
208
Hodges, William, 164
Hoffman, Paul G., 245
Hofstadter, Richard: on business, 13,
234, 237; and consensus, 263
Hogben, Lancelot, 284
Hood, Raymond M., 47
Hook, Sidney, 101
Hoover, Herbert: and Exposition
Internationale des Arts Decoratifs et
Industriels Modernes, 49; and Goethe
Festival, 155, 177, 181, 208

Hopkins, Claude: *Scientific Advertising*,
15–16
Hotel Jerome, *274*; and Aspen Institute,
229, 296; and Aspen photography
conference, 273–275; early history of,
125–127; and Goethe Festival, 181,
197; renovation of, 145–146
Houghton, Arthur A., Jr., 296
House Beautiful, The, 43
Howells, J. M., 47
Hudnut, Joseph, 65
Humanism: and education, 92–93, 98–
99, 215, 306–308; idea of, at Aspen
Institute, 262. *See also* Adler,
Mortimer J.; Aspen Institute for
Humanistic Studies; Chicago
Bildungsideal; Goethe Festival;
Hutchins, Robert Maynard
Humanities: in American culture, 306–
308. *See also* Aspen Institute for
Humanistic Studies; Humanism
Hutchins, Maude (Mrs. Robert M.
Hutchins), 84, 85
Hutchins, Robert Maynard, 85, 87;
affinities of, with other cultural
critics, xv–xvi, 63, 82, 188, 215, 219,
226, 308–309, 311; and Aspen
Institute, 208, 213–214, 219, 226, 231,
232, 247, 248–249, 251; character of,
83–84, 308–309; *The Conflict in
Education*, 256; and consumer
culture, 187, 212; criticism of, 94–95,
98–100, 102–103; as cultural critic,
92–95, 102–103, 113–114, 180, 206–
207, 311; and J. Dewey, 99–100, 103;
educational philosophy of, 86–102,
166, 226; and Fat Man's class, 106–
107; on Goethe, 206–207; and Goethe
Festival, 114–115, 155, 161–162, 173,
175–176, 180, 206–207, 209–210; and
Great Books movement, 110–112;
and *The Great Books of the Western
World*, 107–110; late career of, 245–
246, 306–307; and J. Ortega y Gasset's
The Mission of the University, 215; and
J. Ortega y Gasset's *The Revolt of The*